MW00606288

PROTESTANT SCHOLASTICISM:
ESSAYS IN REASSESSMENT

PROTESTANT SCHOLASTICISM: ESSAYS IN REASSESSMENT

**Edited by
Carl R. Trueman
and
R. Scott Clark**

paternoster
press

Copyright © 1999 Carl R. Trueman and R. Scott Clark

First published in 1999 by Paternoster Press

05 04 03 02 01 00 99   7 6 5 4 3 2 1

Paternoster Press is an imprint of Paternoster Publishing,
P.O. Box 300, Carlisle, Cumbria, CA3 0QS, U.K.
http://www.paternoster-publishing.com

The rights of Carl R. Trueman and R. Scott Clark to be identified as the Editors of
this Work has been asserted by them in accordance with Copyright, Designs and
Patents Act 1998.

*All rights reserved. No part of this publication may be reproduced,
stored in a retrieval system, or transmitted in any form or by any
means, electronic, mechanical, photocopying, recording or otherwise,
without the prior permission of the publisher or a licence permitting
restricted copying. In the U.K. such licences are issued by the
Copyright Licensing Agency,
90 Tottenham Court Road, London W1P 9HE.*

British Library Cataloguing in Publication Data
A catalogue record for this book is available from the British Library

ISBN 0-85364-853-0

Unless otherwise stated, Scripture quotations are taken from the
HOLY BIBLE, NEW INTERNATIONAL VERSION
Copyright © 1973, 1978, 1984 by the International Bible Society.
Used by permission of Hodder and Stoughton Limited. All rights reserved.
'NIV' is a registered trademark of the International Bible Society
UK trademark number 1448790

Cover Design by Mainstream, Lancaster
Typeset by WestKey Ltd, Falmouth, Cornwall
Printed in Great Britain by
Caledonian International Book Manufacturing Ltd, Glasgow

Contents

Acknowledgments

The editors would like to thank Pieter Kwant and the staff at Paternoster for all their help and assistance during the preparation of this book. We would also like to express our appreciation to all the contributors who so generously gave of their time to support this project, who dealt patiently with often difficult questions from the editors, and, in many cases, whose earlier work provided the direct inspiration for the volume.

Finally, the editors wish to dedicate the book to the memory of the Rev Dr Robert D. Preus (1924–95). His own work on post-Reformation Lutheranism was one of the earliest signs that Protestant scholasticism was due for reassessment. Before his death, he had agreed to contribute an essay to this collection and his enthusiastic support in the early stages of this project was most encouraging. He deserves to be recognized as one of the pioneers in this field, with his patient, careful, and dispassionate historical analysis of Protestant orthodoxy having established a standard to which subsequent scholars must aspire. His death leaves a sad void in the current volume.

Contributors

David V.N. Bagchi is Lecturer in the History of Christian Thought at the University of Hull. He is the author of *Luther's Earliest Opponents* and *The Reformation in Print: German Reformation Pamphlets in Translation* (1997), as well as numerous articles on the Lutheran Reformation. He is an expert on Roman Catholic theological reaction to Luther.

Joel R. Beeke is Pastor of Heritage Netherlands Reformed Congregation, Grand Rapids, Michigan, and President and Professor of Systematic Theology and Homiletics at the Puritan Reformed Seminary. He is the author of *Assurance of Faith: Calvin, English Puritanism and the Dutch Second Reformation* and numerous scholarly articles on the Dutch Second Reformation.

Lyle D. Bierma is Professor at Reformed Bible College, Grand Rapids. He is the author of various articles on covenant theology, a book, *German Calvinism in the Confessional Age: The Covenant Theology of Caspar Olevianus*, and the translator and editor of Olevian's *A Firm Foundation*.

R. Scott Clark is Academic Dean and Assistant Professor of Church History, Westminster Theological Seminary, Escondido, California. He has taught at Wheaton College, and is a doctoral candidate in historical theology in Oxford University. He has also written several scholarly essays.

James T. Dennison, Jr. is Librarian and Lecturer in Church History at Westminster Theological Seminary, California. He is the author of *Market Day of the Soul* and editor of Francis Turretin's *Institutes of Elenctic Theology*.

John L. Farthing is Professor at the Steel Center for the Study of Religion and Philosophy, Hendrix College, Arkansas. He is the author of *Thomas Aquinas and Gabriel Biel: Interpretations of St Thomas Aquinas in German Nominalism on the Eve of the Reformation*, as well as numerous scholarly articles on Biel and Zanchi.

W. Robert Godfrey is President and Professor of Church History at Westminster Theological Seminary in California. His PhD thesis from Stanford University, 'Tensions within International Calvinism: The Debate on the Atonement at the Synod of Dordt 1618–1619' continues to attract scholarly attention.

Lowell C. Green is presently Adjunct Professor of History in the State University of New York. He is the author of six books and many scholarly essays focusing on Philip Melanchthon and the Reformation.

Frank A. James III, Reformed Theological Seminary in Orlando, is an editor and translator of the Peter Martyr Library and has edited (with Heiko Oberman) and contributed to *Via Augustini: Augustine in the Later Middle Ages, Renaissance and Reformation*. His Oxford University DPhil thesis 'Praedestinatio Dei: The Intellectual Origins of Peter Martyr Vermigli's Doctrine of Double Predestination' is forthcoming from Oxford University Press.

Martin I. Klauber is a Visiting Professor at Trinity Evangelical Divinity School. He has published a number of articles on the relationship between Reformed scholasticism and rationalism, and a major book, *Between Reformed Scholasticism and Pan-Protestantism: Jean-Alphonse Turretin (1671–1737) and Enlightened Orthodoxy at the Academy of Geneva*.

Richard A. Muller holds the P.J. Zondervan Chair for Doctoral Studies as Professor of Historical Theology at Calvin Theological Seminary. He is the leading authority on Protestant scholasticism and has published numerous scholarly articles and books including *Christ and the Decree: Christology and Predestination in Reformed Theology from Calvin to Perkins* and two volumes of a projected trilogy, *Post-Reformation Reformed Dogmatics*.

John E. Platt is the Chaplain and a fellow of Pembroke College, Oxford, and member of the Faculty of Theology at Oxford University. He has published several authoritative articles on Reformed scholasticism and a major book, *Reformed Thought and Protestant Scholasticism*.

Philip G. Ryken is Associate Pastor, Tenth Presbyterian Church, Philadelphia. He has taught in the Centre for Medieval and Renaissance Studies, Oxford. His Oxford DPhil thesis, 'Thomas Boston (1676–1732): Preacher of the Fourfold State', places Boston in the context of international Calvinism and the development of Reformed theology in Scotland.

Paul R. Schaefer is Assistant Professor of Religion, Northwestern College, Iowa. His doctoral thesis 'The Spiritual Brotherhood on the Habits of the Heart: Cambridge Protestants and the Doctrine of Sanctification from William Perkins to Thomas Shepard' re-examines, among other things, the nature of the Puritan doctrine of assurance.

David P. Scaer is Professor of Systematic Theology at Concordia Theological Seminary, Fort Wayne, Indiana. He is editor of *Concordia Theological Quarterly* and has written the volume on Christology in the series *Confessional Lutheran Dogmatics*. He has also published in numerous scholarly journals.

Donald Sinnema, Trinity Christian College, Illinois, is a well-known scholar of Reformed orthodoxy. He has conducted research into the Synod of Dordt and published numerous articles making a significant contribution to the reassessment of Reformed scholasticism.

David C. Steinmetz, Duke University, is one of the world's leading Reformation scholars. He has written extensively on late Medieval thought and both Lutheran and Reformed wings of the Reformation.

Carl R. Trueman is Lecturer in Historical Theology at the University of Nottingham. He is the author of *Luther's Legacy* and *The Claims of Truth* (a study of the theology of John Owen), as well as a number of scholarly articles on English Protestant theology of the sixteenth and seventeenth centuries.

Introduction

PROTESTANT SCHOLASTICISM: THE NEED FOR REASSESSMENT

This is a volume of *historical* theology, and thus its task is that of historical description, not of systematic or dogmatic evaluation. This is the fundamental distinction between historical and dogmatic or systematic theology. What one ought to believe is a dogmatic judgment. Even the question of the present relevance of orthodoxy to the theological task as pursued in the church and academy today is a matter of dogmatics concerned with the problem of ultimate truth. Historical theology, by contrast, is the discipline of fairly determining and describing what was.

Gerhard Ebeling has complained that historical theology has too often become a refuge for 'those who cannot manage theology'.[1] One might also add that it is too frequently a refuge for those who cannot manage history either, of which much of the literature surrounding Protestant orthodoxy provides classic examples. Why? Because of the way in which scholars have allowed inappropriate theological criteria to shape their historical interpretations. To make this clear, it is necessary to look briefly at the history of theology over the last two hundred years in order to establish the nature of the theological frameworks within which historical analysis frequently takes place.

Post-Kantian theology marked a profound break with and rejection of the Western theological tradition. Where pre-Kantian theology took the Bible as its authoritative starting point, its post-Kantian counterpart, having crossed Lessing's Ugly Ditch, attempted to rescue Christianity from the ravages of the modern historical consciousness and the flux of history.

---

[1] G. Ebeling, *The Study of Theology*, trans. D.A. Priebe (Philadelphia: Fortress, 1978), 67.

Taking its cue from Schleiermacher, liberalism reacted against Protestant scholasticism. Scholasticism was the attempt to adapt the Reformation to the demands of the academy in terms of a precritical world-view. As such, it constituted something of a threat to post-Kantian theology because it was a competing explanation of history and reality which did not depend upon the phenomenal-noumenal distinction for its starting point and yet was not anti-intellectual obscurantism. As every undergraduate theology student knows, post-Kantian theology won the battle, set the trajectories for future debate, and thus wrote the history. Just as the Renaissance tagged the Middle Ages 'dark', modernity labelled orthodoxy 'dead'.

In the twentieth century the image of orthodoxy has been further obscured by the use of the label 'neo-orthodoxy' for the theological movement associated with the names of Karl Barth and Emil Brunner, among others, as if it was a repristination of the old orthodoxy. Barth was himself cognizant of his own break with orthodoxy and did not hold back from sharp criticism of the orthodox when he felt it was necessary.[2] Barthian scholars of Protestant orthodoxy, however, have consistently attempted to cast pre-Enlightenment Reformed theology, particularly that of John Calvin, as fundamentally a proto-Barthian movement in the history of the church.[3] Those theologians who do not fit comfortably within this mould have been relegated by such scholarship either to the rogue's gallery of theological criminals or to the historical-theological ash heap.[4]

[2] See Barth's comments on orthodoxy recorded in Eberhard Busch, *Karl Barth: His Life from Letters and Autobiographical Texts*, trans. John Bowden (Grand Rapids: Eerdmans, 1994), 153–4.

[3] E.g. W. Niesel, *The Theology of John Calvin*, trans. Harold Knight (London: Lutterworth, 1956). The problem with Barthian historiography has been pointed out with some force by James Barr in a recent work: 'Work written from a pro-Barthian standpoint must be judged likely to be biased . . . not because Barthians are necessarily less able in history, but because the Barthian tradition did more than any other theological current to attack the ideal of historical objectivity — especially in biblical exegesis . . . Applying the same principle to their own historical work, which had an important apologetic function, we have to expect it to be biased . . . Barthians asked questions of the older traditions, but they asked them in Barthian form and so obtained Barthian answers. They cannot complain if others discount their work accordingly.' *Biblical Faith and Natural Theology* (Oxford: Clarendon, 1993), 109. For the importance of the Barthianisation of church history for the agendas of Barth's *epigoni*, see Richard A. Muller, 'The Barth Legacy: New Athanasius or Origen Redivivus? A Response to T.F. Torrance', *The Thomist* 54 (1990), 673–704.

[4] For an example of such re-creation of Calvin in Barth's image, combined with a forced distinction between 'covenant' theology and 'federal' theology, see James B. Torrance, 'The Concept of Federal Theology — Was Calvin a Federal Theologian?' in W.H. Neuser (ed.), *Calvinus Sacrae Scripturae Professor: Calvin as Confessor of Holy Scripture* (Grand Rapids: Eerdmans, 1994), 15–41.

The picture, however, is not all black. Since the early 1960s, thanks to the pioneering work of scholars such as Heiko Oberman and David Steinmetz, the academic world has become increasingly aware of the significant points of continuity between medieval philosophy, theology, and exegesis, and the theologies of the Reformation.[5] For example, though Luther and Calvin violently rejected the tradition of nominalist speculation concerning God's absolute power, they accepted implicitly many assumptions about the priority of the divine will inherent in the two-powers distinction. Furthermore, the work of Paul Oskar Kristeller and Charles Schmitt has demonstrated that there was a near-continuous reliance upon Aristotle from the twelfth-century Aristotelian renaissance right through to the early eighteenth century. Yet, at the same time, they have correctly noted the pluriformity of this Aristotelianism.[6] In light of this fact, neither the Reformation, nor the scholastic adaptation of it, appears as the most significant intellectual turning point in modern European history. That honour must be reserved for the Enlightenment's dethronement of Aristotle and the subsequent collapse of the Enlightenment project under the searching light of Immanuel Kant's critical philosophy. To the historian, the continuities in philosophical world-view between the thirteenth and the seventeenth centuries, combined with the watershed nature of the Kantian development would suggest that the theology of Calvin, his Protestant contemporaries and those who succeeded him in the later sixteenth and seventeenth centuries should be assessed in terms of the ongoing Western pre-Kantian tradition, rather than by the criteria formed by post-Kantian theology. It is, one should think, common sense to assume that Calvin's theology would stand in closer relation to his immediate scholastic predecessors and successors than to those who stand in Kant's shadow and within the traditions of critical theology, whether liberal or neo-orthodox, which developed in his wake — and yet such basic historical sensitivity has been conspicuous only by its absence from the mainstream accounts of the development of post-Reformation Protestant theology.[7]

CALVIN AGAINST THE CALVINISTS

Nowhere is this ahistorical *tendenz* more evident than in the body of work which has self-consciously stood in the tradition of Basil Hall's

[5] E.g. Heiko A. Oberman, *The Dawn of the Reformation* (Edinburgh: T. & T. Clark, 1986); David C. Steinmetz, *Luther in Context* (Grand Rapids: Baker, 1995).
[6] See Paul O. Kristeller, *Renaissance Thought: The Classic, Scholastic, and Humanist Strains* (New York: Harper and Row, 1961); Charles B. Schmitt, *Studies in Renaissance Philosophy and Science* (London: Variorum, 1981).
[7] E.g. Ernst Bizer, *Frühorthodoxie und Rationalismus* (Zurich: EVZ, 1963).

essay 'Calvin against the Calvinists' and created an artificial division between the allegedly pristine theology of, for example, John Calvin and its corruption by Theodore Beza and Reformed orthodoxy.[8] The many flaws of this school have been ably and comprehensively exposed by a number of scholars in recent years, especially Richard Muller.[9] His great contribution to this debate has been twofold. First, he has extended and applied to the field of Reformed orthodoxy the insights scholars such as Steinmetz and Oberman have brought to Reformation studies. He has thus refused to judge orthodoxy by anachronistic criteria or by the theology of one or two randomly selected individuals, and has also emphasized the importance of understanding Reformed theology as part of an ongoing Western tradition which extends back through the Middle Ages to the early church. The theologies of the Reformation and the post-Reformation era are neither wholly continuous nor wholly discontinuous with the past — they are, rather, changes in direction within the wider Augustinian, anti-Pelagian tradition of Western theology. As such, the era of orthodoxy must not be set over against its past but must be studied in the context of its medieval and Reformation roots.

Muller's second great contribution is the way in which he has brought to the attention of Protestant scholars a point which has long been a commonplace among Roman Catholic scholars, but which has apparently been overlooked by their Protestant counterparts: that to describe a theology as scholastic is to make a statement about its method not its content.[10] *Pace* the classic definition of scholasticism provided by Brian G. Armstrong,[11] it is clear that the theologies of Thomas Aquinas, Durandus, Scotus, Ockham, and Gabriel Biel, while all enjoying classification as scholastic, seem to possess very little (if any) identity in terms of detailed theological substance. For example, the systems of Aquinas and Biel contain significantly different, if not radically opposed, doctrines of predestination. Yet both can legitimately be classified as scholastic. The same is true of Protestant scholastic systems, e.g. those

---

[8]   Basil Hall, 'Calvin Against the Calvinists' in *John Calvin*, ed. G.E. Duffield (Grand Rapids: Eerdmans, 1966).

[9]   For a good survey and general critique of the older approach to Protestant scholasticism see R.A. Muller, 'Calvin and the "Calvinists": Assessing Continuities and Discontinuities between the Reformation and Orthodoxy', *Calvin Theological Journal* 30 (1995), 345–75, and 31 (1996), 125–60.

[10]   See for example, the discussion of scholasticism by James A. Weisheipl, 'Scholastic Method' in *The New Catholic Encyclopedia* (New York: Catholic University of America, 1967), 12: 1145–6.

[11]   Brian G. Armstrong, *Calvinism and the Amyraut Heresy* (Madison: University of Wisconsin Press, 1969), 31–2.

of Arminius and Ursinus,[12] and this pattern can be repeated with respect to almost any relevant theologian, system, or doctrine which one might select as a test case. It would therefore seem that Roman Catholic theologians have been correct to assert that what these scholastic theologians shared was a way of approaching and arranging their subject matter and not a *weltanschauung* which necessarily determined the nature of the subject matter.

These two insights, one stressing the necessity of understanding Protestant orthodoxy in its own historical-intellectual context, the other ridding the word scholasticism of its pejorative connotations, have effected a change in the scholarship surrounding this area the long-term impact of which should be nothing short of revolutionary.

A MODEST METHODOLOGICAL SUGGESTION

As an exercise in historical theology, this volume assumes that theology is a topic worthy of investigation on its own merits. In contrast to the contemporary infatuation of many historians with exclusively materialist and self-proclaimed 'postmodern' analyses of history, it also assumes that humans act, at least partly, out of theological motives as well as social, economic, and political ones. Historical theology is concerned to locate theologians and theologies within their particular contexts, and in this task history in the more general sense serves primarily to illumine theology, in much the same way that background studies illumine one's interpretation of any historical text.[13] To use the language of modern hermeneutical theory, history provides the means for understanding the horizons of our subjects, points us to which questions can legitimately be asked, and reveals which questions, through their anachronistic presuppositions, are irrelevant. When pursued in this way, using a framework of interpretation sensitive to the critical questions of historical method, historical theology is free to perform an extraordinarily important

---

[12] See R.A. Muller, 'The Federal Motif in Seventeenth Century Arminian Theology', *Nederlands Archief voor Kerkgeschiedenis* 62 (1982), 102–22; *God, Creation and Providence in the Thought of Jacob Arminius* (Grand Rapids: Baker, 1991); 'God, Predestination, and the Integrity of the Created Order: A Note on Patterns in Arminius' Theology' in W. Fred Graham (ed.), *Later Calvinism: International Perspectives*, Sixteenth Century Essays and Studies 22 (Kirksville, Mo.: Sixteenth Century Journal, 1994); 'Arminius and the Scholastic Tradition', *Calvin Theological Journal* 24 (1989), 263–77. See also Eef Dekker, 'Jacobus Arminus and His Logic: Analysis of a Letter', *Journal of Theological Studies* 44 (1993), 118–42.

[13] On the development of historical theology as a discipline see J. Pelikan, *Historical Theology: Continuity and Change in Christian Doctrine* (London: Hutchinson, 1971).

function in the academy and in the church: it relieves the individual of today of the burden of reinventing the Christianity of the past in his or her own image; and it also prevents unhistorical romanticism about earlier epochs in the history of the church, a problem prevalent both in Barthian and, more especially, in conservative pietistic traditions. Careful, thoughtful historical investigation reveals that the church has always been more or less imperfect and that there have been no golden ages, patristic, medieval, or Reformation, despite what conservatives and liberals have asserted to the contrary.

These observations get to the nature of the historiographical problem: the distorting impact which certain idealist models of history have had upon the understanding of post-Reformation theology. For example, one harmful but guiding assumption of much of Reformation and post-Reformation historiography has been that there are 'golden ages' such that the present state of the church pales in comparison to some perceived time when all was right with the church. Often the story is cast as a simple case of 'rise and fall'. The Reformation was a good thing but, in the seventeenth and eighteenth centuries, 'fell' into orthodoxy and scholasticism, which, of course, in fine *1066 and All That* fashion, was self-evidently 'a Very Bad Thing'. Sometimes the golden age is extended to the eve of the Enlightenment, where the rot is seen to set in with Descartes, Hume, etc. — but in both cases the basic presuppositions and framework are the same.

The Golden Age model has two faults. First, it typically smooths out the rough spots in a particular era by treating theology as though it dropped out of the sky, or, perhaps better, straight out of the Bible. It does not. Humans do theology in specific historical, cultural contexts, and theological issues are always more complex than the Golden Age model allows. One does not have to reduce everything to an extreme materialist model of history to acknowledge the truth of this statement. In addition, it does not always allow for the fact that we live in the late twentieth century, not the sixteenth or seventeenth. If one wishes to appropriate the sixteenth or seventeenth century, for example, as a model for contemporary church theology, one must do so without blinkers and with an awareness of the theological, cultural, and philosophical developments between then and now. Ignoring the critical questions of history does not make them go away.

A second model for interpreting the historical development of theology within the church is the Hegelian-inspired dialectical approach, where history is seen as a living organism, with each epoch representing either a positive movement (thesis) a negative reaction (antithesis) or a resulting synthesis. One implication of this model is that any claim to continuity with the past or doctrinal certainty is relativized by the ruthless progress of history. Like those of the Golden Age approach, the presuppositions of this school are also too simplistic. The history of historical theology has shown that whenever scholars have given themselves to the intense study of the primary sources of any given period, they have found that things are too complicated to allow for easy and straightforward taxonomies. Therefore, theologians of a given epoch should not be pressed into a predetermined mould.[14] Having said that, the Hegelian historians have the advantage over the advocates of the Golden Age approach that they recognized the developmental nature of theology: theology is a cumulative enterprise, and there are organic links between thinkers in different eras.

In light of the above, it would seem that a successful explanation of the history of theology must account not only for the 'one', i.e. that which unifies thinkers between epochs, but also for the 'many', i.e. the concrete particulars which distinguish theologians of one era from those in another. To do so, one must account for the development of doctrine. It is the guiding assumption of the editors of this volume, if not all the contributors, that Western theology has a developmental history. Luther and Calvin, for example, built on insights gained from the voluntarist reaction to Thomas. Zwingli, on the other hand, cannot be properly understood without reference to his Thomist background. Yet neither can the Reformation and post-Reformation eras be reduced to a redux of the late medieval theologies. There was a synthesis in Protestantism of patristic, medieval and Reformation insights combined with an appropriation of powerful methodological and philological influences from the Renaissance. If the first stages of the Reformation were the product of a confluence of theological and cultural threads, the development of Protestant scholasticism must be seen as an extension of that process.

Fundamental to understanding the nature of this extension is the historical fact that, in many ways, Protestant scholasticism had a different locus to that of the earlier Reformation: the latter was largely, though not universally, ecclesial in nature, while the former was involved perhaps more centrally in theological and methodological reform of the classroom and university. Thus the later stages of the Reformation had a slightly

---

[14] F.C. Baur (1792–1860) is the most notable proponent of this theory of history. The influential Mercersburg historians, Philip Schaff (1819–1903) and J.W. Nevin (1803–86), learned their dialectical–romantic view of history from J.A.W. Neander (1789–1850). On Schaff see S.R. Graham, *Cosmos in the Chaos: Philip Schaff's Interpretation of Nineteenth Century American Religion* (Grand Rapids: Eerdmans, 1995). On Nevin see J.H. Nichols, *Romanticism in American Theology: Nevin and Schaff at Mercersburg* (Chicago: Chicago University Press, 1961). J.H. Newman (1801–90) is the most notable British practitioner of this method: see his *Essay on the Development of Christian Doctrine* (London, 1845).

more academic and less popular character. This volume is, in part, an attempt to account for that relocation of the Reformation and to delineate its impact.

In the last twenty-five years many scholars, a number of whom are contributing here, have moved away from the traditional models whereby Protestant scholasticism was judged by the standards of later theology, whether Barthian, neo-Calvinist or whatever, to developmental models which attempt to set the movement within the context of its own times and within the ongoing Western theological tradition. A number of very important monographs and articles which adopt this approach have appeared, but until now there has been no attempt to present within a single volume a series of essays representing the best of contemporary scholarly thought on this subject. This volume aims to do just that. It contains essays on aspects of Protestant scholasticism from the Reformation through to the Enlightenment, all written by scholars who are experts within their fields, and many of whom are acknowledged as world authorities.

Much of the work in this field has been done by scholars who have drawn deeply from the historical work of Heiko Oberman, David Steinmetz, and Richard Muller, the last two of whom contribute to this volume. The work of these scholars is represented in the first four sections of the book where, with the exception of David Bagchi's carefully nuanced analysis of Luther, the focus is on Reformed theology. The major subdivisions are based primarily on chronological considerations, but the inclusion of a separate section on British Reformed theology marks an attempt to underline the fact that the theological content of Puritanism was not, as many studies of the subject suggest, a primarily Anglo-Saxon phenomenon but was part of the overall tradition of Reformed theology in the seventeenth century.

It would, however, be indicative of a naive and unhistorical parochialism if the volume concentrated solely on Reformed theology. Lutheran theology, too, was undergoing parallel transformations and development in the period concerned and many Lutheran scholars are now engaged in the substantial reassessment of Lutheran orthodoxy initiated by the ground-breaking work of Robert Preus on Post-Reformation Lutheranism. The editors are thus pleased that American Lutheran scholars Lowell Green and David Scaer, writing from within a very different tradition to that which looks to the work of Steinmetz and Muller, graciously agreed to contribute a section on Lutheran theology to this volume in order to allow for juxtaposition not only of studies of the two great Protestant traditions but also of different scholarly approaches. Readers can then judge for themselves how the two contemporary streams may learn from each other.

It is hoped, in conclusion, that this collection will help to stimulate further research and debate on the issues it confronts and also that it will go some way to sending an unequivocal signal to the scholarly world at large, and to those committed to the unhistorical presuppositions of the old dogmatic approaches in particular, that, to use the words of another protest, 'the times they are a-changing' — if, indeed, they have not changed already.

Carl R. Trueman,   R. Scott Clark,
University of Nottingham.   Wheaton College.

                                    January, 1997.

PART 1
LUTHER AND CALVIN

1

Sic Et Non:
Luther and Scholasticism

D.V.N. Bagchi

INTRODUCTION

There is a case to be made for dating the outbreak of the Protestant
Reformation not to the ninety-five theses on indulgences of October
1517, but to Luther's ninety-seven theses against scholastic theology of a
month earlier. As invitations to academic debate, both sets of theses met
with a resounding silence, though the indulgence theses caught the
popular imagination rather better. It was not until March 1518, at the
annual meeting of the Augustinian order at Heidelberg, that Luther's
anti-scholastic colours were fully recognized, and from that moment his
rejection of the authority of the schoolmen became a capital offence in
the eyes of his opponents.

Luther's aversion to scholasticism and its methods is so much part of
his teaching throughout his life that it is sometimes easy to lose sight of
the fact that his opposition was from the inside. Although condemned by
later Catholic historians as a degenerate form of scholasticism, the *via
moderna* in which he pursued his arts studies was a scholastic training
nonetheless. And yet this same man, who decried the 'pig-theologians'
as worse than the heathen from whom they borrowed their theology,
thought nothing of returning to the scholastic trough when it suited the
exigencies of argument. Whether opposing d'Ailly to Aquinas over
transubstantiation, or exchanging subtle distinctions of the meanings of
'necessity' with that other avowed enemy of school-theology, Erasmus,
or developing the doctrine of ubiquity against the sacramentarians, Luther
demonstrated that he was able and willing to use the very methods he so
execrated in other contexts.

Luther's attitude to the mystical traditions of the late Middle Ages has justly been characterized as 'sic et non'.[1] In his attitude to the scholastic traditions, Luther's 'non' (or, rather, his 'immo'[2]) sounds loud and clear enough. But should we suspect that, as in his own exposition of Jesus's rejection of the Syro-Phoenician woman, behind the 'non' there lies at least some sort of 'sic'?

A SCHOLASTIC REJECTION OF SCHOLASTICISM?

Luther's critique of scholasticism was emphatically that of a scholastic, and not that of a humanist or of an anti-intellectual champion of the 'modern devotion'. Although in recent years it has been shown that his knowledge of Aquinas was not as meagre as was once thought,[3] it is clear that his tertiary education was thoroughly Ockhamist. The arts faculty at Erfurt, where he took his MA in 1505, was dominated by such teachers of the *via moderna* as Bartholomaeus Arnoldi von Usingen and Jodocus Trutfetter,[4] while the theological instruction he received at the

---

[1] See Heiko A. Oberman, 'Simul gemitus et raptus: Luther and mysticism' in idem, *The Dawn of the Reformation* (Edinburgh: T. & T. Clark, 1986), 126–54, esp. 131–41.

[2] On the significance of this word in Luther's early writings, see Heiko A. Oberman ' "Immo": Luthers reformatorische Entdeckungen im Spiegel der Rhetorik', in *Lutheriana: Zum 500. Geburtstag Martin Luthers von den Mitarbeitern der Weimarer Ausgabe*, ed. G. Hammer and K.-H. zur Mühlen, Archiv zur Weimarer Ausgabe, 5 (Cologne and Vienna: Böhlau, 1984), 17–38.

[3] See esp. John L. Farthing, *Thomas Aquinas and Gabriel Biel: Interpretations of St Thomas Aquinas in German Nominalism on the Eve of the Reformation* (Durham, N.C.: Duke University Press, 1988); Denis R. Janz, *Luther on Thomas Aquinas: The Angelic Doctor in the Thought of the Reformer* (Stuttgart: Franz Steiner, 1989); and Otto H. Pesch, *Martin Luther, Thomas von Aquin und die reformatorische Kritik an der Scholastik: Zur Geschichte und Wirkungsgeschichte eines Missverständnisses mit weltgeschichtlichen Folgen* (Göttingen: Vandenhoeck & Ruprecht, 1994).

[4] See W. Urban, 'Die "via moderna" an der Universität Erfurt am Vorabend der Reformation' in *Gregor von Rimini: Werk und Wirkung bis zur Reformation*, ed. H.A. Oberman (Berlin and New York: De Gruyter, 1981), 311–30. For further details on Luther's teachers, see E. Kleineidam, 'Die Bedeutung der Augustinereremiten für die Universität Erfurt im Mittelalter und in der Reformationszeit' in *Scientia Augustiniana: Festschrift für Adolar Zumkeller* (Würzburg: Augustinus, ed. C.P. Meyer and W. Eckermann 1975), 395–422; N. Paulus, *Der Augustiner Bartholomäus Arnoldi von Usingen, Luthers Lehrer und Gegner: Ein Lebensbild* (Freiburg: Herder, 1893); N. Häring, *Die Theologie des Erfurter Augustiner-Eremiten Bartholomäus Arnoldi von Usingen. Beitrag zur Dogmengeschichte der Reformationszeit* (Limburg: Pallotiner, 1939); and G. Plitt, *Jodokus Trutfetter von Eisenach, der Lehrer Luthers in seinem Wirken geschildert* (Erlangen: Deichert, 1876).

Augustinian house in the same city was probably also predominantly Ockhamist, to judge from the presence there of Johann Nathin (a former student of Biel) and Johann von Paltz.[5] This influence is evident in the marginal comments Luther added to an edition of Lombard's *Sentences* in 1509–10, where he shows himself to be in broad agreement with the *via moderna* in rejecting the notion of a created *habitus*.[6] It is still palpable in at least some passages of his Psalms lectures of 1513–15, for instance in his favourable use of the formula 'facienti quod in se est', and of the idea of congruent and condign merit.[7] As late as 1520, long after Luther had decisively rejected scholastic theology, he continued to describe himself as an Ockhamist, a modern, or a terminist, and to speak of the Venerable Inceptor himself as a logician of the highest ability.[8]

It is, however, equally clear that Luther took an increasingly critical stance towards the whole scholastic enterprise. Unfortunately, we lack any record of his first series of lectures, on the *Nicomachaean Ethics*, given as professor of moral philosophy at the University of Wittenberg during his abortive stay there in 1508/9. But by the time he came to lecture on Lombard, a critical attitude towards Aristotle was already emerging, as is shown by his impatience with the application of 'that stinking philosopher, Aristotle' and 'the stinking rules of the logicians', to

---

[5] See B. Hamm, *Frömmigkeitstheologie am Anfang des 16. Jahrhunderts: Studien zu Johannes von Paltz und seinem Umkreis* (Tübingen: J.C.B. Mohr (Paul Siebeck), 1982). None of Nathin's works has survived.

[6] For text, see J.C.F. Knaake (ed.), *D. Martin Luthers Werke: Kritische Gesamtausgabe* (Weimar: Böhlau, 1883–) = *Weimarer Ausgabe* [hereafter *WA*]), 9:28–94. The classic study of Luther's notes on the *Sentences* remains Paul Vignaux, *Luther, commentateur des Sentences (livre I, distinction XVII)* (Paris: J. Vrin, 1935).

[7] See *WA* 4:262.4–7, English translation in *Luther's Works*, ed. J. Pelikan and H.T. Lehmann (Philadelphia: Fortress St Louis: Concordia, 1955–86) [hereafter *LW*], vol. 11, 396; *WA* 4:312.39 = *LW* 11:424; *WA* 4:329.33 = *LW* 11:448f.; *WA* 4:344.4 = *LW* 11:468.

[8] 'Alioqui, cur et meae sectae resisterem, scilicet Occanicae seu Modernorum, quam penitus imbibitam teneo, si verbis voluissem aut vi compesci? Sed satis haec', *Responsio ad condemnationem doctrinalem per Lovaniensis et Coloniensis factam*, 1520 (*WA* 6:195.3–6); 'Nolo tantum respective, sed absolute et certe doceri. Sum enim Occanicae factionis, qui respectus contemnunt, omnia autem absoluta habent, ut sic iocer in istam Moriam', *Adversus execrabilem Antichristi bullam*, 1521 (*WA* 6:600.10–12); 'Occam, magister meus, summus fuit dialecticus', *D. Martin Luthers Werke: Kritische Gesamtausgabe: Tischreden* (Weimar: Böhlau, 1912–21) [hereafter *WA TR*], vol. 2, 516, line 6); 'Occam, quamvis ingenio vicerat omnes et confutavit reliquas vias omnes . . .', (*WA TR* 4:679.24). See also *WA* 38:160.3 ('Mein meister Occam'); 39.I:420.27 ('Magister meus Occam'); 30.II:300.10 = *LW* 34:27 ('Occam, mein lieber Meister'). Given the context, the last example may have been intended ironically.

theology.[9] It is possible that an anti-Aristotelian tradition within the Augustinian Order helped to form Luther's opinions at this stage.[10] Surprisingly, the Psalms lectures reflect little of this upheaval, but the lectures on Romans of 1515–16 reveal an almost obsessive hostility towards scholastic theology. Not only has he finally broken with the nominalist conception of 'doing what is in one',[11] but his personal scorn for the 'stulti, Sautheologen' of the *via moderna* is more marked than ever.[12]

The Romans lectures belong to a phase in Luther's rejection of scholastic theology which includes his annotations on Biel's *Collectorium* on the *Sentences*, made about 1515, and the disputation 'On the Powers and the Will of Man apart from Grace', prepared for Bartholomaeus Bernhardi von Feldkirchen in September 1516.[13] It is clear that this phase saw his opposition to scholasticism become very much sharper. One reason for this sharpening might be his reading for the first time the anti-Pelagian treatises of Augustine, especially *On the Spirit and the Letter*,[14] which seemed to him to put the covenantal theologies of nominalism beyond the pale of orthodoxy.[15] Another might be that he experienced his 'Reformation breakthrough' shortly before, or in the course of, the Romans lectures. If that is the case, then his hitherto fairly conventional antipathy to Aristotle on the grounds of the separateness of theology and philosophy would have given way to the much more specific and personal objection that Aristotle's *Ethics* had encouraged

[9] 'Commentum illud de habitibus opinionem habet ex verbis Aristotelis rancidi philosophi' (*WA* 9:43.4–5); 'sicut rancidae logicorum regulae somniunt' (*WA* 9:47.6). On Luther's attitude to Aristotle see Wilhelm Link, *Das Ringen Luthers um die Freiheit der Theologie von der Philosophie*, ed. Ernst Wolf and Manfred Mezger (Munich: C. Kaiser, 1955²), 160–3; W. Eckermann, 'Die Aristoteleskritik Luthers: Ihre Bedeutung für seine Theologie', *Catholica* 32 (1978), 114–30; and K.-H. zur Mühlen, 'Luther und Aristoteles', *Luther Jahrbuch* 52 (1985), 263–6.
[10] See Adolar Zumkeller, 'Die Augustinertheologien Simon Fidati von Cascia und Hugolin von Orvieto und Martin Luthers Kritik an Aristoteles', *Archiv für Reformationsgeschichte* 54 (1963), 13–37.
[11] *WA* 56:502.32–503.5 = *LW* 25:497.
[12] *WA* 56:274.14 = *LW* 25:261.
[13] For text, see *WA* 1:145–51.
[14] The others were *De peccatorum meritis et remissione, Contra duas epistulas Pelagianorum*, and *Contra Iulianum*. See Luther's letter to Spalatin of 19 October 1516, in *D. Martin Luthers Werke: Kritische Gesamtausgabe: Briefwechsel* (Weimar: Böhlau, 1930) [hereafter *WABr*], vol. 1, 70, lines 8–16, no. 27.
[15] See Leif Grane, *Modus loquendi theologicus: Luthers Kampf um die Erneuerung der Theologie (1515–18)*, Acta Theologica Danica 12 (Leiden: E.J. Brill, 1975), esp. 23–62.

generations of Christians (himself included) to think of the righteousness of God in the 'active', or retributive, sense.[16]

During the academic year 1516/17 it becomes clear that Luther's hostility towards scholastic theology was not the isolated protest of a disenchanted individual, but part of a wider campaign at Wittenberg. His chief ally in this campaign was Andreas Bodenstein von Karlstadt, dean of the arts faculty. Karlstadt, a Thomist, initially took exception to the hot-headed attack on school-theology launched by his younger colleague, and set about the detailed study of Augustine in order to refute him with his own weapons. It had the opposite effect, and in April 1517 Karlstadt published 151 theses, the first blast of Wittenberg's trumpet against scholasticism. Naturally there were differences at this stage between Luther's and Karlstadt's ideas, but these differences are significant only in the light of later developments:[17] at the time, Luther clearly saw Karlstadt's theses as a decisive event, and sent copies to friends (including Christoph Scheurl at Nuremberg[18]), and a few days later wrote a famous letter to Lang in triumphal mood:

> Our theology and St Augustine proceed apace and are dominant in our university, by the grace of God. Aristotle declines steadily and is heading for total oblivion. All object to hearing lectures on the text-books of the Sentences, and no one can expect an audience who does not advance this theology — that is, the Bible or St Augustine, or some other doctor with ecclesiastical authority.[19]

In September 1517, Luther made his first contribution to the renewal of theology which was designed to have an impact beyond Wittenberg. His theses for Franz Günther, known since the middle of the nineteenth century as 'the Disputation against Scholastic Theology', share Karlstadt's intention of depicting scholastic theology as Pelagian.[20] It would be satisfying to think of Karlstadt the renegade Thomist and Luther the

---

[16]   For this argument, see Alister E. McGrath, *Luther's Theology of the Cross: Martin Luther's Theological Breakthrough* (Oxford: Blackwell, 1985), 136–41.

[17]   For an account of the theses, which also includes most of the text, see Ernst Kähler, *Karlstadt und Augustin: Der Kommentar des Andreas Bodenstein von Karlstadt zu Augustins Schrift De spiritu et litera*, Hallische Monographien 19 (Halle: Niemeyer, 1952), 8–37.

[18]   See Luther's letter to Scheurl, 6 May 1517 (*WABr* 1:93f., no. 38).

[19]   Luther to Johann Lang, 18 May 1517 (*WABr* 1:98f., no. 41).

[20]   For text, see *WA* 1:224–8 = *LW* 31:9–16 = *Luther: Early Theological Works*, Library of Christian Classics [hereafter *LCC*] (London: SCM, 1962), ed. James Atkinson, 266–73. The most extensive study of these theses can be found in Leif Grane, *Contra Gabrielem: Luthers Auseinandersetzung mit Gabriel Biel in der Disputatio contra scholasticam theologiam 1517* (Copenhagen: Gyldendal, 1962).

renegade Ockhamist fighting each on his own front, one 'contra Capreolum' and one 'contra Gabrielem'; but the stronger impression is that Karlstadt is at this stage the senior partner, who sets out a programme for an Augustinian reform of theology, while Luther is left with the more restricted and negative task of battering the old theology to death.[21] So the second blast of Wittenberg's trumpet had to wait until the following May. In the meantime, Luther had achieved wide celebrity, not (as he had hoped) for his attack on scholastic theology, but for his engagement with an aspect of pastoral theology. When Luther was offered centre-stage at the congress of Augustinians at Heidelberg, it must have been puzzling to his expectant hearers that he chose not to defend his position on indulgences, but to develop his anti-scholasticism into a positive theology of the cross.[22] Of course, for Luther the contemporary shortcomings of speculative and pastoral theology were two sides of the same coin.

The Heidelberg Disputation contained nothing in its anti-scholasticism which Luther had not essayed before; but in its polemical contrast between the *theologia crucis* and the *theologia gloriae* it succeeded in unchurching the schoolmen to an extent that few critics had even attempted. A young Dominican who was present that day, Martin Bucer, certainly felt that Luther had taken a decisive step forward in saying openly what Erasmus had only hinted at. Luther for his part felt that the theology of the cross was gaining support amongst such young men as Bucer, even as it was losing the support of the old.[23] He was thinking of his Erfurt arts professors: Trutfetter, who had diplomatically sported his oak when his notorious former student called on his way back from Heidelberg, and Usingen, whom Luther failed to win over on the same journey. While still in Erfurt, Luther wrote to Trutfetter to dispel any hard feelings, and the result is perhaps the most poignant and revealing of all his voluminous correspondence of the time. Poignant, because Luther clearly feels that he is developing his master's own insights — 'Permit me to treat the schoolmen as you yourself have treated them' (that is, accepting their authority only where it is consonant with Scripture and the Fathers); revealing, because this letter contains a clear statement of Luther's motive in attacking scholastic theology:

> I simply believe that it is impossible to reform the Church, unless the canons, decretals, scholastic theology, philosophy, logic, as we now have them, be eradicated completely and other studies substituted; and I

[21]   See Karl Bauer, *Die Wittenberger Universitätstheologie und die Anfänge der deutschen Reformation* (Tübingen: J.C.B. Mohr (Paul Siebeck), 1928), 46.

[22]   For text, see *WA* 1:353–74. English translations in *LW* 31:39–70 and *LCC* 16:266–73.

[23]   Luther to Spalatin, 18 May 1518 (*WABr* 1:174.42–7, no. 75).

proceed accordingly in that conviction, when I pray God each day that this may happen immediately, and the purest study of the Bible and the holy fathers be recalled. You think I am no logician, and perhaps I'm not; but this I know, that I fear no-one's logic in defending this conviction.[24]

Despite the *ad hominem* tone of this explanation of his actions, there is no reason to doubt the sincerity of Luther's belief that he was merely taking Trutfetter's own approach to its conclusion. Trutfetter had apparently followed Augustine in distinguishing sharply between canonical and apocryphal books: the former are to be treated with faith, the latter with judgment.[25] We know that Trutfetter and Usingen also made a more fundamental distinction between the necessary truths of revelation and experience and the accidental truths of speculative reason.[26] This is broadly identical with Luther's own position in the spring of 1518, except that his teachers' qualitative distinction becomes in Luther's hands a polemical separation.

Luther's debt to his scholastic teachers found practical expression in the course of the indulgence controversy. I do not mean by this simply that he conducted the controversy according to the rules of scholastic disputation, following the *propositiones* of October 1517 with their *resolutiones* the following year, and then engaging at last in a live and public debate with Karlstadt and Eck in 1519. Much more striking are his repeated assertions, as a precondition for debate, that consonance with Scripture, with the Fathers, with canon law, and with reason and experience, be accepted (in that order) as the basis on which the validity of arguments were to be tested. What is missing from this list of 'ecclesiastical' authorities is of course the teaching of scholastic theologians. 'For the sake of argument', he asks that such teaching be regarded as 'mere opinions', to be accepted or rejected merely on the basis of reason and experience, where they are not supported by the first three authorities.[27] The task of the theologian (as he reminded the Master of the Sacred Palace, Sylvester Prierias!) is to put forward the truth of the gospel and of the church, not his own opinions.[28]

---

[24] Luther to Jodocus Trutfetter, 9 May 1518 (*WABr* 1:170.33–40, no. 74).

[25] *WABr* 1:171–4.

[26] See Urban, 'Via moderna', 325.

[27] See the *Resolutiones disputationum de indulgentiarum virtute*, 1518 (*WA* 1:529–628, at 529.30–530.12), translated as *Explanations of the Ninety-five Theses* (*LW* 31:83–252, at 83); also *Ad dialogum Silvestri Prieratis de potestate papae responsio*, 1518 (*WA* 1:647–86, at 647.17–648.1).

[28] *Ad dialogum Prieratis responsio*, *WA* 1:648.2–9: 'Nam si apud Iureconsultos proverbium recipitur "Turpe est Iuristam loqui sine textu", tu vide, quam sit honorificum Theologum (qui maxime omnium debet) loqui sine textu, quem Apostolus iubet calceatum esse pedibus in praeparatione Euangelii et Episcopum

The *Explanations of the Ninety-five Theses* and the *Response to Prierias* were not published until August 1518. But Luther made the same point for a lay audience as early as the preceding March. In a little-known but highly significant sermon which pithily summarized his thoughts on indulgences, in the vernacular, he made a sharp distinction between unfounded opinions and the certainty offered by Scripture and the church. Something of the flavour of the *Sermon on Indulgence and Grace* can be got from the first and penultimate paragraphs:

> You should know that some recent teachers, such as the Master of the Sentences, St Thomas, and their followers divide the sacrament of penance into three parts . . . This division stems from their own opinion, and is scarcely, or rather not at all, based on Holy Scripture, or on the ancient, holy Christian teachers . . . On these points I have no doubts, for they are well enough grounded in Holy Scripture, and you should have no doubts about them either. Let the scholastic doctors be scholastic. Even added together, their opinions could not substantiate one sermon.[29]

Luther's motivation is clear. In attacking scholasticism he believed that he was bringing back to the Church (in the sense of both clergy and laity) a firm basis both for theological certainty and religious faith. But the hierarchy of authorities which alone could restore such certainty was itself 'a scholastic distinction'. It was a debt which, in his poignant, parting letter to Trutfetter, Luther was ready to acknowledge.

---

potentem, non in syllogismis et opinionibus hominum, sed in doctrina sana, nimirum ea, quam alibi divinitus inspiratam vocat. Hoc enim consilium si fuisset servatum, minus nunc Ecclesia haberet inutilium quaestionum et opinionum, et plus Euangelii et Christianae veritatis.' One is reminded of a passage from Luther's letter to the bishop of Brandenburg on 13 February 1518, which Leif Grane sees as highly significant for Luther's re-asserting of a proper theological *modus loquendi*: 'Porro scholasticis doctoribus et canonistis constat nullam deberi a nobis fidem, dum suas opinantur opiniones. Et, ut vulgo dicitur: Turpe est Iuristam loqui sine textu. At multo turpius est Theologum loqui sine textu. Non Aristotelis dico, Nam hunc plus, valde, nimis, satis loquuntur, sed nostro, id est sacrae scripturae, Canonum, Ecclesiasticorum patrum.' (*WABr* 1:139.27–32, no. 32). See Grane, *Modus loquendi theologicus*, 143. Luther's belief that scholastic theology produced only opinions, not certitude, remained strong throughout his life. As late as the lectures on Genesis, from his last decade, he could write, 'Ideo Scholastica Theologia nihil aliud est quam opinio' (*WA* 44:732.1–3) — though now lawyers and Jews are mentioned in the same breath as schoolmen!

[29]   *Ein Sermon von den Ablass und Gnade*, 1518 (*WA* 1:243–46, at 243.4–10 and 246.27–30).

A RETURN TO SCHOLASTICISM?

To suggest that Luther's rejection of scholasticism was itself in a sense 'scholastic' is by no means to suggest that it was incomplete or insincere. It is difficult to imagine a more absolute renunciation. And yet there remains the fact that in later years Luther frequently returned to scholastic ways of arguing. He was quite unselfconscious on such occasions and clearly felt no need to explain himself. There were of course the disputations which continued at Wittenberg throughout Luther's life and to which he was an enthusiastic contributor.[30] But there were also the scholastic distinctions which he frequently made in his writings against opponents. In the *Babylonian Captivity of the Church* of 1520, he used the Ockhamist Pierre d'Ailly's critique of transubstantiation as the basis of his own view, namely that after consecration the bread and wine remain in their natural substances alongside the body and blood of Christ. It is true that he does distance himself, partly by referring to his discovery of d'Ailly as in the past ('some years ago, when I was drinking in scholastic theology'), partly by denying the ability of any philosophy to grasp what can be grasped only by faith. Here he does not try to clinch an argument by using a scholastic authority, but only to point to the existence of a variety of 'opinions', of which transubstantiation is just one.[31]

The second example is of a distinction proper. In this treatise on justification against Latomus, written from the Wartburg in 1521, Luther made a number of distinctions. One, on the believer as both righteous and a sinner, he had made for some time.[32] Another, between 'grace' and 'gift' (that is, between God's favour towards us and the change which that

---

[30]   See H. Hermenlink, 'Luther als Disputator' in *WA* 39.II: xxxiii–xxxvii; and E. Wolf, 'Zur wissenschaftsgeschichtlichen Bedeutung der Disputationen an der Wittenberger Universität im 16. Jahrhundert' in idem (ed.), *Peregrinatio II: Studien zur reformatorischen Theologie, zum Kirchenrecht und Sozialethik* (Münster, 1965), 38–51.

[31]   *WA* 6:508–12 = *LW* 36:28–35. For a detailed discussion of Luther's treatment of transubstantiation in this connection, see Leif Grane, 'Luthers Kritik an Thomas von Aquin in De captivitate Babylonica', *Zeitschrift für Kirchengeschichte* 80 (1969), 1–13; and, more briefly, idem, 'Luther and scholasticism' in *Luther and Learning*, ed. Marilyn J. Harran (Selinsgrove: Susquehanna University Press, 1985), 52–68, at 64.

[32]   Interestingly, Luther used Aristotelian categories — against the scholastics — to establish the doctrine of 'simul iustus et peccator' in the Romans lectures (see *WA* 56:441.24–442.14 = *LW* 25:433f.). He returned to such distinctions for the same purpose throughout his life. See the Psalms lectures of 1538, where he again deployed Aristotelian categories to defend the principle of extrinsic righteousness (*WA* 40.II:518.7); and the promotion disputation of 3 July 1545, *WA* 39.II:340.1–9 (where he cites the *moderni* approvingly) and 39.II:363.1–4. Similar arguments can be found in *WA TR* 1:5.17–27, no. 11; 533.5–21, no. 1057.

effects inwardly), took on a new significance, though he had interpreted Romans 5:15–17 according to this distinction in his Romans lectures. Most interestingly of all, he introduces a series of distinctions in order to show how the Christian can both be suffering under sin, and yet be victorious over it in Christ. The sophists, he goes on, 'know nothing at all of what quality sin has when categorized by quantity, quality, relation, action, and passion'.[33] These categories may be those of Quintilian rather than of Aristotle; but Luther's use of them is still remarkable, especially so since in the same treatise he explicitly aligns his own approach with 'the simple, Pauline way of understanding and speaking [modum intelligendi et loquendi] which *needs no distinctions* and is wonderfully attractive and clear'.[34] Again, Luther demonstrates no embarrassment at the apparent dissonance between his rejection of scholasticism and his use of its methods and *modus loquendi*.

The third example is the very strange one of his encounter with Erasmus over free will, in which the two most famous anti-scholastics of their day traded scholastic terms. When dealing with the question of whether Judas betrayed Christ by free will (in which case he deserved punishment) or by God's coercion (in which case he did not), Erasmus distinguished between a necessity of consequence (*necessitas consequentiae*, sometimes referred to as conditional necessity) and a necessity of the thing consequent (*necessitas consequentis*, or absolute necessity). If and while A is the case, then B cannot be the case — that is the necessity of consequence; but it does not follow that B could not, under other circumstances, have been the case, so there is no absolute necessity of the thing consequent. The point of this distinction — and his use of it clearly causes Erasmus some embarrassment — is that the betrayal happened necessarily in the sense that God infallibly knew of it; but Judas could have acted differently, in which case God would infallibly have known that instead. Luther had never accepted this distinction as a worthwhile one, and his position in *The Bondage of the Will* was no

---

[33] *WA* 8:88.3–6 = *LW* 32:201 = *LCC* 16:336.

[34] *WA* 8:107.38–40 = *LW* 32:229f. = *LCC* 16:351 (my emphasis). On Luther's engagement with the scholastic 'manner of speaking' and his struggle to recover a characteristically theological (i.e. Pauline/Augustinian) manner of speaking, see Grane, *Modus loquendi theologicus*; *passim*, esp. 142f. On the history of this discussion in late scholasticism, see Heiko A. Oberman, *Werden und Wertung der Reformation*, Spätscholastik und Reformation 2 (Tübingen: J.C.B. Mohr (Paul Siebeck), 1977), 120–34. For an interesting view of scholastic philosophy as providing an inappropriate grammar for theology, see the richly documented essay by Walter Mostert, 'Luthers Verhältnis zur theologischen und philosophischen Ueberlieferung' in *Leben und Werk Martin Luthers von 1526 bis 1546. Festgabe zu seinem 500. Geburtstag* 1, ed. H. Junghans (Göttingen: Vandenhoeck & Ruprecht, 1983), 347–68, at 360–2.

different.[35] His response was to counter with another traditional distinction, between a necessity of force (*necessitas coactionis*) and a necessity of immutability (*necessitas immutabilitatis*). Had Judas been compelled against his will to betray his Lord, then the question of reward or punishment hardly arises. But the fact that he had no choice in the matter was the result not of any external force but of the impulse of his own depraved nature which he could not change unaided. So he did not sin freely, but he did sin voluntarily.[36] It has been pointed out that Luther misunderstood both these distinctions, and that in fact his own position was closer to that of Aquinas, which he believed he was rejecting.[37] But for our purposes it is significant not that he misused a distinction in *The Bondage of the Will*, but that he used one at all.

What can we deduce from these examples about Luther's repeated recourse to scholastic distinctions, long after he had rejected scholasticism itself? Was he aping his opponents in order to ridicule them? Was he simply playing one devilish delusion off against another? If so, then his playful use of such distinctions raises no serious difficulties. But while he was certainly capable of ridiculing such methods,[38] the examples quoted above serve important functions in the development of his argument in each case. In *The Babylonian Captivity*, Pierre d'Ailly is invoked to demonstrate that transubstantiation is not the only way of applying Aristotelian physics to the problem of Christ's presence. Here Luther does use a scholastic argument in a negative way, to counter another scholastic argument; but there is no suggestion of mockery, or that d'Ailly himself did not have a good case. In *The Bondage of the Will*, Luther was much more conscious of his own style, knowing that the controversy with

---

[35] For his discussion in *The Bondage of the Will*, see *WA* 18:616.13–619.15 = *LW* 33:39–41 = *LCC* 17:120f. For his earlier rejection of the distinction, see the Romans lectures (*WA* 56:382.21–383.19 = *LW* 25:372f. = *LCC* 15:248–50), and the *Disputation against Scholastic Theology*, thesis 32 (*WA* 1:225 = *LW* 31:11 = *LCC* 16:269).

[36] See *WA* 18:693.30–6 = *LW* 33:151f. = *LCC* 17:211f.

[37] See Harry J. McSorley, *Luther: Right or Wrong? An Ecumenical-Theological Study of Luther's Major Work, The Bondage of the Will* (New York: Newman/Minneapolis: Augsburg, 1969), 313–29. For further unconscious parallels between Luther and Aquinas, see the important work by Denis R. Janz, *Luther and Late Medieval Thomism: A Study in Theological Anthropology* (Waterloo, Ontario: Wilfrid Laurier University Press, 1983).

[38] An example of *reductio* can be found in his comic treatment of the scholastic doctrine of concomitance in *Ein Bericht an einem guten Freund von beider Gestalt des Sakraments aufs Bischofs zu Meißen Mandat* of 1528 (*WA* 26:560–618). See my 'Diversity or Disunity? A Reformation Controversy Over Communion in Both Kinds' in *Unity and Diversity in the Church*, ed. R.N. Swanson, Studies in Church History 32 (Oxford: Blackwell, 1996), 207–19, esp. 211f.

Erasmus would be a very public one. Here he is on his best literary and theological behaviour, and the result is not always representative of Luther in full spate. We may not therefore be able to deduce much from this work, but again we can at least say that the distinction between *necessitas coactionis* and *necessitas immutabilitatis* was put forward in all seriousness as an integral part of his argument. The treatise *Against Latomus* was written under very different circumstances. Alone in the Wartburg, with the Bible as his only theological text, he was thrown back onto the fundamentals of his belief, and the treatise itself, though long, contains only what is strictly essential. So it is especially revealing that his use of 'categories' forms part of an explicit attack on the whole scholastic enterprise. It is evident that Luther saw no conflict between good theology and good logic: rather, scholastic theology was poor because it was based on poor logic. Again, we can say that Luther's use of the scholastic method as an antidote to scholastic theology was meant seriously, not ironically.

We may conclude that while *theologia scholastica* was always to be opposed to the *theologia crucis*, the *modus loquendi scholasticus* was not always for Luther contrary to the *modus loquendi theologicus*. Far more important than method was content, context, and motive. Even in the course of his most devastating attack on scholasticism, the Heidelberg Disputation, Luther was careful to make this clear:

> In the same way as the evil of sexual desire cannot be used well except by those who are married, so no-one can philosophize well unless he is foolish, that is, a Christian. The reason is that, as sexual desire is a perverted wish for pleasure, so philosophy is a perverted love of knowledge, unless helped by the grace of Christ; not because philosophy or pleasure are evil in themselves, but because desire for either is wrong unless it be Christian. Indeed, all our bodily and spiritual powers are such that they pervertedly desire their object, namely God's good creation [sc. rather than God himself].[39]

SUMMARY

In order to understand Luther's equivocal approach to scholasticism, we must set it in the context of his approach to a whole range of theological sources and methods. As with mysticism, with allegory, and later with the Fathers, so with scholasticism: Luther could combine a critical, at

---

[39] *Heidelberg Disputation*, philosophical thesis 2 (*WA* 59:409.20–410.6). On the implications of this thesis, see Anna Vind, ' "Men de har intet forstaaet om Kristus . . .": om Luthers opør med den skolastiske teologi', *Dansk Teologisk Tidsskrift* 59 (1996), 27–49, at 45.

times hostile, attitude towards them with a selective reliance upon them. This was possible because the decisive matter for Luther was consonance with Scripture. In themselves, or when used to express what he regarded as unbiblical theology, such sources and methods were not permissible; but wherever they were in accordance with Scripture, or could be used in such a way, they were to be approved. This 'sic et non' position was of course the lesson he had learned at the feet of Trutfetter and Usingen, who had established the Ockhamist principle of a reductive approach to authorities: theological sources are not to be multiplied beyond necessity.

Within this wider context, scholasticism nevertheless had a special place for Luther. The ostentatious rejection of scholastic methods was a luxury he could afford when concentrating on the key issue of the gospel, and when the cause of the gospel and the humanist cause seemed identical, especially in the aftermath of the Leipzig Disputation.[40] But whenever he attempted a more sustained presentation of his views, it became necessary to use scholastic distinctions. It is tempting to ask whether, had he composed a systematic formulation of his theology, he would have had even readier recourse to scholastic logic and categories, or even to an 'Aristoteles Christianus',[41] as Melanchthon and others had later. It is impossible to answer this hypothetical question with any certainty: it may even be the case that his distrust of scholasticism is precisely what prevented him from attempting any such summa, and what enabled him to resist what has been called 'the natural craving of the human spirit for a clear, transparent and definite system'.[42] But it is possible to say that Luther's own writings contained within them the seeds of a Protestant scholasticism, seeds that could easily be propagated in more favourable soil.

---

[40] On the importance of the period after Leipzig for drawing up the lines of battle between scholastics and humanists (and on the difficulties posed by such terms), see David V.N. Bagchi, *Luther's Earliest Opponents: Catholic Controversialists, 1518–1525* (Minneapolis: Fortress, 1991), 69–91.

[41] Luther, of course, never went this far. But he did regard Aristotle as preferable to the scholastics, because he never committed the blasphemy of applying his categories to divine matters (*WA* 40.I:411.6f.).

[42] Josef Pieper, 'The philosophical act' in idem, *Leisure, The Basis of Culture* (1952), 131, quoted in A. Louth, *Discerning the Mystery: An Essay on the Nature of Theology* (Oxford: Clarendon, 1983), 146.

2

The Scholastic Calvin

David C. Steinmetz

No one, so far as I know, has ever seriously disputed the claim that John Calvin was deeply influenced by the ideals and methods of Renaissance humanism. Like many humanists, Calvin aspired to be a *homo trilinguus*, a master of Greek, Latin, and Hebrew. In this respect he surpassed even Erasmus, who was master only of Latin and Greek. Before turning from law to theology, he edited an ancient classical text by the Stoic philosopher, Seneca, though he is less remembered for his study of Roman antiquity than for his commentaries, lectures, and sermons on the Bible. He read carefully the writings of the early church Fathers, annotating the Latin translation of Chrysostom for his own use. He was interested in the rhetorical analysis of biblical texts, albeit to a much lesser degree than Philip Melanchthon, whose rhetorical analysis of Paul was widely imitated by other commentators. In the controversy between humanists and scholastics, he joined the chorus of humanists in their noisy and not always well-founded criticism of the methods and aspirations of scholastic theologians. In short, there is no reason to dispute the thesis that Calvin, like many of the early Protestant reformers, found the intellectual agenda of the humanists congenial and embraced many of their methods and goals.

The relationship of Calvin to scholasticism is a far more vexed and difficult issue to resolve. Calvin, after all, had studied law at Orleans and Bourges, not theology at Paris.[1] Unlike Martin Luther, who had undergone a full scholastic theological education at Erfurt and Wittenberg, Calvin was largely an autodidact, who seems to have taught himself the theology he taught to others. Some historians like Reuter and Torrance

---

[1] For a brief introduction to the life of Calvin see my *Calvin in Context* (New York and Oxford: Oxford University Press, 1995), 3–22.

have thought they could detect in the theology of Calvin echoes of the Scottish theologian, John Major, who lectured on theology at Paris during the period in which Calvin was earning his arts degree.[2] There is, however, no evidence that Calvin ever attended lectures given by Major or participated in any disputation at which Major presided. Other historians saw the telltale marks of scholastic theology in Calvin's thought without agreeing about its source. Whereas, for example, Alister McGrath proposed that Calvin may have been influenced by late medieval nominalism and Augustinianism in the form of the so-called *schola Augustiniana moderna*, Heiko Oberman, who had written many of the books on which McGrath based his conclusions, thought the evidence suggested rather the influence of the theology of John Duns Scotus.[3] No one, however, defended the notion that Calvin should be thought of as a scholastic theologian, in spite of the fact that undoubted elements of scholastic theology could be found in his writings. William Bouwsma characterized Calvin's method as Erasmian, while McGrath described it merely as humanist.[4] The phrase, 'the scholastic Calvin', is in the view of most historians an oxymoron.

Unfortunately, the attempt to understand Calvin's relationship to scholasticism has been complicated by the fact that some Reformation historians have accepted almost uncritically and at face value the characterization of scholasticism by its enemies.[5] For such historians scholasticism was invariably arid, speculative, subservient to Aristotelian philosophy, philosophical rather than biblical, absorbed with trivial questions, and devoted to logic-chopping. Early Protestant theology, according to this understanding, was biblical and exegetical rather than rational and speculative. It represented in its deepest impulses a departure from scholasticism and a way of doing theology that was antithetical to

---

[2] Karl Reuter, *Das Grundverständnis der Theologie Calvins* (Neukirchen, 1963); Thomas F. Torrance, *The Hermeneutics of John Calvin* (Edinburgh: Scottish Academic, 1988).

[3] Alister E. McGrath, *A Life of Calvin* (Oxford and Cambridge, Mass.: Blackwell, 1990); Heiko A. Oberman, *Initia Calvini: The Matrix of Calvin's Reformation* (Amsterdam: Koninklijke Nederlandse Akademie van Wetenschappen, 1991), 117, 121. Also in *Calvinas Sacrae Scripturae Professor: Calvin as Confessor of Holy Scripture*, ed. Wilhelm Neuser (Grand Rapids: Eerdmans, 1994), 114–25.

[4] William J. Bouwsma, *John Calvin: A Sixteenth-Century Portrait* (New York: Oxford University Press, 1988); McGrath, op. cit., 148.

[5] James Overfield's important study *Humanism and Scholasticism in Late Medieval Germany* (Princeton: Princeton University Press, 1984) provides a useful warning against taking the rhetoric of the humanists against the scholastics at face value. Also important in this connection is Paul Oskar Kristeller, *Medieval Aspects of Renaissance Learning*, ed. and trans. E.P. Mahoney (Durham, N.C.: Duke University Press, 1974).

it. To return to scholasticism, as Protestant theologians in the late sixteenth and early seventeenth centuries did, was by definition to betray the original theological vision of the early Reformation. For all of these reasons, historians who held such views argued that John Calvin was not and, indeed, could not have been a scholastic theologian. At most he was a humanist lightly touched by some scholastic ideas.

The difficulty with this characterization is not that it is completely false, but that it is so inaccurate as to be dangerously misleading. It rests on assumptions about the nature of medieval scholasticism in general and scholastic theology in particular that demonstrate little understanding of what the scholastic method was or how it was implemented in the theological faculties of Europe, especially at the University of Paris. Although Oxford and Cambridge followed a slightly different plan for theological education, Paris served as the model for many universities throughout Europe. What I intend to do in this essay is first to describe scholasticism and the scholastic method as briefly and as accurately as I can and then to re-examine Calvin's relationship to it. What I hope to show is that Calvin's relationship to it was both more positive and more profound than is commonly assumed. While it is clear that Calvin was not a scholastic in one sense, it is not so clear that he was not a scholastic in another.

I

Scholastic theology was not the only form of theology developed in medieval Europe. Jean Leclercq argued years ago that there were two main ways of pursuing Christian theology in the Middle Ages, scholastic and monastic.[6] Scholastic theology was a relatively late method developed first in cathedral schools in the eleventh and twelfth centuries and further refined thereafter in such early European universities as Oxford, Cambridge and Paris. Monastic theology represented a much older way of doing theology that had been preserved in Cistercian and other Benedictine communities. Monastic theologians did not draw distinctions, pose questions or preside at disputations. They wrote theology as it had always been written; namely, as hymns, essays, prayers, liturgy, commentaries, and sermons. Bernard of Clairvaux, whose sermons and treatises on the spiritual life were widely read outside monastic circles, may be taken as a representative of monastic theology at its best. Indeed, his writings were so universally admired that they became an important source for scholastic theology as well.

[6]   Jean Leclercq, *The Love of Learning and the Desire for God: A Study of Monastic Culture* (New York: Fordham University Press, 1961).

Scholastic theology was, as the name implies, theology as it was pursued in schools. The schools in question had not been organized for general lay education but for the formation of a clerical elite that could provide theological and institutional leadership for the church in the Latin West. Most parish priests never saw the inside of a university and were trained for their work in a more rudimentary way at a local level. But secular and religious masters at theological faculties in Paris, Oxford, and Cambridge lectured to young men who would become the bishops, archdeacons, priors, and provincials of the next generation. It was a task that engaged some of the finest theological minds in the history of the Christian church from Albert the Great and Thomas Aquinas to John Duns Scotus and Gregory of Rimini.

The aim of scholastic theology was to provide a leadership that had been steeped in the theology and exegesis of the early Christian church. To that end two textbooks were required reading for all theological candidates and their teachers. The required textbook for dogmatic theology was the *Sentences* of Peter Lombard, the required textbook for exegesis was the *Glossa Ordinaria* or *Ordinary Gloss*. The content of each book consisted in large part of quotations from and summaries of selected writings of early Christian Fathers with a scattering of citations from later writers. Peter Lombard reflected the traditional inclination of the Western Catholic Church, when he cited heavily in his *Sentences* the writings of St Augustine, the most important of the Latin Christian Fathers. The basic curriculum of theological education consisted of extended commentaries, oral and written, by university lecturers on these two mainly patristic sourcebooks.

The *Sentences* of Peter Lombard represented a shift in form and structure from patristic theology. Lombard organized theology into topics and arranged his sources according to the themes they discussed. Organizing theology according to topics took what had been an unstructured and nearly unmanageable body of early Christian theology preserved in sermons, letters and essays, gave it a coherent structure, and, by doing so, made it easier to teach to beginning students in a classroom setting. Ordering theology by topic also uncovered unexpected disagreements, some real and some only apparent, among early Christian Fathers. By doing so, it forced Christian theologians to face the antinomies and tensions in their own tradition. They could no longer assume that earlier authorities spoke with one unified voice. The existence of undeniable differences compelled them to make discriminating judgments and to seek for a resolution of what they regarded as only apparent contradictions.

Lombard organized his four books of *Sentences* according to two distinctions in the theology of St Augustine: the distinction between two kinds of loving as indicated by two Latin verbs, *uti* and *frui*, and the distinction between signs (*signa*) and things (*res*).[7] The verb *frui* means to love a thing with the love of enjoyment. Things can be enjoyed if they are loved as ends and not as the means towards some other higher end.[8] In Augustine's view only God could be loved with a love of enjoyment since only God could be loved for himself alone. The verb *uti* means to love a thing not for itself, but as a means towards something else. Because everything that is not God — that is, the whole realm of creatures — could only be loved as a means that deflects one's final love towards God, the verb *uti* describes the love that is owed to creation. The first three books of the *Sentences* deal with things to be loved and the fourth book deals with signs. Book One deals with things to be enjoyed; i.e. it deals with the Triune God who is to be loved with the love of enjoyment. Book Two deals with things to be used as means; i.e. it deals with creation, which is to be loved with the love of use. Book Three deals with things to be loved both as an end and as a means; i.e. it deals with Jesus Christ, the God-man, who insofar as he is divine may be enjoyed and insofar as he is a creature used. And finally, Book Four deals with signs; i.e. it deals with the church's sacraments.

Lecturers on the *Sentences* did not feel an obligation merely to repeat the arguments, authorities, and formulations advanced by Peter Lombard but pressed beyond him by posing new questions and drawing further distinctions. Scholastic theologians were well aware that asking the right questions is the first and indispensable step in arriving at a knowledge of the truth. They were also well aware that rhetorical solutions that glossed over the difficulties in an issue with a homiletical nostrum did not advance the church's knowledge. Their ideal was to proceed by careful argument firmly rooted in the texts Lombard had assembled to a more adequate grasp of Christian truth, never raising their voices in anger when their arguments failed or appealing to the prejudices of their readers or listeners. Sometimes their inquiries took them to the boundaries of human knowledge, as when, for example, they asked whether God could by an act of his almighty power and without violating his own sense of justice, to say nothing of ours, send Judas to heaven and Peter to hell? And if he could not, what did it mean to say that God was omnipotent?[9] Often their questions focused on practical issues of pastoral care. How, asked some scholastic masters, could a Catholic

---

[7]   On the structure of the *Sentences* see Gerhard Ebeling, 'The Hermeneutical Locus of the Doctrine of God in Peter Lombard and Thomas Aquinas' in Ernst Käsemann et al., *Distinctive Protestant and Catholic Themes Reconsidered* (New York: Harper and Row, 1967).

[8]   Augustine, *De doctrina christiana* I.iii.3.

[9]   For a survey of literature on the question of God's omnipotence and the relation of this discussion to Calvin's theology, see my 'Calvin and the Absolute Power of God', *Journal of Medieval and Renaissance Studies* 18.1 (Spring, 1988), 65–79.

boy and girl, each of whom had been cleansed from original sin by the sacrament of baptism, communicate an original sin they did not have to their baby? Or, for that matter, how could water, which by its nature washes away dirt, wash away original sin, which lies beyond the capacity of nature?[10] Exegesis alone could not answer such questions. Scholastic masters, while grounding their arguments in the Bible and tradition, hoped so to pattern the minds of their students with the logic of Christian faith that they could witness to the gospel without losing themselves in unresolved contradictions, logical absurdities, imprecise definitions, or maudlin sentimentality. Clear thinking about theological issues was an important skill for a university don to cultivate. It was an equally important skill for a bishop, entrusted with the care of souls.

To further careful thinking about difficult issues theological faculties sponsored ordinary and quodlibetal disputations. Ordinary disputations tackled questions set by the theological curriculum, while quodlibetal disputations dealt with topics chosen at the discretion of the principal teacher or master. Students debated the issues in dispute — e.g. whether a habit of grace is necessary for the justification of a sinner or whether the love that is poured into the heart of a penitent sinner is uncreated grace (i.e. the Holy Spirit) or created grace (i.e. an infused habit).[11] Masters spoke last, commenting on the debate and the positions argued by the debaters and resolving the issues that had been raised as they understood them. While argument in the sense of a noisy row was excluded in principle, if not always in fact, argument in the sense of a sharp exchange of contrary opinions was welcomed. Through such disciplined argument theological students and their teachers hoped to achieve a firmer grasp of difficult theological problems.

The second major element in the scholastic theological programme was its exegetical component.[12] Medieval theologians did not draw a sharp distinction, as we would, between biblical exegesis and dogmatic theology. The words 'theology' and 'sacred page' could be used interchangeably, since biblical interpretation was by definition theological and dogmatic theology exegetical. The texts, of course, differed. Exegesis

---

[10] No one has written more helpfully on these matters than William J. Courtenay, 'Covenant and Causality in Pierre d'Ailly', *Speculum* 46 (1971), 94–119; 'The King and the Leaden Coin: The Economic Background of Sine Qua Non Causality', *Traditio 28* (1972), 185–209.

[11] I *Sent.* d. 17.

[12] The most helpful treatment of this subject I have found is the as yet unpublished essay by the Director of the Medieval Institute at Notre Dame, John Van Engen, 'Studying Scripture in the Early University'. See also my forthcoming essay, 'Divided by a Common Past: The Reshaping of the Christian Exegetical Tradition in the Sixteenth Century', *Journal of Medieval and Early Modern Studies*.

proper (in our sense) required the text of the *Ordinary Gloss* as its foundation, while dogmatic lectures (again in our sense) regularly took the form of commentary on the *Sentences*. Exegetical lectures followed the text of whatever biblical book was under discussion from the first verse of the first chapter to the last verse of the last chapter. Theological lectures followed the order of distinctions or topics in the *Sentences*, moving from subject to subject rather than from verse to verse. At the same time it should be noted that a fair amount of the patristic material in the *Sentences* had been culled by Peter Lombard from the *Ordinary Gloss*.[13]

The theological curriculum reflected the dual emphasis on exegesis and dogmatics. In order to become a Master of Theology a candidate needed to become first a Bachelor of the Bible and then a Bachelor of the Sentences.[14] In England the order was reversed, perhaps in order to demonstrate that dealing directly with the biblical text was, after all, a higher task than dealing with a merely human compendium like the *Sentences*. At any rate, only after lecturing on the Bible and the *Sentences* under the supervision of a Master, could a student be promoted to the degree of Doctor of Theology. While a newly-minted Doctor had many duties, he was free to lecture either on the Bible or on the *Sentences* of Peter Lombard. In the early scholastic period he would have been expected to lecture primarily on the literal sense of the Bible.[15] His students had already been taken by a teaching assistant (the *cursor* or *baccalaureus biblicus*) through a quick survey of the glossed biblical text. It was his duty to open up the mysteries of divine revelation by a thorough attention to the Latin text that presupposed his mastery of text, glosses, and the theological distinctions in Lombard.

There were, however, questions that could not be answered on the basis of the biblical exegesis alone. While the scholastics thought the Bible taught a rudimentary anthropology and psychology, they did not think they could derive an analysis of the powers of the human soul from the Bible. But an analysis of the powers of the soul might in fact be important in order to understand the nature of contrition or the possibility of union of the soul with God in this life. Calvin agreed with the scholastics that the philosophers taught things about the nature and powers of the human

---

[13] This fact is clearly evident from the notes and apparatus of Ignatius Brady in the critical edition of Lombard's *Sentences, Magistri Petri Lombardi Sententiae in IV Libris Distinctae*, Spicilegium Bonaventurianum, 5 (Grottaferrata, 1981).

[14] James Overfield provides a useful summary of the scholastic curriculum in his *Humanism*, 44–9.

[15] Overfield cites evidence from Frankfurt and Ingolstadt that leads him to conclude that late scholasticism may have devoted more attention to lectures on the *Sentences* than lectures on the Bible, op. cit., 47.

soul that were useful for Christians to know. God is, after all, the Creator and Redeemer of heaven and earth and all that they contain. Yet not everything necessary and useful to know about heaven and earth can be found in the pages of the Bible. Therefore scholastic theologians made free use of the philosophers, not as a substitute for divine revelation and never willingly in contradiction to it. Philosophy was a good gift of God to human beings made in the rational image of God and like God capable of creative thought.

Early scholasticism was very eclectic in its use of philosophy. There is very little in Peter Lombard that could be described as philosophical except the philosophy inherent in the writings of the Church Fathers themselves. Later scholasticism became far more philosophically sophisticated, though probably without overcoming entirely a kind of philosophical eclecticism. It is probably never possible or even desirable for Christian theologians to become overly loyal to a single philosopher, since the odd shape of the Christian faith forces a kind of philosophical eclecticism on its serious practitioners. No philosophy — not the philosophy of Aristotle or Plato or Kant or Hegel or Kierkegaard — is exactly cut to the shape of divine revelation. The Aristotle whom Christian scholastics adopted was an Aristotle who had been baptized, chastened and corrected by Christian theology, and shorn of his most incorrigibly pagan convictions. Thomas Aquinas, to take a famous example, is frequently described as an Aristotelian. But Thomas was not so loyal to the opinions of Aristotle that he did not abandon them when what he regarded as better opinions could be found elsewhere. One has only to consider how important the theme of participation was to Thomas to see that he, too, could not afford the luxury of unswerving loyalty to one philosopher. Philosophy was the scholastic theologian's tool, not his principal subject matter. The tune to which he danced was played by a different piper.

It is important to keep clearly in mind how important biblical exegesis was to the scholastic enterprise. The essence of scholasticism cannot be found in distinctions, questions, and disputations alone. Nor was exegesis scholastic only when the lecturer drew a distinction, composed a syllogism, or raised a disputed question. Central to the scholastic enterprise were lectures on the Latin text of the whole Bible as glossed by the early Fathers. Thomas Aquinas was not more scholastic when he presided at disputations concerning the nature of truth than when he lectured on the literal sense of Job. Albert the Great did not embody scholastic ideals when he mused on the nature of water and depart from them when he expounded the prophet Isaiah. Scholastic theology pursued its own vision of the exegetical task. It was not identical with the humanist vision, but it was not altogether different either.

II

Anyone who reads a page of the *Collectorium concerning Four Books of Sentences* by the fifteenth-century German theologian, Gabriel Biel, and compares it with a page of the *Institutes of the Christian Religion* by John Calvin will be struck by the differences. Whereas the Latin of Biel is simple and spare and ordered strictly to the explanation of the issue under consideration, the Latin of Calvin is more elegant, using a far wider range of rhetorical devices and effects not only to explain but also to convince, cajole, scold, challenge, and move his readers. Although Calvin preferred the scholastic convention of disagreeing with one's enemies anonymously, he could even attack and abuse his opponents by name, calling, for example, such a relatively harmless and reform-minded prelate as the late Albert Pigge, that 'dead dog Pighius'. While Calvin, like Biel, cited authorities, disputed issues, and raised questions, he did not use them as organizing principles but embedded them in the body of his exposition. Furthermore, Calvin did not comment on the text of Peter Lombard — or, indeed, on any theological textbook — even though there are some structural similarities between the four books of *Sentences* and the four books of the *Institutes*, including the order and placement of some topics.

If we compare Calvin's biblical commentaries with late medieval lectures on the Bible, we see similar differences. Calvin did not comment on the glossed Latin text but on the unglossed Greek and Hebrew text. For Calvin, who even took the Hebrew and Greek Bibles with him into the pulpit, the Bible could not be properly understood without a mastery of the original languages in which it was written. Although some medieval theologians like Nicholas of Lyra and Paul of Burgos could read Hebrew and even cited rabbinical traditions in their exposition of Scripture, mastery of languages was far less important to most scholastic theologians than mastery of the glosses, a collected treasury of traditional wisdom derived for the most part from the ancient church. Similarly, the fact that Calvin read an unglossed Hebrew or Greek text did not mean that he prepared his own interpretations of the Bible without first reading commentaries on the passage he was expounding, including commentaries by ancient Christian Fathers. Anyone who doubts this fact has only to compare Calvin's exposition of Romans 4 with the antecedent exegetical tradition to see how great his dependence was on earlier tradition, not only for great themes and insights but also for smaller bits of exegetical lore.[16] Calvin's Hebrew and Greek Bible was formally but not materially unglossed. His library, if not the margins of his Hebrew and Greek text, was filled with the work of glossators, ancient and modern.

[16]   See my *Calvin in Context*, 64–78.

Calvin made only limited use of philosophy. It is obvious from what he wrote that he had read philosophy and approved of themes and ideas from various philosophers. He appealed to an innate sense of divinity, which he derived from Cicero rather than from St Paul, and used the notion to clarify what Paul had written about the Gentiles in Romans 1:18–32.[17] He employed a causal scheme borrowed from Aristotle to set in order the causes of salvation, accepting as well a scholastic distinction between consequent necessity and necessity of the consequence.[18] He commended philosophers for their analysis of the powers of the soul and, although he did not single out one philosopher for special commendation, his general recommendation surely covered Aristotle's *De anima* on which his friend Melanchthon had written a commentary.[19]

Still any historians who attempt to reconstruct Calvin's metaphysics from his collected works have set themselves a nearly impossible task. Like most of the Protestant theologians of his generation (Melanchthon, Zanchi, and Musculus are obvious, if partial, exceptions) Calvin set out to write a theology that was wholly exegetical. If he did not entirely succeed (and no-one who professes the doctrine of the Trinity can entirely succeed), it was not for lack of resolution. Like many early Protestants he was in the grip of an exegetical optimism that proved not altogether workable in practice. Melanchthon abandoned philosophy only to take it up again. Calvin discovered that some philosophical distinctions, including many of the distinctions drawn by the schoolmen, were too useful to be discarded lightly. If one objects that there is still very little philosophy in Calvin's late theological and exegetical writings, the obvious reply is that there is even less in Peter Lombard's.

Yet, in spite of Calvin's resolution to avoid what he regarded as the failings of scholasticism, anyone who reads the preface to his *Commentary on Romans* will be struck by the similarity between his bipolar programme for writing theological and exegetical works and the bipolar theological and exegetical agenda of medieval scholasticism.[20] Like the scholastics and unlike the early Christian Fathers, Calvin announced his intention to write not only exegesis (with, perhaps, occasional writings on limited themes) but also a book which organized theology by topic. Topical

---

[17] *Institutes,* I.xxx.1.

[18] For the fourfold cause of salvation see ibid. III.xiv.17; on the two kinds of necessity see ibid. I.xvi.9.

[19] Ibid. I.xv.6 in which Calvin both criticizes and commends the philosophers. For an excellent treatment of Melanchthon on the soul, see Sachiko Kusukawa, *The Transformation of Natural Philosophy: The Case of Philip Melanchthon* (Cambridge: Cambridge University Press, 1995), 75–123.

[20] T.H.L. Parker (ed.), *Iohannis Calvini Commentarius in Epistolam Pauli ad Romanos* (Leiden: E.J. Brill, 1981), 1–4.

discussions would allow Calvin to address complex doctrinal issues in a separate volume without interrupting the flow of exegesis in his commentaries. At the same time such topical discussions could provide an indispensable frame of reference within which to read and comprehend Scripture. The commentaries would provide a running gloss on the biblical text, while the organization of exegetical materials by topic would enable Calvin to explain everything relevant to each doctrinal issue in one place. The clearest difference between Calvin's plan and the programme of medieval scholasticism was that Calvin did not comment on the two main textbooks of medieval scholasticism, the *Ordinary Gloss* and the *Sentences* of Peter Lombard. Of course, as I have already indicated, this difference may be more apparent than real. Calvin read widely in the biblical exegesis of the early Fathers and carried on a lively debate with antecedent Christian tradition both in his commentaries and in the *Institutes*. Sometimes he read the Fathers in compendia like the *Corpus of Canon Law*; sometimes he read them in critical editions. Sometimes he quoted them; sometimes he refuted them. What he did not do was ignore them.[21]

If we look at the text of the *Institutes*, we find ample evidence of Calvin's positive and negative relationship to scholasticism. No one has done a better job of analysing the Latin and French texts than Richard Muller, who has demonstrated how deeply embedded in the fabric of the *Institutes* were distinctions, questions, and disputations.[22] Moreover, Muller has refined the earlier thesis of Armand LaVallee concerning the identity of the anonymous scholastics Calvin scorned by arguing that Calvin may sometimes not have had the great scholastic doctors in mind (and certainly not the early scholastic doctors) but a few unnamed teachers at the Sorbonne who had earned Calvin's contempt. What appears to the casual reader to be a blanket condemnation of scholasticism may prove in certain cases to be nothing of the kind, but to have a quite local point of reference. Calvin may condemn an entire phylum in order to squash a single specimen.

The question also has to be raised whether Calvin has in certain cases understood the scholastic theologians correctly. For example, in treating

---

[21] In this connection it is well worth reading the careful analysis of Calvin's use of the Fathers by David Pareus in the late sixteenth century. See David Pareus, *Libri Duo: I. Calvinus Orthodoxus de Sacrosancta Trinitate: et de aeterna Christi Divinitate. II. Solida Expositio XXXIIX. Difficilimorum Scripturae Locorum et Oraculorum: et de recta ratione applicandi Oracula Prophetica ad Christum. Oppositi Pseudocalvino Iudaizanti nuper a quodam emisso* (Neustadt: Matthaeus Harnisch, 1595).

[22] See the paper presented by Richard A. Muller at the Calvin Congress in Edinburgh, 1994, 'Scholasticism in Calvin: A Question of Relation and Disjunction'. A revised form of this paper will appear in his forthcoming book, *The Unaccommodated Calvin* (New York and Oxford: Oxford University Press).

the scholastic distinction between the absolute and the ordained power of God, Calvin misstated what the scholastics meant by the use of this distinction, restated what he regarded as the correct answer (which was, more or less, what the scholastics taught when they drew the distinction), and concluded, quite wrongly, that he and the scholastics were worlds apart.[23] Either Calvin did not understand the distinction and simply made a mistake; or he understood the distinction correctly but was disingenuous and misstated the position of the scholastics in order to score a cheap point; or he first encountered this distinction in the teaching of a third party, who had himself misunderstood what the scholastics intended and so misled Calvin. I am inclined in this case to apply the hermeneutic of charity and to assume that Calvin, who after all was educated as a lawyer rather than as a theologian, made an honest mistake and misrepresented the scholastics unwittingly. However, the point I want to emphasize is that Calvin and the scholastics were in agreement on the substance of the issue, even though Calvin himself was convinced that they differed.

The number of scholastic themes one can find in Calvin's *Institutes* is fairly impressive. Take, for example, what he has to say about predestination. In outlining his doctrine of predestination, Calvin reiterated points that had first been made by Augustine and repeated in the great Augustinian tradition of the medieval church. If one compares Calvin's doctrine of predestination with the teaching of Thomas Aquinas and John Duns Scotus, one will undoubtedly be impressed by how close they were to each other, in large measure because each remained close to Augustine.[24] All three, for example, rejected as Pelagian the notion that predestination was based on God's foreknowledge of human good works or even of a good use of grace. However, on other issues on which Scotus differed with Thomas Aquinas, Calvin unfailingly chose the position of Scotus. Like Scotus and unlike Thomas, Calvin asserted predestination was first to glory and only then to grace and that whatever God willed was by that very fact righteous and just, propositions that Thomas could not accept in the form in which Scotus and Calvin taught them.[25]

III

I want to conclude, however, not by focusing on the many ways in which Calvin, who spoke disparagingly of scholasticism, nevertheless embraced ideas, distinctions, and methods that were characteristic of it. What I want to do is suggest another way to approach this issue, one that focuses on

---

[23]   *Institutes,* III.xxiii.2. See Steinmetz, *Calvin in Context,* 40–52.
[24]   Steinmetz, *Calvin in Context,* 141–56.
[25]   For the relevent texts by Calvin see *Institutes,* III.xxii.1, 9; III.xxiii.2.

the parish rather than on the university as the locus for the pursuit of a kind of school theology. When Calvin was asked to define the church, he took the famous dictum of Cyprian — one cannot have God for a father who does not have the church for a mother — and modified it to describe the church as both mother and school.[26] Scholastic theology was, as the name implies, theology appropriate to a school. If, as Calvin argued, the church was a school as well as a nurturing mother, then it was essential to craft a theology appropriate to it.

Medieval scholastic theology was also developed for a particular kind of school. The medieval school was not a public school open to laity. It was not even a clerical school open to all of the clergy. It was an elite school for the training of the church's leadership. Some of the young clergy who studied theology at such schools became teachers themselves. Most were recruited to serve in positions of leadership in their diocese or order.

The parish was not regarded in the medieval church as the appropriate place for the pursuit of scholastic theology. The parish priest was frequently a man of limited education, often not much different from the people he served. He said prayers for the community, baptized their children, married their couples, blessed their homes, and buried their dead. He presided at worship and heard their annual confession before Easter mass.[27] He might preach or he might not. Lay people could always hear a sermon in a Dominican or Franciscan church if there were one nearby. Some might even be lucky enough to live in a larger town with a well-known preacher supported by public funds. But theology was not as central to the life of the late medieval community as it would become in early Protestant churches. The local parish was less an assembly room for the theological education of the laity than a sacred space for the celebration of religious mysteries. On the parish level the church was a mother, but only in a very restricted sense a school.

For a relatively small group of clergy, however, the church was school in the full sense of the term. Young men who studied in a university faculty of theology or in a *studium generale* of their order formed an elite corps capable of dealing with advanced theological topics. They heard lectures on the glossed Bible and on the *Sentences* of Peter Lombard, both from teaching assistants earning their first degrees and from established

---

[26]   Ibid. IV.i.4.

[27]   On penitential practice in the parish in Austria and Bavaria see the illuminating study by W. David Myers, *'Poor, Sinning Folk': Confession and Conscience in Counter-Reformation Germany* (Ithaca and London: Cornell University Press, 1996). See also chapter 2, 'How the Plowman Learned His Paternoster' in Eamon Duffy, *The Stripping of the Altars: Traditional Religion in England 1400–1580* (New Haven and London: Yale University Press, 1992), 53–87.

theologians. They participated in disputations the laity would never have understood on topics of incredible difficulty. While the laity heard sermons on limited portions of Scripture, they studied large sections of the Bible, analysing them chapter by chapter. Unlike preachers who limited themselves to the pericopal lesson of the day, university lecturers discussed entire books of the Bible, examining both the Latin text and the patristic glosses which formed the indispensable context of proper exegesis.

Calvin knew perfectly well that not every member of the church was capable of theological reflection at an advanced level. Many of his sermons dealt with exegetical questions at a somewhat lower level of difficulty than his commentaries. Even his French translation of the *Institutes*, prepared for people of lesser culture who did not read Latin, added explanations that were missing in the Latin text. Nevertheless, the fact that Calvin regarded the church as both mother and school, meant that in his view all Christians, no matter how limited their capacity, had a theological task to discharge. They could not sidestep their theological responsibility by relying on implicit faith and claiming, as they had once done in the old church, that they believed whatever the church taught.[28] That was far too indolent a faith. The church was a school, not only for an elite, but also for quite ordinary people. The broadening of access to theological education may also help to explain Calvin's impatience with what he regarded as excessive speculation in medieval scholasticism. A clerical elite could spare the time to consider questions that were only experiments in thought. But a church focused on the theological education of ordinary men and women, particularly ordinary men and women who had been incorrectly formed in the Christian faith by the late medieval church, could not afford such a luxury.[29]

The curriculum Calvin envisioned for the school of faith followed a bipolar model, similar to the model developed by early scholasticism. While the laity were not expected to buy or read glossed Bibles (the Geneva Bible of 1602 is a notable exception), Calvin prepared and printed his own extended glosses on the biblical text, which, together with vernacular Bibles, were available for sale at reasonable prices. Theological issues raised in his commentaries and sermons were discussed in the *Institutes*, which also served as an introduction to further study of the Bible. While not all the laity could buy, read, and comprehend such theological and exegetical works, especially if they were in Latin, many certainly could. What the laity could not read, could be read and discussed

---

28 *Institutes*, III.ii.2–5.
29 In this connection see my forthcoming essay, 'Luther and Formation in Faith' in the Acta of the Lilly Foundation Conference on the Formation of Peoples in Faith held at the University of Notre Dame in 1995.

by pastors, whose pastoral office had been reconceived in a church that regarded itself as both mother and school.

Not everything, of course, was reconceived. Many of the functions of the old parish priest were still discharged by the new Reformed parson, who baptized, catechized, married, and interred his parishioners. The new minister presided at the eucharist four times a year and preached at every worship service; though preaching, which had been a peripheral duty in the late medieval church now became central, while the celebration of the eucharist, which had been primary, became comparatively infrequent. Moreover, Calvin and his allies were unwilling to restrict themselves in their preaching to a few comments on pericopal lessons. Unlike the old parish priest who preceded them but like the former university lecturer whom they emulated, the new parsons preached through an entire book of the Bible, chapter by chapter, phrase by phrase, omitting nothing. The kind of thorough exegesis that had been limited in medieval scholasticism to a clerical elite was now offered on a somewhat more elementary level by Calvin to all the faithful. The Calvinist ideal was to place a learned glossator in every pulpit. The local parish became less a sacred space for the celebration of religious mysteries than an assembly room for the theological education of the laity. Historians should not be surprised that the pastor in Reformed churches was often known as a teaching elder. Teaching became a central function of the parish minister in a church that was both mother and school.

In short, the relationship of Calvin to scholasticism is a good deal more complicated that we might first have thought. If we raise only the limited question of Calvin's attitude towards scholasticism in the late medieval church, we can say that Calvin despised it, respected it, borrowed from it, misrepresented it, and emulated it. Indeed, his own bipolar theological programme of theology and exegesis bore a striking resemblance to the bipolar programme of the scholastic theologians. If, however, we focus on Calvin's understanding of the nature of the church, we find that he regarded it as a school of faith in which all the laity were called to exercise their theological responsibility before God. It could be argued — and I am inclined to argue it — that Calvin's reconception of theology as a school theology for the church represents a democratization and expansion of the scholastic ideal. The time is therefore overdue for historians and theologians to acknowledge what they can no longer credibly deny; namely, that the phrase, 'the scholastic Calvin' is not an oxymoron. Even if Calvin was not a scholastic in the sense Duns Scotus was (and there is a sense in which he clearly was not), he was undeniably a *scholasticus* in another equally important sense, a schoolmaster in the church that he regarded as both mother and school.

PART 2
EARLY REFORMED
ORTHODOXY

1

The Use and Abuse of a Document:
Beza's *Tabula Praedestinationis*, The Bolsec Controversy, and the Origins of Reformed Orthodoxy

Richard A. Muller

The understanding of Beza's *Summa totius christianismi* or, as it is often called, *Tabula praedestinationis*, as a system or as a prospectus for a system, beginning with Heppe's use of the diagram in several places as proof that later Reformed theology gravitated towards a predestinarian system,[1] and continuing in Dantine's and Kickel's analyses of Beza as a rationalistic predestinarian,[2] rests both on the nineteenth-century central-dogma theory and on a misreading of Beza's title, *Summa totius christianismi*, as indicating a *Summa theologiae*.[3] Even so, the identification of Beza's *Tabula*

---

[1] Cf. Heinrich Heppe, *Theodore Beza: Leben und ausgewählte Schriften* (Elberfeld, 1861), 320–38 (the *Tabula* followed by a German translation of its explanatory text) with idem, 'Der Charakter der deutsch-reformierten Kirche und das Verhältniss derselben zum Luthertum und zum Calvinismus', *Theologische Studien und Kritiken*, 1850 (Heft 3), 672; and idem, *Reformed Dogmatics Set Out and Illustrated from the Sources*, rev. and ed. by Ernst Bizer, trans. G.T. Thomson (London, 1950/Grand Rapids: Baker, 1978), 147–8.

[2] Johannes Dantine, 'Das christologische Problem in Rahmen der Prädestinationslehre von Theodor Beza', *Zeitschrift für Kirchengeschichte* LXXVII (1966), 81–96; idem, 'Les Tabelles sur la doctrine de la prédestination par Théodore de Bèze', *Revue de théologie et de philosophie* XVI (1966), 365–77; and Walter Kickel, *Vernunft und Offenbarung bei Theodor Beza* (Neukirchen: Neukirchner, 1967), 136–46.

[3] On the problem of the central dogma theory, see Richard A. Muller, 'Calvin and the "Calvinists": Assessing Continuities and Discontinuities between the Reformation and Orthodoxy, Part I', *Calvin Theological Journal* 30 (1995), 345–75; 'Part II', *Calvin Theological Journal* 31 (1996), 128–9, 151–7.

as a primary source of Protestant scholasticism,[4] is at best a gross exaggeration. There appears to be no firm ground in the materials of later sixteenth- or of seventeenth-century Reformed theology for assuming that any of Beza's contemporaries or successors interpreted the *Tabula* as a system of doctrine in outline.[5] Nonetheless, despite the increasing weight of evidence and argument against such interpretations of Beza's *Tabula* and against the notion of predestination as a central dogma, the old hypothesis continues to be advanced,[6] and, therefore, to require some response by way of examination of the document in question.

As Bray indicated, the title ought probably to be understood as 'the sum total of the Christian life'.[7] The *Tabula* simply is not a full systematic design: it does not mention all 'doctrines' and, therefore, did not and could not indicate their sequence.[8] What it does is offer the relationship of the various elements of the *ordo salutis* to the divine decree, with an emphasis on Christ and on the graciously given faith that receives Christ. The general focus of the treatise — much like the focus of the differently ordered *Confession de la foy* or the *Brieve confession de foy* — is on soteriological issues.

In the case of the *Tabula*,[9] moreover, the specific focus is not, as in the

---

[4]   E.g. Basil Hall, 'Calvin Against the Calvinists' in *John Calvin*, ed. Gervase Duffield (Grand Rapids: Eerdmans, 1966), 23–7; Ernst Bizer, *Frühorthodoxie und Rationalismus* (Zurich: EVZ, 1963), 7–9.

[5]   The one potential example of such use of the *Tabula* is William Perkins' *A Golden Chaine*, but see Richard A. Muller, 'Perkins' *A Golden Chaine*: Predestinarian System or Schematized *Ordo Salutis*?', *Sixteenth Century Journal* 9 (April 1978), 69–81. Nor will it suffice to state, without any documentation, that the *Tabula* could have been understood in this way: thus, James B. Torrance, 'The Concept of Federal Theology: Was Calvin a Federal Theologian?' in *Calvinus Sacrae Scripturae Professor: Die Referate des Internationalen Kongresses für Calvinforschung vom 20. bis 23. August 1990 in Grand Rapids*, ed. Wilhelm H. Neuser (Grand Rapids: Eerdmans, 1994), 15–41, esp. 19–20, 24, 38–40.

[6]   Thus, Philip C. Holtrop, *The Bolsec Controversy on Predestination, from 1551 to 1555*, 2 vols. (Lewiston: Edwin Mellen, 1993), I, 28–9, especially n. 99 (p. 42); II, 842–5, 857, 874, et passim.

[7]   J.S. Bray, *Theodore Beza's Doctrine*, (Nienwkoop: Bibliotheca Homanistica et Reformatorica 12, 1975), 72.

[8]   Cf. ibid. 71, contra Ian McPhee, 'Conserver or Transformer of Calvin's Theology? A Study of the Origins and Development of Theodore Beza's Thought, 1550–1570' (PhD diss., Cambridge University, 1979), 301.

[9]   See Theodore Beza, *Confession de la foy chrestienne, contenant la confirmation d'icelle, et la refutation des superstitions contraires* (Geneva, 1558; 1561[2]); in modern French: *Confession de foi du chrétien*, ed. with an intro. by Michel Réveillaud, *La Revue Réformée* VI/23–4 (March and April, 1955), 1–180; and idem, *Autre brieve confession de foy* (Geneva, 1561); and the discussion of these documents in Richard A. Muller, *Christ and the Decree: Christology and Predestination in Reformed Theology from Calvin to Perkins* (Durham, N.C.: Labyrinth, 1986/Grand Rapids: Baker, 1988), 83–96.

two confessions, on summarizing the entire faith in order to manifest its soteriological centre, but summarizing only the order of the causes of salvation and damnation in order to show the positive relationship between the soteriological implications of the doctrine of the decrees and Christian preaching.[10] Of course, Beza does explicitly declare that 'the ultimate end of the counsel of God is neither the salvation of the elect nor the destruction of the reprobate but his own glory, as set forth both in those redeemed by [his] mercy and in those condemned by [his] righteous judgment'.[11] Such is his teaching — but this teaching in no way undermines the hortatory, homiletical, and soteriological focus of the document: it is, in fact, the reason for that focus. Beza's fundamental intention is to demonstrate how such a doctrine belongs to Christian instruction and is a support of piety. In short, the intention of the *Tabula* is to show that the doctrine of the decree and its execution, as presented through the collation of biblical texts, is a source of consolation and strength — in this particular context, against the claims of Bolsec that the doctrine was not based on a simple reading of Scripture and was a monstrous distortion of the gospel.

THE ORIGIN AND CONTEXT OF BEZA'S *TABULA PRAEDESTINATIONIS*: THE BOLSEC CONTROVERSY

Although Theodore Beza's famous *Chart* or *Table of Predestination* (*Tabula praedestinationis*) was first published, with its explanatory text, in 1555, the beginnings of Beza's effort to produce such a clear and precise definition of the doctrine of the divine decrees came several years earlier, in the context of the Bolsec controversy.[12] From his post in Lausanne, Beza had been one of Calvin's chief theological supporters in that controversy from its inception in 1551.[13] From the perspective of the formal process against

---

[10]   Theodore Beza, *Summa totius christianismi, sive descriptio and distributio causarum salutis electorum and exitii reproborum, ex sacris literis collecta* [*Tabula praedestinationis*] (Geneva, 1555); also in idem, *Tractationes theologicae*, 3 vols. (Geneva, 1570–82), I, 170–205. Subsequent references will note both chapter and aphorism and the page in Beza's *Tractationes*.

[11]   *Tabula*, III. v.

[12]   Cf. Paul F. Geizendorf, *Théodore de Bèze* (Geneva, John Jullier 1967), 74–5; McPhee, 'Conserver or Transformer of Calvin's Theology? A Study of the Origins and Development of Theodore Beza's Thought, 1550–1570', (PhD diss.: Cambridge University, 1977), 66–84; and Holtrop, *Bolsec Controversy*, 842.

[13]   Documentation of nearly the entire Bolsec affair is readily accessible in *Registres de la Compagnie des Pasteurs de Genève au temps de Calvin*, ed. R.M. Kingdon and J.-F. Bergier, 2 vols. (Geneva: Droz, 1962–4), I, 80–131, most of which, in turn, is translated in *The Register of the Company of Pastors of Geneva in the Time of Calvin*, ed. and trans. Philip E. Hughes (Grand Rapids: Eerdmans, 1966), 137–86. The materials from the *Registres* together with other documents from the archives of Geneva

Bolsec, the controversy was over shortly after it began. There were incidents in March and May of 1551, but the main controversy began in mid-October and by the end of December Bolsec had been banished from Geneva. The Genevan controversy, thus, ran for barely two and a half months.

The brevity of the Genevan debate is not, however, an index of the gravity of the controversy. Both Roget and Choisy surmised that Bolsec, who (although trained as a physician) fancied himself a theologian and enjoyed controversy, had been engaged by Calvin's political adversaries to cause trouble in the city.[14] Bolsec's complaints drew on themes that had earlier plagued Calvin in his debates with Pighius and with the Libertines,[15] and they clearly moved beyond the theological into the political realm in their implication that Calvin could not preach with any authority. Beyond this local ecclesio-political problem, there was also the

---

belonging to the civil side of the process are found in *Actes du Procès intenté par Calvin et les autres ministres de Genève à Jérôme Bolsec de Paris* in *CO* 8, col. 144–248. A full account of the trial including most of the documentation was also printed in Henri Fazy, *Procès de Jérôme Bolsec publié d'aprés les documents originaux* in *Mémoires de l'Institut nationale genevois* 10 (1865), 3–74. Fazy's analysis is coloured by his insistence that 'the principle [of] free inquiry' and 'the doctrine [of] predestination' are the opposing and irreconcilable sides of 'Calvinist Protestantism'. Bolsec, he declares, was merely the victim of Calvin's predestinarian intolerance after Calvin chose to favor this 'humiliating doctrine' rather than to proceed in the emancipation of the human spirit! Careful presentations on the controversy appear in Amedée Roget, *Histoire du peuple de Genève, depuis la Reforme jusqu'à l'Escalade*, 7 vols. (Geneva: John Jullien, 1870–83), III, 157–206; IV, 204–10; and Eugène Choisy, *La théocratie à Genève au temps de Calvin* (Geneva: Eggimann, 1897), 98–129, 165–73. The most balanced, albeit brief, account of the controversy in English remains that in Williston Walker, *John Calvin: The Organizer of Reformed Protestantism (1509–1564)* (1906; repr. with a bibliographical essay by John T. McNeill; New York: Schocken, 1969), 314–20. Far greater detail, accompanied, however, by excessive authorial editorializing from a neo-orthodox perspective and by tendentious argumentation, paralleling that of Fazy, on behalf of Bolsec and his theology, is found in Holtrop, *Bolsec Controversy*; cf. my review of Holtrop in *Calvin Theological Journal* 29/2 (1994), 581–9.

[14]   Roget, *Histoire du peuple de Genève*, III, 158; Choisy, *La théocratie à Genève*, 113.

[15]   The first part of Calvin's response to Pighius, the *Defensio sanae et orthodoxae doctrinae de servitute et liberatione humani arbitrii adversus calumnias Alberti Pighii Campensis* [1543] in *CO* 6, col. 225–404, can now be studied in translation: John Calvin, *The Bondage and Liberation of the Will: A Defense of the Orthodox Doctrine of Human Choice against Pighius*, ed. A.N.S. Lane, trans. G.I. Davies, Texts and Studies in Reformation and Post-Reformation Thought, (Grand Rapids: Baker, 1996). The treatise against the Libertines, *Contre la secte phantastique et furieuse des Libertins que se nomment Spirituels* [1545] in *CO* 7, cols. 149–248; tran. in John Calvin, *Treatises Against the Anabaptists and Against the Libertines*, trans. and ed. Benjamin W. Farley (Grand Rapids: Baker, 1982), 159–326.

problem of the relationship between Geneva and the other Swiss cities and cantons, notably Berne, whose army both offered protection to and threatened the independence of Geneva. Indeed, it was to Bernese territory that Bolsec went after his expulsion from Geneva and it was to the Bernese that he continued to complain concerning Calvin's teachings, well into 1555.

Beza's personal involvement in the controversy was marginal, inasmuch as he remained in Lausanne throughout the debate, only arriving in Geneva in 1558, nearly three years after the debate finally came to its genuine conclusion. Yet, as Beza's correspondence documents, he was a consistent and eloquent ally of Calvin who eventually lent his literary skills to the resolution of the debate. Indeed, the probable chronology of Beza's work on his chart of the decree and its execution and on the accompanying explanation parallels that of the extended controversy. There is, in the first place, a series of epistolary comments and queries concerning the doctrine of predestination from Beza to his two theological 'fathers', Calvin and Bullinger, that date from the time of the Bolsec controversy and deal with issues explicitly resolved in the *Tabula*: Beza to Bullinger (29 Oct. 1551; 12 Jan. 1552) and Beza to Calvin (21 Jan. 1552), the last of which also, most probably, refers to the *Tabula*.[16] In other words, Beza began to query his mentors about predestination within two weeks of the major incident leading to the Bolsec controversy and he most probably had an initial draft of the *Tabula* in hand a month after Bolsec's ejection from Geneva. The trial took two months, Beza's first formulation appeared in three. Specific references to the *Tabula* at various stages of its development are found in letters of Bullinger to Calvin (25 Oct. 1554),[17] Haller to Bullinger (17 Nov. 1554),[18] Beza to Vermigli (March 1555),[19] and a letter to Calvin dated 29 July 1555 most certainly refers to the completed document in a penultimate stage of composition.[20]

Towards the close of discussions with Berne, in October 1554, the Genevan clergy wrote letters of protest against continued attacks on Calvin's doctrine.[21] The Bernese Senate responded and, in addition, instructed the clergy of French-speaking classis under their jurisdiction to refrain from controversial subjects.[22] Finally, in March and early April

---

[16]   *Correspondence de Théodore de Bèze* (Geneva: Droz, 1960), I, 71–3, 76–80, 81–4; cf. McPhee, 'Conserver or Transformer', 68.
[17]   *CO* 15, col. 296.
[18]   Ibid. col. 316.
[19]   *Correspondence de Théodore de Bèze*, I, 153.
[20]   Ibid. 169–173.
[21]   *CO* 15, col. 250–2, 256–8 (Hughes, *Register*, 299–303).
[22]   Ibid. col. 313–14, 319–20.

1555, Calvin, Henry Aulbert, Francoys Chamoys, Raymond Chauvet, and Jehan Mascard were sent as ambassadors to Berne to deal with residual debate over predestination and the continued claims emanating from Bolsec, from André Zébedée (a minister of Nyon) and Jean Lange (pastor of Bursins), that Calvin was a heretic. In the end, the Bernese approved of Calvin's teaching while at the same time encouraging their own clergy not to involve themselves in dissentions and not to attempt to penetrate the deep secrets of God.[23]

The composition of the document, therefore, between ca. 1551 and 1555, corresponds precisely to the time of the Bolsec controversy, with its publication at the time of the final Genevan discussions with Berne. Historians have concluded that Beza first circulated the chart among the Swiss Reformers for advice and criticism, perhaps before he made public the 'Brief explication' that now accompanies it — given that the letter from Peter Martyr Vermigli to Beza, dated March 1555, suggests to Beza that he offer some written explanation of his chart of the decrees. Vermigli 'praised and exceedingly approved' of Beza's 'tables or pictures', but cautioned moderation and, by way of explanation, noted 'notwithstanding that I see in these [tables] a methodical division of the topic (*methodicam partitionem*), and have attentively observed a sound method of teaching (*didaktiken rationem*), they cannot fully embrace the entirety of the doctrine, as long as some explanation is not added and places from the holy text are not appended; I am nonetheless able to discern the lion by the claws . . .'[24] Inasmuch, however, as Beza's letter to Calvin of 21 January 1552 mentions 'certain chapters' on predestination by Beza,[25] it may also be possible that Vermigli was simply confirming a query from Beza concerning the advisability of juxtaposing his already written 'chapters' with the table — in which case Beza's work on the 'aphorisms' of the *Tabula* began at about the time that Bolsec was exiled.

It was also at this time, as also recorded in this letter of 21 January, that Beza offered a series of critical comments on Calvin's treatise *Concerning the Eternal Predestination of God* and offered a brief description of his own debates in the Lausanne classis. Beza first indicates his complete agreement with Calvin's teachings, but then notes that the treatise itself may not provide a formally suitable response. Beza suggests that Calvin follow Bullinger's advice, as provided in a now lost letter concerning Calvin's *Concerning the*

---

[23]   Cf. ibid. col. 537–52 with Kingdon and Bergier, *Registres*, II, 59–63 (Hughes, *Register*, 305–6).

[24]   *Correspondence de Théodore de Bèze* (Geneva: Droz, 1960), I, 153; cf. Bray, *Theodore Beza's Doctrine of Predestination*, 71; McPhee, 'Conserver or Transformer', 67–8. The phrase, 'the lion from the claws' is, as the editors of Beza's correspondence indicate, drawn from Erasmus' *Adagiorum chiliades*, I.34.

[25]   *Correspondence de Théodore de Bèze*, I, 82–3.

Eternal Predestination of God. Both Bullinger and Beza felt that the treatise, directed explicitly against Calvin's old adversary, Pighius, was too much based on the form of the latter's work and that, by attempting to respond to all objections in Pighius' own order, it failed as a positive exposition of doctrine. The doctrine must, Beza continues, be 'methodically treated' — as he himself has done in the 'chapters' that he wrote on the subject when the controversy first broke forth. Once he had worked through Calvin's treatise, Beza edited his own work and brought both the proof-texts (*probationes*) and refutations of objections into a suitable order.[26]

From Beza's perspective his *Tabula* and, probably, the written explanation of it, offered a methodical approach to the issue and, therefore, the proper form of a dogmatic response, if not to Pighius, certainly to Bolsec, whose teaching, such as it was, had been formulated in a series of brief articles.[27] Arguably, Beza advocated in polemics the very style of *brevitas et facilitas* that Calvin had advocated so strongly for his commentaries.[28] (Calvin had, of course, responded verbally to Bolsec's accusations during the interrogation process and the Genevan clergy had pronounced at some length on Bolsec's comments to them, but neither was a formal publication.[29]) In addition, the homiletical emphasis of Beza's explanatory text functioned as a response to the Bernese prohibition of preaching on the doctrine of predestination.

The letter of 17 November 1554 to Bullinger from Berthold Haller indicates that François Sampaulier, the pastor of Vevai or Vevey (some ten miles east of Lausanne on the shore of Lake Geneva), had seen some form of the *Tabula*. Sampaulier was probably one of those members of the Lausanne classis who had denied the use of distinctions such as that between reprobation and damnation. Sampaulier (or Sampaulinus) clearly did hold that reprobation was grounded in a foreknowledge of the fall.[30] Haller had not seen the chart, but he comments that, according to Sampaulier, the 'figure' demonstrated that 'all things, even evil things, rest upon God himself as the first cause of all things'. Haller makes no comment of his own, but the reported words of Sampaulier

---

[26] Ibid.

[27] Cf. 'Articles que nous avons extraitz des propos tenuz . . . par un nommé maistre Hierosme', 'Les Responces et confessions de Me Jherome Borset', and 'Les responces de Me Jherome', and 'Articles proposée par Hierome Bolcet' in Kingdon and Bergier, *Registres*, 85–6, 88–90, 90–3, 104–6 (Hughes, *Register*, 142–5, 146–9, 150–3, 163–5).

[28] Richard Gamble, '*Brevitas et facilitas*: Toward an Understanding of Calvin's Hermeneutic', *Westminster Theological Journal* 47 (1985), 1–17.

[29] 'Les repliques que font les Ministres de la Parolle de Dieu', 'Résponse de Calvin' in Kingdon and Bergier, *Registres*, 95–103, 106–7 (Hughes, *Register*, 153–62, 166–7).

[30] See Beza to Calvin, 29 July 1555, in *Correspondence de Théodore de Bèze*, I, 170.

are certainly pejorative — and they did have an influence on the composition of the *Tabula*.[31] Thus, Beza's chart does in fact enter into the discussions of the Bernese over the Genevan doctrine of predestination. Indeed, it appears, as far as Sampaulier was concerned, to offer evidence of the justice of Bolsec's charges.

In addition to these rather striking references to and parallels with the arguments of the *Tabula* from the time of the debate, we also have the circumstantial evidence from the literary history of Calvin's writing at the time of the debate with Bolsec: Beza's *Tabula* appeared in print at the very end of the controversy, as a final answer to the annoying Bolsec and his sets of articles for debate, while Calvin busied himself with other writing projects. At the time, Calvin appears to have assumed that he had answered Bolsec well enough in his *Congrégation [sur] l'élection éternelle de Dieu* of 18 December 1551. Indeed, Calvin's major polemical works on predestination, written at the time of the controversy, do not directly address Bolsec at all. The so-called *Consensus Genevensis* (1552), which is the second portion of Calvin's treatise against the Roman Catholic theologian Albert Pighius (augmented by polemic against Georgius of Sicily), offers a more or less confessional solution to the Bolsec controversy but does not so much as mention Bolsec's charges, although, certainly, the oblique comment in Calvin's prefatory remarks, concerning a troublesome person, is a reference to Maître Jerome.[32] Calvin's later works on the same subject, *A Brief Reply in Refutation of the Calumnies of a Certain Worthless Person* (1557)[33] and *On the Secret Providence of God* (1558)[34] respond to Sebastian Castellio, while the *Treatise of the Eternal Predestination of God* (1560) is a series of three sermons directed against no particular adversary.[35] Calvin could

---

[31]   *CO* 15, col. 316.

[32]   John Calvin, *De aeterna Dei praedestinatione* in *CO* 8, col. 249–366, trans. as *Concerning the Eternal Predestination of God*, with an intro. by J.K.S. Reid (London: James Clarke, 1961), 50; and idem, *Calvin's Calvinism: Treatises on the Eternal Predestination of God and the Secret Providence of God*, trans. Henry Cole (London, 1856; repr. Grand Rapids: Reformed Free Publishing Association, n.d.), 13–186, 223–56; cf. the discussion in W. De Greef, *The Writings of John Calvin* (Grand Rapids: Baker, 1993), 158–9.

[33]   John Calvin, *Brevis responsio Io. Calvini ad diluenda nebulonis cuiusdam calumnias* in *CO* 9, col. 257–66, trans. as *A Brief Reply in Refutation of the Calumnies of a Certain Worthless Person* in *Calvin's Calvinism*, 187–206.

[34]   John Calvin, *Calumniae nebulonis cuiusdam, quibus odio et invidia gravare conatus est doctrinam Ioh. Calvini de occulta Dei providentia. Ioannis Calvini ad easdem responsio* in *CO* 9, cols. 269–318, trans. as *On the Secret Providence of God* by Cole, in *Calvin's Calvinism*, 257–350.

[35]   *Traité de la prédestination éternelle de dieu, par laquelle les uns sont éleuz à salut, les autres laissez en leur condemnation* (Geneva, 1560); also published as *Treze sermons traitans de l'élection gratuite de Dieu en Iacob et de la réiection en Esau* (Geneva, 1562) in

have easily been struck by Beza's methodological comments and, in the midst of his technical responses to an adversary far more skilled in theology than Bolsec, left the task of answering Bolsec's articles on predestination and its relation to sin and grace to his younger ally and future associate. This pattern — if this is indeed what occurred — would become typical of the working-relationship between Calvin and Beza, as evidenced also in the case of Castellio, to whom Beza replied at length in 1558,[36] and in the cases of François Baudouin,[37] Joachim Westphal, and Tilemann Heshusius.[38]

THE *TABULA PRAEDESTINATIONIS* AS AN ANSWER TO BOLSEC

Although it ought to be fairly obvious that no large-scale or cohesive 'theology of Bolsec' can be reconstructed from the rather scanty materials found in the *Registres* and *Actes du procès*, a reasonably consistent account of his views on predestination can be presented on the basis of the three kinds of statement found in the documents: we have, in other words, Bolsec's own express arguments, his own responses to accusations, and the report of other elements in his teaching found in the sets of articles of interrogation. These latter remain significant as an index to his thought insofar as he did not deny their content: for example, he gave every indication of accepting as accurate the report that he had identified Zwingli's and Calvin's teachings as 'Manicheean' and as making God the author of sin. So too, he let stand the articles of accusation in which he

---

CO 58, cols. 1–206; note the translation, *Thirteen Sermons of Maister Iohn Calvin, Entreating of the Free Election of God in Iacob, and of Reprobation in Esau. A treatise wherein every Christian may see the excellent benefites of God towardes his Children, and his marvellous iudgements towardes the reprobate*, trans. Iohn Fielde (London, 1579); cf. the discussion in De Greef, *Writings of John Calvin*, 114, 178.

[36] *Ad sycophantarum quorumdam calumnias, quibus unicum salutis nostrae fundamentum, id est aeternam Dei praedestinationem evertere nititur, responsio Theodori Bezae Vezelii* (Geneva, 1558); cf. De Greef, *Writings of John Calvin*, (Grand Rapids: Baker 1993) 178.

[37] Cf. ibid. 208.

[38] Calvin wrote three treatises in response to Westphal beginning in 1555 and concluding with his *Ultima admonitio Ioannis Calvini ad Ioachimum Westphalum* (Geneva, 1557); Westphal responded to this 'final admonition', and was answered in Theodore Beza, *De coena Domini, plana et perspicua tractatio. In qua Ioachimi Westphali calumniae postremum editae refelluntur* (Geneva, 1559); similarly, as the eucharistic controversy continued, Calvin wrote his *Dilucida explicatio sanae doctrinae de vera participatione carnis et sanguinis Christi in sacra coena ad discutiendas Heshusii nebulas* (Geneva, 1561) but further debate was handled by Beza; cf. De Greef, *Writings of John Calvin*, 190–3.

was reported as claiming that God elected and reprobated in view of his knowledge of human obedience and rebellion, that election rested on foreknowledge of belief, and that reprobation followed on human rebellion — in fact, he chose to answer these charges somewhat evasively.[39]

In addition, Bolsec's views on predestination must not be abstracted from their context. Most of his theological expressions have strong affinities with the late medieval theological milieu (as, of course, does Calvin's own teaching on predestination),[40] and in particular with views and definitions belonging to that milieu but also, in the later Middle Ages as well as in the mid-sixteenth century, standing in opposition or at least juxtaposition to the tradition represented by Calvin. Whereas Calvin's thought stood firmly in the Augustinian tradition and certainly reflected the patterns of late medieval monergism,[41] Bolsec's views reflected patterns resident in the synergistic theology of the later Middle Ages, against which the Reformers had protested. The controversy between Calvin and Bolsec was not, therefore, an epochal conflict — neither presented or intended to present new theological opinions. The debate was one heard over and over during the era of the Reformation — the confrontation between a revived Augustinian monergism focused on salvation by grace alone and a comfortable, entrenched synergism that assumed divine foreknowledge of human choice as the basis for salvation.

Nor, indeed, was the controversy between Calvin and Bolsec of great moment in the development of Calvin's thought: there was nothing that Calvin needed to say in response to Bolsec that was not either already said in his debates with Pighius and the Libertines or in the Romans commentary and the major *locus* on predestination added to the *Institutes* in 1539 — or that would not be said shortly in the continuation of his argument against Pighius and the debate with Castellio. It was, surely, the Bolsec controversy and Bolsec's vague and amateurish advocacy of what Calvin took to be a Pighian line of argument that stimulated further response to Pighius — just as it was the Bolsec controversy, with its

---

[39]   Cf. Kingdon and Bergier, *Registres*, 85 (article 2), 87 (questions 4–5), 88 (responses to 4 and 5), 91 (responses to 4 and 5). The last of these responses will be considered at greater length below.

[40]   On the medieval background, see the classic essay of J.B. Mozley, *A Treatise on the Augustinian Doctrine of Predestination*, (New York, 1878²): Mozley was hard put to find substantive differences between the doctrines of predestinaton taught by Augustine, Aquinas, and Calvin.

[41]   Albeit any effort to establish a clear line of influence or a late medieval pedigree for Calvin must fail for lack of documentation: see Alexandre Ganoczy, *The Young Calvin*, trans. David Foxgrover and Wade Provo (Philadelphia: Westminster, 1987), 173–8; and Heiko A. Oberman, 'Initia Calvini: the Matrix of Calvin's Reformation' in *Calvinus Sacrae Scripturae Professor: Calvin as Confessor of Holy Scripture* ed. Wilhelm Neuser (Grand Rapids: Eerdmans, 1994), 114–25.

significant ecclesial and political implications that led Calvin and his ministerial allies to present the second response to Pighius as a theological consensus of the Genevan clergy. But this ecclesio-political significance points us once again to the conclusion that Bolsec's impact on Genevan affairs did not rest on any significant new theological insight on his part and that, in Calvin's view, the written response to Bolsec's actual claims could be left, as the controversy wound down, to his faithful assistant, Theodore Beza.

The substance of Bolsec's points against Calvin and of his answers to the various questions posed for him by his Genevan questioners bears out these generalizations. In the very first article 'extracted' from his statements by the Genevan authorities, Bolsec opposes a doctrine of predestination from before the creation of the world that does not rest the divine will on foreknowledge of 'who would believe and those who would be faithless'. Similarly, in the second article, Bolsec is cited as holding that election was grounded 'on consideration of those who would obey the Gospel' and reprobation on consideration 'of rebellion' against the will of God. So also, from Bolsec's insistence on the priority of unbelief to divine condemnation, the Genevan authorities concluded — without any subsequent objection from the accused — that Bolsec assumed 'unbelief must precede reprobation in order'.[42] Bolsec states, moreover, that 'faith does not depend on election, rather we ought to consider faith and election together, for before man can be considered elect of God, it is necessary that he be loved, and before we consider him loved of God, it is necessary that we recognize in virtue of whom we are loved by God, namely Jesus Christ whom God has given, with whom there is neither before nor after'.[43] He subsequently comments 'it is not proper to state that God has foreknowledge of one thing more than of another, for in him there is neither past nor future, but all things are present'.[44]

Two issues here demand consideration. First, Bolsec does not at all oppose the notion of a God acting 'in history' to that of a God decreeing eternally.[45] The contrast he makes is between a view of the distinction between eternity and time that argues the priority of God's eternity over time and one that does not. In Bolsec's answer, the eternal act of election

---

[42] Kingdon and Bergier, *Registres*, 109 (Hughes, *Register*, 143); Hughes' rendering of 'que l'incredulité precede en ordre la reprobation' as 'that in order of time unbelief must precede reprobation' cannot be followed, inasmuch as the issue is not the eternity of the divine will (Bolsec never denied this) but whether the eternal will of God is grounded on foreknowledge: the issue, therefore, is not the order of time but the logical order of objects known and willed by God — or, indeed, whether or not God elects graciously apart from merits in the creature.

[43] Kingdon and Bergier, *Registres*, 91.

[44] Ibid. 92.

[45] Contra Holtrop, *Bolsec Controversy*, I, 62–3.

respects neither 'past nor future' and relates to a Christ with 'whom there is neither before nor after'. There is, in short, a simultaneity of election and faith, given the non-temporal character of eternity. Bolsec's comments here, moreover, bear a very strong resemblance to the Boethian argument for the non-necessitating nature of certain divine foreknowledge, particularly as it had been advocated by Calvin's adversary of a decade before, Albertus Pighius.[46] Since eternity is not a time 'before time', but an eternal presence, what God knows of our temporal acts is in fact a present knowing. As McPhee notes, the answer does not resolve the problem posed by the question: the Genevan ministers were surprised by Bolsec's failure to acknowledge a distinction between temporal and logical order. Eternity is not temporally before time and so not temporally ordered with it — but there is nonetheless 'an order' or priority that can be identified. This is something, the ministers commented, that even 'children in school' grasped easily.[47]

Second, Bolsec relies on very traditional formulae in his statement that 'before man can be considered elect of God it is necessary that he be loved . . .' We read in Aquinas' article on predestination and election 'that love precedes election in the order of reason, and election precedes predestination'. 'Whence all the predestinate', Thomas concludes, 'are objects of election and love.'[48] Bolsec's understanding of the priority of love over election, moreover, echoes those particular medieval scholastic models in which the order of terms is love, election, predestination and in which 'predestination' is defined strictly as God's positive will towards his elect and 'reprobation' left as the term indicating the ordained end of those who are not loved by God. This terminology of the predestined elect and the foreknown reprobate is present, with a synergistic implication, in the theology of Gabriel Biel and Johann Eck — who identified the elect as the *praedestinati* and the reprobate as the foreknown (*praesciti*), foreknown, that is, as unresponsive or resistant to God's grace.[49] What is more, given that the sequence of divine love, election, predestination could be used either monergistically or synergistically, it also carried over

---

[46] Albertus Pighius, *De libero hominis arbitrio et divina gratia* (Cologne, 1542), 133v; cf. McPhee, 'Conserver or Transformer', 24–7.

[47] Kingdon and Bergier, *Registres*, 100 (reply to point 10); cf. McPhee, 'Conserver or Transformer', 10.

[48] Thomas Aquinas, *Summa Theologiae*, Ia, q.23, a.5.

[49] Cf. Gabriel Biel, *Epithoma pariter et collectorium circa quattuor sententiarum libros* (Tübingen, 1501), I, dist. 40, q. 1, art. 1 with Johann Eck, *In primum librum Sententiarum annotatiumculae*, ed. Walter Moore (Leiden: E.J. Brill, 1976), dist. 40 (pp. 110–14); and see Heiko A. Oberman, *The Harvest of Medieval Theology: Gabriel Biel and Late Medieval Nominalism* (Grand Rapids: Eerdmans, 1967[rev.]), 187–91, 194–5.

into the Reformation in the theology of Thomistically trained monergists like Vermigli.[50]

Bolsec's doctrine itself, insofar as it can be elicited from the documents of the controversy, can best be characterized as a mild synergism. McPhee hesitates on this point on the ground of Bolsec's teaching of the priority of grace in salvation,[51] although it ought to be clear that the priority of grace is an assumption shared by monergists and synergists alike in the tradition. Thus, although there is a certain degree of similarity between Bolsec's view of reprobation and Bullinger's, Bullinger himself did not hesitate to block a synergistic interpretation of his theology by grounding faith itself in unmerited grace.[52] What Bolsec certainly shared with Bullinger, albeit from a different vantage point, was a distaste for the parallelism of election and reprobation in Calvin's doctrine of predestination.

The text of the *Tabula* itself, moreover, identifies its purpose — quite different from the caricatures presented by Hall, Dantine, Kickel, and Holtrop. Beza does not begin in his own words, but in the words of Augustine. The citations concern the problems that some have in encountering the doctrine of predestination and the necessity, notwithstanding, of preaching the doctrine 'so that they who have ears may hear and glory in the grace of God rather than in themselves'.[53] The doctrine of predestination, rightly understood, according both to Augustine and Beza, focuses our attention on the grace of God in salvation and away from a Pelagian self-glorification or, as in the case of Bolsec, a synergistic diminution of God's grace and of the depth of the problem of human sinfulness. After citing Augustine, Beza moves to an explicit statement of his own purpose in writing:

> These are the thoughts of the most excellent Augustine. They pose for us two limitations: first, that we discuss this topic as the Word of God prescribes; second, that we explain — skillfully and for edification — precisely what Scripture teaches concerning these things. We will, therefore, speak briefly of both these issues — first concerning the doctrine itself, second concerning its use and application.[54]

---

50 Vermigli, *Loci communes*, III.i.10–11; cf. J.C. McLelland, 'The Reformed Doctrine of Predestination according to Peter Martyr', *Scottish Journal of Theology* 8 (1955) 255–71; with Muller, *Christ and the Decree*, 62–7.
51 McPhee, 'Conserver or Transformer', 12–13.
52 Heinrich Bullinger, *Decades*, 5 vols. (Cambridge: Cambridge University Press, 1849), I.iv (vol. I, 84–5, 87); IV.iv (vol. III, 189–90); cf. Cornelis P. Venema, 'Heinrich Bullinger's Correspondence on Calvin's Doctrine of Predestination, 1551–1553', *Sixteenth Century Journal* 17/4 (1986), 435–50, which makes a similar point with reference to Bullinger's correspondence during the Bolsec controversy.
53 Beza, *Tabula*, I.ii.
54 Ibid. I.iv–v.

The purpose of the *Tabula*, then, is the exposition of the doctrine of predestination with a view to Christian edification, with attention to the place of the doctrine in the church and in preaching, and with emphasis on the 'application' of the doctrine — which is to say, on the issue of Christian faith and piety, particularly as they raise the question of the ground and assurance of salvation. The concern is intensely soteriological and — as the explanatory text of the *Tabula* evidences — strongly christological. Nor, indeed, does Beza's teaching that the glory of God is the ultimate goal of the eternal decree run in any way counter to the central soteriological interest, the pedagogical and homiletical emphasis, or the fundamental christological assumptions of the treatise.

The style or genre of the *Tabula* is also quite significant to its assessment: not only is the document interesting from the perspective of the chart, it is also a rather unique production in view of its division of the text of its chapters into 'aphorisms' each followed by a series of biblical proofs. The translator and editor of the English version of the *Tabula*, *A Briefe Declaration of the Chiefe Poyntes of Christian Religion*, appears to have viewed this structure as somewhat inaesthetic or at least ungainly, particularly given the tendency of the shorter aphorisms to belong to a fairly continuous argument and even to stand as clauses within larger sentences often stretching across several aphorisms. As a result, the aphorisms disappear in the translation and the chapters are presented as continuous arguments, with the biblical proofs appearing merely as citations, foot-noted in the text, and listed at the conclusion of each chapter. Beza, however, surely had a reason for his somewhat curious organization of the work — and it is most certainly a reason that arose directly out of the historical context of the document in the Bolsec controversy.

Bolsec had proposed a series of articles for debate with Calvin in which he had demanded that Calvin 'answer categorically and without human reasons or vain similitudes, but simply according to the Word of God'.[55] In his first article, Bolsec had asked,

> whether [Calvin] does not confess that all the articles of faith and the doctrines that are taught in the Church of our Lord ought to be proved authoritatively by many direct and evident testimonies from the whole of Scripture which cannot be twisted to a different meaning?
>
> And whether he does not confess that it is improper to speak of God otherwise than Holy Scripture teaches, and that it is impermissible to augment or diminish the Word, but simply accept what is given there?[56]

In this context, Beza's extended lists of 'Proofs from the Word of God' should be understood as an explicit response to Bolsec's fundamental challenge.

55   Kingdon and Bergier, *Registres*, 104 (Hughes, *Register*, 163).
56   Ibid.

THE *TABULA* AND THE *APHORISMS*: AN ANALYSIS OF BEZA'S DOCTRINE

Both in his *Tabula* and in the accompanying *aphorismi*, Beza exhibits a foundational use of a distinction between the eternal decree and its execution in time which ought not to be viewed as itself proof positive of a speculative impulse, an incipient supralapsarianism, a direct reliance on the medieval scholastic tradition, or a departure from Calvin. For although the distinction between the eternal decree of God and its execution that is fundamental to the *Tabula* could have been elicited from virtually any of the later medieval scholastic theologians and could even have been found in a treatise by Luther's mentor, Johann von Staupitz, Beza in all probability simply borrowed the concept from Calvin himself. In any case, the distinction is certainly not, as Bray claimed, a point of divergence between Beza and Calvin: at very least, the distinction is a feature belonging to Calvin's and Beza's theology that represents a continuity with medieval, and with later Protestant, scholasticism.[57]

Calvin had, early on, explicitly used the distinction in his commentary on Romans (1540).[58] Moreover, in his commentary on Ephesians (1548) he had given it precisely the form in which it is adopted in Beza's *Tabula*: 'The decree (*decretum*) was eternal and ever-fixed, but it must be enacted in Christ, because in him it was purposed.'[59] So also in the commentary on John (1553), Calvin writes:

> If God wills to save by faith those whom he has elected, and in this way confirms and executes his eternal decree, whosoever is not satisfied with Christ but enquires curiously about eternal predestination desires, as far as lies in him, to be saved contrary to God's purpose. The election of God in itself is hidden and secret: the Lord manifests it by the calling with which he honors us.[60]

---

[57] Contra Bray, *Theodore Beza's Doctrine*, 90–3; cf. Muller, *Christ and the Decree*, 21.

[58] *Commentary on Romans*, 11:34, *CO* 49, 231: 'Tenenda vero est quam nuper attuli distinctio inter arcanum Dei consilium et voluntatem in scriptura patefactam'.

[59] *Commentary on Ephesians*, 3:11, *CO* 51, 183: 'fuisse aeternum semperque fixum decretum, sed quod debuerit in Christo sanciri, quia in ipso statutum erat'.

[60] *Commentary on John*, 6:40, *CO* 47, 147: 'Quod si Deus fide servari vult quos elegit et aeternum suum decretum hoc modo sancit ac exsequitur, quisquis non contentus Christo de aeterna praedestinatione curiose inquirit, quantum in se est, praeter Dei consilium salvus esse appetit. Electio Dei per se occulta est et arcana: eam Dominus vocatione qua nos dignatur patefacit'. Cf. Commentary on John 10:16, *CO* 47, 244: 'Nam arcanum Dei consilium, quo ordinati sunt ad vitam homines, tandem suo tempore patefacit vocatio'.

The distinction is also clearly implied throughout the *Institutes*: Calvin writes, for example, 'God, in his secret counsel, freely chooses whom he will . . . [but] his gratuitous election is only half displayed till we come to particular individuals, to whom God not only offers salvation, but assigns it' and, in the same chapter, 'by an eternal and immutable counsel, God has once and for all determined, both whom he would admit to salvation, and whom he would condemn to destruction . . . in the elect, we consider calling as an evidence of election'.[61] Indeed, there is one place in the *Institutes* at which Calvin specifically has recourse to the distinction: against the Stoic doctrine of an inexorable fate defined by 'perpetual chain of causes . . . contained in nature', Calvin states, 'we hold that God is the disposer and ruler of all things, — that from the remotest eternity, according to his own wisdom, he decreed what he was to do, and now by his power executes what he has decreed'.[62] It is worth noting that, especially in this last use, Calvin sees the distinction as a barrier to fatalism.

Beza, thus, not only most probably drew the distinction between the decree and its execution directly from Calvin, he also most probably intended to echo, throughout the *Tabula*, the more lengthy arguments presented on the same points of doctrine in Calvin's *Institutes*. By way of example, the general thrust of the *Tabula*, enunciated in its first chapter, is to argue the utility of the doctrine of predestination, to ground his discussion in the very practical problem that not all who hear the gospel respond to it, and to base the entire discussion on Scripture in order to guarantee the truth of what is preached: these are precisely the issues addressed in Calvin's introduction to the doctrine of predestination in the *Institutes*.[63] Calvin's other introductory concern, that the order or direction of discussion begin with what has been revealed rather than attempt to penetrate the 'labyrinth' of the divine decree, is also a primary emphasis of Beza's argument. Indeed, Beza not only frames his discussion of the order of proper discussion with precisely these concerns — even to the point of echoing Calvin's language — he also makes clear that his distinction between the eternal decree and its execution in time is but another way of making the anti-speculative point by offering as the title of his second chapter, 'Concerning God's eternal counsel, hidden in Himself, and subsequently known from its effects'.[64]

Beza's use of the distinction in the *Tabula* also points back to his letter to Calvin of 29 July 1555. There he had queried whether he ought to emphasize the decree itself as prior to all secondary causes or the execution

---

[61] Calvin, *Institutes*, III.xxi.7.

[62] Ibid. I.xvi.8.

[63] Cf. Beza, *Tabula*, I.[i–v] and ibid., VIII with Calvin, *Institutes*, III.xxi.1–2.

[64] Cf. Calvin, *Institutes*, III.xxi.1 with Beza, *Tabula*, II, title and VII.[iii, v–vi].

of the decree and, therefore, the order of the secondary causes.[65] Unfortunately no response from Calvin is extant, so that whatever recommendations Calvin may have made concerning the arrangement of the table and the contents of Beza's explanatory text remain a mystery. What is clear, however, is that Beza, for whatever reason, shifted his approach between the time of the letter and the final draft of the *Tabula* and chose not to emphasize one or the other but both of these perspectives.

Part of the reason for Beza's emphasis on both aspects of the problem and, specifically, on the distinction between the decree and its execution, may well have been the Swiss Reformed response to the debate, including the response that he received from within his own classis at Lausanne. Sampaulier and others not only argued that reprobation rested on divine foreknowledge of human fault in the fall, they also refused to make distinctions between reprobation and damnation, proximate and remote causes, efficient and privative causes, and between issues of order and issues of temporal priority.[66] These arguments are clearly related: distinctions between reprobation and damnation and remote and proximate causality parallel the distinction between the decree and its execution in time.

Some distinction must be noted here between the arguments of Sampaulier and those of Bolsec. Whereas Sampaulier had been quite willing to acknowledge an eternal decree of utterly gratuitous election, he has been unwilling to allow a parallel eternal decree of reprobation. The latter he refused to distinguish from damnation and sought to lodge in the divine foreknowledge of human sin.[67] The point closely resembles the single predestinarianism of the *Second Helvetic Confession*, with, however, the addition of an explicit reference to foreknowledge of the fall.[68] Bolsec, by way of contrast, denied both an eternal decree of reprobation and a genuinely gratuitous eternal decree of election and demanded that both sides of predestination cohere with human choice, whether of unbelief or of faith.[69] Bolsec also denied that the divine decree invariably preceded and grounded the divine foreknowledge.[70]

Bolsec's barely veiled synergism is also discernible in his protest against Saint-André's teaching that 'the elect who have been ordained

---

[65] *Correspondence de Théodore de Bèze*, I, 170.
[66] Ibid. *82*.
[67] Ibid. 170.
[68] *Second Helvetic Confession*, X.1, 2; cf. ibid., XVI.1, where faith is defined as itself 'the mere gift of God'. Note the stricter definition of predestination in Bullinger, *Decades*.
[69] Cf. 'Articles extraitz' 3, 4 with 'Responces et confessions de Me Jherome Borset', 5 in Kingdon and Bergier, *Registres*, I, 85 (Hughes, *Register*, 143, 151).
[70] 'Articles proposés par Hierome Bolset' in ibid. 105 (Hughes, *Register*, 165).

and determined by God for salvation are made by God to believe and receive his Word, while the others whom God has rejected from the beginning and determined to damn are not able to receive this Word' and in his assertion that the 'will of God' cannot be 'the cause both of the reception of faith and of the rejection of faith' or of 'the perdition of the damned'.[71] For Bolsec, the faith that is coordinate with election is the ground of 'the union of man with [God's] Son'. Faith, in turn, is possible only if God 'changes [man's] heart of stone' by grace — but 'God offers grace to all'.[72] In response, moreover, to two very specific queries of the Genevan clergy — 'Whether the entire race of Adam and all of humanity is not so corrupt that none can aspire to the good, unless God draws them' and 'Whether this grace of drawing is not special to some, which is to say, to those whom God has adopted before the creation of the world' — Bolsec had initially identified the first as an error and had evaded answering the second but, on being queried again, answered simply 'Yes' to the former and, in response to the latter, denied special grace in the name of a resistible grace offered generally to all.[73]

Bolsec's statements make clear why, unlike Sampaulier, Beza viewed the introduction of distinctions, such as that between reprobation and damnation, as necessary — and, indeed, why 'Master Jerome' came to be called 'the master muddler'. Beza well knew that failure to make such distinctions, whether among the Reformed or in the theology of one such as Bolsec, when coupled with the belief that damnation was the result of human sinfulness, could lead towards synergism or towards a doctrine of divine partiality. Beza also recognized that a theology emphasizing divine sovereignty but lacking these distinctions would be unable to explain the presence of sin in a satisfactory manner: the omnipotent God wills all things, but equally clearly the omnipotent God does not will all things in precisely the same sense. Even so, all of these distinctions do appear in the *Tabula*: namely, a very careful distinction between the glory of God in the revelation of his mercy and justice as final cause of election and reprobation, and therefore subsequent in temporal sequence but prior in order to all means of salvation; and a very clear distinction between the eternal divine reprobation grounded only in God's will and the final damnation rooted in the freely chosen wickedness of the reprobate.[74]

Given this emphasis of the diagram and its explanation of the distinction between the decree and its execution, and of the fact that the decree

---

[71] *Actes du Procès*, *CO* 8, col. 152, 156–7 and Kingdon and Bergier, *Registres*, 88–9.

[72] Kingdon and Bergier, *Registres*, 92 (Bolsec's ninth response).

[73] Ibid. 87 (questions 7 and 8); 89 and 91 (Bolsec's two sets of responses).

[74] Beza, *Tabula*, II.1, 5–6; III.3–5.

remains hidden while its execution is revealed, the *Tabula* clearly ought not to be taken either as a prospectus for an *a priori* or deductive theological system or as evidence of Beza's interest in using the decree itself as a speculative principle for theological argumentation. The avowed purpose of the treatise — to respond to the claim that predestination has no practical or religious value and ought not to be preached — points in the other direction. Even so, Beza's concluding observations on the right method for teaching the doctrine of predestination explicitly recommend the method of Paul's Epistle to the Romans which, according to Beza, begins with the lower degrees of the execution of the decree, specifically with the Law, and proceeds through the remission of sins, to the 'higher' points of doctrine.[75] Beza's own instructions, therefore, militate against beginning preaching or instruction at the top of the *Tabula* with 'God whose ways are past finding out'.[76]

Comparison with Calvin's *Institutes* is instructive. As Dowey has pointed out, Calvin rather consciously chose to follow an order of knowing (*ordo cognoscendi*) in the organization and argument of his *Institutes* rather than the order of being (*ordo essendi*) or order of causes from first efficient cause, by way of secondary or intermediate causality, to the goal or final cause of all things.[77] Of course, as the order and arrangement of the final edition of the *Institutes* makes clear, these distinctions concerning order do not point to two utterly incompatible patterns: an *ordo cognoscendi*, rightly conceived, ought to reveal the *ordo essendi*. In addition, given the credal patterning of the final edition of the *Institutes*, and its consequent movement from the doctrine of God to creation and providence, human nature, the fall, sin, the distinction between Old and New Testaments, Christology, the work of redemption, and the final judgment, the *ordo essendi* is quite evidently present in the organizational structure of the *Institutes* and, given also Calvin's approach to the problem of the knowledge of God in each of these various topics, the *ordo essendi* corresponds quite closely to the *ordo cognoscendi*.

Perhaps the instance in which the two orders diverge most clearly, however, is the doctrine of predestination. If positioned according to the *ordo essendi*, the doctrine of predestination would most naturally occur immediately following the doctrine of God or, as some theologians have understood it, in connection with the issue of what may be predicated of God — i.e. among the divine attributes. If placed, however, according to an *ordo cognoscendi*, the doctrine arguably would fall into an *a posteriori*

---

[75] Ibid. VII.

[76] Beza, *Tabula* in *Tractationes*, I, 170.

[77] Cf. Edward Dowey, *The Knowledge of God in Calvin's Theology* (New York: Columbia University Press, 1952/Grand Rapids: Eerdmans, 1995[3]), 218, 241.

location — so that the location itself would indicate that the predestination of individuals is not known to them by an examination of the divine
decrees in eternity but by the examination of the order of salvation and
its relation to one's self. Thus, predestination is known in and through
the examination of faith rather than through rational meditation on the
nature of God. In the final edition of the *Institutes*, Calvin appears to have
chosen the latter pattern. In his chart of the decrees and their execution
Beza appears to have chosen the former.

Nonetheless, from what we have already noted about the interrelationship of the two orders, the contrast ought not to be overstated. For
all his emphasis on faith and on the order by which divine truths are
known, Calvin insisted — notably, in his answer to Bolsec — that 'the
will of God, as supreme cause is the necessity of all things'.[78] Similarly,
Calvin had argued that in order to understand Christ's merit, 'we go back
to God's ordinance, the first cause'.[79] Calvin also quite consistently
indicated that 'election precedes faith as to the divine order, but it is
understood by faith'.[80] He also recognized that, although the initial
understanding of election must follow this *ordo cognoscendi*, once election
was understood and believed, the *ordo essendi* must also be taught and
confessed in order that believers should not be misled by an exclusive
emphasis on the effects of God's will:

> If we try to penetrate to God's eternal ordination, that deep abyss will
> swallow us up. But when God has made plain his ordination to us, we
> must climb higher, lest the effect overwhelm the cause. For when Scripture
> teaches that we are illumined according as God has chosen us, what is
> more absurd and unworthy than for our eyes to be so dazzled by the
> brilliance of this light as to refuse to be mindful of election?[81]

In other words, it is precisely the result of following out the *ordo cognoscendi*
that believers are instructed in the *ordo essendi* and come to the recognition
that 'predestination [is] God's eternal decree, by which he compacted
with himself what he willed to become of each human being'.[82]

The logic of Calvin's position is, in fact, most expertly presented in
Beza's *Tabula* when the chart is read in close connection with its explanation. The chart itself is clearly the result of a full examination of the order
of salvation in terms of the question of ultimate (first and final) causality
and its relationship to secondary causes and means. It moves from God and

---

[78]   Kingdon and Bergier, *Registres*, 107; (Hughes, *Register*, 166).
[79]   Calvin, *Institutes*, II.xvii.1.
[80]   Calvin, *De aeterna praedestinatione dei* in CO, VIII,318, my translation; cf. Calvin,
Concerning the Eternal Predestination of God, 127 and *Institutes*, III.xxi.5, 7; xxiv.1, 3;
IV.i.2.
[81]   Calvin, *Institutes*, III.xxiv.3.
[82]   Ibid. xxi.5.

the eternal decree, through the life of fallen humanity and work of redemption, towards the final judgment and the future reward of the elect and the reprobate — in short, the *ordo essendi*. But Beza very clearly indicates in his explanation that believers *do not* learn of their election by following the arrangement of the chart from top to bottom! Like Calvin, Beza points towards secondary causality as the beginning of our knowledge and as the immediate focus of our piety — the place where the divine will is known. This common interest is particularly apparent in a comparison of Beza's *Tabula* with Calvin's *Concerning the Eternal Predestination of God*. Calvin indicates, for example, that 'since God manifests his power through means and inferior causes, it is not to be separated from them'.[83]

Indeed, Beza writes that 'unless there is some significant reason to do otherwise' believers 'should ascend from the lowest degrees up to the highest, just as Paul does in the Epistle to the Romans' — from the pedagogical use of the law, to forgiveness of sins, faith, justification, and so forth. Beza even cautions, echoing the language of Calvin's comments on our understanding of the causal order, that believers ought not to examine it without proper training: 'For the brightness of the divine majesty suddenly or impetuously presented to the eyes — unless one has been accustomed to it by long and frequent exposure — will render one so blind that afterward even the understanding of lesser things will be impossible'.[84] Beza warns against beginning a study of the doctrine with either first or final causality — either the beginning or end, height or depth. Such an approach ignores the means of salvation as the proper beginning of a knowledge of God's will. This *a posteriori* approach dictated by Paul, Beza indicates, is the 'proper path through all of theology'.[85] In other words, on Beza's own testimony in his explanation of the *Tabula*, the causal order of the *Tabula* was not to be understood as establishing the initial or primary order of theological investigation.

Of course, Beza's comments are concerned with the initial pattern of teaching or knowing and do not rule out other orders: thus, for those so schooled in theology and exegesis that they will not take 'offense' at the doctrine, it is entirely possible to mirror the *ordo essendi* in an alternative *ordo cognoscendi*.[86] (In other words, while there can be only one *ordo essendi*, there can easily be more than a single *ordo cognoscendi* — just as the study of Scripture, catechetical instruction, and theological systems have different orders and arrangements. Beza's preference in teaching the doctrine of predestination at the initial, almost catechetical level and, presumably, in preaching, is clearly for an *a posteriori* rather than an *a priori* order.)

---

83   Calvin, *Concerning the Eternal Predestination of God*, 170.
84   Beza, *Tabula*, VII.[5].
85   Ibid. [6].
86   Ibid.

This anti-speculative, *a posteriori* emphasis on the proximate causes and the effects of predestination is hardly unique to the *Tabula* or bound by its apologetic purpose. Beza's other writings on the subject confirm that this was his basic approach: this is the view taken in his enormously influential *Annotationes in Novum Testamentum*, which also carried over into the notes of the *Geneva Bible*:

> Having established the doctrine of the eternall predestination of God on both parts, that is, as well of the reprobate as of the elect, he commeth now to shew the use of it, teaching us that we ought not to seeke the testimony of the secret counsel of God, but by the vocation which is made manifest, and set foorth in the Church, propounding unto us, the example of the Jewes and Gentiles, that the doctrine may be better perceived.[87]

As I have noted elsewhere, the frequently heard comment that Calvin removed the doctrine of predestination from its usual placement in the doctrine of God and positioned it in his soteriology (and that Beza, in his *Tabula*, returned predestination to its *a priori* placement) is a rather imprecise assessment of the two documents and their relationship.[88] In terms of the restructuring of the *Institutes* that took place in 1559, Calvin removed the doctrine of providence from its *a posteriori* placement with predestination (where it had been since 1539) and located it in relation to the doctrine of God, thereby establishing clear causal *foci* both in his discussion of the relationship between God and the created order and in his presentation of the order of salvation. Inasmuch as Beza's *Tabula* was written in 1555, it could not be expected to have reflected this restructuring, whatever its significance for the understanding of predestination. Moreover, Calvin's movement of providence into relation to the doctrine of God in the 1559 *Institutes* in fact brings the order and arrangement of the *Institutes* into closer relationship to the arrangement of Beza's chart — even though, as we have already shown, the chart was not intended as a model for a system of theology.

Beza's doctrinal exposition in the *Tabula* not only observes the suggestions he made to Calvin concerning the order of argument (that it follow the natural order of the subject rather than the order of an opponent's argument), it also evidences a desire for terminological clarity and careful distinction between ideas that look past the style of Calvin's *Institutes* towards the scholastic approaches of early Reformed orthodoxy. The *Tabula* itself, of course, does not provide an example of scholastic method, but its effort to attain clarity of doctrinal definition partakes of

---

[87]   *Geneva Bible* (1602), in loc.; cf. *Annotationes*, in loc.: '. . . cujus docet quaerendum esse testimonium non in arcano Dei, nec in ulla nostra dignitate, sed in voluntate Dei nobis patefacta, id est in efficaci vocatione. . . .'
[88]   Cf. Muller, *Christ and the Decree*, 22–5, 79, 84.

the movement of Reformed theology towards confessional orthodoxy and doctrinal precision. Thus, while Calvin avoided the traditional distinction between divine will and permission and has not always clearly distinguished between the causality of reprobation and the causality of damnation, Beza sought to answer the objections of Bolsec and others, like Sampaulinus, with a more perspicuous division of the subject.

A primary example of Beza's concern for clear distinction is his strict understanding of reprobation as belonging to the eternal divine decree and of damnation as the immediate result not of the decree but of voluntary human intransigence in sin.[89] Certainly, part of Beza's reason for clarifying this particular distinction lay in the desire to vindicate his and Calvin's theology from Bolsec's charge that he had made 'the will and decree of eternal God' the 'cause of the sins that the wicked commit and of their perdition'.[90] According to the transcript of the initial interrogation that took place in prison, Bolsec had explained his outburst on the ground that Manicheism was again rampant in the Genevan doctrine that 'the will and immutable decree of God is the single cause of all that is and will be'.[91] Certainly neither Calvin nor Saint-André had intended so to rest sin on the divine causality as to remove the blame for sin and the ground for damnation from human beings: Calvin had insisted that the original righteousness of Adam and Eve served to 'vindicate God's justice from every accusation' and that 'Adam could have stood if he wished, seeing that he fell solely by his own will'.[92] Nonetheless, Calvin had denied, or at least qualified, the traditional language of divine permission on the assumption that the will of God must be 'the highest and first cause of all things' and that therefore both the fall of Adam and the subsequent corruption of the human race had been predestined by God.[93] In addition, as Sinnema has noted, Calvin resolved this problem of divine will and human responsibility for damnation by recourse to a distinction between remote and proximate causality: 'we should contemplate the evident cause of condemnation in the corrupt nature of humanity — which is closer to us — rather than seek a hidden and utterly incomprehensible cause in God's predestination'.[94] Thus, although human beings are responsible for their own fallenness and damnation, God's will, understood specifically as the decree of reprobation, remains fully in the background of the fall, sin, and damnation.

---

[89]   Beza, *Tabula*, V.i–ii.
[90]   Kingdon and Bergier, *Registres*, 104 (Hughes, *Register*, 163).
[91]   *Actes du Procès*, *CO* 8, col. 153.
[92]   Calvin, *Institutes*, I.xv.1, 8.
[93]   Ibid. I.xvi.8, cf. III.xxiii.7–8.
[94]   Ibid. III.xxiii.8; cf. D. Sinnema, 'The Issue of Reprobation at the Synod of Dort (1618-19) in Light of the History of this Doctrine' (PhD diss.: St Michael's College, 1985), 61–2, 69–70.

Beza's application of the distinction between the decree and its execution to the problem of reprobation and damnation, therefore, both followed positively a major thrust of Calvin's own argumentation and offered a clearer perspective on a significant point of contention between Calvin and Bolsec. On the one hand, Beza could postulate a double decree of election and reprobation and declare that God eternally willed to create human beings 'of two utterly different kinds' — the one destined for glory, the other destined for wrath. Even so, Beza adds, Scripture sometimes ascends above the level of secondary or proximate causes to the eternal purpose of God in order to reveal the ground of election and reprobation in the divine will, apart from any foreknowledge of good or evil, indeed, of sin itself in the creature.[95] He does, thus, use Calvin's distinction between remote and proximate causality (albeit explicitly only with reference to election), but associates it more closely with the distinction between the eternal decree and its execution in time. Beza can, as a result, note a distinction between the decree or 'purpose to reprobate' and the final 'reprobation itself': in the case of the latter act, an act belonging to the execution of the decree, the causes of destruction lie entirely in the 'corruption, faithlessness, and iniquity' of the reprobate themselves.[96] Or, again, in his discussion of the execution of the decree Beza can declare that 'the entire fault leading to the damnation of the reprobate lay in the reprobate themselves' inasmuch as God did not create human beings in sin and inasmuch as the first pair 'willingly and freely rebelled against God' without either 'external constraint' or 'internal impulsion or necessity'.[97] These events must, of course, occur within the divine providence and, if by divine permission, not by 'a bare or idle permission' or 'contrary to the will of God'. Yet it remains the case that sin arose in such a way that 'the entire blame' rests on the sinner. This is so, Beza argues because 'the will of the first human being intervenes' causally 'between the hidden and incomprehensible will of God and the corruption of the human race'.[98]

As for the issue of Beza's broader systematic concerns, a simple perusal of the text of the *Tabula* confirms the fact that the only doctrine present in the *Tabula* other than its announced doctrinal topic, predestination, is the doctrine of Christ.[99] This characteristic of the document serves, by itself, to dismiss the claims that it is the prospectus for a predestinarian system of theology: there is no adumbration of a doctrine of God; there

---

[95] Beza, *Tabula*, II.2, 4–5.
[96] Ibid. II.6.
[97] Ibid. III.2–3.
[98] Ibid. III.5–6.
[99] Cf. Muller, *Christ and the Decree*, 82; note the undocumented criticism of this conclusion in Holtrop, *Bolsec Controversy*, 35, n. 25–6; 38, n. 57.

is reference to the creation of the world in relation to the doctrine of predestination but no doctrine of creation; there is no ecclesiology, no doctrine of the sacraments, no fully developed eschatology — in short, no theological system. Instead there is a consistent reference to Christ as the one in whom election is accomplished and a specific development of virtually an entire Christology in Beza's fourth chapter. Thus, in Beza's second chapter, the subject of which is the eternal counsel of God, Beza declares that election is the 'primary source' or foundation of the salvation of the children of God. And, he adds, it is precisely because of this foundation of salvation in the eternal decree that Scripture does not simply indicate the 'fruits of faith' as a ground of assurance or rest with the discussion of 'second and proximate causes, namely faith and vocation, *but ascends to Christ himself, in whom, as our Head, we are indeed elected and adopted*; and then mounts up even to the eternal purpose'.[100] Beza will not, in other words, mention the eternal decree without at the same time indicating that election is grounded in Christ.

Similarly, when Beza indicates, at the conclusion of the same chapter, that a distinction must be made between the 'eternal purpose to elect' and election 'as it is appointed in Christ', he points to the christological focus of subsequent chapters: there can be no enactment or execution of election apart from Christ, in whom the eternal Word is incarnate.[101] Indeed, this relationship between the divine intention to save and the incarnation provides the focus of Beza's fourth chapter. Here the pattern of enactment or execution of election focuses, first and foremost, on the need for a mediator — and, in the form and substance of its argument, echoes the initial arguments of Calvin's Christology. Since God is both merciful and just, it was 'necessary' that a mediator be appointed to 'restore' human beings 'to their integrity'. This soteriological need was met by the incarnation: 'the two natures were joined in the one Jesus Christ, in order that the entire corruption of humanity might be wholly renewed in one person'.[102]

---

[100] *Tabula*, II.iv.

[101] Ibid. II.vii.

[102] Ibid. IV.i, iii; cf. Calvin, *Institutes*, II.xii.1: 'It deeply concerned us that he who was to be our Mediator should be very God and very man. If the necessity be inquired into, it was not what is commonly termed simple or absolute, but flowed from the divine decree on which the salvation of man depended. What was best for us, our most merciful Father determined. Our iniquities, like a cloud intervening between him and us, having utterly alienated us from the kingdom of heaven, none but a person reaching him could be the medium of restoring peace. But who could reach him? Could any of the sons of Adam? . . . if the Godhead did not itself descend to us, it being impossible for us to ascend. Thus the son of God behoved to become our Emmanuel, i.e., God with us; and in such a way, that by mutual union his divinity and our nature might be combined; otherwise, neither was the proximity

Beza follows these aphorisms on the Person of Christ with a discussion of Christ's work and its application to the elect,[103] and then proceeds to a brief statement of the beginnings of the *ordo salutis* in the pedagogical function of the law: salvation begins with the condemnation of sin and the terror of judgment. But this negative work of God also points to Christ: 'he does not offer his counsel in such a manner that they remain in terror, but so that through contemplation of the magnitude of danger that surrounds them, they might turn and take refuge in the sole mediator, Jesus Christ'.[104] This focus on Christ and identification of the foundation of salvation as laid in Christ pervades the remainder of the chapter. Indeed, the central christological emphasis of Beza's argument only serves to indicate the underlying purpose of the treatise — to outline the right method of teaching the doctrine of predestination as a basis for assurance.

Although a clear supralapsarian tendency is present, this is not the fully developed supralapsarian teaching of the early seventeenth-century controversy. Dijk and others, certainly and with some justice, view Beza's formulations as a point of transition between supralapsarian aspects in Calvin's thought and a more strictly defined doctrinal model.[105] Nonetheless, contrary to the implication of Dijk's statements, Calvin did, very much like Beza, include the fall — together with everything else belonging to the finite order — in the divine decree, generally understood. Indeed, the basis of Beza's argument on this point is precisely the same as Calvin's: that nothing happens 'by a bare or idle permission in some way separated from [God's] will and decree'.[106] Beza, moreover, offers no speculation concerning the way in which God eternally conceives the as-yet-to-be-created human race in relation to the decree of salvation — i.e. as creatable and liable or as created and fallen. In fact, the text of Beza's *Tabula*, very much like the text of his letter to Calvin concerning the *Tabula*, avoids placing any qualifications on humanity: Beza identifies the 'lump' of Romans 9:21 as 'the human race not yet formed', indeed prior to the divine determination to form it. Humanity is not considered as fallen or as fallible, or even as created.[107]

near enough, nor the affinity strong enough, to give us hope that God would dwell with us; so great was the repugnance between our pollution and the spotless purity of God'. Beza's first three aphorisms (*Tabula*, IV.i–iii) are virtually a paraphrase of Calvin's point.

[103]   *Tabula*, IV.iv–vi.

[104]   Ibid. vii; similarly, IV.viii.

[105]   Cf. K. Dijk, *De strijd over Infra- en Supralapsarisme in de Gereformeerde Kerken van Nederland* (Kampen: Kok, 1912), 30–1; with K.T. Nösgen, *Symbolik oder Konfessionelle Prinzipienlehre* (Gütersloh, 1879), 253; H.E. Weber, *Reformation, Orthodoxie, und Rationalismus* (Gütersloh: Bertelsmann, 1951), II. 81, 83.

[106]   Cf. Beza, *Tabula*, III.5 with Calvin, *Institutes*, III.xxiii.4, 7, 8; also note Beza, *Tabula*, II.1; III.4.

[107]   *Correspondence de Théodore de Bèze*, I, 170.

From one perspective, this is a supra-supralapsarianism, but from another it is simply a refusal to ask any of the questions posed by the later debate. The radically supralapsarian tone is offset by the phrase immediately following, that God justly decrees 'to condemn for their own corruption and its fruits'. Whereas, technically, Beza is here certainly speaking of the execution of the decree, he does not explicitly make the point.[108] It ought also to be noted here that Beza's supralapsarian tendency is coupled in the *Tabula* not with a highly speculative interest in the content of the divine decree but with an anti-speculative emphasis on the temporal execution of the divine purpose.

Without diminishing the very real differences in emphasis between the supra- and infralapsarian varieties of the Reformed doctrine of predestination, it is important to note also their fundamental agreement. Modern discussions of the infralapsarian definition as less 'harsh' than the supralapsarian form often miss the point that the results of the two definitions are identical: the infralapsarian form does not argue that more human beings are brought into the kingdom, nor does it leave any opening for the human will in matters of salvation. It merely identifies the human objects of the eternal decree differently — as created and fallen rather than as creatable and liable. This common intention of the two definitions was, moreover, pointed out at the very beginning of the Arminian controversy by Francis Junius in his response to a series of issues and questions raised privately by Arminius in a letter: according to Junius, the various monergistic definitions of predestination 'differ ... more in the manner of speaking than in the substance of the matter'.[109]

In continuity with this line of argument and in contrast with both Augustine and Calvin, Beza argues that 'original sin and all else that might be attributed to Esau by reason of his birth are excluded as causes of God's hatred' by the Pauline argument of Romans 9:13.[110] But, once again, this conclusion is not so much a product of a supralapsarian logic of the eternal decree as the result of Beza's assumption that God's decree is grounded on no temporal causes: as he had previously indicated, the divine decrees are indifferent, arising 'purely from God's good pleasure' or, as he later comments, 'nor indeed does Paul respond that God so willed because he

---

[108] Cf., ibid. 171 with Beza, *Tabula*, III.6.

[109] Arminius, *Amica collatio* in *Opera Theologica*, (Leiden, 1629), 479 (*The Works of James Arminius* (London, 1828) III, 46).

[110] Cf. Beza, *Tabula*, II.5, proof 2, with Augustine, *Ad Simplicianum*, II.18 and Calvin, *Commentary on Romans*, 9:13, in loc. (*CO* 49, col. 179; *CTS Romans*, 352); and note the pointedly infralapsarian interpretation in Calvin, *Commentary on Romans*, 9:11, in loc. (*CO* 49, col. 178; *CTS Romans*, 349): 'When therefore he says, that neither of them had done any good or evil, what he took as granted must be added, — that they were both the children of Adam, by sinful nature, and endued with no particle of righteousness'.

foresaw that they would be corrupt, and that the cause of the decree was grounded in their depravity'.[111]

By itself, therefore, the *Tabula* does not easily fulfill the requirements of the 'predestinarian system' and, in the context of Beza's other writings, it cannot at all be interpreted in that manner. Indeed, when Beza did write his 'general summary' of Christian doctrine, the *Confessio christianae religionis* of 1558, he did not use predestination either as a 'central dogma' or as an architectonic principle for the organization of the whole body of Christian beliefs.[112] Nor can it be said that Beza's approach to the causal language of the decree and its execution is substantively different from Calvin's: certainly, Beza's greater clarity of argument and design stands on common methodological ground with Reformed orthodoxy, but his causal language and its doctrinal implications are integral to the context of argument in 1555 and clearly parallel to Calvin's own intentions. Beza's *Tabula* did become emblematic of the nineteenth-century notion of a deductive, decretal theological system characteristic of later Reformed orthodoxy, but the treatise itself gives no substance to the myth.

So too, the all too frequently heard comment that after Calvin had definitively removed the doctrine of predestination from the context of the doctrine of God, Beza returned the doctrine of the decrees to that *a priori* placement in his theological system, utterly misreads the *Tabula*. In the first place, the date of the *Tabula* is 1555, four years before Calvin created the arrangement of the *Institutes* in which predestination appears following the doctrines of faith and regeneration. Beza's point of reference for his teaching in the *Tabula* would have been the Latin text of 1550 or the somewhat augmented French edition of 1551.[113] Beza certainly had access to Calvin's *Concerning the Eternal Predestination of God* (1552). Beza could also have looked to Calvin's *Treatise on Free Choice against Pighius* (1543) and perhaps the *Articuli de praedestinatione*.[114] The definitions found in these works of Calvin offered Beza strong precedent for the ordering of the causes of salvation and damnation found in his *Tabula*. And, of course, in the second place, Beza's *Tabula* does not argue any particular order of doctrine to be followed in a theological system. Nonetheless, Beza's advocacy of a Pauline order of

---

[111]   Beza, *Tabula*, II.3; II.5, proof 2.

[112]   Cf. Muller, *Christ and the Decree*, 83–96.

[113]   Cf. F. Wendel, *Calvin: the Origins and Development of his Religious Thought*, (London: Fontana, 1963), 117–18 on the 1551 French text.

[114]   *CO* 9, col. 713–14. The articles are from an undated autograph of Calvin's found in the library of Geneva. Reid argues that the 'uncompromising' tone of the articles 'may be held to argue a comparatively late date'. There is virtually no statement in the articles, however, that cannot be paralleled by statements or arguments in the 1539 *Institutes* or the *Commentary on Ephesians* (1543).

teaching, moving from sin to law, grace, and only then to predestination, arguably echoes the actual order of topics in the 1539 *Institutes*, an order which remained intact in 1559. These conclusions leave us with a document that does not point very far beyond its own time — and which certainly does not offer any clear prototype for the grand-scale dogmatic systems of later Reformed orthodoxy. The primary basis for a right understanding of the *Tabula* must be consideration of its genre and purpose in its historical context, not the purpose to which it might be directed by nineteenth-century theologians in search of their own central dogmas.

2

Peter Martyr Vermigli:
At the Crossroads of Late Medieval Scholasticism, Christian Humanism and Resurgent Augustinianism

Frank A. James III

INTRODUCTION

In the mid-sixteenth century, Italian Catholic theologians did not usually receive a warm welcome into the Protestant communion.[1] What is more, we are not accustomed to tracing the origins of Reformed theology to Padua, Naples and Lucca. But then, few scholars have reckoned with Peter Martyr Vermigli (1499–1562). Our study concentrates on one of the leading lights from that constellation of theologians who gave formative shape to early Reformed theology. He embodied a rare combination in sixteenth-century Europe — an Italian Roman Catholic theologian who became one of the leading Protestant Reformers of his day. No other theologian

[1] Martyr's immediate acceptance by Protestant theologians was quite remarkable because, from the outset of the Reformation movement, Italians were viewed with suspicion by the northern reformers. Calvin's own distrust of Italians is displayed in a letter of 19 April 1543 to Conrad Pellican, in which Calvin refers to Vermigli's Italian compatriot and fellow apostate, Bernadino Ochino. Shortly after Ochino's unexpected arrival in Geneva, Calvin wrote: 'Because I do not trust Italian spirits, I have conversed with Ochino about individual points of our faith.' *Calvini opera* (*CR*) 39.462. The same is true of Luther whose anti-Italian bias manifested itself in his assessment of the Papal legate, Cardinal Cajetan (Tommaso de Vio), in October 1518: 'He is an Italian, and that is what he remains.' *D. Martin Luthers Werke: Briefwechsel* (*WA Br*) (Weimar: Böhlau, 1930–78), 1.209.

[2] The only other contender would be Pier Paolo Vergerio, Bishop of Capodistria. Although he had risen to rank of bishop, Vergerio never reached the status of Vermigli as a major Protestant theologian. See Anne Jacobson Schutte, *Pier Paolo Vergerio: The Making of an Italian Reformer* (Geneva: Droz, 1977).

of the sixteenth century stood out so prominently in both camps.[2] In his capacity as a Protestant, Vermigli's sphere of influence extended to some of the major centres of the Reformation movement: Bucer's Strasbourg, Archbishop Cranmer's Oxford (where he was Regius Professor of Divinity from 1547–53) and Bullinger's Zurich. Indeed, his importance was such that one Protestant contemporary, Joseph Justus Scaliger, could say, 'the two most excellent theologians of our times are John Calvin and Peter Martyr'.[3]

Vermigli's extraordinary career strategically placed him at the intellectual and religious crossroads of the sixteenth century, where late medieval scholasticism, Christian humanism and resurgent Augustinianism intersect. Although scholars have tended to concentrate on Calvin as the standard-bearer of Reformed theology, more recent historical analysis has suggested that the Genevan reformer was only one among several religious thinkers who gave form to the Reformed tradition. Besides Calvin, Bullinger, Musculus and others, Vermigli has now been recognized as one of the 'codifiers' of Reformed theology.[4]

In recent years, renewed attention has been given to the relations between the early Reformed tradition and its later seventeenth-century expression. Vermigli has emerged as one of the central characters in this scholarly conversation. As a result, Vermigli has acquired a number of interesting labels, such as 'pioneer of Calvinist Thomism', 'Protestant Humanist' and 'intensified Augustinian'. Our task will be to examine each of these labels and to determine how they apply to Peter Martyr Vermigli.

PIONEER OF CALVINIST THOMISM[5]

The question of Vermigli's scholasticism inevitably begins with a consideration of his years at the University of Padua, where he received a thorough grounding in Thomism.[6] Vermigli spent nearly eight years at the Augustinian monastery of S. Giovanni di Verdara in Padua where the theological curriculum was integrated with that of the

---

[3] Gordon Huelin, 'Peter Martyr and the English Reformation' (PhD diss. University of London, 1954), 178.

[4] Richard A. Muller, *Post-Reformation Reformed Dogmatics*, 3 vols. (Grand Rapids: Baker 1987–), 1.14.

[5] J.P. Donnelly, 'Calvinist Thomism', *Viator* 7 (1976), 441-5.

[6] Philip McNair, *Peter Martyr in Italy* (Oxford: Oxford University Press, 1967), 106. See also McNair, 'Biographical Introduction: Peter Martyr Vermigli' in *Early Writings: Creed, Scripture and Church*, Peter Martyr Library, ed. by J.C. McLelland (Kirksville: Thomas Jefferson University Press and Sixteenth Century Journal Publishers, 1994), 5.

famous university.[7] By the time of Vermigli's arrival in 1518, the reputation of the University of Padua had outstripped that of its main progenitor, the University of Bologna.[8] In 1490, two chairs of theology and two in metaphysics had been entrusted to the Dominicans and the Franciscans. Antonino Poppi is undoubtedly correct when he states, 'theology in Padua finds its splendid origins in the monasteries of the Dominicans and Franciscans'.[9] As one would expect, the Dominicans taught theology and metaphysics according to the *via Thomae*, and the Franciscans according to the *via Scoti*.[10]

According to Josiah Simler, Vermigli's contemporary and first biographer, he studied under two Dominicans at Padua, from which it may be inferred that he was regularly present at their lectures at the Dominican monastery of S. Agostino.[11] From an examination of the *Rotuli* of the University of Padua during Vermigli's student years, we can identify the two Dominican theologians. The University Professor of Theology in the *via Thomae* was the Dominican, Gaspare Mansueti da Perugia, while his fellow Dominican, Alberto Pascaleo da Udine, served as the Professor of Metaphysics.[12] There is little doubt that these are the two Dominicans who introduced the young Vermigli to the thought of Thomas Aquinas.

Drawing upon his Paduan education, the balance of recent scholarship has tended to portray Vermigli as a kind of proto-Protestant scholastic, who served as an important theological bridge between late medieval and Reformed scholasticism. It was Brian Armstrong who set in motion the interpretation of Vermigli as one of the three 'early reformers who most evidently inclined towards the budding Protestant scholasticism' (along

---

[7]   Hastings Rashdall, *The Universities of Europe in the Middle Ages* (Oxford, 1895), II, part 1, 21. Cf. Antonino Poppi, 'La Teologia nell'Universita e nelle Scuole' in *Storia e Cultura al Santo di Padova: Fra Il XIII e Il XX Secolo* 3 ed. Antonino Poppi, (Vicenza, 1976), 14.

[8]   A.B. Cobban, *The Medieval Universities: Their Development and Organization* (London: Methuen, 1975), 48–74.

[9]   Poppi, 'La Teologia', 3: 'la teologia a Padova trova il suo splendido inizio nella sede dei Domenicani e dei Francescani'. Cf. Rashdall, *Universities*, I.252–3.

[10]   Giovanni Brotto and Gasparo Zonta, *La facoltà teologica dell'Università di Padova* (Padua, 1922), 129–31. The chair of metaphysics was established sometime around 1442 and was entrusted to the Dominicans 'rinforzare la posizione del tomismo'. In 1490 the chairs of metaphysics and theology were subdivided, so that in each discipline new chairs were created *in via Thomae* and *in via Scoti*.

[11]   Josiah Simler, *Oratio de vita et obitu viri optimi, praestantissimi Theologi D. Petri Martyris Vermilii* . . . (Zurich, 1562) (unpaginated), third page.

[12]   Archivio Antico dell'Universita di Padova, MS. 651. fols. 29r–65r contain the University *Rotuli* for the years 1519–26. Cf. McNair, *Peter Martyr in Italy*, 103–4.

with Theodore Beza and Girolamo Zanchi).[13] This 'villainous triumvirate', it was argued, cast an Aristotelian spell upon the Reformed tradition,
resulting in the displacement of the essentially biblical vision of Calvin
with a philosophical orientation and a reliance on speculative reason. As
the senior member of this trio, Vermigli emerges as the Italian Aristotelian
inaugurator of Reformed scholasticism.[14]

Subsequently, and with more caution, John Patrick Donnelly moderated Armstrong's assessment of Vermigli's scholasticism.[15] While acknowledging that Vermigli's theology rested upon a Pauline foundation and
was buttressed by Augustine's anti-Pelagian writings, Donnelly judged
that Thomas Aquinas was the primary medieval inspiration. The points
of agreement between Vermigli and Thomas, argues Donnelly, are
'probably instances of direct borrowing'.[16] Based upon his analysis,
Donnelly concludes that Vermigli was a kind of 'Calvinist Thomist'.[17]
According to Donnelly, 'Jerome Zanchi was the most thoroughgoing and
influential in pioneering Calvinist scholasticism, Theodore Beza was the
best known and most prolific, but Vermigli was the first and the
inspiration of all who came after.'[18]

As Donnelly acknowledges, the question of Vermigli's scholasticism
turns on the matter of how one understands scholasticism.[19] Many have
lamented the difficulty of defining scholasticism.[20] If one takes a more
traditional view, as articulated by Brian Armstrong, scholasticism involves
the assumption that reason is equal (or superior) to faith and lays stress on
the use of Aristotelian categories in the rational defence of a theological
system. Measured against Armstrong's definition of scholasticism,
Vermigli exhibits little or only a partial correspondence.[21]

---

[13] Brian G. Armstrong, *Calvinism and the Amyraut Heresy: Protestant Scholasticism and Humanism in Seventeenth-Century France* (Madison: University of Wisconsin Press, 1969), 38.

[14] Armstrong, *Calvinism and the Amyraut Heresy*, 129. At the time of his assessment, Armstrong admitted Vermigli's scholasticism awaited positive demonstration. How-ever, he concluded: 'There is little doubt in my mind that this [Vermigli's scholasticism] existed'.

[15] J.P. Donnelly, *Calvinism and Scholasticism in Vermigli's Doctrine of Man and Grace* (Leiden: E.J. Brill, 1976), 29, readily admits that his study 'is primarily concerned with the scholastic side of Martyr'.

[16] Donnelly, *Calvinism and Scholasticism*, 126. Donnelly's stress on Vermigli's Thomistic origins is even more emphatic in his article 'Calvinist Thomism', 443.

[17] J.P. Donnelly, 'Calvinist Thomism', *Viator* 7 (1976), 452.

[18] Donnelly, *Calvinism and Scholasticism*, 207.

[19] Ibid. 198.

[20] Martin Grabmann, *Die Geschichte der scholastischen Methode* (Berlin: Akademie, 1957), I.28–37. Cf. Bengt Hagglund, *History of Theology* (St Louis: Concordia, 1968), 299–300.

[21] Donnelly, *Calvinism and Scholasticism*, 197–202.

Since the early work of Armstrong, progress has been made towards a more complete definition of scholasticism. The important efforts of Charles Schmitt and Richard Muller have been particularly helpful.[22] Both make the fundamental point that scholasticism was primarily a method of teaching or writing rather than a philosophical orientation. Schmitt defines scholasticism as 'a method of study and of teaching developed and used within the framework of institutional instruction and pedagogy'.[23] This characterization of scholasticism finds solid confirmation in Vermigli. There was in Vermigli a general concern for clarity, precise definition and logically presented argumentation and, when appropriate, syllogism, scholastic terminology and Aristotelian causality. Simler informs us that while at Padua, Vermigli 'loved and esteemed [Aristotle] by reason of the method'.[24] Here Simler specifically indicates that Vermigli's appreciation of Aristotle was due to his *method*.

Even within the parameters of this improved definition, however, important qualifications are required in the case of Vermigli.[25] The first qualification is that the same Vermigli who appreciates Aristotle's method also severely critiques Aristotle's views. In his lectures on the *Nichomachean Ethics* of Aristotle, Vermigli concludes nearly every chapter by showing the points where Aristotle differs from the Scriptures.[26] Marvin Anderson has also taken pains to identify specific instances where Vermigli opposes Aristotle.[27] Furthermore, Vermigli was quite sweeping in his criticism of the theological ideas of the leading late medieval scholastic theologians. He says of Lombard, Thomas, Scotus and Ockham — 'they filled everything with darkness'.[28] To the mind of Vermigli, it would seem that the scholastic method could be used as a vehicle for good theology or bad.

---

[22] Charles B. Schmitt, 'Towards a Reassessment of Renaissance Aristotelianism', *History of Science* II (1973), 159–93; and Richard Muller, *Scholasticism and Orthodoxy in the Reformed Tradition: An Attempt at Definition* (Grand Rapids: Calvin Theological Seminary, 1995), 1–8.

[23] Schmitt, 'Renaissance Aristotelianism', 161.

[24] *Oratio*, fourth page.

[25] See Richard Muller, *An Attempt at Definition*, 4. See also Muller's important two-part article, 'Calvin and the "Calvinists": Assessing Continuities and Discontinuities between the Reformation and Orthodoxy', *Calvin Theological Journal* 30 (1995), 345–75; and 31 (1995), 125–60.

[26] *In primum, secundum, et initium tertii libri Ethicorum Aristotelis ad Nichomachum . . . Commentarius doctissimus* (Zurich, 1563), 292–6. Cf. J.P. Donnelly, 'The Social and Ethical Thought of Peter Martyr Vermigli' in *Peter Martyr and Italian Reform*, ed. J.C. McLelland (Waterloo, Ontario: Wilfred Laurier University Press, 1980), 117.

[27] Anderson, 'Peter Martyr Vermigli: Protestant Humanist' in *Peter Martyr and Italian Reform*, esp. 69–77.

[28] Vermigli, *Exhortatio ad iuventutem*, in *Loci Communes* (London, 1583), 1050.

A second qualification is that Vermigli always made reason subservient to the authority of Scripture. Richard Muller has adroitly drawn attention to the important fact that 'all of the scholastic thinkers . . . whether medieval or Protestant, assumed the priority of Scripture over reason and philosophy'.[29] If it is true of late medieval theologians that the scholastic method was subservient to the authority of the Bible and careful exegesis, it is nowhere more vividly illustrated than in the work of Vermigli. The principle of the ultimate authority of Scripture and the necessity to engage in careful exegesis of the Scripture was manifested on virtually every page of his commentaries. Indeed if there was one overriding precept, one essential doctrine, one foundational presupposition at the heart of Vermigli's theology, it was the commitment to the final authority of scripture.[30]

With these qualifications in mind, it seems appropriate to characterize Vermigli as a scholastic with respect to his methodology. This is not to suggest that he was only a scholastic or even that he was primarily a scholastic. There were many intellectual tributaries which flowed into and gave shape to Vermigli's theological system.

PROTESTANT HUMANIST[31]

Donnelly's characterization of Vermigli as a 'Calvinist scholastic' provoked a protest from another Vermigli scholar.[32] In opposition to Donnelly, Marvin Anderson argued that Vermigli's primary orientation was humanistic and biblical.[33] While admitting that Vermigli did employ philosophical categories, Anderson urges that one must at the same time recognize the limitations which Vermigli himself placed upon such categories. For Anderson, the interpretative problems could begin to be

---

[29] Muller, 'An Attempt at Definition', 10.

[30] Vermigli, *In Epistolam S. Pauli Apostoli ad Romanos commentarii doctissimi* (Basel, 1558), dedicatory epistle to Sir Anthony Cooke, unpaginated. Vermigli variously describes the Scriptures as 'oracles from heaven', 'God's books' or simply 'God's words'. At one point he states: 'We will speak to men, not with the words of men but with the words of God'.

[31] Anderson, 'Peter Martyr Vermigli: Protestant Humanist' in *Peter Martyr Vermigli and Italian Reform*, 65–84.

[32] Anderson, 'Protestant Humanist' 65–84. Cf. Alexandre Ganoczy, *La Bibliothèque de l'Académie de Calvin* (Geneva: Droz, 1969), 19–27. Ganoczy's reconstruction and analysis of Vermigli's library supports Anderson's portrayal of Vermigli as a humanist. Ganoczy notes (23–4): 'Parmi les oeuvres des grands théologiens, on note l'absence prèsque totale des scolastiques . . . Enfin le nombre et la variété des éditions, études et travaux dus aux humanistes contemporains sont frappants.'

[33] Anderson, 'Protestant Humanist', 68–70.

resolved if one recognized Vermigli's own distinction between form and content. 'No matter how similar his patterns of thought may be to Aristotelian categories or indeed his view of man to Thomistic psychology, Vermigli himself drove a wedge between the motives of ethical philosophy and the gospel of salvation by faith alone.'[34] It is important to note that Donnelly, whose focus was confined to an investigation of Vermigli's scholasticism, recognized that Vermigli's theology was 'at once humanist and scholastic'.[35] How can Vermigli exhibit both a scholastic and humanistic methodology? Two matters require reconsideration — a re-examination of Vermigli's Paduan education and his vocation as a biblical exegete.

First, it must be noted that besides scholasticism, there was another intellectual current running through Vermigli's Paduan years, namely, Christian humanism.[36] The evidence for this intellectual strain in the monastery of the Augustinian canons is somewhat circumstantial but persuasive overall. Of particular importance is the fact that the university community was frequented by well-known humanists such as Pietro Bembo, Reginald Pole, and Marcantonio Flaminio, whose ideas almost certainly infiltrated S. Giovanni di Verdara.[37] Also important is the fact that Vermigli's own prior, Alberto da Verona, was a dedicated humanist.[38] Finally, the research of Paolo Sambin indicates that the formation of the library at S. Giovanni di Verdara reveals a significant interest in the humanist tradition.[39] These influences are reinforced by the demonstrable fact that a humanist orientation was amply reflected in Vermigli's later thought.

Secondly, one needs to grant full recognition of Vermigli's life-long vocation as a biblical exegete and commentator. If one is to begin to understand Vermigli one must appreciate that he was first and foremost a man of the book — a biblical scholar. His entire catalogue of publications was an expression of a self-conscious attempt to derive his theology directly from the Scriptures. He lectured on many books of the Bible at Protestant academies in Strasbourg, Zurich and the University of Oxford. During his lifetime, his commentaries on 1 Corinthians, Romans and

---

[34]   Ibid. 83.

[35]   Donnelly, *Calvinism and Scholasticism*, 201–202.

[36]   D. Fenlon, *Heresy and Obedience in Tridentine Italy: Cardinal Pole and the Counter-Reformation* (Cambridge: Cambridge University Press, 1972), 26.

[37]   McNair, *Peter Martyr in Italy*, 96–100.

[38]   *Biblioteca Classense*, Ravenna, Acta Capitularia, MS. 220, fols. 11v, 49r, 73r, refers to his election as the Rector General in the years 1505, 1516 and 1519, thus revealing how important a figure Alberto da Verona was among the Augustinian canons. Cf. McNair, *Peter Martyr in Italy*, 88.

[39]   Paolo Sambin, 'Biblioteca di S. Giovanni di Verdara', 265–6, notes, for example, that the library contained Petrarch's *De remediis* and his *De vita solitaria*.

Judges were published and a number of his lectures on biblical books were published posthumously as commentaries — Genesis, Lamentations, 1 and 2 Samuel, 1 and 2 Kings.[40] Although Vermigli had wide-ranging theological and polemical interests to which he devoted many pages, there can be little doubt that his first and primary calling was as a biblical commentator.[41] Along with Calvin and Bullinger, Vermigli was among the leading representatives of the Reformed tradition of Protestant biblical commentators.

As a biblical exegete, he exhibits and exemplifies a pronounced humanistic orientation, with its strong emphasis on philology, patristics, and exegesis.[42] Vermigli's own method of biblical commentary shared with his fellow Protestants the commitment to the Renaissance notion of *ad fontes*,[43] that is, going back to the original sources, as well as the conviction which is summed up in the phrase *Scriptura Scripturae interpres*. In accord with his humanist biblical methodology, Vermigli expressly states that his aim as biblical commentator was to 'make plain the words' of the biblical writer. He sought to elucidate what he described in the preface to his commentary on 1 Corinthians as the *verum genuinumque sensum Scripturae*.[44] In his desire to present the plain meaning of the text, Vermigli was recognized for the unusual clarity of his biblical commentaries. In his own day Beza contrasted Vermigli's clarity to Bucer's prolixity.[45] Josiah Simler, Vermigli's successor in Zurich, made the same observation[46]. Even Vermigli's opponents noted the clarity of his writings. Cornelius Schulting, a Catholic controversialist, declared that Vermigli's *Loci Communes* displayed a 'greater perspicuity' than Calvin's *Institutes*.[47]

Also in good humanist style, Vermigli's exegesis does not occur in an historical vacuum; rather, he constantly made reference to the Church

[40]   Cf. Klaus Sturm, *Die Theologie Peter Martyr Vermiglis während seines ersten Aufenthalts in Strassburg 1542–1547* (Neukirchen: Neukirchener, 1971), 30–7.

[41]   Frank A. James III, 'The Biblical Scholarship of Peter Martyr Vermigli (1499–1562)' in *Major Biblical Interpreters*, ed. Donald McKim (Downers Grove: InterVarsity Press, forthcoming). Cf. John L. Thompson, 'The Survival of Allegorical Argumentation in Peter Martyr Vermigli's Old Testament Exegesis' in *Biblical Interpretation in the Era of the Reformation*, ed. Richard A. Muller and John L. Thompson (Grand Rapids: Eerdmans, 1996), 255–8.

[42]   Anderson, 'Protestant Humanist', 69–71. Cf. Muller, 'Calvin and the "Calvinists" ', I.366; and Muller, *An Attempt at Definition*, 6–7, 11, 27–8.

[43]   Vermigli, *Exhortatio ad iuventutem*, 1050, writes: 'Redeamus obsecro, redeamus ad primos scripturarum fontes'.

[44]   Vermigli, *In selectissimam S. Pauli Priorem ad Corinth. Epistolam Commentarij . . .* (Zurich, 1551), preface.

[45]   Théodore de Bèze, *Correspondence*, (Geneva: Droz, 1960), VI, 115.

[46]   Simler, *Oratio*, fourth page.

[47]   Cornelius Schulting, *Bibliothecae catholicae et orthodoxae*, vol. 1, sig. Ai.

Fathers, both Greek and Latin. Although unheralded today, he was one of the great patristic scholars of the first half of the sixteenth century.[48] Among the galaxy of Church Fathers cited in his writings, none was more luminous than St Augustine.

The juxtaposition of humanist and scholastic strains in Vermigli's methodology reflects what a growing number of modern scholars have come to recognize about theologians of the sixteenth century — namely, that late medieval scholasticism and Renaissance humanism are not mutually exclusive. Like so many of his Protestant contemporaries, Vermigli displayed the confluence of scholasticism and humanism. Indeed, in Vermigli one finds remarkable confirmation of Kristeller's insight that it is a mistake to pit these two methods against one another.[49] Certainly one cannot ignore the existence of distinguishable patterns between humanists and scholastics, nor can one fail to acknowledge that at times there were controversies between advocates of the two approaches.[50] One must not, however, exaggerate the differences.[51] It has been increasingly recognized that the two methodological approaches 'peacefully coexisted' not only at universities, but also in the thought of individual theologians. For the most part, both were employed to serve

---

[48] J.C. McLelland, *The Visible Words of God: A Study in the Theology of Peter Martyr* (Edinburgh: Oliver & Boyd/Grand Rapids: Eerdmans, 1957), 267–71.

[49] P.O. Kristeller, *Renaissance Thought: The Classic, Scholastic, and Humanist Strains* (New York: Harper and Row, 1955), 92–119. Cf. James Overfield, *Humanism and Scholasticism in Late Medieval Germany* (Princeton: Princeton University Press, 1984), Erika Rummel, *The Humanist-Scholastic Debate in the Renaissance and Reformation* (Cambridge, Mass.: Harvard University Press, 1995) and Charles Nauert, *Humanism and the Culture of Renaissance Europe* (Cambridge, Mass.: Harvard University Press, 1995).

[50] C. Nauert, *Humanism and the Culture of Renaissance Europe*, 20: 'Humanism was not a comprehensive system of philosophy . . . but a distinct method of intellectual procedure. Since scholasticism also was essentially an intellectual method rather than a single set of doctrines or conclusions, a subtle clash of intellectual methods underlies the many overt and accidental causes for the conflicts between humanists and scholastics.' See also Nauert, 'The Clash of the Humanists and Scholastics: An Approach to Pre-Reformation Controversies', *Sixteenth Century Journal* 4 (1973), 2–5; L. Boehm, 'Humanistische Bildungsbewegungen und mittelalterliche Universitätsverfassung: Aspekte zur frühneuzeitlichen Reformgeschichte der deutschen Universitäten' in *The Universities of the Late Middle Ages*, ed. J. Ijsewijn (Louvain: Leuven University Press, 1978), 320; and Erika Rummel, *Humanist-Scholastic Debate*, 16–18.

[51] See P.O. Kristeller, *Renaissance Thought*, 114; L. Spitz, 'Humanism and the Protestant Reformation' in *Renaissance Humanism* 3, ed. A. Rabil (Philadelphia: University of Pennsylvania Press, 1988), 393; Winfried Trusen, 'Johannes Reuchlin und die Fakultäten' in *Der Humanismus und die oberen Fakultäten*, ed. G. Keil et al. (Weinheim Acta Humaniosa, VCH, 1987), 115.

theological interests, although neither method was necessarily tied to a particular theological or philosophical viewpoint.

Still more, however, needs to be said about this methodological coexistence in Vermigli. First, it must be understood that scholastic language was a common inheritance for all theological discourse among the sixteenth-century reformers. Like other reformers, Vermigli employed scholastic terms in his commentaries and theological treatises, since such terms were the established form of theological interaction. This is true not only of Vermigli, but of Calvin as well. Calvin, not generally categorized as a scholastic, nevertheless employed fourfold Aristotelian causality in his discussion of predestination in his Commentary on Ephesians.[52] Thus, in virtually all Protestant theological exposition, there was a fundamental continuity between humanism and scholasticism.[53]

Second, Vermigli's subject matter determined his methodological approach. For example, when opposing the medieval doctrine of transubstantiation, as he did with Gardiner, Vermigli employed a more distinctively scholastic approach.[54] The nature of the subject matter (transubstantiation) and Gardiner's approach determined the language, manner and terminology of Vermigli's analysis. Since the doctrine of transubstantiation was developed and defended on the basis of Aristotelian categories, Vermigli interacted with those categories in order to deal effectively with the opposing arguments. In his *Confutio*, Gardiner established the terms of the debate by employing the Aristotelian distinction between *substantia* and *accidentia*.[55] Vermigli took him to task precisely on his understanding of Aristotle, which by the nature of the case required Vermigli to employ Aristotelian language.[56]

---

[52] Calvin's comments on Ephesians 1 in *Calvin's New Testament Commentaries: Galatians, Ephesians, Philippians and Colossians*, ed. D.W. Torrance and T.F. Torrance, trans. T.H.L. Parker (Grand Rapids: Eerdmans, 1965), 126–30.

[53] Vermigli was not alone in this respect. At the very beginning of the humanistic movement in the fourteenth century, scholastic strains were evident even in the first humanists. The leading Florentine humanist, Coluccio Salutati (1331–1406) employed scholastic terminology in his theological writings. One finds for example, that Salutati's *De verecundia* evidences 'a curious blend of scholasticism and humanism'. R. Witt, *Hercules at the Crossroads: The Life, Works, and Thought of Coluccio Salutati* (Durham: Duke University Press, 1983), 256, 298–9.

[54] Donnelly, *Calvinism and Scholasticism*, 196.

[55] M. Anton. Constantius [Stephen Gardiner], *Confutatio cavillationum . . . a impiis Capernaitis*. See Vermigli, *Defensio*, Obj. 10–11. Cf. J.C. McLelland, *Visible Words of God*, 181–202; and Salvatore Corda, *Veritas Sacramenti: A Study in Vermigli's Doctrine of the Lord's Supper* (Zurich: Theologischer, 1975), 114ff.

[56] Vermigli, *Defensio Doctrinae veteris et Apostolicae de sacrosancto Eucharistiae Sacramento . . . adversus Stephani Gardineri . . . librum* (Zurich, 1559), especially fols. 235–59.

Third, there was in Vermigli a fusion of humanism and scholasticism. Charles Schmitt observes: 'One major reason for the longevity of the Aristotelian dominance and a continued reliance on that system lies in its ability to adapt itself and to absorb many novel elements.'[57] One way the flexibility of the Aristotelian tradition was shown was its ability to absorb various new materials, thus developing through its interaction with outside influences.

Perhaps the most notable manifestation of Vermigli's methodological fusion of humanism and scholasticism was found in his use of *loci communes*. These *loci* were systematic theological expositions of the biblical text. In his more extensive *loci*, after having completed the grammatical-historical exegesis and having consulted with the patristic and other commentators (such as rabbi's in his Old Testament commentaries), Vermigli brings the main exegetical and patristic considerations together into a theological essay. For him, it was vital to appreciate that theological formulation was preceded and grounded upon biblical exegesis — a conviction shared with all Protestants. This biblical-theological interaction can be seen in his Romans commentary, where Vermigli placed his extensive *locus* on predestination at the end of his comments on the ninth chapter of St Paul's epistle. It was only after having completed his exegesis of chapters eight and nine that Vermigli then drew out the theological significance of the doctrine of predestination.[58] An important fact in understanding the interrelationship between humanism and scholasticism is that both the medieval scholastic and Renaissance humanist hermeneutical traditions traced their origins to Aristotle. Vermigli's *loci* methodology was not new. Melanchthon had already employed a version of this approach in his *Loci Communes* of 1521. Melanchthon had borrowed the essence of the *loci* method from Rudolf Agricola, who took it from Cicero, who adapted it from the *topoi* (places) of Aristotle. So even the humanist tradition ultimately traces its ancestry to Aristotle's *topoi* methodology. This goes a long way in explaining why many humanist-trained Protestant reformers still retained traces of Aristotelianism. It would appear that the Reformation movement in part continued the trends of medieval Aristotelianism and in part received new direction under the influence of Renaissance humanism. One sees in Vermigli's hermeneutic this new combination of elements of the old methodology joined with a new philological orientation and infused with a new theological motive. Thus Vermigli's method of biblical interpretation was not so much a rejection of scholastic methodology as a reconfiguration of scholastic and humanist approaches in the service of new theological convictions.

---

[57] Schmitt, 'Renaissance Aristotelianism', 178.

[58] Frank A. James III, *Peter Martyr Vermigli and Predestination: The Augustinian Inheritance of an Italian Reformer* (Oxford University Press, forthcoming).

INTENSIFIED AUGUSTINIAN[59]

The importance of Vermigli's university education should not obscure the fact that Vermigli also received a theological education within the walls of S. Giovanni di Verdara which drew heavily upon the teaching of Augustine.[60] Indeed, S. Giovanni di Verdara has been described as a 'stronghold of Augustinianism'.[61] In a monastic order that traced its origins to the Bishop of Hippo and which lived according to the Rule of St Augustine, it is not surprising that Augustine was well represented in the library, as he had been in Badia Fiesolana, where Vermigli had studied earlier.[62] Any organized curriculum for theological study would have placed considerable emphasis on the writings of their spiritual patron.

There is no question that Vermigli employed scholastic methodology. Nor is there any doubt about his indebtedness to humanism. It is our contention, however, that both intellectual methods were utilized to serve an Augustinian theology. If these two intellectual movements are pictured as tributaries in the thought of Vermigli, then Augustinianism is the deep and wide river in which they converge. It must not be forgotten that Vermigli, whether Catholic reformist or Protestant theologian, was an Augustinian by vocation and conviction. This theological commitment was the motivation behind his education, his flight from Roman Catholicism, and his success as a Protestant reformer. Under the umbrella of Augustinianism, one finds room for Aristotelian methodology, humanist philology and Protestant theology. Thus there was a continuity not only of method, but also of theological content between Vermigli and late medieval Augustinianism. Indeed, the methods of scholasticism and humanism served the content of an intensified Augustinianism. This continuity of theological content is seen particularly well in Vermigli's absorption of the distinctive doctrine of *gemina praedestinatio* from the late medieval Augustinian, Gregory of Rimini.[63]

We know that Vermigli read and appreciated the theology of Gregory of Rimini while a student at Padua. Simler, whose source must have been

---

[59] James, *Peter Martyr Vermigli.*

[60] McNair, *Peter Martyr in Italy,* 121.

[61] Paolo Sambin, 'Intorno a Nicoletto Vernia', *Rinascimento* 3 (1952), 262–3, cited by McNair, *Peter Martyr in Italy,* 94.

[62] See Paolo Sambin, 'La formazione quattrocentesca della Biblioteca di S. Giovanni di Verdara in Padova', *Atti dell'Instituto Veneto di Scienze Lettere ed Arti,* Classe di scienze morali e lettere, 114 (1955–6), 263–80; and Rudolf Blum, *La biblioteca della Badia Fiorentina,* Studi e Testi 155 (Rome, 1951).

[63] Frank A. James III, 'A Late Medieval Parallel in Reformation Thought: *Gemina Praedestinatio* in Gregory of Rimini and Peter Martyr Vermigli' in *Via Augustini: Augustine in the Later Middle Ages, Renaissance and Reformation,* ed. H.A. Oberman and F.A. James III (Leiden: E.J. Brill, 1991), 157–88.

Vermigli himself, makes this clear.[64] As a *baccalaureus sententiarum*, Vermigli must have first encountered Gregory as one of the important commentators on Lombard's *Sentences*. Corroborating this line of Gregorian influence is the fact that Gregory's commentary on the *Sentences* was frequently reprinted as a textbook and readily available in northern Italy. It was reprinted eleven times at major educational centres in Europe from 1481 to 1522. Of these reprintings, four were in northern Italy.[65] So, if Vermigli's course of study followed the standard pattern, he would have first become acquainted with Gregory's commentary on Lombard's *Sentences* as an auditor of ordinary lectures on the *Sentences*. That places Vermigli's introduction to Gregory of Rimini in the early 1520s.

Gregory figured prominently in the fourteenth-century Augustinian resurgence on two fronts: the recovery of the whole corpus of Augustine's writings, thus freeing theologians from reliance on various medieval *compendia*, and the critical excision of apocryphal material. As Gregory makes clear in *distinctio* 40–1 of his commentary, he was a devoted follower of Augustine's doctrine of predestination.[66] Damasus Trapp describes Gregory of Rimini as 'the first Augustinian of Augustine'.[67] Although they were dealing with different historical manifestations of perceived Pelagianism, there are remarkable parallels between the fourteenth-century predestinarianism of Gregory and that of Vermigli in the sixteenth century. Time and again, the same issues are isolated and resolved with the same theological conclusions, often employing the same terms, and always based upon the same twin sources of Scripture and Augustine. One of the most basic parallels between the two theologians is the construction of the doctrine of predestination within a causal nexus. Indeed, both treatments are, at their core, extended theological essays differentiating the *causa* from the *effectus* of predestination. In order to argue the Augustinian case properly, they turned to the powerful imagery of Romans 9 and took the *ordo salutis* schema in Romans 8:28–30 as the constitutive framework for the doctrine of predestination.[68]

A comparison of their formal definitions of predestination illustrates the structural parallel. After acknowledging Augustine's classic definition (*quod praedestinatio est gratiae praeparatio*), Gregory offers his own definition of predestination:

---

[64]   *Oratio*, fourth page.

[65]   See F. Stegmuller, *Reportorium Commentariorum in Sententias Petri Lombardi* 6 (Wurzburg: F. Schöningh 1947), 2 vols, I, 178.

[66]   Gregory of Rinini, *Gregorii Ariminesis*, OESA Lectura Super Primum et Secundum Sententiarum, ed. Damasus Trapp and Venicio Marcolino, 7 vols (Berlin, 1979–87), 1 Sent. dist. 40–1 q. 1 art. 2 (III, 335).

[67]   Damasus Trapp, 'Augustinian Theology of the Fourteenth Century: Notes on Editions, Marginalia, Opinions and Book-Lore', *Augustiniana* 6 (1956), 181.

[68]   James, *Peter Martyr Vermigli*.

it [predestination] is the eternal purpose of God concerning the grace to be given and this grace, which Augustine tells us is the 'effect of predestination', is threefold: calling, justification and glorification.[69]

Vermigli's formal definition was more detailed but follows precisely the same structure.

Predestination is the most wise purpose of God by which He has decreed firmly from before all eternity, to call those whom He has loved in Christ to the adoption of sons, to be justified by faith, and subsequently to glorify through good works, those who shall be conformed to the image of the Son of God, that in them the glory and mercy of the Creator might be declared.[70]

The same cause-and-effect structure is evident. Further, both definitions represent the eternal *propositum Dei* as the ultimate cause of predestination which in turn produces the following soteric effects: vocation, justification and glorification. Notably, both employed precisely the same words to explain the cause and the effects of divine predestination.

If there is a single theological idea which reveals continuity of theological content between Gregory and Vermigli, it was their understanding of reprobation. One of the most distinctive aspects of their predestinarian systems was the forthright affirmation of unconditional reprobation. It was this dark side of the *propositum Dei* that distinguished them from nearly every other late medieval 'school' of thought and which united them theologically.[71] Gregory defined reprobation as 'the eternal purpose of God (*propositum Dei*) whereby He preordained not to give grace; moreover, He preordained a just eternal punishment for sins.'[72] Vermigli's definition was more elaborate but presses in the same

---

[69] *Lectura*, 1 Sent. dist. 40–1 q. 1 art. 2 (III, 321): 'id est praeordinatio vel electio seu propositum dei aeternum dandae gratiae, et ideo ipsa, ut ibi dicit Augustinus, "est praedestinationis effectus". Haec autem gratia in generali est triplex, scilicet vocatio, iustificatio et glorificatio.'

[70] *Romanos*, 411: 'Dico igitur, praedestinationem esse sapientissimum propositum Dei, quo ante omnem aeternitatem decrevit constanter, eos, quos dilexit in Christo, vocare ad adoptionem filiorum, ad iustificationem ex fide, et tandem ad gloriam per opera bona, quo conformes fiant imagini filii Dei, utque in illis declaretur gloria, et misericordia creatoris.'

[71] Indeed, Gordon Leff suggests that the primary reason that Gregory is remembered in later generations is because of this foreboding doctrine of reprobation. Gordon Leff, *Gregory of Rimini: Tradition and Innovation in Fourteenth Century Thought* (Manchester: Manchester University Press, 1961), 196.

[72] *Lectura*, 1 Sent. dist. 40–1 q. 1 art. 1 (III, 322): 'aeternum dei propositum, quo praeordinavit talem non dare gratiam, praeordinavit autem iustam pro peccatis aeternam poenam.'

direction.[73] At five crucial junctures, their definitions ran parallel. First, the *propositum Dei* was the ultimate cause of reprobation. Second, reprobation was construed passively, that is to say, it is a withholding of divine mercy. Third, reprobation was distinguished from punishment which is based on sins. Fourth, reprobation entails the inevitability of human sin. Finally, eternal reprobation is absolutely just.[74]

Virtually all late medieval theologians resisted a full-fledged doctrine of reprobation. Neither Gregory nor Vermigli follows this tendency. Demonstrating the first parallel, both were unequivocal in their assertion that reprobation is not dependent upon foreseen sins and that the sovereign will of God is the ultimate and exclusive cause of reprobation. Against the backdrop of Pierre Auriole's concepts of *causa positiva* and *causa privativa*, Gregory maintained that just as there is no foreseen *causa positiva* or *causa privativa* for predestination, neither are there foreseen temporal causes for reprobation. With the example of Jacob and Esau in view, Gregory resolutely declared: 'Just as God predestined eternally those whom He willed and did this not because of some future merits of theirs, so also He eternally reprobated those whom He willed, not because of their future demerits.'[75] Exhibiting much the same perspective as Gregory and very nearly the same words, Vermigli declared: 'What we have already demonstrated with regard to predestination, that it does not depend on foreseen works, we also affirm with regard to reprobation, that it does not depend on foreseen sins.'[76] Gregory and Vermigli upheld the same Augustinian doctrine against what they judged to be heterodox forces.

There can be no doubt that both Gregory and Vermigli taught a doctrine of *gemina praedestinatio*.[77] Both accepted as valid the same line of reasoning, that if the divine will, possessed of perfect wisdom, power and sovereignty, predestines some, it necessarily implies a corresponding

---

[73] *Romanos*, 413.

[74] See James, *Peter Martyr Vermigli*.

[75] *Lectura*, 1 Sent. dist. 40–1 q. 1 art. 2 (III, 343): 'sicut deus, quos voluit, ab aeterno praedestinavit et non propter merita aliqua futura, ita, quos voluit, ab aeterno reprobavit non propter demerita eorum futura.'

[76] *Romanos*, 426: 'Quod hactenus probauimus de praedestinatione, eam videlicet ab operibus praeuisis non pendere: idem etiam de reprobatione asserimus, quoniam nec ipsa pendet a praeuisis peccatis, modo intelligas per reprobationem non extremam damnationem, sed illud imum aeternum Dei propositum non miserendi'.

[77] There is a general consensus that Gregory taught a doctrine of double predestination. See Martin Schüler, *Prädestination, Sünde und Freiheit bei Gregor von Rimini* (Stuttgart: W. Kohlhammer, 1934), 46ff.; Heiko Oberman, *Archbishop Thomas Bradwardine, a Fourteenth Century Augustinian: A Study of His Theology in its Historical Context* (Utrecht: Kemink, 1957), 219; and Gordon Leff, *Gregory of Rimini*, 197. As for Vermigli, see Frank A. James III, *Peter Martyr Vermigli and Predestination*, (forthcoming); and Donnelly, *Calvinism and Scholasticism*, 132.

reprobation of the rest. With both, this logic was nurtured by the Pauline juxtaposition of Jacob's election and Esau's rejection with the imagery of the potter and the clay in Romans 9. For Gregory and Vermigli, the central core of the doctrine of double predestination was the *propositum Dei*. With equal ultimacy, divine reprobation and divine predestination issue from the same *propositum Dei*. It was this distinctive parallel that suggests theological continuity.

Especially significant is the fact that Vermigli read Gregory precisely at the formative stage of his theological development. This stands in distinction with Luther's training, in which he did not encounter Gregory's writings until well after his formal theological training had concluded. Indeed, it is for this reason that Steinmetz and others have hesitated to recognize the intellectual link between the Augustinianism of Gregory and that of Luther.[78] Given Steinmetz's important reservations concerning Gregory and Luther, Vermigli's early introduction to Gregory of Rimini is not only a crucial factor in the proper interpretation of the intellectual origins of Vermigli's doctrine of predestination, but also of historiographical importance.[79] If there was a connection between the intensive, academic Augustinianism of Gregory of Rimini and the Reformation of the sixteenth century, Vermigli emerges as a hitherto unknown intellectual conduit.

CONCLUSION

It was Vermigli's Augustinianism which provided the intellectual link between his late medieval scholasticism with its humanist modification and his role as a 'codifier' of Reformed scholasticism. Each of these designations (scholastic, humanist, Augustinian) illuminates a fundamental truth about

---

[78] See Heiko Oberman, 'Headwaters of the Reformation: *Initia Lutheri — Initia Reformationis*' in *Luther and the Dawn of the Modern Era*, ed. Heiko A. Oberman (Leiden: E.J. Brill, 1974), 40–88; and more recently, in his *Initia Calvini: The Matrix of Calvin's Reformation* (Amsterdam: Koninklijke Nederlandse Akademie van Wetenschappen, 1991), 8–9. Oberman has been strongly opposed by David Steinmetz, *Luther and Staupitz: An Essay in the Intellectual Origins of the Protestant Reformation* (Durham: Duke University Press, 1980), 13–34; and Leif Grane, 'Lutherforschung und Geistesgeschichte: Auseinandersetzung mit Heiko A. Oberman', *Archiv für Reformationsgeschichte* 68 (1977), 56–109. From a Roman Catholic perspective, Adolar Zumkeller also rejects any connection between Luther and late medieval Augustinianism. See his 'Augustinian School of Theology' in *Sacramentum Mundi: An Encyclopedia of Theology*, ed. Karl Rahner et al. (London: Burns & Oates, 1968), I.129.

[79] David Steinmetz, 'Luther and the Late Medieval Augustinians: Another Look', *Concordia Theological Monthly* 44 (1973), 245–60.

a more complete understanding of the proper significance of Vermigli and his contributions to the development of post-Reformation theology. (i) Both scholastic and humanist methods were operative in the Reformation. (ii) And while the theological method and emphases may vary in nuance and emphasis, the Augustinian content remained intact by and large. Indeed, only when all the various pieces of the puzzle are brought together does an accurate portrait begin to emerge. Furthermore, it helps modern scholars to understand the enormous complexity of the intellectual influences upon him, as well as his influence on subsequent Reformed theology. He was a pivotal theologian and one of the most important vehicles for understanding the intellectual origins of the Reformation itself, as well as one of the most important vehicles for understanding subsequent theological developments in the Reformed tradition. Scholasticism, humanism and Augustinianism are intellectual tributaries which flowed into the theological tradition we designate Reformed orthodoxy. Indeed, one cannot fully understand Reformed orthodoxy without taking cognizance of the scholastic, humanist and Augustinian strains in the thought of Peter Martyr Vermigli.

3

Patristics, Exegesis, and the Eucharist in the Theology of Girolamo Zanchi

John L. Farthing

INTRODUCTION

Sola Scriptura made it inevitable that exegetical and dogmatic tasks would be closely interwoven in the work of the heirs of the first-generation Reformers. It is not at all surprising to find a close linkage between exegesis and dogmatics both in the biblical commentaries and in the topical treatises of Girolamo Zanchi (1516–90), the Italian refugee who, along with Peter Martyr Vermigli (1500–62), became a pivotal figure in the formation of Reformed orthodoxy in the latter half of the sixteenth century.[1]

---

[1] Recent scholarship has witnessed a reappraisal of the significance of Zanchi's place in the early history of Reformed scholasticism. Cf. R.A. Muller, *Christ and the Decree: Christology and Predestination in Reformed Theology from Calvin to Perkins* (Durham, N.C.: Labyrinth, 1986/Grand Rapids: Baker, 1988), 110–25; N. Shepherd, 'Zanchius on Saving Faith', *Westminster Theological Journal* 36 (1973), 31–47; J.P. Donnelly, 'Calvinist Thomism', *Viator* 7 (1976), 441–55; C.J. Burchill, 'Girolamo Zanchi: Portrait of a Reformed Theologian and His Work', *Sixteenth Century Journal* 15 (1984), 185–207; J.L. Farthing, '*De coniugio spirituali:* Jerome Zanchi on Ephesians 5.22–33', *Sixteenth Century Journal* 24 (1993), 621–52; idem, 'Christ and the Eschaton: The Reformed Eschatology of Jerome Zanchi' in *Later Calvinism: International Perspectives*, ed. W. Fred Graham, Sixteenth Century Essays and Studies idem, 22 (Kirksville, Mo. Sixteenth Century Journal, 1994), 333–54; idem, '*Foedus evangelicum:* Jerome Zanchi and the Covenant', *Calvin Theological Journal* 29 (1994), 149–67; and 'Holy Harlotry: Jerome Zanchi and the Exegetical History of Gomer (Hosea 1–3)' in *Biblical Interpretation in the Era of the Reformation: Essays Presented to David C. Steinmetz in Honor of His Sixtieth Birthday*, ed. Richard A. Muller and John L. Thompson (Grand Rapids: Eerdmans, 1996), 292–312.

In the decades following 1524, controversies and schisms within Protestantism made clear the limitations of 'Scripture alone' as a basis for consensus. In anti-Roman polemics, *sola Scriptura* proved to be an effective device for criticizing the structures and dynamics of late medieval Catholicism, but the ecumenical failures at Maulbronn (1564) and Montbéliard (1586) made it clear that proof-texting alone could not provide the basis on which a unified Protestant alternative could be constructed. Especially on questions involving the eucharist and Christology, irreconcilable hermeneutical differences unleashed among the Reformers' heirs a powerful centrifugal impulse; it quickly became clear that simple appeals to the biblical text could not form an adequate basis for Protestant unity. In the 'Introduction' to his excellent translation of Peter Martyr Vermigli's *Dialogus de utraque in Christo natura* (1561), John Patrick Donnelly notes that this hermeneutical impasse required both the Lutherans and the Reformed, for all their slogans about the sole authority of Scripture, to make further appeals to the authority of early Church Fathers (especially Augustine and Cyril) as aids to a proper interpretation of the biblical text.[2] Although the Fathers play a somewhat less prominent role in Zanchi's work than in Vermigli's, it remains true that his interpretation of key eucharistic texts is informed, if not shaped, by a careful reading of the patristic exegetical tradition.

Since Zanchi is equally serious about his work as an exegete and as a dogmatician, we should consider his interpretation of Scripture and of the Fathers in samples from the two genres in which he seems most at home — commentaries and topical essays *(loci)*. Here we will consider selections from his commentaries (on Colossians and Philippians) and the systematic discussion of the eucharist in his *De coena Domini*.

EXEGESIS AND EUCHARIST: ZANCHI ON COLOSSIANS 3: 1–2 AND PHILIPPIANS 1:23

A. Colossians 3:1–2: *Si igitur surrexistis cum Christo, quae sursum* (sunt) *quaerite: ubi Christus est. Quae sursum* (sunt) *sapite* φϱονεῖτε *non quae super terram.*

Zanchi sees in the language of verses 1–2, especially in its emphatic distinction between what is above *(sursum, τὰ ἄνω)* and what is below *(in terra, τῆς γῆς)*, a clear indication of where the corporeal humanity of Christ is — and is not — located: 'Therefore Christ', he argues, 'is only

---

[2]   Peter Martyr Vermigli, *Dialogue on the Two Natures of Christ*, trans. John Patrick Donnelly, *Sixteenth Century Essays and Studies*, (Kirksville, Mo.: Sixteenth Century Journal, 1995), xxi.

in heaven'.[3] Only a theologian far less careful than Zanchi, however, would leave that statement unqualified. His radical view of Christ's deity leads him at once to add the necessary qualifications; he does not intend to affirm a doctrine of the 'real absence' of Christ from this world.

> But how is it that [Christ] is only in heaven and not elsewhere? I answer: it is by his corporeal presence and according to that nature in which he arose and also ascended into heaven. By his deity, indeed, he is in all places; by his grace and his regenerating Spirit, moreover, he is in all the saints . . . And he is everywhere by his word, by the signification of himself and of his will in the preaching of the Gospel. Finally, he is present in his representation in the Sacraments. But as far as his body is concerned, by a corporeal presence, he is only in heaven.[4]

For if we are to seek Christ above (because that is where he exists in his humanity), then his physical body is not to be sought or found on the earth, since, according to a clear apostolic witness, that is where his humanity, hence his finite body, does *not* exist.[5] The apostle's language, then, is incompatible with the claim that the body of the risen Christ is capable of existing on earth.

The text clearly identifies the one place where Christ's body is — 'sitting at the right hand of God' *(in dextra Dei sedens)*. Zanchi cites John of Damascus to the effect that this session at the Father's right hand is a function of Christ's glorification in the flesh *(secundum carnem)*. In view of Hebrews 8:1–2, Zanchi argues that the corporeal presence of Christ in heaven is a precondition for his service as our High Priest. For if Christ were exercising his priesthood on earth, the order of his priesthood would have to be either Levitical or Melchisedechean. But neither of those alternatives is possible. For the Levitical priesthood was an earthly type of the heavenly archetype, whereas Christ, who was not of the tribe of Levi, was not the type but was himself the archetype. On the other hand, whatever is earthly is temporal, but Christ is a priest after the order of Melchisedec 'forever' *(in aeternum* — Ps. 110[:4]); his priesthood is eternal, hence heavenly. As far as Christ's humanity is concerned, therefore, it is not only permissible but crucial to affirm that 'He is not on earth, but in heaven'.[6]

---

[3]   D. *Hieronymi Zanchii in epistolam ad Colossenses commentarius* [hereafter *In Col.*] 9 in *Operum theologicorum*, 8 vols. (Geneva, 1617) VI, 323: 'Atqui Christus sursum in coelo est, scilicet tantum'.

[4]   *In Col.* 3.1–2, 323.

[5]   Ibid.: 'Si ideo quaerere debemus quae sursum sunt, quia ibi Christus est suo corpore, ergo quaerenda nobis non sunt quae sunt super terram, quia super terram non est Christus'.

[6]   Ibid. *324.*

B. Philippians 1:23: *Coarctor enim ex iis duobus, desiderium habens dissolvi et esse cum Christi.*

Zanchi's commentary on Philippians 1:12–27 ends with a discussion of doctrinal themes. The tenth doctrinal excursus 'on the communication of properties' *(De communicatione idiomatum)* lays the groundwork for the eleventh, 'on the real existence of the human nature of Christ only in heaven', intended as a refutation of the ubiquitarians *(De reali humanae naturae Christi, in coelo tantum existentia, contra Ubiquitarios)*. On the communication of idioms, Zanchi's basic claim is that whatever is said of either nature may be predicated of the whole person, but what is proper to one nature cannot be predicated of the other.[7] He illustrates this principle by referring to Paul's death-wish in Philippians 1:23. When Paul said that he wished to be 'dissolved', that is, to die, it was not his body but his soul that so wished; yet the desire is predicated of the whole person of Paul. When he spoke of his wish to be with Christ, he was clearly referring not to his body (which, Paul knew, was headed for the grave[8]) but to his soul; yet this desire is predicated of the whole person. But since Paul's death preceded the resurrection, Zanchi finds it laughable *(annon rideretur)* that anyone should use this language as a basis for arguing that Paul's postmortem state would find him in heaven with Christ, in a bodily way as well as spiritually. But that is the same kind of mistake that ubiquitarians make: when Christ promises to 'be with you always, even to the end of the age' (Matt. 28:20) or to be present 'where two or three are gathered in my name' (Matt. 18:20), 'They conclude, "He is everywhere not only according to his deity but even according to his humanity".'[9] If whatever is predicated of one nature can be predicated of the whole person but not of the other nature, the distinction between the two natures of Christ must not be blurred by attributing omnipresence to his humanity. Christ is everywhere in his divinity but not in his humanity, just as Paul expects his soul to be with Christ after death, even while his body lies in the grave awaiting the day of resurrection.

Paul desires to die in order to be with Christ. That would be pointless, Zanchi argues, if the ubiquitarians were right. For in that case being with Christ in heaven would not involve a more intimate connection with him than is already available on earth. Clearly Paul's longing is to be present to Christ's bodily humanity, since by his divinity Christ is already present to Paul and Paul to Christ.[10] If the human body and soul of Christ

---

[7] *D. Hieronymi Zanchii in Epistolam ad Philippenses commentarius* (hereafter *In Phil.*) in *Operum theologicorum VI*, 54.

[8] *In Phil. 1.12–27*, 54.

[9] Ibid.

[10] Ibid. *1.23*, 56.

were present on earth, as the ubiquitarians claim, there would be no need for Paul to choose between staying with the brethren and departing to be with Christ. That Paul is torn between the two implies that he cannot experience both at the same time. There must be a way of being with Christ in heaven that is not available on earth; that makes sense, however, only if we assume that the corporeal humanity of Christ is located in heaven and is available there but not elsewhere.[11] To be with Christ in the fullest sense, with respect to his humanity as well as his divinity, is to be in the literal presence of Christ's human flesh and human soul. Zanchi cites 2 Cor. 5:6 ('As long as we are in this body, we are absent from the Lord'), which he interprets in light of the longing that Christ expressed when he said to the disciples in John 17:24, 'I want you to be where I also am'. Such language makes sense, according to Zanchi, only if it is recognized that as long as believers are in this present world there is a dimension of Christ's presence which they can only anticipate. That is why both Paul and Christ express the longing for a physical intimacy that is available only in heaven, where Christ's finite, bodily humanity is located. The doctrine of ubiquity, according to Zanchi, renders such a longing unintelligible.

Zanchi goes on to argue that, if Christ's body were ubiquitous, Paul's desire for death would be pointless, and thus immoral;[12] by subverting the teleological point of Paul's wish to die, the ubiquitarians have rendered it not just meaningless but sinful. It is unlawful to separate soul from body except for some godly purpose; hence entertaining the desire to do so is likewise unlawful. It is, in fact, a sin against nature and against nature's Author.[13] In Paul's case, moreover, it would have also been an act of selfishness and thus a sin against charity. If it were possible to be with Christ (in his humanity) while remaining on earth for the sake of the brethren, it would be uncharitable, hence sinful, for Paul to entertain the desire to die, for in that case nothing would be gained that might justify the loss that the brethren in Philippi would sustain by his dying. The doctrine of ubiquity implies that Paul's wish to die involves a sin against nature and God, but also against Paul's brothers and sisters in Christ. Such a consequence, in Zanchi's view, is the ultimate *reductio ad absurdum* of any ubiquitarian Christology.[14]

Anticipating a possible response to this line of criticism, Zanchi considers the possibility that Paul was already present to Christ's humanity, although

---

[11] Ibid. *1.23*, 55–6.

[12] Ibid. *1.23*, 54.

[13] Ibid.: 'Nemo simpliciter appetit, aut appetere potest vel debet, dissolvi seu mori, quia hoc pugnat cum natura, et per se bonum non est neque esse potest. Quod si quis hoc facerer, peccaret in Naturam et in Deum naturae autorem.'

[14] Ibid. *2.23*, 56.

less intensely than would be the case after death. 'But you will say, The Apostle was indeed, even then, with the soul and body of Christ, but not as perfectly as would be the case if his soul had been separated from his body. It was for this reason — for the sake of a more perfect presence and union with the humanity of Christ — that he wished for his soul to be freed from his body.'[15] But Zanchi notes that Paul makes no reference to a more or less perfect mode of presence with the humanity of Christ; he speaks simply about the terms of the possibility of being literally with Christ in his corporeality. Paul 'is teaching that as long as the soul remains in the flesh, that is, in the body, it can indeed be in Christ and Christ in it (that is, by faith and by the Holy Spirit). But to be WITH Christ (that is, to be in the actual presence of Christ, where his body and soul specifically dwell), is not possible, as he explains in II Cor. 5[:6]'[16] by saying that *as long as we are in the body, we are away from the Lord.* In any case, on ubiquitarian grounds, the notion of being more or less present to him strikes Zanchi as incoherent. Ubiquity implies that in his humanity Christ is *already* present to Paul, and presumably to every other creature as well, in the most perfect way possible, that is, substantially.[17] There would then be no greater or more perfect presence with Christ to be experienced beyond this earthly life.

An additional absurdity implied by the ubiquitarian view arises from considering the condition in which Paul presently finds himself now that he has received what he wished for. Now that Paul's soul has been separated from his body, he is fully present to the actual soul and body of Christ. But if the humanity of Christ were ubiquitous, then Paul would have to be everywhere too, or else he would not be fully *with Christ.* Paul would have to share in the ubiquity of Christ's body in order to be fully present to him. But the absurdity involved in speaking of *the ubiquity of Paul's body* strikes Zanchi as too obvious to call for a refutation. On the other hand, if Christ's humanity differed from Paul's in this respect, the disproportion between the infinite body of Christ and the finite body of Paul constitutes a qualitative difference that renders a full union between Christ and Paul unthinkable.[18] Zanchi objects to the doctrine of the ubiquity of Christ's body, then, on grounds that it destroys the ontological

---

[15]   Ibid. *1.23*, 56: 'At inquies, Erat quidem Apostolus, etiam tum, cum anima et corpore Christi praesentibus praesens, sed non quam perfecte quam si anima fuisset a corpore separata. Hoc igitur ob causam, hoc est, propter perfectiorem praesentiam et coniunctionem cum humanitate Christi, cupiebat solvi animam a corpore.'

[16]   Ibid. *1.23*, 57: 'Et docet dum anima manet in carne, id est, in corpore, posse quidem eam esse in Christo et Christum in ea, per fidem nimirum et per Spiritum Sanctum; verum esse CUM Christo, id est, reapse praesentem esse apud Christum, ut exponit II Cor. 5, hoc est apud eius animam et corpus per speciem, non posse'.

[17]   Ibid.

[18]   Ibid.

precondition of the possibility of a true and complete union between Christ and believers.

In classic Protestant form, Zanchi worries about ways in which the doctrine of ubiquity might become, in effect, an invitation to idolatry. He claims that by elevating the created humanity of Christ to the point at which it assumes a defining characteristic of divinity, ubiquitarianism blurs the distinction between creature and Creator. Only the divine can be omnipresent; to say that the body of Christ can be in more than one place at the same time is to subvert the ontological distinction between God and everything else, which is the essence of idolatry. By suggesting that his humanity is of the same nature as his divinity, those who claim that the body of Christ is omnipresent are treating a created reality as if it were divine; thus they stand convicted of not just heresy but idolatry as well.[19]

Do the ubiquitarians know something about the nature of Christ that Paul did not know? Paul makes no mention of the ubiquity of Christ's body. How, then, could that doctrine be required for salvation?

> If he does not mention it (as, in truth, he does not), it is not relevant to our salvation *(neque ad salutem facit)* to know that Christ in his human nature is everywhere. For the Apostle takes note of whatever pertains to our salvation, and the whole mystery of godliness was revealed to him; indeed, he knew secret things that it is not lawful for a man to speak. Are our ubiquitarians wiser than Paul? If Paul paid no attention to this [doctrine of] ubiquity, why do they force it on us as necessary for salvation?[20]

By the end of Zanchi's comments on Philippians 1:23, the ubiquitarians stand accused of an exegetical carelessness that undermines piety while generating manifold absurdities, along with heresy, idolatry, and an imposition on the Christian conscience that is without biblical warrant.

EXEGETICAL-EUCHARISTIC PATTERNS IN ZANCHI'S SYSTEMATIC THEOLOGY: *DE CULTU DEI EXTERNO: DE COENA DOMINI*

In his discussion of appropriate forms of external worship, Zanchi undertakes a close analysis of the words with which Christ instituted the eucharist *(Hoc est corpus meum)*. At once it becomes clear that to

---

[19] Ibid.: 'Ita tandem quocunque te vertas, rem creatam exaequabis creatori, et ex creatura facies Deum.'.
[20] Ibid. *1.23*, 56.

regard Zanchi's sacramental theology as a 'mere memorialism' is to misunderstand him completely. In the words of institution, he argues, *This (Hoc)* must be understood as a reference to the sacramental bread, not only because it was to the bread that Jesus was referring *(suo subiecto)* when he uttered the word *Hoc*, but also because the predicate, *corpus meum*, is mystically linked with the subject by way of the copulative verb, *est*.[21]

Yet this relationship, Zanchi insists, is mystical and sacramental, not material. The sacrament consists of three elements: bread, wine, and the Word. Zanchi considers it obvious that the joining of the Word to the bread and to the body of Christ takes place not in substance but only by way of a signifying relationship; this becomes his model for understanding the relation of the bread to the body of Christ and the wine to his blood. 'Therefore in the sacraments, that which is signified is not joined to that which signifies it except by a union that takes place through a mystical relation. This, however, is the sacramental union.'[22] Thus for Zanchi the union of *res* with *signum* is actual, yet noncorporeal.

For Christ said not only, 'This is my body', but also 'Do this in memory of me'. Since memory is a function of mind rather than of flesh, Zanchi finds here a signal pointing towards a mystical, spiritual, sacramental union, rather than a material or physical union, of the bread and wine, on the one hand, with the body and blood of Christ, on the other.

This view of the eucharist Zanchi finds confirmed in the liturgy of the ancient church. The *Sursum corda* ('Lift up your hearts') implies that the real, substantial body and blood of Christ are not actually to be found on the altar.[23] It is the nature and function of sacraments to lead our souls beyond what the sacramental matter is in itself to that which is signified by it. The sacrament could not thus point beyond itself to the reality signified by it if that reality were already joined ontologically *(realiter et substantialiter)* to the sacramental elements.

When unbelievers consume the elements, therefore, they receive bread and wine, but not the body and blood of Christ; there can be no *manducatio impiorum* because linkage between the elements and the body of Christ is sacramental and spiritual, not corporeal. It is by a special

---

[21] *De cultu Dei externo, in expl. secundi praecepti* in *Operum theologicorum IV*: 434: 'primum quidem suo subiecto refertur ad panem; panis enim est illud de quo dixit, *Hoc.*' Zanchi's fuller treatment of the eucharist, *De coena Domini*, is a part of his analysis of sacraments in general and follows his treatment of baptism. All of this is embedded in his discussion of the second commandment and the external worship of God; see *Operum theologicorum, IV*: 444–57.

[22] *De cultu Dei externo*, 435.

[23] Ibid.

operation of the Holy Spirit, not by natural processes of digestion and metabolism, that the true body and blood of Christ are imparted to believers.[24] It is by his eternal Spirit — that is, by his divinity — that Christ has offered himself to the Father as a perfect sacrifice for the sins of the elect (Hebr. 9:14); it is by the same Spirit that Christ works in the hearts of the elect to make his body and blood savingly available to them. The parallel between baptism and eucharist points to a spiritual rather than a corporeal eating of the flesh of Christ: 'Just as in baptism the washing of the conscience from sin is spiritual, so the true eating of Christ's body must also be spiritual'.[25]

Christ's finite humanity is literally located in heaven; believers partake of his body and blood when their minds are elevated by the Spirit to make contact with Christ's body in the one place where it actually is, namely, in heaven. What this implies is that the body of Christ is not eaten physically, since the mouth of the body can eat things only as they *now* exist, not as they existed at some point in the past. In the Supper Christ offers believers his *broken* body and his *shed* blood, but since the resurrection *his body and blood no longer exist in that form*. The purpose of the Supper is to join us not to a lifeless corpse but to *a living Christ* — whose body is broken and whose blood is shed no longer!

With the mouth of the body we eat things not as they once were but as they are now. The body of Christ, however, is now alive, not bloodless, and his blood is now in his veins, not poured out. If, therefore, the body is not given to be eaten except insofar as it is bloodless and dead, and the blood is not given to be drunk except insofar as it is poured out from the body, they are given separately from each other. Neither, however, exists in such a state; the body is alive with its blood and the blood is in the veins of the body. The mouth of the body, however, cannot receive things except as they now exist; clearly a mind endowed with faith is what is required for eating the dead body of Christ and drinking his poured out

---

[24] *De coena Domini* in *Oper. Theol.* VII, 452: 'Adiecimus opera Spiritus sancti nobis communicari corpus et sanguinem Christi . . .' Citing 1 Cor. 12:13, Zanchi argues that the role of the Spirit in baptism is precisely parallel to what takes place in the eucharist. 'Et enim ἐν ἑνὶ πνεύματι nos omnes in unum corpus baptizati fuimus. Deinde de Coena:καὶ πάντες εἰς ἓν πνεῦμα ἐβαπτίσθημεν repetenda est particula ἐν ἑνὶ πνεύματι. Per totum enim caput ostendit per unum et eundem Spiritum distribui omnia dona coelestia, et omnia Ecclesiae membra in unum coniungi, foveri, conservari. Illud vero εἰς ἓν πνεῦμα respondet superiori membro de baptismate, εἰς ἓν σῶμα . Est enim elegans allusio ad corpus et animam, seu Spiritum humanum, quasi dicat non solum in unum corpus sub capite Christo unimur omnes in baptismate per Spiritum Sanctum sed etiam in unum Spiritum ceu in animam unam potamur et vivificamur in coena per eundem scilicet Spiritum.'

[25] Ibid. 453.

blood. For it is the mind endowed with faith that remembers and embraces things that are in the past — namely, that Christ has given his body and shed his blood for us — which is precisely what it means to eat and drink the body and blood of Christ . . .[26]

Only the believing mind remembers and embraces Christ's saving work; hence it is only the faithful who partake of the body and blood of Christ.

Although Zanchi is generally eager to make common cause with Augustine's sacramental theology, he does not hesitate to reject Augustine's assumption that it is possible for the impious to receive the sacrament. On the contrary, he insists, since the full sacrament consists of the Word, the element, *and the sacramental reality that it signifies,* unbelievers — who by definition do not partake of the sacramental reality (Christ) — do not receive the sacrament at all. Zanchi is happy to associate himself with the dictum of Augustine that the element apart from the Word constitutes no sacrament,[27] but when Augustine claims that the godless are capable of receiving the sacrament (even though they do not receive the body and blood of Christ[28]), Zanchi registers his dissent. He does so, however, in a way that enables him to present his doctrine as a *more subtle* reading of Augustine:

> But we have shown that the complete sacrament consists of three things: the element, the Word, and the spiritual reality [signified in the sacrament] . . . Thus in the strictest sense *(proprie),* even as the sacrament is not received by one who receives the element without the Word or the Word without the element, so one who receives both of these but not the [sacramental] reality may not be said to receive a complete or full sacrament. But what Augustine said [about the impious receiving the sacrament] takes the term 'sacrament' loosely *(improprie)* as a way of talking about the sacramental sign.[29]

Thus Zanchi manages to interpret Augustine in a way that safeguards his view that 'the true body of Christ is eaten only by the godly'.[30] For the substance of the sacrament is *Christ,* whom the reprobate do not and cannot receive.[31] Only *true disciples* are nourished by the *true body and blood* of Christ. Here Zanchi buttresses the connection between eucharist and

---

26 Ibid. 451.
27 Ibid. 436: 'Et ideo Augustinus dicit, *Accedit verbum ad elementum et fit sacramentum*'.
28 Cf. Augustine, *Tract. 26,* on John 6:41–59 in *NPNF,* series I, vol. 7, 173 [18].
29 *De coena Domini,* 436.
30 Ibid. 451.
31 Ibid. 444.

ecclesiastical discipline by invoking the authority of Justin Martyr's *First Apology*.[32]

When the elect receive the sacramental elements in faith, therefore, what they receive is nothing less than the true body and true blood of the one who is himself the inner reality of the eucharist, and that reality is linked sacramentally to the material elements of bread and wine. Christ's language — *Hoc est corpus meum* — is simply too clear to be evaded or allegorized away.[33] We must confess, therefore, that 'the bread is the true body of Christ',[34] not substantially but sacramentally, not to the lips but to faith. The effect of receiving the sacrament, after all, is a twofold union — with Christ *and with all other Christians*. Union with fellow believers makes us one body with them; this union is effected, however, not carnally but spiritually. In just the same way, believers' access to the body and blood of Christ in the eucharist is spiritual, not carnal.[35]

What is received in this spiritual manner, however, is nothing less than the true body *(verum corpus)* and the true blood *(verus sanguis)* of Christ. Zanchi is as emphatic as any Lutheran about the actuality of the body and blood offered to the faithful in the Supper. Citing the brutally realistic language of John 6:53–8 (along with Paul's less shocking language of 'participation' in 1 Cor. 10:16), Zanchi insists that the encounter with Christ's body and blood is not merely imaginative or figurative or symbolic. Multiplying adjectival and adverbial forms of *verus*, Zanchi waxes eloquent in thematizing the actuality of the believer's participation in the body and blood of the Lord. He is quick to insist, however, that any interpretation of John 6:53 in which the linkage between bread and the flesh of Christ is understood substantially and physically rather than sacramentally involves precisely the kind of moral scandal — in this case, cannibalism — that Augustine identifies as a mark of eisegesis.[36] By

---

[32] Ibid. 447: 'Ideo Iustinus in Apol. secunda *[sic]* ait ad Coenam Domini non solitum fuisse admitti nisi qui primo concederet nostram doctrinam esse veram, 2. qui ablutus esset lavacro regenerationis in remissionem peccatorum, 3. qui denique sic vivat ut Christus docuit.' Zanchi's reference to the *Second Apology* is erroneous; what he has given, in fact, is a careful citation of Justin's remarks in the *First Apology*, c. 66 (*ANF*, I, 185).

[33] *De coena Domini*, 444: 'Verba institutionis enim aperta sunt quibus non mentitur: *Accipite, edite, hoc est corpus meum.*'

[34] Ibid.: 'Oportet igitur fateri panem esse corpus Christi verum.'

[35] Ibid. 449: 'Ideo sicut inter nos uniti sumus et sumus unum corpus non per unionem carnalem quasi unus homo penetret in alterum, sed per spiritualem, quia omnes unimur vinculo Spiritus sancti, qui est Spiritus fidei et charitatis, sic etiam non unimur Christo carnaliter, quasi Christus suo corpore penetret in nostra corpora ullo modo, vel subtili vel crasso, sed unimur spiritualiter, hoc est per ipsius Spiritum.'

[36] Ibid. 453; cf. Augustine, *De doctrina christiana* III, c. 16 (24) in *NPNF*, series 1, vol. 2, 563.

receiving the Supper in faith, the elect partake not only of signs but also of the realities signified by them, namely, the true body and blood of Christ; what they receive is the true body and blood, but these are received *not cannibalistically (by the mouth of the body) but spiritually (by faith)*. They are received, in other words, not corporeally but sacramentally. (That a 'true body' should be received in a non-bodily way may strike ubiquitarians as curious or even oxymoronic, but it is surely no more paradoxical than Paul's notion of a 'spiritual body' (σῶμα ρνευματικόν) in 1 Cor. 15:44.)

The spiritual point of receiving the eucharist is a deepening of intimacy with the living Christ whose body and blood are offered to the faithful: 'We eat the dead [body] in order to be united to the living [body of Christ]. For union is the effect of partaking. That is why Christ said, "Whoever eats my flesh abides in me" [John 6:56]'.[37] Here the mystic/pietist strand in Zanchi's thought helps to shape his eucharistic theology.

> For this is the reason why he instituted this sacrament and commanded that bread and wine should be eaten and drunk by the mouth of the body, so that, aided by these outward symbols and by the outward eating and drinking of them, our minds should be lifted up to contemplate the body of Christ that was handed over for us and the blood of Christ that was shed for us, and that we should embrace them by faith, applying them to ourselves by a spiritual eating and drinking, to the end that we should grow more and more to be one with Christ *(magis ac magis in unum cum Christo coalescamus)*, being nourished by this spiritual food.[38]

Zanchi's emphasis on the spiritual way in which the body and blood are received can hardly be viewed as disguising a dualistic contempt for the body. Zanchi is comfortable with creaturely corporeality; his perspective is consistently wholistic and incarnational rather than dualistic.[39] He concludes his commentary on Colossians 2, in fact, with an extensive, enthusiastic vindication of human corporeality.[40] Zanchi's insistence on the finitude of Christ's body implies a positive view of finite bodiliness; Christologically and eucharistically, he seeks to preserve an ontological basis of the incarnational theme of God's coming to confront us precisely in our own corporeal finitude. The promise of salvation, after all, includes 'even your mortal bodies' (Rom. 8:11):

---

[37]   *De coena Domini*, 451.

[38]   Ibid. 451–2.

[39]   The prominence of marital and sexual metaphors in Zanchi's theology makes it clear that he is not trapped in a grim asceticism. Cf. Farthing, '*De coniugio spirituali*', 345–6, and '*Foedus evangelicum*: Jerome Zanchi on the Covenant', *Calvin Theological Journal* 29 (1994) 157–62.

[40]   *In Col.*, 320–1.

as the Fathers say, our bodies are nourished and nurtured for the resurrection by the flesh of Christ. This does not mean that the flesh that is in heaven corporeally penetrates our bodies and nourishes them; it means, rather, that, by the power of the Spirit of Christ, we are more and more joined to Christ our Head, so that as a result life flows more and more into us, not only to bring our souls to life but also to prepare and dispose our bodies for the blessed resurrection, while we are daily purged from sin and made suitable to be temples of the Holy Spirit.[41]

For Zanchi, two points are critical. (a) It is the true body and blood of Christ that are available to believers in the Supper, since that is the only way in which the eucharist could bind them 'more and more' into a solidarity with him, but (b) the true body and blood are received sacramentally, that is, in a spiritual way, since otherwise the ontological distance between Christ's body and ours would render this union impossible.

ZANCHI IN CONTEXT

Whether he is working topically or exegetically, Zanchi does not do his theology in a vacuum. In his Christology and eucharistic theology, Zanchi remains in dialogue with both his predecessors and contemporaries. While a full assessment of Zanchi's relation to his dialogue-partners is beyond the scope of this essay, the following suggestions may serve as a first step in that direction.

Zanchi and the Fathers

Patrology plays a role in Zanchi's eucharistic theology that is significant but hardly determinative. His use of materials borrowed from the Fathers is less central to his eucharistic thought than is the case, for instance, with his fellow-expatriate Italian, Peter Martyr Vermigli.[42] It is hardly surprising to find that among the Fathers cited both in his commentaries on Colossians and Philippians and in his *De coena Domini*, Augustine is by far the most important. Since Augustine did not propound a single unambiguous view of the eucharist, Zanchi, no less than the ubiquitarians, is able to find materials in Augustine that are helpful in the articulation of his own

---

[41] *De coena Domini*, 453.

[42] Cf. Joseph C. McLelland, *The Visible Words of God* (Grand Rapids: Eerdmans; Edinburgh: Oliver & Boyd, 1957), especially, 'Appendix B', 267–71. A perusal of the *Dialogue on the Two Natures of Christ* quickly indicates that Vermigli's patristic erudition far exceeds anything that Zanchi sees fit to put on display in the eucharistic materials that we have examined here.

Reformed perspective. He is happy to associate himself with Augustine's authority whenever possible. He does not hesitate to correct Augustine's view of the *manducatio impiorum*, but he does so in the gentlest way possible.

Next to Augustine, Zanchi's favorite patristic authorities are Justin Martyr, who is cited in favour of a rigorous view of the religious and moral prerequisite for admission to the Lord's table,[43] and John Chrysostom, from whom he draws much of the unitive thrust of his interpretation of the eucharist as a sharing (κοινωνία) in Christ's own life through a deepening of believers' communion with each other as members of the one Body of Christ.[44] One cannot be sure about the degree to which Zanchi's interpretation of the text is shaped by his reading of the Fathers. His intent, however, is clear; his basic loyalty is to the text, and he appeals to the Fathers to confirm or illustrate conclusions that he has reached on sound exegetical grounds.

Luther, Calvin, and Zanchi

In the eucharistic materials reviewed here, Zanchi once mentions Luther by name, but Calvin's name is never invoked. Yet the Lutherans are clearly the ubiquitarians against whom he is writing, while Calvin's spirit hovers over virtually every paragraph in Zanchi's eucharistic treatises. His one reference to Luther, nonetheless, is relatively generous. He notes that Luther's early interpretation of the eucharist *(initio, ante acriorem pugnam)* emphasized faith's appropriation of Christ's death as the token (λυτρόν) of our redemption,[45] which involves partaking of the body and blood of Christ in a spiritual rather than a material way.[46] Zanchi's language makes it clear that he wishes to associate himself with Luther at this point; it also suggests that the trajectory of Luther's later teachings (which the Reformed tradition finds problematic) must be attributed, in part, to the polemical temper of the times.

In his view of the eucharistic partaking of Christ's body and blood, and especially in his emphasis on the role of the Holy Spirit (so that this partaking can no longer be understood materialistically), Zanchi does not see fit to buttress his position with citations from Calvin; the contours of his understanding of the eucharist, however, are unmistakably

---

[43]   See above, n. 32.

[44]   *De coena Domini*, 454. Zanchi claims the authority of the Fathers for this view, mentioning, in particular, Oecumenius, Photius, and Chrysostom. Cf. Chrysostom's *Homily 46* on John 6:41–2 in *NPNF*, series I, vol. 14, 166 [3], *Homily 32* on Matt. 9:27–30 in *NPNF*, series I, vol. 10, 218, and *Homily 24* on 1 Cor. 10:13 in *NPNF*, series I, vol. 12, 139–40.

[45]   *De coena Domini*, 446–7.

[46]   Cf. 'Epistel des Sontags Septuagesime: I Corinth. 9', *WA* 17/2:134–5; 'Am tag des heiligen warleichnams Christi, Euangelion Iohannis, vj.', *WA* 17/2:435–41.

Calvinistic.[47] In his insistence that the Supper is not just a reminder of a transaction in the past but an instrument through which God offers believers the body and blood of Christ in the present, Zanchi is making common cause with Calvin's critique of Zwingli's eucharistic doctrine.[48] In his rejection of the *manducatio infidelium*, Zanchi allies himself with Calvin's critique of the view articulated by the Lutheran pastor at Heidelberg, Tilemann Hesshusen.[49]

With respect to Zanchi's Pauline exegesis, we may note that in the *Institutes* Calvin's sole reference to Philippians 1:23–4 occurs in connection with a discussion of proper attitudes towards death;[50] here Calvin does not invoke Paul's language to the Philippians, as does Zanchi, for Christological and eucharistic purposes. At four points in the *Institutes* Calvin cites Colossians 3:1–2. Three of these references, however, occur in the context of exhorting Christians to spiritual earnestness and the avoidance of earthly distractions from the heavenly pursuit; the question of ubiquity is left unmentioned.[51]

Calvin's final citation of Colossians 3:1–2 is found at the beginning of his systematic refutation of ubiquitarianism: Calvin sees in Colossians 3:1 a reference to the session at the Father's right hand.[52] Again, though, Calvin passes up the opportunity to derive from this text, as Zanchi does, a recitation of the absurdities involved in the claim that Christ's body is present on earth as well as in heaven. Zanchi's appropriation of Colossians 3:1–2 clearly goes beyond what Calvin sees fit to say about the text, although it is equally clear that his use of Colossians 3:1–2 is in complete harmony with the larger thrust of Calvin's doctrines of Christ and the eucharist. Zanchi is not merely repeating Calvin's exegesis, but neither does he in any sense betray or distort Calvin's intention. Similarly, in his commentaries on Colossians and Philippians, Calvin does not seize the opportunity, as does Zanchi, to address questions of ubiquity and the eucharist. On the other hand, nothing in Zanchi's exegesis marks a point of conflict with Calvin's.[53]

---

[47] *Institutes*, 4.17.19. See Killian McDonnell, *John Calvin, the Church, and the Eucharist* (Princeton: Princeton University Press, 1967), 206–93; Cf. Karl-Heinz zur Mühlen, 'Christology' in *Oxford Encyclopedia of the Reformation*, 1:317.

[48] Cf. David C. Steinmetz, *Calvin in Context*, 173.

[49] Steinmetz, *Calvin in Context*, 179–80.

[50] *Institutes* 3.9.4.

[51] *Institutes* 2.16.13; 3.6.3; 3.16.2.

[52] *Institutes* 4.17.36

[53] Cf. *Calvin's Commentaries: The Epistles of Paul the Apostle to the Galatians, Ephesians, Philippians and Colossians* ed. D.W. Torrance and T.F. Torrance, trans. T.H.L. Parker (Grand Rapids: Eerdmans, 1965), 345–6 (on Col. 3:1–2) and 239–40 (on Phil.1:23). Zanchi's critique of ubiquity clearly serves the christological and soteriological interests that inform Calvin's doctrine of the eucharist; cf. Killian McDonnell, *John Calvin, the Church, and the Eucharist*, 211.

Zanchi and his Contemporaries

Zanchi refers the reader to his predecessor at Heidelberg, Zacharias Ursinus (1534–83), the editor of the Heidelberg Catechism, for a fuller discussion of the κοινωνία with God and with fellow-believers, that is available in the eucharist.[54] Although Zanchi makes no explicit reference to the commentary on the Heidelberg Catechism by its co-author, Caspar Olevianus, his eucharistic theology is entirely compatible with the view articulated in the discussion of article 82 in *A Firm Foundation*, published by Olevianus in 1567.[55]

An Augustinian view of the eucharist as the visible Word of God *(verbum Dei visibile)* — which both expresses and reinforces a deeply incarnational understanding of how God is available to humanity — finds its most persuasive articulation in the writings of Zanchi's fellow-expatriate, Peter Martyr Vermigli. The incarnational thrust of Zanchi's spirituality leads him to embrace this view of the eucharist as the Word made visible.[56] Without invoking St Augustine or Vermigli by name, Zanchi insists that the visible and invisible forms of the Word constitute an indissoluble unity: 'The audible Word must not and cannot be separated from the visible Word.'[57] Exegetically, it is worth noting that in the *Dialogue*, while Peter Martyr does not have recourse to Paul's language in Philippians 1:23, he does invoke Colossians 3:1 in his critique of the ubiquitarians.[58] Here again Zanchi makes common cause with Vermigli, although his treatment of the text is understandably more extensive (since he deals with Colossians 3:1 in a genre — commentary — that provides opportunities for a fuller exposition than one would expect to meet in a dialogue devoted to a larger theme).

If preaching and the eucharist are equally forms of the Word,[59] partaking of the body and blood of Christ through faith has the same purpose — and the same effect — as does the faithful hearing of the evangelical proclamation. In preaching and in celebration of the eucharist, the same goal is in view: eternal life, which involves the full humanity of both body and soul, through union with Christ in his full, corporeal

---

[54] *De coena Domini*, 455. Cf. Péry André, *The Heidelberg Catechism with Commentary*, trans. A.O. Miller and M.E. Osterhaven (Philadelphia: United Church, 1962), 132–3 (q. 79).

[55] Caspar Olevianus, *A Firm Foundation: An Aid to Interpreting the Heidelberg Catechism*, trans. and ed., L.D. Bierma, Texts and Studies in Reformation and Post-Reformation Thought, 1 (Grand Rapids: Baker, 1995), 61–2 (qq. 82–3).

[56] Cf. McLelland, *The Visible Words of God*, 128–38.

[57] *De coena Domini*, 448: 'Non enim verbum audibile a visibili separari debet aut potest.'

[58] Vernigligi, *Dialogue*, topic 7: 165–6.

[59] *De coena Domini*, 454.

humanity, and with one another in his body, the church.[60] Zanchi's spirituality includes a concern for the subjective perception of new life in Christ as well as for the objective reality that is made available to believers in the preaching and in the sacramental life of the church. The purpose of the sacrament is not only to make Christ redemptively present to believers but also to enable them to grow 'more and more each day' *(magis ac magis quotidie)* into an ever more intense awareness *(vividius)* of Christ's presence.[61] Zanchi is convinced that the effect of this perception will be to activate the transformative effects of charity, in both its vertical and its horizontal dimensions. (That is part of what is implied, he notes, in the use of the term ἀγάπη as a way of referring to the eucharist: 'For it is a sacrament not only of faith but also of love'.[62]) Thus the patrology and exegesis that underlie Zanchi's doctrine of the eucharist are clearly in service to a spirituality that stands among the sources of what would become, in the following century, a full-fledged, self-conscious Reformed pietism in the work of figures such as Willem Teellinck (1579–1629), Jodocus van Lodensteyn (1620–77), Theodorus à Brakel (1608–69), and Willem à Brakel (1635–1711) in the Netherlands, along with Theodor Untereyck (1635–93), Joachim Neander (1650–80), and Friedrich Adolph Lampe (1683–1729) in Germany.[63]

---

[60] See above, n. 58. Cf. *De coena Domini*, 454: The bread of the eucharist is 'id quo seu per quod nos adducimur in κοινωνίαν, id est, societatem et unionem corporis Christi, vel potius adducti magis ac magis coalescamus cum ipso et inter nos tanquam membra sub uno capite Christo.'

[61] Ibid. 445.

[62] Ibid. 456.

[63] I have previously noted the mystic/pietist element in Zanchi's exegesis; see *De coniugio spirituali*, 650–2; *Foedus evangelicum*, 161; 'Christ and the Eschaton', 346–56. Cf. Eric Lund, 'Second Age of Reformation: Lutheran and Reformed Spirituality, 1550–1700' in *Christian Spirituality 3, Post-Reformation and Modern*, ed. Louis Dupré and Don E. Saliers (New York: Crossroad, 1989), 213–39, esp., 232–3; F. Ernest Stoeffler, 'Pietism' in Mircea Eliade, *Encyclopedia of Religion 2*, (New York/London: Macmillan, 1987), 324–6.

4

Law and Grace in Ursinus' Doctrine of the Natural Covenant:
A Reappraisal

Lyle D. Bierma

INTRODUCTION

Scholars have long recognized the contributions of Heidelberg theologian Zacharias Ursinus to the development of Reformed covenant theology in the sixteenth century.[1] Already in the mid-1800s Heppe identified Ursinus as a major architect of the 'federal-theological dogmatics' that appeared in the Palatinate in the 1560s,[2] and since then nearly every survey of the history of covenant theology has included his name.[3] Today it is

[1] Ursinus, who is perhaps best known as the primary author of the Heidelberg Catechism (1563), was born in Breslau, Silesia, in 1534. After spending seven years (1550–7) in Wittenberg as a student of Philip Melanchthon, he embarked on a study tour of the major centres of Reformed Protestantism before returning to his native Breslau to teach at the St Elizabeth Gymnasium (1558–60). From there he was invited to Heidelberg, where he served as professor both at the university (1562–8) and at the theological seminary known as the Sapience College (1561–77). When Heidelberg reverted to strict Lutheranism in 1576, Ursinus took a post as lecturer at the Reformed academy in Neustadt until his death in 1583. For a full account of Ursinus' life and writings, see Karl Sudhoff, *C. Olevianus und Z. Ursinus: Leben und ausgewählte Schriften* (Elberfeld: Friderichs, 1857); G. Bouwmeester, *Zacharias Ursinus en de Heidelbergse Catechismus* (The Hague: Willem de Zwijgerstichting, 1954); and Derk Visser, *Zacharias Ursinus, the Reluctant Reformer: His Life and Times* (New York: United Church, 1983).

[2] Heinrich Heppe, *Dogmatik des deutschen Protestantismus im sechzehnten Jahrhundert*, 3 vols. (Gotha: Friedrich Andreas Perthes, 1857), 1:158–60, 142–4.

[3] See, for example, Gerhardus Vos, *De Verbondsleer in de Gereformeerde Theologie* (Grand Rapids: 'Democrat', 1891), 6, 8; Gottlob Schrenk, *Gottesreich und Bund im älteren Protestantismus, vornehmlich bei Johannes Cocceius* (Gütersloh: Bertelsmann,

widely acknowledged that the covenant idea played a significant, even structural, role in Ursinus' theology and that it was he who introduced the term, if not the concept, of a *foedus naturale* ('natural covenant', later known as the covenant of works) into Reformed theology.[4]

No such consensus exists, however, about the relationship between Ursinus' doctrine of the natural covenant and the emerging Reformed scholasticism of the second half of the sixteenth century. In a 1935 monograph on the covenant of works, N. Diemer argued that the *foedus naturale* in Ursinus was no different from that of his predecessors Bullinger and Calvin, both of whom had broken sharply with the medieval scholastic view of the prelapsarian state of Adam. The 'pure Reformed standpoint' of Bullinger, Calvin, and Ursinus was compromised only when the Herborn theologians, Johannes Cocceius, and others in the late sixteenth and seventeenth centuries began to slip back very close to the scholastic position of the Middle Ages.[5]

The dominant view in recent scholarship, however, has been that Ursinus' concept of the *foedus naturale* was illustrative of a larger shift of emphasis from grace to law in early Reformed orthodoxy. This was first suggested by Karl Barth, who in a long excursus on the history of covenant theology in the *Church Dogmatics* portrayed the Cocceian federal theology of the seventeenth century as an advance on both the medieval and the Protestant forms of scholasticism that preceded it.[6] However, with

---

1923), 57–9; Otto Ritschl, *Dogmengeschichte des Protestantismus* 3, *Die reformierte Theologie des 16. und des 17. Jahrhunderts in ihrer Entstehung und Entwicklung* (Göttingen: Vandenhoeck & Ruprecht, 1926), 416–17; N. Diemer, *Het scheppingsverbond met Adam (het verbond der werken) bij de theologen der 16e, 17e en 18e eeuw in Zwitserland, Duitschland, Nederland en Engeland* (Kampen: J.H. Kok, 1935), 18–19; Karl Barth, *Church Dogmatics* 4, *The Doctrine of Reconciliation*, pt. 1, trans. Geoffrey W. Bromiley (Edinburgh: T. & T. Clark, 1956), 54, 49, 62; J. Wayne Baker, *Heinrich Bullinger and the Covenant: The Other Reformed Tradition* (Athens, Ohio: Ohio University Press, 1980), 202–3; Stephen Strehle, *Calvinism, Federalism, and Scholasticism: A Study of the Reformed Doctrine of Covenant* (Berne: Peter Lang, 1988), 163–7; David A. Weir, *The Origins of the Federal Theology in Sixteenth-Century Reformation Thought* (Oxford: Clarendon, 1990), 99–114; David N.J. Poole, *The History of the Covenant Concept from the Bible to Johannes Cloppenburg* (San Francisco: Mellen, 1992), 127–38; and C. Graafland, *Van Calvijn tot Comrie: Oorsprong en ontwikkeling van de leer van het verbond in het Gereformeerd Protestantisme*, 2 vols. (Zoetermeer: Boekencentrum, 1994), 2:11–41.

[4] On covenant as a structural principle in Ursinus' theology, see August Lang, *Der Heidelberger Katechismus und vier verwandte Katechismen* (Leipzig: Deichert, 1907), LXIVff., and Graafland, *Van Calvijn tot Comrie*, 13. On the *foedus naturale* in Ursinus, see the works listed in n. 3 above, esp. those by Diemer, Weir and Graafland.

[5] Diemer, *Scheppingsverbond met Adam*, 7–19.

[6] Barth, *Church Dogmatics*, 4.1:55.

Ursinus' introduction of the covenant of works into Reformed theology in the previous century, exegesis in the Protestant tradition was 'invaded by a mode of thought' that Cocceius was never able to overcome. This mode of thinking, which became a standard feature in the Reformed scholastics before Cocceius, began exclusively with human beings and their works (the covenant of works), not God and his grace (the covenant of grace). The idea of a God who from the very beginning turns to humanity in grace was now eclipsed, for in the covenant of works God is pledged to humanity only by virtue of the latter's prior goodness. The covenant of works had become the primary covenant, the framework and standard of reference for the covenant of grace.[7]

Barth's line of argument was adopted and amplified by others,[8] but most elaborately by Holmes Rolston III in 1972 in *John Calvin Versus The Westminster Confession*.[9] The thrust of Rolston's argument is summarized in the title of the book. Like many giants of the faith before him, Calvin had broken free of a legalistic religious tradition when he rediscovered the primacy of the grace of God. The very legalism from which Calvin had escaped, however, reemerged in the 'Reformed orthodoxy' of his disciples and was given full confessional status in the Westminster Confession of 1647.[10] Nowhere could this be more clearly seen than in the double covenant idea (covenant of works, covenant of grace), which was 'totally absent from Calvin' but arose within the next two generations among such relatively obscure theologians as Zacharias Ursinus.[11] Whereas Calvin had highlighted the primacy of divine grace in God's creation of the world and in the original relationship between God and humanity, Ursinus and the Reformed orthodox theologians shifted the emphasis to human worth and ability with their doctrine of a covenant of works. The primal covenant relationship between God and humanity was no longer gracious but legal. The covenant of works was a doctrine not first of all of grace but of law, justice, duty, merit, contract, and reward.[12] Hence the theologies of Calvin and the Calvinists who succeeded him were as opposed to each other as grace and law: 'Reformed orthodoxy ha[d] fallen into a legalism that [wa]s wholly uncharacteristic of the Reformer himself'.[13]

---

[7]   Ibid. 61–4.

[8]   See, for example, Donald J. Bruggink, 'Calvin and Federal Theology', *Reformed Review* 13 (1959), 15–22.

[9]   (Richmond, Va. John Knox, 1972). A synopsis of this study appeared as idem, 'Responsible Man in Reformed Theology: Calvin versus the *Westminster Confession*', *Scottish Journal of Theology* 23 (1970), 129–56.

[10]   *Calvin Versus The Westminster Confession*, 6, 11–12, 57–8, 114–15.

[11]   Ibid. 11–12.

[12]   Ibid. 16–17, 23, 36.

[13]   Ibid. 36, 58.

Interpretations vary widely, therefore, on how the *foedus naturale* in Ursinus is related to the rise of Reformed orthodoxy in the second half of the sixteenth century. A similar lack of consensus can be found in the research on Ursinus' doctrine of the covenant of grace,[14] but because of limited space this essay will treat only the alleged priority of law over grace in his natural covenant, a view that continues to appear in the secondary literature but has received little critical attention.[15] We shall argue that, for two reasons, such an approach is unsatisfactory.

THE NATURAL COVENANT IN URSINUS' WRITINGS

First of all, what is sometimes overlooked in this discussion is that the natural covenant plays a relatively insignificant role in Ursinus' theology as a whole. The terms *foedus naturale* and *foedus in creatione* appear in only one of his theological writings, the *Summa Theologiae* of 1561 or 1562 (often called the *Catechesis maior* [hereafter *Cma*]), and there in only three of the 323 questions and answers:

Cma **10 Q.** *What does the divine law teach?*
A. It teaches the kind of covenant God established with human beings in creation [*quale in creatione foedus cum homine Deus iniverit*] . . .

Cma **36 Q.** *What is the difference between the law and the gospel?*
A. The law contains the natural covenant established by God with humanity in creation [*foedus naturale, in creatione a Deo cum hominibus initum*], that is, it is known by human beings by nature, it requires perfect

---

[14] Interpretation of the relationship between Ursinus' doctrine of the covenant of grace and the post-Reformation doctrine of predestination, for example, falls across a wide spectrum. At one end stands Heinrich Heppe (*Dogmatik des deutschen Protestantismus*, 1:139–60), who considered Ursinus' 'German Reformed federal theology' to be the direct opposite of a 'Calvinian-scholastic theology' that elevated double predestination to a central place in its system. In the middle of the spectrum we find Gottlob Schrenk (*Gottesreich und Bund*, 55–6), for whom the covenant theology of Ursinus and his Heidelberg colleague Olevianus reflected some scholastic influence but still served to soften the rigid forms of post-Calvinian predestinarian teaching. At the opposite end from Heppe, finally, is J. Wayne Baker (*Heinrich Bullinger and the Covenant*, 203), who in an appendix entitled 'Calvinist Orthodoxy and the Paralysis of the Covenant Idea', identified Ursinus as a Reformed scholastic theologian whose 'conditional covenant was subsumed by his doctrine of double predestination'.
[15] Recent secondary literature includes James B. Torrance, 'Covenant or Contract? A Study of the Theological Background of Worship in Seventeenth-Century

obedience from us to God, and promises eternal life to those who keep it but threatens eternal punishment to those who do not . . .

Cma 135 Q. *Why is it necessary that the satisfaction and righteousness of Christ be imputed to us for us to be righteous before God?*

A. Because God, who is immutably righteous and true, wants to receive us into the covenant of grace in such a way that he nevertheless does nothing against the covenant established in creation [*foedus in creatione initum*] . . .[16]

By contrast, the covenant of *grace* is mentioned at least thirty-eight times in the *Cma*,[17] and serves as an integrating theme, if not the structural principle, of the work.[18]

After the *Cma*, which did not appear in print until 1584,[19] Ursinus never made reference to the natural covenant again. In fact, the entire covenant idea receded into the background in the *Catechesis minor* (1562), the Heidelberg Catechism (1563), and the *Summa religionis christianae*, an

---

Scotland', *Scottish Journal of Theology* 23 (1970), 51–76; idem, 'Strengths and Weaknesses of the Westminster Theology' in *The Westminster Confession*, ed. Alasdair Heron (Edinburgh: St Andrews, 1982), 40–53; idem, 'Calvin and Puritanism in England and Scotland: Some Basic Concepts in the Development of "Federal Theology" ' in *Calvinus Reformator*, ed. W. Neuser (Potchefstroom: Potchefstroom University for Christian Higher Education, 1982), 264–77; idem, 'Interpreting the Word by the Light of Christ or the Light of Nature? Calvin, Calvinism, and Barth' in *Calviniana: Ideas and Influence of Jean Calvin*, ed. Robert V. Schnucker (Kirksville, Mo.: Sixteenth Century Journal, 1988), 255–67; Robert Letham, 'The *Foedus Operum*: Some Factors Accounting for Its Development', *Sixteenth Century Journal* 14, (1983), 459–61, 467; Weir, *Origins of the Federal Theology*, 6–7; and Poole, *History of the Covenant Concept*, 127. Peter Lillback ('Ursinus' Development of the Covenant of Creation: A Debt to Melanchthon or Calvin?', *Westminster Theological Journal* 43 [1981]: 247–88) makes a strong case for continuity between Calvin and Ursinus, but not in response to the long-standing argument for discontinuity. Richard A. Muller ('The Covenant of Works and the Stability of Divine Law in Seventeenth-Century Orthodoxy: A Study in the Theology of Herman Witsius and Wilhelmus à Brakel', *Calvin Theological Journal* 29 [1994], 75–101) offers a trenchant critique of Holmes and Torrance as their thesis relates to the seventeenth-century Reformed theologians Witsius and Brakel.

[16] For the Latin text of *Cma* 10, 36, and 135, see Lang, *Der Heidelberger Katechismus*, 153, 156, 171. I have followed an unpublished English translation by John Medendorp and Fred H. Klooster, although I have made some alterations based on the Latin text.

[17] *Cma* 1, 2, 10, 30–7, 39, 72–4, 87, 132, 135, 141–2, 148, 150, 223–4, 265–6, 274, 276–7, 279, 281, 284, 293–6, 306, 323 (in Lang, *Der Heidelberger Katechismus*, 152–99).

[18] See n. 4 above and Lyle D. Bierma, *German Calvinism in the Confessional Age: The Covenant Theology of Caspar Olevianus* (Durham, N.C.: Labyrinth, 1996), 22, 61.

[19] In *Volumen Tractationum theologicarum* (1584; rep. Neustadt: Harnisch, 1587).

incomplete set of loci lectures delivered sometime before 1568 and first published in 1584.[20] It resurfaced in his lectures on the HC but only in the introduction, in scattered references in the sections on the sacraments, and in a short excursus on the covenant of grace placed after the doctrine of the mediator.[21]

This abrupt change in Ursinus' use of the covenant idea has long piqued the curiosity of scholars and has led to a variety of explanations. One possibility is that Ursinus was under external pressure to tone down the doctrine of the covenant in both the *Cmi* (the main source for the HC) and the HC itself. According to Lang, some have argued that Frederick III of the Palatinate was trying to keep his territorial catechism in line with the (altered) Augsburg Confession by avoiding any reference to 'signs of the covenant', which in some ears might sound too Zwinglian. Lang himself suggested that it was only the *foedus naturale* that some found to be a stumbling block but that because of the close relationship between the natural and gracious covenants, the entire covenant idea had to be sacrificed to remove the offensive part.[22]

---

[20]   In the *Catechesis minor* (hereafter cited as *Cmi*) the term *foedus* is found only three times (*Cmi* 55, 63, 71 [in Lang, *Der Heidelberger Katechismus*, 208, 210, 212]]). In the Heidelberg Catechism (hereafter cited as HC) *bund* appears only twice (HC 74, 82 [in Lang, *Der Heidelberger Katechismus*, 29, 34]). In the *Summa religionis christianae* (hereafter cited as *Sum. relig.*) *foedus* appears in two places (in *Volumen Tractationum theologicarum* [1587 ed.], 2, 278). All are references to the covenant of *grace*.

[21]   Ursinus' lectures on the HC appeared in print in several different versions, all published after his death. *Doctrinae Christianae Compendium* (Geneva, Leiden, 1584; Cambridge, 1585; London, 1586) and *Explicationum catecheticarum* (Neustadt, 1585; Cambridge, 1587) were early versions of his commentary on the HC based on student lecture notes. David Pareus, Ursinus' former student, spent a lifetime revising and publishing a number of editions of this commentary under three different titles: *Explicationes catecheticae*, which appeared in at least six editions from 1591–1608 and was also included as *Explicationes catecheseos* in the first volume of Q. Reuter's *Ursini . . . opera theologica* (Heidelberg, 1612); *Corpus doctrinae orthodoxae* (Heidelberg 1612, 1616); and *Corpus doctrinae Christianae* (Heidelberg 1621, 1623, 1634, 1651). According to T.D. Smid ('Bibliographische Opmerkingen over de *Explicationes catecheticae* van Zacharias Ursinus', *Gereformeerd Theologisch Tijdschrift* 41 [1940], 241), the editions of 1634 and 1651 are without a doubt the most reliable. My citations are taken from *Corpus doctrinae Christianae* (Hannover, 1634; hereafter cited as *Corp. doct.*). For the English translation, I have followed G.W. Williard's *The Commentary of Dr. Zacharias Ursinus on the Heidelberg Catechism* (1851; reprint, Grand Rapids: Eerdmans, 1954; hereafter cited as *Commentary*), although I have made some corrections based on the Latin text. For references to the covenant of grace in the lectures on the HC, see *Corp. doct.*, 2–3, 96–100, 394–404, 418, 464 (*Commentary*, 2–3, 96–100, 366–76, 387–8, 430).

[22]   Lang, *Der Heidelberger Katechismus*, LXXVIII–LXXIX.

Another possibility is that the covenant concept virtually disappeared in the *Cmi* and the HC and then reappeared in Ursinus' commentary (lectures) on the HC because of the different audiences for which these documents were prepared. The *Cma* and lectures on the HC were technical theological works designed for theological instruction at the university and seminary, whereas the *Cmi* and HC were simpler documents written for a more general audience. For Ursinus, covenant served as an important concept in the weighty theological discussions of the classroom, but such doctrinal complexities did not need to be foisted upon the laity.[23]

Neither one of these possibilities is entirely satisfactory. If Ursinus was bowing to external pressure to play down the covenant theme in the official catechism of the Palatinate, why then does covenant not play as significant a role in the later loci lectures and commentary on the HC, which had no official status, as it did in the *Cma*? The same question applies to the suggestion by Sturm and Graafland that Ursinus was not always writing for the same audience. If he intended to develop the doctrine of the covenant only for a theologically sophisticated readership, why is covenant not given the same prominence in his later scholarly works that it had in the *Cma*? And why does the *foedus naturale* not reappear?

A more satisfactory explanation is that the change in Ursinus' treatment of the covenant in his scholarly corpus was part of a process of theological maturation. As Visser has pointed out, the *Cma*, in which covenant serves as a dominant motif, was published not only after Ursinus' death but contrary to his deathbed wish. Apparently it represented only a provisional stage in his thinking. A fuller, more definitive version of his theology can be found in his lectures on the HC, and thus any 'interpretation of the *Maior's* summary statements [should be done] with the aid of the relevant commentaries on the Heidelberg *Catechism*'.[24] This mature theological treatment of covenant in the commentary on the HC, however, involves more than just the elimination of the language of a natural covenant. As Graafland has demonstrated elsewhere in his study, the distinction between law and gospel (to which the *foedus naturale* and *foedus gratiae* are linked in the *Cma*) is less sharply drawn in the commentary, and the unity of the *one* covenant of grace in its two administrations is more heavily accented.[25]

---

[23] Erdmann Sturm, *Der junge Zacharias Ursinus: Sein Weg vom Philippismus zum Calvinismus* (Neukirchen: Neukirchener, 1972), 238–41, 253; Graafland, *Van Calvijn tot Comrie*, 2:13–14. Graafland (ibid. 14) does grant the possibility that the covenant reappears in Ursinus' lectures on the HC because he was prevented from including this theme in the HC itself.

[24] Derk Visser, 'The Covenant in Zacharias Ursinus', *Sixteenth Century Journal* 18 (1987), 533.

[25] Graafland, *Van Calvijn tot Comrie*, 2:27–9.

Whatever the reason for these changes in Ursinus' treatment of covenant — political and theological pressures from the outside, the audiences he was addressing, development in his own doctrinal thinking, or some combination of the above — there is no evidence here that his doctrine of the *foedus naturale* exemplifies a shift of emphasis from grace to law in early Reformed orthodoxy. His references to a covenant established at creation are early, few, and fleeting.[26] The only shift to be noted here is in Ursinus himself, a shift away from the terminology of a natural covenant and to a greater stress on the unity of the covenant of grace.

URSINUS AND CALVIN ON THE NATURAL COVENANT

Second, the *foedus naturale* may play a relatively minor role in Ursinus' theology, but where it does appear, it does not represent a radical departure from the teaching of Calvin. Rolston claimed that the concept of a covenant of works developed by the Reformed scholastics is 'not only absent from Calvin but alien to his thought', because for Calvin the original relationship between God and humanity is primarily gracious, not legal.[27] This conclusion, however, is not supported by the evidence. Much of Ursinus' doctrine of the natural covenant can be found already in Calvin, and much of the gracious character of Calvin's view of humanity's primal relation to God can be found again in Ursinus.

Rolston himself concedes that 'the original divine order and its subsequent inversion by sin are concepts in Calvin very nearly parallel to the later notion of a covenant of works and the breaking of that covenant by sin'.[28] He also acknowledges the elements of law, commandment, conditionality, probation, judgment, and promise in Calvin's understanding of the original relationship between God and humanity, elements that 'could be isolated as an incipient covenant of works'.[29] But as

---

[26] Cf. Graafland's conclusion (ibid. 2:29) that 'het zogenaamde natuurverbond toch niet een wezenlijke en in ieder geval geen blijvende plaats in Ursinus' verbondsdenken heeft ingenomen'.

[27] Rolston, *Calvin versus The Westminster Confession*, 34–6.

[28] Ibid., 23. Cf. Rolston's comment a few pages later (ibid. 27) that 'here Calvin parallels what his successors were to term a general covenant with all men'.

[29] Ibid., 42–3. For these elements in Calvin, see, for example, *Institutes of the Christian Religion* (1559), ed. John T. McNeill and trans. Ford Lewis Battles, Library of Christian Classics, vols. 20–1 (Philadelphia: Westminster, 1960), 2.1.4, 2.6.1; *Commentaries on . . . Genesis* 1:26 (Calvin Translation Society ed. [1979] 1:91–6, *Calvini Opera* 23:25–7), 2:7 (CTS 1:111–13, *CO* 23:35–6), 2:9 (CTS 1:115–18, *CO* 23:37–9), 2:16 (CTS 1:125–8, *CO* 23:44–6), 3:6 (CTS 1:151–7, *CO* 23:59–63), 3:19 (CTS 1:175–80, *CO* 23:74–7).

the research of Diemer, Helm, and especially Lillback has demonstrated, those aspects of Ursinus' *foedus naturale* and the later covenant of works that are found already in Calvin go beyond the elements identified by Rolston.[30] For one thing, although Calvin never employs the terms *foedus naturale* or *foedus operum*, there are at least two places in his writings where he seems to think of God's pre-fall relationship with humanity as a covenant. In his commentary on Hosea 6:7, he states:

> Others explain the words thus, 'They have transgressed as Adam the covenant'. But the word, Adam, we know, is taken indefinitely for men. This exposition is frigid and diluted, 'They have transgressed as Adam the covenant'; that is, they have followed or imitated the example of their father Adam, who had immediately at the beginning transgressed God's commandment. I do not stop to refute this comment; for we see that it is in itself vapid.[31]

Calvin, of course, is rejecting an interpretation of this text that would support an Adamic covenant, but only on linguistic grounds related to the word 'adam'; he does not deny the notion of an Adamic covenant per se. In fact, he seems to accept the idea of a pre-fall covenant by interchanging *foedus* with 'commandment', a word he uses elsewhere to describe the probationary test of the first parents.[32]

The other context in which Calvin refers to Adam's pre-fall situation as a covenant is his discussion of the sacraments in Book 4 of the *Institutes*. When God gave Adam and Eve the tree of life and Noah and his descendants the rainbow, they regarded these signs as sacraments 'because they had a mark engraved upon them by God's Word, so that they were proofs and seals of his *covenants*'.[33] This sign of the tree of life was intended 'to lead him to the knowledge of divine grace',[34] but it was still the sign of a covenant that also included a command, a test, and a penalty.

Another dimension of later covenant theology that is adumbrated in Calvin is the principle of federal headship, according to which Adam served as the representative head of the human race in his covenant relationship with God before the fall. Obedience or disobedience to God's probationary command in Eden would determine the fate of all of

---

[30] Diemer, *Scheppingsverbond met Adam*, 16–18; Paul Helm, 'Calvin and the Covenant: Unity and Continuity', *Evangelical Quarterly* 55 (1983), 71–7; Lillback, 'Ursinus' Development of the Covenant of Creation', 270–86; and idem, 'The Binding of God: Calvin's Role in the Development of Covenant Theology' (PhD diss., Westminster Theological Seminary, 1985), 446–84.

[31] *Commentaries on . . . Hosea* 6:7 (CTS 13:235, CO 42:332–3).

[32] See the references listed in n. 29 above.

[33] Calvin, *Institutes*, 4.14.18 (italics added).

[34] Calvin, *Comm. Gen.*, 2:9 (CTS 1:117, CO 23:38).

Adam's descendants, not (or not only) because the whole human race was seminally present in Adam but because God had appointed Adam to represent all humanity. According to Calvin,

> the beginning of corruption in Adam was such that it was conveyed in a perpetual stream from the ancestors into their descendants. For the contagion does not take its origin from the substance of the flesh or soul, but because it had been so ordained by God that the first man should at one and the same time have and lose, both for himself and for his descendants, the gifts that God had bestowed upon him.[35]

> In the same way Christ, the second Adam, represented (elect) humanity in living obediently before the law of God and in taking upon himself the penalty for the first Adam's representative disobedience.[36]

Whether this line of argument can be characterized as 'thorough-going federalistic'[37] or only as a 'rather incidental side of Calvin's thought'[38] is still an open question. And it is certainly true that Calvin does not discuss Adam's federal headship in explicitly covenantal terms. Nevertheless, like so many other aspects of the later covenant of works, this incipient federalism represents a strand of thinking in Calvin that reappears in almost identical form in Ursinus a generation later and in a more developed way in later Reformed covenant thought.[39]

According to Rolston, the most significant difference between Calvin and 'the Calvinists' who followed him was that the latter 'failed to understand and retain Calvin's concept of the grace of God as primary even in this primal and general relation between God and man; very soon the principle of it was no longer grace, but law'.[40] Rolston himself provides ample evidence from Calvin of the primacy of God's grace in the pre-fall relationship with humanity.[41] What he fails to realize,

---

[35] *Institutes*, 2.1.7. Cf. also Calvin, *Comm. Gen.*, 3:6 (CTS 1:155–6, CO 23:62), and *Commentary . . . on John 3:6* (CTS 17:113, CO 47:57).

[36] Calvin, *Institutes*, 2.12.3.

[37] Lillback, 'Ursinus' Development of the Covenant of Creation', 280.

[38] Helm, 'Calvin and the Covenant', 72.

[39] Ursinus, *Corp. doct.*, 43 (*Commentary*, 40–1): '[Original sin] transit enim neque per corpus, neque per animam, sed per totius hominis generationem immundam, propter culpam primorum parentum, propter quam Deus justo judicio, animas dum creat, simul privat originali rectitudine et donis, quae parentibus hac lege contulerat, ut et posteris ea conferrent vel perderent, si ipsi ea retinerent vel amitterent.' Cf. also *Corp. doct.*, 46 (*Commentary*, 43). For the federal headship principle in later Reformed covenant theology, see Heppe, *Reformed Dogmatics Set Out and Illustrated from the Sources*, rev. and ed. Ernst Bizer, trans. G.T. Thomson (1950; rep. with a foreword by Karl Barth, Grand Rapids: Baker, 1978), 291, 313–15.

[40] Rolston, *Calvin versus The Westminster Confession*, 36.

[41] Ibid. 23–45.

however, is that Ursinus too always presents this primal relationship in the context of divine grace — in both the *Cma* and the commentary on the HC.[42]

The very first reference to the *foedus naturale* in the *Cma*, for example, can only be understood in light of the entire question and answer in which it occurs (*Cma* 10) and of the six questions and answers that follow (*Cma* 11–16). The first half of the answer in *Cma* 10 is divided into three parts, each of which is then further explained in a corresponding part in the second half of the answer:

> Q. *What does the divine law teach?*
>
> A. It teaches (a) the kind of covenant God established with human beings in creation, (b) how they behaved in keeping it, and (c) what God requires of them after establishing the new covenant of grace with them. That is, (a) what kind of human beings God created and for what purpose, (b) into what state they have fallen, and (c) how they must conduct themselves, now that they are reconciled to God.[43]

The kind of covenant that God established with humanity at creation, therefore, can be understood by looking at the nature and purpose of created humanity. Human beings were created in the image of God (*Cma* 11), that is, with 'a true knowledge of God and the divine will and the inclination and desire of the whole person to live according to this knowledge [will?] alone' (*Cma* 12).[44] The purpose for which we were created was to worship God with our whole lives (*Cma* 13), that is, to obey God according to his law with the purpose of honoring him (*Cma* 14). The summary of this law and obedience is love for God and neighbour (*Cma* 15), which includes acknowledging God alone as creator, provider, and saviour (*Cma* 16).[45] For Ursinus, therefore, the call to obedience, the promise of life, and the threat of punishment in the covenant established at creation (*Cma* 36)[46] are not arbitrary. They are consistent with the very purpose for which God created human beings: to relate to him in loving obedience.

This is a relationship surrounded by grace. That the law was 'known by human beings by nature' in the natural covenant (*Cma* 36) was rooted in the fact that God had created human beings in his image, that

---

[42]　Ernest F. Kevan (*The Grace of Law: A Study in Puritan Theology* [Grand Rapids: Baker, 1965], 112–13) makes a similar point about the Reformed covenant theologians of the seventeenth century.

[43]　In Lang, *Der Heidelberger Katechismus*, 153.

[44]　'Vera Dei et divinae voluntatis agnitio, et secundum hanc solam vivendi, totius hominis inclinatio et studium'. In Lang, *Der Heidelberger Katechismus*, 153.

[45]　Ibid. 153–4.

[46]　Ibid. 156.

is, with a 'true knowledge of God and the divine will' (*Cma* 12). In addition, meeting the requirement of obedience in the natural covenant was possible, once again, only because God had created human beings in his image, in a state of righteousness and holiness that reflected these qualities in his own being (cf. *Cmi* 8, HC 6).[47] He had graciously equipped them with the ability to keep the law, with the inclination and desire to worship him with their whole lives (*Cma* 12; cf. *Cmi* 8, HC 9). This knowledge, ability, and desire were 'gifts' (*gaben*) from God's hand (HC 9).[48] Indeed, as Ursinus puts it in a parallel passage in *Cmi* 8, when Adam and Eve fell, 'they robbed themselves and all their descendants of that *grace* of God'.[49]

Even though, as we have already seen, the terminology of natural covenant disappears from Ursinus' writings after the *Cma* of 1561/62, the content of this doctrine can still be found in his lectures on the HC. According to *Cma* 36, the law, which contains the natural covenant, is known by nature, requires obedience, promises eternal life, and threatens eternal punishment. In his HC lectures, however, Ursinus uses virtually identical language to describe the moral law but with no explicit reference to the natural covenant:

> The moral law is . . . known by nature, engraven upon the hearts of creatures endowed with reason in their creation, . . . binding all intelligent creatures to perfect obedience and conformity to the law, . . . promising the favour of God and eternal life to all those who render perfect obedience; and at the same time denouncing the wrath of God and everlasting punishment upon all those who do not render this obedience.[50]

The same is true of Ursinus' treatment of the creation and fall of humanity. In *Cma* 10 he had identified 'the kind of covenant God established with human beings in creation [and] how they behaved in keeping it' with 'what kind of human beings God created and for what purpose, [and] into what state they have fallen'.[51] In the catechetical lectures, the covenant framework is gone, but Ursinus still discusses at some length the nature and purpose of the creation of human beings and their fall into sin.[52] And he still maintains that in the Garden of Eden God 'put humanity on trial', placing Adam and Eve under a 'command', promising 'eternal

---

[47]   Ibid. 201, 6.

[48]   Ibid. 7.

[49]   'voluntaria inobedientia se et universam posteritatem suam illa Dei gratia spoliarunt' ibid. 210 (emphasis added).

[50]   *Corp. doct.*, 521 (*Commentary*, 490–1). Cf. also *Corp. doct.*, 528 (*Commentary*, 497–8).

[51]   See n. 43 above.

[52]   *Corp. doct.*, 29–38 (*Commentary*, 27–36).

life' and threatening 'punishment' — all elements that Ursinus had formerly identified as covenantal.[53]

What is noteworthy about these passages in the *Corp. doct.*, however, is that although the language of covenant is now missing, the language of grace is certainly not. According to Ursinus, one of the reasons for examining the doctrine of humanity as created is 'so that we may acknowledge our ingratitude for the *benefits* we received' from God at creation.[54] What are these benefits? Primarily our being created in the image of God, that is, our being created 'good, wise, just, holy, happy, and lord of all other creatures'.[55] All our inclinations, desires, and actions were properly regulated and controlled; our wills, hearts, and 'external parts' were perfectly conformed to the law of God.[56] These were not only the 'ends' for which we were created, but the 'properties and conditions' with which we were created, the 'proper form' of humanity. This form of humanity — happiness, knowing God aright, glorifying God — is related to the purpose of our creation, that we might forever know and praise God.[57] In the creation of humanity, therefore, God manifested himself as the master architect: form was perfectly suited to function.

These original endowments Ursinus explicitly identifies as divine grace. Already in the loci lectures of the 1560s, he had characterized the *originalis iustitia* with which we were created — conformity with God, perfect obedience to the entire divine law, divine acceptance — as a state in which we could not persist without God's grace (*gratiam*) to us.[58] According to his HC lectures, the 'benefits' (*beneficiis*) of being created in the image of God and for eternal life were not only 'good things' (*bona*) from God but divine *gratia*, a grace that we repaid with ingratitude by listening to the devil rather than to God.[59] In fact, it was God's withholding or withdrawal of that grace at the time of the first temptation that led to the fall of the human race. God had put us to the test to demonstrate that we cannot do or retain anything good apart from his preservation and control. He wished to teach us that left to ourselves, apart from his grace of original righteousness, we are weak and incapable of resisting the temptation of the devil. This withdrawal of grace, however, does not mean that God was the cause of the fall. That would have been true only if three conditions had applied: if God had been obligated not to withdraw

---

[53]	Ibid. 36–37 (*Commentary*, 33–4).

[54]	'Ut agnoscamus nostram ingratitudinem pro acceptis beneficiis' ibid. 29 (*Commentary*, 27; emphasis added).

[55]	Ibid. 30 (*Commentary*, 28).

[56]	Ibid 34 (*Commentary*, 32).

[57]	Ibid. 31 (*Commentary*, 29).

[58]	*Sum. relig.*, 154, 223.

[59]	*Corp. doct.*, 36 (*Commentary*, 34).

this grace, if his motives in so doing were malicious, and if we had wanted to retain that grace. But God was under no obligation to preserve that grace in humanity, his motive was not malicious (it was only to put morally responsible creatures to the test), and he withheld such grace at the time of temptation only because Adam and Eve had wilfully *rejected* it in the first place. They were guilty, therefore, not just of falling but of spurning the divine grace that would have prevented that fall.[60]

Once again, there is no evidence here of a shift of emphasis from grace to law. In those passages in which Ursinus discusses the pre-fall relationship between humanity and God — sometimes in covenantal terms, sometimes not — he consistently places this relationship in the context of divine grace. For him grace is not just a redemptive concept; it is manifest already in the original righteousness conferred by God at creation and repudiated by us at the fall.

CONCLUSION

In sum, Ursinus' doctrine of the natural covenant offers no indication of the priority of law over grace that, according to Barth, Bruggink, Rolston, and Torrance, is characteristic of Reformed covenant theology after Calvin. The *foedus naturale* is a relatively minor doctrine in Ursinus' theology and is muted in his later writings by the disappearance of the terminology of natural covenant and by a heavier accent on the unity of the one covenant of grace. Furthermore, many of the 'legal' elements of Ursinus' creation covenant are anticipated already in Calvin, and Calvin's emphasis on divine grace in the prelapsarian relationship with Adam clearly resurfaces in Ursinus. Certainly so far as the pre-fall covenant is concerned, there is more continuity between Calvin and Ursinus than discontinuity.

These conclusions are consistent with those of other research on the early history of the covenant of works — not only other studies that have argued for continuity in this doctrine between Calvin and Ursinus,[61] but those that have found such continuity also between Calvin and the seventeenth-century scholastics Witsius and Brakel[62] and between Calvin and the later Calvinists more generally.[63] But our conclusions also support

---

[60]   Ibid. 37 *(Commentary*, 34–5).
[61]   Diemer, *Scheppingsverbond met Adam*, 7–19; Lillback, 'Ursinus' Development of the Covenant of Creation', 270–86; and idem, 'The Binding of God', 446–84. In my judgment, however, Diemer exaggerates the disjunction between the medieval scholastics and the reformers and between the reformers and the later Reformed scholastics.
[62]   Muller, 'Covenant of Works and the Stability of Divine Law'.
[63]   Helm, 'Calvin and the Covenant'.

a recent line of research that is questioning the whole view of Reformed orthodoxy with which Barth, Bruggink, Rolston, and Torrance were operating in their treatment of Ursinus' natural covenant. Barth, and especially some of the neo-orthodox theologians that followed him, have driven a wedge between Calvin's theology as a whole and that of the later Calvinists, contrasting the biblical Christocentrism of Calvin with the Aristotelian predestinarianism of the Reformed scholastics, and Calvin's theology of grace with the legalism of the federal theologians.[64] In their view, the disjunction they have found between Calvin and Ursinus on the *foedus naturale* is part of a much larger rift between the Reformation and Reformed orthodoxy. Our findings, however, corroborate Muller's thesis that these dichotomies are too sharply drawn and reveal more about the theological assumptions of Neo-orthodoxy than of Reformed orthodoxy.[65] In other words, the similarity we have discovered between Calvin and Ursinus on the natural covenant is not an isolated case; it is but one example of fundamental doctrinal continuity in the midst of development and change as Reformed theology made the transition from the age of reformation to the age of orthodoxy.

---

[64] Muller, 'Calvin and the "Calvinists": Assessing Continuities and Discontinuities between the Reformation and Orthodoxy', *Calvin Theological Journal* 30 (1995), 349–50, 353–4, 356–7; *Calvin Theological Journal* 31 (1996), 147–51.

[65] Muller, 'Calvin and the "Calvinists" '. Cf. idem, *Christ and the Decree: Christology and Predestination in Reformed Theology from Calvin to Perkins* (Durham, N.C.: Labyrinth, 1986; repr. Grand Rapids: Baker, 1988); idem, *Post-Reformation Reformed Dogmatics 2, Holy Scripture: The Cognitive Foundation of Theology* (Grand Rapids: Baker, 1993).

5

The Authority of Reason in the Later Reformation:
Scholasticism in Caspar Olevian and Antoine de La Faye

R.S. Clark

INTRODUCTION

To historians of doctrine, scholasticism has often appeared to be one of the dangers which Protestant theologians must navigate in order to remain Protestant. Scholasticism is usually said to entail a certain amount of rationalism. By *rationalism* I mean a system of thought in which human reason is supreme, the fulcrum by which all other authority is levered. As to whether later Calvinism slipped into the abyss of scholastic rationalism there have been two basic schools of thought. In the nineteenth century scholars generally agreed that whereas Luther's 'central dogma' was justification, Calvin's was predestination and the later Calvinists were thought to be, in the main, faithful to their master. Ritschl spoke of Calvin's 'dogmatic precision': his system was said to contain an 'inner logic' which inevitably worked itself out.[1] This perception of Calvin has also coloured scholarship on Reformed orthodoxy. Thus Reinhold Seeberg's summary of Reformed orthodoxy was headed: 'Triumph of the Doctrine of Predestination'.[2]

In this century, however, Calvin's image in scholarly literature has undergone a remarkable transformation. The search for Calvin's central dogma seems to have been abandoned by most and he is now routinely described in terms once reserved for Luther. Another way of describing

---

[1]   Albrecht Ritschl, *A Critical History of the Christian Doctrine of Justification and Reconciliation*, trans. John S. Black (Edinburgh: T. & T. Clark, 1872), 206.
[2]   Reinhold Seeberg, *Textbook of the History of Doctrines*, 2 vols., trans. Charles E. Hay (Philadelphia: Lutheran Publication Society, 1905), 2:420.

this sea-change in historiography would be to say that whereas in the days of the 'central dogma' Calvin and the Calvinists were viewed as scholastics, now Calvin has come to be viewed almost entirely in the light of his relations to humanism. The later Calvinists, however, have not fared so well. Already in the mid-nineteenth century Heinrich Heppe was portraying not only Calvin, but also Beza as an Aristotelian rationalist.[3] With the passing of the central dogma interpretation of Calvin, the view that Beza was the spoiler of pristine Calvinism quickly gained momentum and has been repeated by E. Bizer, H.-E. Weber, O. Gründler, B.G. Armstrong, J.B. Torrance, R.T. Kendall, and more recently by D.A. Weir.[4] According to this view, the Reformed scholastics took their cues from Beza, Ursinus, Peter Martyr and Zanchi, not Calvin, in fashioning a determinist predestinarian theology starting from the decrees rather than sacred Scripture.

Not surprisingly, since the 1970s a small group of scholars has been challenging this rather narrow characterization of later Calvinism. Just as post-World War I scholarship rehabilitated Calvin this group of scholars have begun the task of rehabilitating Protestant scholasticism. Robert D. Preus began with a two-volume reconsideration of scholastic Lutheranism.[5] Jill Raitt approached Theodore Beza through his theology of the sacraments[6] and more recently the massive research of Richard Muller[7] has demonstrated rather convincingly that the sources show no such 'ration-

---

[3] Heinrich Heppe, *Geschichte des deutschen Protestantismus in den Jahren 1555–1581*, 3 vols. (Marburg, 1852–9).

[4] See E. Bizer, *Frühorthodoxie und Rationalismus* (Zurich: EVZ, 1963); H.-E. Weber, *Reformation, Orthodoxie, und Rationalismus* (Gütersloh: Bertelsmann 1951 Darmstadt: Wissenschaftliche Buchgesellschaft, 1966); O. Gründler, 'Thomism and Calvinism in the Theology of Girolamo Zanchi' (ThD thesis, Princeton Theological Seminary, 1961); B.G. Armstrong, *Calvinism and the Amyraut Heresy: Protestant Scholasticism and Humanism in Seventeenth-Century France* (Madison: University of Wisconsin Press, 1969); J.B. Torrance, 'The Concept of Federal Theology — Was Calvin a Federal Theologian?' in W.H. Neuser (ed.), *Calvinus Sacrae Scripturae Professor* (Grand Rapids: Eerdmans, 1994); R.T. Kendall, *Calvin and English Calvinism to 1649* (Oxford: Oxford University Press, 1979); D.A. Weir, *The Origins of the Federal Theology in Sixteenth Century Reformation Thought* (Oxford: Clarendon, 1990).

[5] Robert D. Preus, *The Theology of Post-Reformation Lutheranism*, 2 vols. (St Louis: Concordia, 1970–1), 1:19.

[6] Jill Raitt, *The Colloquy of Montbéliard: Religion and Politics in the Sixteenth Century* (Oxford: Oxford University Press, 1993); idem, *The Eucharistic Theology of Theodore Beza* (Chambersburg: American Academy of Religion, 1972).

[7] Richard A. Muller, 'Perkins' *A Golden Chaine*: Predestinarian System or Schematized *Ordo Salutis?*', *Sixteenth Century Journal* 9 (1978), 69–81; idem, '*Duplex Cognitio Dei* in the Theology of Early Reformed Orthodoxy', *Sixteenth Century Journal* 10 (1979), 51–61; idem, *Christ and the Decree: Christology and Predestination in Reformed Theology from Calvin to Perkins* (Durham, N.C.: Labyrinth, 1986/Grand Rapids: Baker, 1988); idem, '*Fides* and *Cognitio* in Relation to the Problem of

alism'. Rather, research has shown that in varying degrees, both early and later Reformers made use of Aristotle when it suited their purposes and that the move towards a more sophisticated theological method did not necessarily entail a regression to rationalism.[8] Which of the Protestant scholastics placed reason on a par with revelation? If one looks closely at Peter Martyr, Zanchi, Ursinus, or Polanus it is difficult to find them actually giving to fallen human reason the same authority as revelation.[9] As Muller

---

Intellect and Will in the Theology of John Calvin', *Calvin Theological Journal* 25 (1990), 207–24; idem, *Post-Reformation Reformed Dogmatics*, 3 vols. (Grand Rapids: Baker, 1987).

[8]   John Platt, *Reformed Thought and Protestant Scholasticism: The Arguments for the Existence of God in Dutch Theology, 1575-1650* (Leiden: E.J. Brill, 1982); Lyle D. Bierma, 'The Covenant Theology of Caspar Olevian' (PhD diss., Duke University, 1980), idem, 'Federal Theology in the Sixteenth Century: Two Traditions?', *Westminster Theological Journal* 45 (1983), 304–21; Ian McPhee, 'Conserver or Transformer of Calvin's Theology? A Study of the Origins and Development of Theodore Beza's Thought 1550–1570' (PhD diss. Cambridge University, 1979); John Patrick Donnelly, 'Calvinist Thomism,' *Viator* 7 (1976), 441–5.

[9]   On Vermigli see John Patrick Donnelly, *Calvinism and Scholasticism in Vermigli's Doctrine of Man and Grace* (Leiden: E.J. Brill, 1976); idem, 'Italian Influences on the Development of Calvinist Scholasticism', SCJ 7 (1976), 81–101; Frank A. James III, 'Praedestinatio Dei: The Intellectual Origins of Peter Martyr Vermigli's Doctrine of Double Predestination' (DPhil diss. Oxford University, 1993); idem, 'A Late Medieval Parallel in Reformation Thought: *Gemina Praedestinatio* in Gregory of Rimini and Peter Martyr Vermigli' in *Via Augustini: Augustine in the Later Middle Ages, Renaissance and Reformation*, ed. H.A. Oberman, Frank A. James III (Leiden: E.J. Brill, 1991).

On Zanchi see Muller, *Christ and the Decree*, 110–21; John. L. Farthing, '*Foedus evangelicum*: Jerome Zanchi on the Covenant', *Calvin Theological Journal* 29 (1994): 149–67; idem, '*De coniugio spirituali*: Jerome Zanchi on Ephesians 5:22–33', *Sixteenth Century Journal* 24 (1993), 621–52; idem, 'Christ and the Eschaton: The Reformed Eschatology of Jerome Zanchi' in *Later Calvinism: International Perspectives*, ed. W. Fred Graham, Sixteenth Century Essays and Studies 22 (1994), 333–54.

On Ursinus see Derk Visser, *Zacharias Ursinus, the Reluctant Reformer: His Life and Times* (New York: United Church, 1983); idem, 'Zacharias Ursinus and the Palatinate Reformation' in *Controversy and Conciliation: The Palatinate Reformation, 1559–1618*, ed. Derk Visser (Pittsburgh: Pickwick, 1986); John Patrick Donnelly, 'Immortality and Method in Ursinus' Theological Ambiance' in *Controversy and Conciliation*; Christopher J. Burchill, 'On the Consolation of a Christian Scholar: Zacharias Ursinus (1534–83) and the Reformation in Heidelberg', *Journal of Ecclesiastical History* 37 (1986), 565–83; Lyle D. Bierma, 'The Covenant Theology of Caspar Olevian', 77–92; Muller, *Christ and the Decree*, 97–109.

On Polanus see Muller, *Christ and the Decree*, 130–59; Robert Letham, 'Amandus Polanus: A Neglected Theologian', *Sixteenth Century Journal* 21 (1990), 463–76. See also Richard A. Muller, 'Scholasticism Protestant and Catholic: Francis Turretin on the Object and Principles of Theology', *Church History* 55 (1986), 203–5.

notes, reason was consistently given an instrumental function whereas revelation was given magisterial authority.[10] The distinction is one of *method* versus alleged rationalistic *Zeitgeist*.[11] This restraint is in marked contrast to the Remonstrants who, unlike the Calvinist scholastics, did attempt to resolve the paradox of divine sovereignty and human responsibility.[12]

I wish to continue this process of reconsideration of later Calvinism by examining two transitional figures who contributed to the development of Reformed orthodoxy: Caspar Olevian and Antoine de La Faye. I will argue that, properly understood, these two men were Protestant scholastics, with the emphasis on *Protestant*, and that the work of both men challenges the Bizer–Armstrong portrayal of Calvinist scholasticism. My thesis is that these Protestants made self-conscious use of scholastic methods in order to adapt the gains of the early reformers to the demands of the schools.[13]

BIOGRAPHICAL DETAILS

Caspar Olevian (1536–87) helped to form the nucleus of two major later Calvinist theological faculties: the Heidelberg theologians (1560–76) and the Herborn theologians (1576–87). He received his university education in Paris, Orleans, and Bourges (1550–7); his theological education in Geneva and Zurich. He is interesting for the purposes of this paper because he is most closely associated with the Heidelberg Catechism (1563) of which he was one of the primary authors and editors. He was known to international Calvinism for the federal theology contained in his three commentaries on the Apostles' Creed and his commentaries on the Pauline epistles. He was regarded by Heppe as part of the Melanchthonian reaction to Calvin's predestinarianism. D.A. Weir has renewed a version of this argument in his book. On the other hand, Olevian has also been described by Karl Barth as one in whom he could hear 'the voice of Calvin again'.[14] I too hear the voice of Calvin in Olevian, but it is not as though that voice has not been mediated through Protestant

---

[10]   Muller, *Post-Reformation*, 1:91–2; idem, '*Vera philosophia cum sacra theologia nusquam pugnat*: Keckermann on Philosophy, Theology, and the Problem of Double Truth', *Sixteenth Century Journal* 15 (1984), 341–65.

[11]   John Patrick Donnelly, 'Calvinist Thomism', 452.

[12]   Richard A. Muller, 'God, Predestination, and the Integrity of the Created Order: A Note on Patterns in Arminius' Theology' in *Later Calvinism*, ed. W. Fred Graham.

[13]   William J. Bouwsma, 'The Two Faces of Humanism' in *Itinerarium Italicum: The Profile of the Italian Renaissance in the Mirror of its European Transformations*, ed. H.A. Oberman and T.A. Brady (Leiden: E.J. Brill, 1975), 3–61.

[14]   Karl Barth, *Church Dogmatics*, 13 vols., ed. G.W. Bromiley and T.F. Torrance, trans. G.W. Bromiley (Edinburgh: T. & T. Clark, 1956), 4:1.59; Heinrich Heppe, *Geschichte 1555–1581*; D.A. Weir, *The Orgins of the Federal Theology*; Hans Emil

scholasticism. What is significant is that whether Olevian has been interpreted as 'Calvinist' or not, he has always been interpreted as a sort of 'anti-scholastic'.

Olevian's partner, for the purposes of this essay, Antoine de La Faye, is something of a Melchizedekian figure in that we know nothing of his past before he appeared in Geneva in 1561, and his biographers cannot agree whether he died in 1616, 1617 or 1618. He served as a regent, professor, and rector in the Academy. He was a member of the Company of Pastors and of Beza's team at the Colloquy of Montbéliard, a delegate to the national Synod of Montauban in 1594, and published widely over a fifty-year period.[15]

REFORMED SCHOLASTICISM

In order to divorce Calvin from later Calvinism, some scholars have oversimplified the phenomenon of Reformed scholasticism. In fact, the differences between Reformed scholastics and non-scholastics are mainly methodological, not theological. Muller correctly describes the rise of Reformed scholasticism as a self-consciously Protestant *methodological* adaptation of the Reformation to the classroom. Protestant scholasticism was primarily a method and not a metaphysic.[16] He defines scholasticism as a 'technical and logical approach to theological system' which subdivided the loci into component parts and subjected those subdivisions to analysis

---

Weber, *Reformation, Orthodoxie und Rationalismus*; Ernst Bizer, *Frühorthodoxie und Rationalismus*. A version of this thesis is summarized by W.A. Brown, 'Covenant Theology' in *The Encyclopaedia of Religion and Ethics*, ed. James Hastings (Edinburgh: T. & T. Clark, 1911), Vol 4, 216-24.

[15] S. Stelling-Michaud (ed.), *Le Livre Du Recteur de L'Académie de Genève (1559–1878)* 2 vols. (Geneva: Droz, 1959), 1:78. It does not appear that La Faye was ever a student in Geneva. Eugene Haag, *La France Protestante, ou Vies des protestants français qui se sont fait un nom dans l'histoire*, 9 vols. (Paris: J. Cherbuliez, 1846–59), s.v. 'La Faye, Antoine de'; Paul F. Geizendorf, *Théodore de Bèze* (Geneva: Jullien, 1967), 395–7; Jill Raitt, *The Colloquy of Montbéliard*, 73. Haag credits to La Faye nineteen books. Among them are, *Disputatio verbo Dei* (1591); *Disputatio de traditionibus adversus earum defensores pontificios* (1592); *Disputatio de Christo Mediatore* (1597); *De legitima et falsa sanctorum spiritum adoratione* (1601); *Disputatio de bonis operibus* (1601); *Geneva Liberata* (1603); *Enchiridion theologicum aphorista methodo compositum ex disputationibus* (1605); *De vera Christi ecclesia* (1606); *De vita et obitu clarissimi viri D. Theodori Bezae* (1606); *Emblemata et epigrammata miscellanea selecta ex stromatis peripateticis* (1610). La Faye also wrote commentaries on Romans (1608–9); 1 Timothy (1609) and Ecclesiastes (1609).

[16] On scholasticism as method, see J.A. Weisheipl, 'Scholastic Method' in *The New Catholic Encyclopedia* (New York: Catholic University of America, 1967), 12:1145–6.

by propositions. It was a method designed to facilitate clarity in debate and to make use of Scripture and the broader Christian tradition. Its goal was to provide 'an adequate technical theology for schools, seminaries and universities' and the church with 'right teaching', literally, 'orthodoxy'.[17] From this perspective, the discursive method of Calvin's *Institutes* or Olevian's commentaries, though still propositional, was something of an historical parenthesis in a larger period which was dominated by the scholastic method from the late twelfth century through the late eighteenth century. In fact, according to Walter Ong, the entire period, including the discursive parenthesis, was continually under the influence of Aristotle.[18] By defining scholasticism broadly as a method and distinguishing method from substance, Muller is able to argue that Protestant scholasticism was indeed Protestant and not a duplication of medieval theology.[19] It is probably most accurate to see Protestant scholasticism as both an adaptation of medieval methods and a synthesis of late Renaissance humanism, with the result that later Calvinism was able to move fluently between the discursive mode of the *Institutes* and more recognizably scholastic modes of expression.

Otto Gründler's influential thesis 'Thomism and Calvinism in the Theology of Girolamo Zanchi' is an excellent example of confusion of methodology with metaphysic. Gründler's mode of operation throughout is to review, for example, Zanchi's doctrine of Scripture, show how it was ultimately Thomistic, and then contrast this Thomistic Protestantism with a pristine anti-Thomistic Calvin.[20] For Gründler, to be associated with Thomas or borrow from Thomas in any way is sub-Protestant and sub-Calvinian. What Gründler never explained was *how* or *why* Zanchi used Thomas. Gründler omitted any sympathetic discussion of Zanchi's motives for his method or consideration of the historical circumstances in which Zanchi wrote and ministered.[21]

[17] R.A. Muller, *Dictionary of Latin and Greek Theological Terms* (Grand Rapids: Baker, 1985), 8.

[18] Walter J. Ong, *Ramus: Method and the Decay of Dialogue* (Cambridge, Mass.: Harvard University Press, 1958); cf. Muller, *Post-Reformation*, 1:39.

[19] Muller, *Post-Reformation*, 1:18–52.

[20] David A. Weir, *The Origins of the Federal Theology*, 74, relies upon Gründler's work as part of his two-stream interpretation of Reformed federalism. Cf., Richard A. Muller, *Post-Reformation 2, Holy Scripture: The Cognitive Foundation of Theology*.

[21] The work of Norman Shepherd, Richard Muller, Christopher J. Burchill and John Farthing has provided a valuable corrective to the one-sided analysis of Gründler and others. See Norman Shepherd, 'Zanchius on Saving Faith', *Westminster Theological Journal* 36 (1973), 31–47; Richard Muller, *Christ and the Decree*, 110–21; Christopher J. Burchill, 'Girolamo Zanchi: Portrait of a Reformed Theologian and His Work', *Sixteenth Century Journal* 15 (1984), 185–207; John Farthing, '*De coniugio spirituali*'; idem, 'Christ and the Eschaton'; idem, '*Foedus evangelicum*'.

In fact, Gründler admitted that at *crucial points* Zanchi sharply departed from Thomas. For example, Gründler noted that Zanchi failed to make use of Thomas' five ways at the appropriate place.[22] Nor was Zanchi as consistent as Thomas in his definition of faith.[23] He observed that Zanchi stopped short of Thomas' full analysis of the distinction between *esse* and *essentia* and that Zanchi did not distinguish, as Thomas did, between two senses of *esse*.[24] Yet, in none of these instances, did Gründler ask *why* Zanchi departed from Thomas, nor did he account for the consequences of Zanchi's departures from Thomas. These were crucial omissions on Gründler's part. The most natural explanation was that Zanchi's *Calvinism* or, more broadly, his Protestantism conditioned his use of Thomas.[25] What Gründler unintentionally proved was that Zanchi made selective, critical use of Thomas because it served his apologetic purposes. As Farthing and others have more recently noted, 'the contrast between Calvin and Zanchi has been exaggerated' and the 'continuities between Zanchi's perspective and Calvin's are numerous, significant, and profound'.[26]

There is no clearer evidence of the existence of the scholastic method in the sixteenth century than the many colloquies and disputations which were held throughout the century.[27] The colloquy and the disputation were essentially identical except that colloquies were usually conducted under the auspices of the church and disputations in the divinity schools. The disputation was a fixed part of academic life in the great universities of Europe such as Oxford, Cambridge and Heidelberg. All incepting doctors proposed and defended theses. The *disputatio* had been the accepted mode of resolving intellectual disagreements and demonstrating academic proficiency in the West since Anselm.[28] The doctrinal history of the Reformation is in part a history of *colloquia*. Jill Raitt's, *The Colloquy of Montbéliard* has shown that the colloquy could even be dramatic.[29]

Implicit in much of the criticism of Protestant scholasticism seems to be the assumption that the Protestant scholastics were not conscious of

---

[22]   Gründler, 'Thomism and Calvinism', 95.

[23]   Ibid. 92–3.

[24]   Ibid. 101.

[25]   Farthing, *De coniugio spirituali*, 622. In 'Foedus evangelicum', 151, Farthing described Gründler's argument as 'fatally flawed'.

[26]   Farthing, *De coniugio spirituali*, 622. See Arvin Vos, *Aquinas, Calvin and Contemporary Protestant Thought: A Critique of the Views of Thomas Aquinas* (Grand Rapids: Eerdmans, 1985).

[27]   J.A. Weisheipl, 'Scholastic Method'.

[28]   Pierre Fraenkel, *De l'Écriture à la dispute* (Lausanne: Revue de theologie et de philosophie, 1977), 1–9; Ian McPhee, 'Conserver or Transformer of Calvin's Theology?', v–xxix.

[29]   Jill Raitt, *The Colloquy of Montbéliard*.

their appropriation and modification of scholastic methodology. Donald Sinnema's research has shown, however, that Reformed orthodoxy adopted the scholastic method only after critical reflection.[30] In fact, the Reformed orthodox were not unwitting victims of a resurgent scholasticism. Rather, they made a conscious decision to use the scholastic method to accomplish their purposes. We will see that, for example, La Faye's introduction to the 1586 *Theses Theologiae* contained an impressive example of this pedagogical sophistication.[31] In fact, the Protestant scholastics routinely distinguished themselves and their method from the medieval scholastics.[32] There was ample precedent for this late Reformation and early orthodox move towards the use of Aristotle in theology. A.E. McGrath has shown that the medieval theologians did approximately the same thing to Augustine, while remaining faithful to the 'dogmatic content' of his theology.[33] The consolidation of the Reformation required increased professionalization and technical philosophical skill on the part of the orthodox Reformed.[34] Otto Weber says,

> nothing could be more incorrect than to understand the dogmatics of Orthodoxy merely as Protestant Aristotelianism. This would mean a misunderstanding of Orthodoxy's intention, which was to preserve the Reformation approach which had become a tradition and a legacy, and to order everything conceptual in it.[35]

OLEVIAN AND SCHOLASTICISM

To my knowledge Caspar Olevian has never been described as a Protestant scholastic. This is for two reasons. First, because the definition of scholasticism has been too narrow and second because he has been read

---

[30]   Donald Sinnema, 'Reformed Scholasticism and the Synod of Dort (1618–19)' in B.J. van der Walt (ed.), *John Calvin's Institutes: His Opus Magnum* (Potchefstroom: Potchefstroom University, 1986).

[31]   Translated and published in English as *Propositions and Principles of Divinitie propounded and disputed in the universitie of Geneva, by certaine students of Divinitie there, under M. Theod. Beza, and M. Anthonie Faius, professors of Divinitie* (Edinburgh, 1591). La Faye wrote the epistle dedicatory for the *Theses Theologiae* in June 1586, just nine months after writing the preface to *De substantia*.

[32]   Muller, *Post-Reformation*, 1:81

[33]   Alister E. McGrath, 'Augustinianism? A Critical Assessment of the So-Called "Medieval Augustinian Tradition" on Justification', *Augustiniana* 31 (1981), 252–3.

[34]   John Patrick Donnelly, *Calvinism and Scholasticism;* Kristian Jensen, 'Protestant Rivalry: Metaphysics and Rhetoric in Germany, c.1590–1620', in *Journal of Ecclesiastical History* 41 (1990), 28, 42–3; McPhee, 'Conserver or Transformer of Calvin's Theology?', xvi, xvii.

[35]   Otto Weber, *Foundations of Dogmatics*, 2 vols., trans. Darrell L. Guder (Grand Rapids: Eerdmans, 1981–2), 1:113.

selectively. Yet he began his academic career teaching Aristotelian logic using Melanchthon's *Dialectices* (1547) and he participated in several colloquies in defence of the Catechism while in Heidelberg. His two handbooks of logic, written for his students in Wittenberg, demonstrate familiarity with the *disputatio*.[36]

The dominant interpretation of Olevian is reflected in Jürgen Moltmann's influential 1957 article, 'On the Meaning of Peter Ramus for Philosophy and Theology in Calvinism'.[37] Moltmann revived the Heppe thesis by arguing that Olevian was a Ramist who reacted to harsh, Bezan, metaphysical, predestinarianism.[38] As Walter Ong has shown, however, the attempt to distinguish between Aristotelians (e.g. Beza) and Ramists (e.g. Ames) using rationalism as the criterion is fundamentally flawed. In the case of Olevian's *De inventione dialecticae* (1583) it is impossible sharply to distinguish between Ramism and Aristotelianism. There is abundant evidence of Aristotle's influence on Olevian. In *De inventione*, Olevian made use of all the categories of Aristotle's *Organon*: Substance, Quantity, Quality, Relation, Place, Time, Posture/Position, State/Condition, Action and Affection.[39] He translated Aristotle's *ousia* with *substantia* and followed the Stagirite's definition.[40] He also used, however, an obviously Ramist chart and his arrangement of the material is almost indistinguishable from Book One of Piscator's Ramist *Animadversiones*.[41] In *De inventione*, he used the same bipartite definition of dialectic, *inventio* (discovery) and *iudicium* (arrangement) as Piscator.[42] He followed Ramus in defining method as *doctrina* or teaching;[43] and he also followed Ramus' 'corpuscular epistemology' which regarded 'everything, mental and physical, as composed of corpuscular units or "simples" '.[44] These 'simples' were said to be *individua* and clusters of simples he defined as *genera*.

---

[36] *Fundamenta dialecticae breviter consignata e praelectionibus* (Frankfurt, 1581); *De inventione dialecticae liber, e praelectionibus Gapari Oleviani excerptus* (Geneva, 1583).

[37] Jürgen Moltmann, 'Zur Bedeutung des Petrus Ramus für Philosphie und Theologie im Calvinismus', *Zeitschrift für Kirchengeschichte* 68 (1957), 295–318.

[38] Compare Moltmann's article with J.I. Good, *The Heidelberg Catechism in Its Newest Light* (Philadelphia: Reformed Church in the United States, 1914); J.T. McNeill, *History and Character of Calvinism* (New York: Oxford University Press, 1954) 391. Cf., Walter J. Ong, *Ramus*.

[39] Aristotle, *The Organon*, 2 vols., trans. Harold P. Cooke (London: William Heinemann, 1949), 13–17; see *Aristotelis Opera, Organon, Categoriae*, 2.11^{a}–4.19^{b}.

[40] Aristotle, *The Organon*, 20–35; Bierma, 'The Covenant Theology of Caspar Olevian', 232.

[41] *De inventione*, 168.

[42] *Animadversiones* (Frankfurt, 1582), 12. *De Inventione*, 3. *Iudicium* is usually translated with 'judgment' or 'conclusion'. In using 'arrangement', I am following Ong, *Ramus*, 183–4.

[43] Ong, *Ramus*, 162.

[44] Ibid. 203.

He was eclectic and the relations between Aristotelianism and Ramism in *De inventione* are too complex to permit easy categorization.

Thus, Bierma was only partly correct when he said, in response to Moltmann, that Olevian was Aristotelian in logical method but not in his metaphysics or epistemology.[45] It is true that Olevian was no Aristotelian in his metaphysics. Olevian was, however, Aristotelian in dialectic and Ramist in rhetoric. Even if it could be shown that Olevian was in fact a 'Ramist' in the way that Moltmann claimed, it would mean little since Ramus identified rhetoric with dialectic, *so that he had no distinctive metaphysic* over against Aristotle and regarded the *usus* of logic as the 'real exercise' of dialectic.[46] This was because Ramism was more a pedagogical technique than a dialectical theory or metaphysic. Moltmann, like Heppe, failed to account for the complexity of sixteenth century thought in this regard. Because it is really just a re-organisation of Aristotle, Ramism should not be seen as a sort of proto-Schleiermacherian reaction to Aristotle.[47]

Bierma has also argued that *De inventione* shows substantial identity to Melanchthon's 1547 *Dialectices* (which Olevian used as a textbook in Trier) as proof that Olevian could not have been 'Ramist' but must have been exclusively Aristotelian.[48] Such a dichotomy is misguided, however, because Ramus also borrowed heavily from Melanchthon's *Dialectices*.[49] Throughout *De inventione* Olevian mixed obviously Aristotelian substance with Ramist presentation. He followed Aristotle by dividing each question into *simplex* and *coniuncta* parts, distinguishing between cause and effect and between form and substance. However, under each head he also included *regulae argumentandi, lumen argumentorum* and the *usus*, all pedagogical devices supplied by Ramus.

In *De inventione*, Olevian defined *substantia* in six articles.[50] In the opening remarks he defined substance as 'being' because 'being proper' belongs to it. God (incorporeal, infinite and indivisible substance) and created substances share this definition. In the *ordo substantiarum* there were corporeal and incorporeal substances. Corporeal and incorporeal substances were subdivided into perfectly and imperfectly mixed substances. Perfectly mixed corporeal substances could be further subdivided into animate and inanimate substances. Animate substances included the

---

[45] Bierma, 'Covenant Theology of Caspar Olevian', 229–38.

[46] Ong, *Ramus*, 172–3.

[47] Muller, *Christ and the Decree*, 180–2.

[48] Bierma, 'Covenant Theology of Caspar Olevian', 233–5; see idem, 'The Role of Covenant Theology in Early Reformed Orthodoxy', *Sixteenth Century Journal* 21 (1990), 458–9.

[49] Ong, *Ramus*, 236–9, 299.

[50] Caspar Olevian, *De inventione*, Cap. 39, Articles 1–6, 167–70.

sentient and the non-sentient. Among sentient beings there were *rationalis* (e.g. humans) and *irrationalis* (e.g. horses). It was most important for Olevian that one distinguish properly between *primas substantias* and *secundas substantias*. Primary substances were indivisible and 'secondary substances' were composite. So, though he used the Ramist definition of *species* and *genera* it was Aristotle's definition of *substantia* on which he relied.[51]

There are three explanations for this phenomenon of Aristotelianism mixed with Ramism. First, in the period 1577–87 Olevian was, like Ramus (1515–72), a teacher of teenage boys and needed simple, clear, pedagogical tools. Second, Ong has shown that Ramism was no intellectual revolution. Ramism was not even a particularly novel or creative anti-Aristotelian method, despite Ramus' claims, but rather a synthesis of older mild criticisms of Aristotle made first by Peter of Spain and Rudolph Agricola. Ong called the product of these criticisms 'arts scholasticism', which he distinguished from theological scholasticism.[52]

Arts scholasticism was far more widespread than theological scholasticism. It 'centered on logic' and its philosophy was 'terminism'. Ong showed that because the Arts faculty at Paris, where Ramus taught, was warned away from theology, the parts of the Aristotelian corpus with which it dealt were circumscribed. The result was that those sections in Aristotle deemed to deal with metaphysics were off-limits and the 'Aristotle with whom Ramus dealt was far less a metaphysical Aristotle (in the modern sense) than an arts-course Aristotle'.[53]

It is significant to note that *De inventione* was a logic textbook geared for *future preachers* because it illustrates the fact that Olevian thought it was important to pass along a good dose of Aristotle to future preachers so that they would be most effective in the pulpit. His Aristotelianism served his theology and so his use of Aristotle is tempered with criticism.[54] According to Olevian, if we prudently distinguish substances from accidents, we will distinguish between the promised eternal indwelling of the Holy Spirit and Aristotle's *bonus motus*.

> One must prudently distinguish between substance and accidents. Thus when Christ promised to us the Paraclete, He did not promise 'good movements of the heart or consolation' — that would be confusing effect

---

[51] *De inventione*, 167: 'Substantia est ens, quod proprium esse habet, nec est in alio, ut habens conservationem in suo esse a subiecto. Haec definitio communis est Deo et creatis substantiis. Differunt primae substantiae et secundae substantiae apud Aristotelem. Primas substantias vocat individua, ut hunc hominem, hanc arborem. Secundas substantias vocat species et genera'.

[52] Ong, *Ramus*, 7–9, 61–2, 98–112, 132, 240.

[53] Ibid. 144.

[54] John Patrick Donnelly, 'Immortality and Method', 187–91.

with cause — as much as the author of them himself . . . When Scripture says the same about angels, it speaks not about good movements, but about good spiritual subsistences . . . Thus the 'insanity' of the Sadducees is apparent, who imagined angels to be the good movements of the heart.[55]

For Olevian, Christ, through his Spirit, is *substantia* who moves us as well.

Olevian also argued that primary, indivisible substances were *extra intellectum*, whereas from secondary substances, according to God's eternal will, one can discern God's existence.[56] Thus, what under this category Aristotle called *ousia*, the Church has called *essentia* and used it to explain the Trinity.[57]

All this is to show that Olevian *was* capable of using a more scholastic dialectical method. If we define scholasticism as primarily a method of instruction, then we may fairly call Olevian a scholastic. To call him a scholastic is to say he worked in the *schola* — put plainly, he was a teacher. Like most dedicated teachers he made use of the best equipment to hand to do the job. In the last quarter of the sixteenth century Aristotle, with a few Ramist charts thrown in, was the only teaching aid on the market.

OLEVIAN DE DEO

In the earlier literature on Protestant scholasticism it was understood that discussion of God *in se* (in himself) constituted evidence of scholasticism. Were one to find such discussion in theologians not heretofore considered scholastic, the definition of the term would need to be revised.

In his *Expositio symboli apostolici* (1576), in addressing matters preparatory to his exposition of the Apostles' Creed, Olevian provided a 'description of God' (*descriptio Dei*) and a discussion of the divine attributes apart from Christology.[58] He had no qualms about discussing God apart

---

[55] 'Inter entia etiam ipsa prudenter discernendae substantiae ab accidentibus, ut cum Christus promittit, se nobis Paracletum missurum qui in nobis sit, et maneat nobiscum in aeternum, non promittit tantum bonos motus cordis seu consolatione, sed ipsum authorem, omnis consolationis fontem, nempe causam cum effectu. Item cum Scriptura loquitur de Angelis, non loquitur de bonis motibus, sed spirituibus bonis subsistentibus . . . Hic apparet insania Saducaeorum, qui Angelos fingebant esse bonos motus cordis.' *De Inventione*, 169, art. 2. See Muller, *Dictionary of Latin and Greek Theological Terms*, s.v., 'motus'.

[56] *De inventione*, 169.3; 170.4, 'Etsi autem secundae substantiae extra intellectum nihil sint: tamen utile est videre seriem in hac tota universitate rerum, quam intellectu seu mente circumferentis discernimus Deum a rebus creatis, a quibus in aeternum discerni vult'.

[57] *De inventione*, 170.5.

[58] Casper Olevian, *Expositio symboli apostolici* (Frankfurt, 1576), 19.

from the incarnation. For Olevian, to answer the question, 'who is God' was to discuss the nature of God proper, the Trinity, and then the incarnation. It is also remarkable that he located this doctrine not under Christology, but after his partition of the Creed and before his exposition of the article 'I believe in God the Father' and his discussion of the Trinity. As part of his defence of his Calvinist doctrine of providence, he argued that the God who redeems us is the same God who manifests as much power in preserving us presently as he did in the first creation.[59] Part of the Father's universal government includes the gathering of the church 'by the word of the gospel' (*voce Euangelii*) and 'the internal word of the Son'.[60] The covenant (*foedus*) is a source of comfort for the elect only because the God who made it is omnipotent. In short, God's electing power and decree are but subsets of his universal power (*potentia*) over all things.[61]

Olevian believed that Christians must know what God is, in himself, in order to believe in him.[62] There were certain propositions about the divine nature, logical predicates of the term 'God' which he, with the Western theological tradition, accepted as properly belonging to the concept of God. He considered that it is only when we know who God is in himself that we can appreciate the magnitude of his grace in condescending to promise 'by an everlasting covenant that he will be a God unto us'.[63]

THESES THEOLOGICAE

The other assumption about later Calvinism which I wish to criticise is the assumption that Calvin's biblicist humanism was victimized by later Calvinist Aristotelianism. In this regard it is most interesting to notice, in the dedication of the *Theses Theologicae*, Antoine de La Faye's clever defence of the necessity of the system of the *disputatio* as a means of propagating and preserving the truth, i.e. Reformed orthodoxy.[64] La Faye says:

---

[59]   *Expositio*, 59. 'certo statuet quotide mane and vesperi non minorem potentiam in conservatione and gubernatione rerum omnium Deum exerere, quam in prima creatione'.

[60]   Ibid.

[61]   Ibid. 48. 'Credo me habere foedus cum Deo omnipotente, qui and omnipotentia sua omnia quae vult in toto mundo effeciat, and quincuncque non vult sive non decrevit, impediat'.

[62]   Ibid. 25.

[63]   Ibid. 20, '. . . qui promisit foedere sempiterno se fore nobis in Deum'.

[64]   *Theses Theologicae in schola Genevensi ab aliquot sacrarum literarum studiosis sub DD. Theod. Beza and Antonio Fayo S.S. theologiae professoribus propositae et disputatae. In*

It has long been the complaint of very many, that those whom they call the Schoolmen and Disputers, have given the study of the Holy Scriptures, not only a great injury, but even a death wound. And therefore it may seem wonderful to some, that the custom of disputing divine matters, is retained in these Churches and Schools, which are reformed according to the pure word of God.[65]

Is it not true, in the nature of the case, that by *disputing* matters of sacred doctrine one places them in the realm of philosophy thus thereby making them less than certain? La Faye concedes that the medieval scholastics did this very thing, 'in the very first beginning of the Church there was a very sore blow given to religion, by those who being swollen up by the pride of human reasonings, would rather submit Christ unto their judgments, than themselves unto his majesty'.[66] Too often the Schoolmen,

> have altogether drunk up and consumed the juice and moisture of godliness, so that there remained nothing for them, but the dry and withered bark: and it has brought forth so many controversies and diversities of opinions, which teach and learn nothing else, but brawls and parts taking.[67]

La Faye based his defence of the *disputatio* on a sharp distinction between that which belongs to Pythagoras and that which has been spoken by 'Jehovah by his Prophets and Apostles in his word written'.[68] The blame for the association of the *disputatio* with the corruption of the gospel lies not with the *disputatio* itself, but rather with the medieval scholastics who failed to distinguish, according to La Faye, between opinion and revelation. Because they were 'over curious (which is not to be commended)' it does not follow that 'therefore careful diligence should be disliked'.[69]

La Faye gave four reasons why the disputation system should be used by reformed theological students. (1) Because divinity consists of holy things, care is required. (2) The writings of Scripture are full of sharp disputations (especially the Pauline epistles). The only way biblical

---

quibus methodica locorum communium S.S. theologiae epitome continetur (Geneva, 1586). Translated and published in English as *Propositions and Principles of Divinitie propounded and disputed in the universitie of Geneva, by certaine students of Divinitie there, under M. Theod. Beza, and M. Anthonie Faius, professors of Divinitie* (Edinburgh, 1591). I am not aware of another analysis of La Faye's dedicatory epistle to the *Theses Theologicae.*

[65]   Ibid. ii.
[66]   Ibid. iii.
[67]   Ibid.
[68]   Ibid. ii.
[69]   Ibid. v.

disputations can be discussed is by the 'use of reasoning'. (3) Our Lord himself disputed with 'Doctors, Pharisees, Sadducees, etc.' as Paul disputed with 'the Jews, with the Philosophers, with the brethren'. (4) The Fathers also disputed, e.g. Irenaeus against the 'Gnostics', Tertullian against the Marcionites, Athanasius against the 'Arians' and Nazianzen, Cyril, Theodoret, Hilary, Augustine and many others, 'almost against innumerable heresies'.[70]

His list shows that he was aware that by using and defending the *disputatio* he and the Academy might be identified with the medieval schoolmen and therefore he was at pains to cast himself and his students as heirs of the patristic polemic tradition. It was not the method, but its subversion which was the problem. He proposed a three-step remedy for the disease which ailed the medieval scholastic system. Disputations become profitable, when nothing else is considered in them but: (1) the ways of the Lord which are mercy and truth; (2) deceit, subtlety, self-love and desire of victory is removed; (3) the desire of the truth, the love and reverence of God's majesty joined with modesty and singleness is used therein.[71]

La Faye envisioned the Reformed disputation system as a gathering for fraternal, theological and moral correction. All Christian teachers have a responsibility to

> frame and fashion their scholars so that they timely season them with the juice of these virtues in such sort, as when afterwards they shall come abroad from their private studies, to any public calling, they may perpetually retain those virtues.[72]

Though it was a mild exaggeration to equate the more informal biblical disputes (e.g. Jesus and the Pharisees) with the classroom *disputatio*, La Faye's defence of the use of the scholastic method in the Calvinist academy shows that he was aware of the increasing need for doctrinal and apologetic precision required by the changing ecclesiastical and political circumstances in which the academy existed.

CONCLUSION

Caspar Olevian and Antoine de La Faye exemplify the difficulties associated with the traditional (Heppe–Bizer–Barth–Armstrong) approach to Protestant scholasticism. Olevian has historically been read either as an anti-Aristotelian anti-Calvinist Melanchthonian (Heppe–Moltmann) or

---

[70] Ibid.
[71] Ibid. v, vi.
[72] Ibid. vi.

Calvinist–Humanist anti-scholastic (Barth–Weir). In fact, he was a full-blooded 'Calvinist' who combined Calvin's discursive method with a functional Aristotelian dialectic. Olevian is interesting because he breaks the mould and should cause us to re-evaluate our understanding of who is and is not scholastic, and question whether Armstrong's claim that there is a 'scholastic' mentality stands up.

La Faye is interesting because he challenges the notion that Reformed scholasticism was unconsciously taken hostage by Aristotelian–Bezan scholasticism. In fact, later Calvinists were sophisticated theologically and philosophically and made a calculated use of scholastic methods and pedagogy in their attempt to fit the Reformation to the *schola*.

6

The Distinction Between Scholastic and Popular:
Andreas Hyperius and Reformed Scholasticism

Donald Sinnema

INTRODUCTION

Recent studies on Reformed scholasticism have made significant advances in understanding its characteristics and development. A fuller historical understanding of Reformed scholasticism, however, requires closer study of how its sixteenth and seventeenth century representatives actually understood this phenomenon. One key to such an historical understanding is their usage of the term 'scholasticus'. The term was used in three basic senses: in general reference to 'school' matters; in reference to medieval 'scholastics'; and in reference to the teaching style and methods of the universities.[1] The third sense, which lies at the heart of scholasticism, requires closer analysis. What exactly did theologians of Reformed orthodoxy mean when they spoke of a 'scholastic' method or way of treating theology?

It was rather common for Reformed theologians of the Post-Reformation period to make a distinction between a 'scholastic' and 'popular' treatment of theology. This distinction, which has not been duly recognized, provides a significant clue to understanding the character and limits of Reformed scholasticism. The scholastic-popular distinction itself was by no means new in the sixteenth century. It can be found, for example, in medieval homiletic manuals where 'popular

---

[1] See my 'Reformed Scholasticism and the Synod of Dort (1618–19)' in *John Calvin's Institutes: His Opus Magnum*, ed. Van der Walt (Potchefstroom: Potchefstroom University, 1986), 467–506, esp. 469–72.

interpretation' and 'scholastic interpretation' referred to preaching in the parish and preaching in the university.[2]

Marburg theologian Andreas Hyperius (1511–64) offered a carefully developed formulation of this distinction, and was only the second theologian in the Reformed tradition to do so.[3] His contemporary Calvin, for example, never explicitly used this distinction in his *Institutes*; his writings were generally marked by a humanist rather than scholastic style.[4] Hyperius considered both the scholastic and popular ways of treating theology to be legitimate. He stood at the beginning of the period of Reformed scholasticism and, since his formulation of the scholastic-popular distinction legitimized the scholastic approach, had considerable impact on this emerging movement.

HYPERIUS' FORMULATION OF THE DISTINCTION

It appears that Hyperius first developed the scholastic-popular distinction sometime between 1546 and 1552 while preparing a book about the way to do theological studies.[5] When he later discussed this distinction again in *De formandis concionibus sacris*, published in 1553, he stated:

> Since we said several things about the scholastic interpretation (*interpretatione scholastica*) of the Scriptures when we deliberated on the way of

---

[2]   Edward Cecil Meyer, 'The First Protestant Handbook on Preaching: An Analysis of the *De formandis concionibus sacris seu de interpretatione scripturarum populari libri II* of Andreas Hyperius in Relation to Medieval Homiletical Manuals' (PhD diss. Boston University, 1967), 141.

[3]   H. Bullinger's *Studiorum ratio* (1527) being the first. Hyperius received a humanist education in Paris; after two years of travel he spent four years in England, and in 1541 arrived at Marburg where he served as professor of theology for the rest of his life. For his life see Gerhard Krause, *Andreas Gerhard Hyperius: Leben, Bilder, Schriften* (Tübingen: Mohr, 1977). Theologically Hyperius stood within the Reformed tradition, but represented a rather independent stance, like Bucer. See Willem van't Spijker, *Principe, Methode en Functie van de Theologie bij Andreas Hyperius* (Kampen: Kok, 1990), 36. For literature on Hyperius see Gerhard Krause, 'Andreas Hyperius in der Forschung seit 1900', *Theologische Rundschau* 34 (1969), 262–341.

[4]   In his commentary on Genesis 1:15–16 Calvin did use a somewhat similar distinction when he stated that Moses did not write philosophically (*philosophice*) about creation but popularly (*populariter*): *Corpus Reformatorum*, LI:21–2.

[5]   Hyperius probably presented this material in lectures at Marburg University. It was later published in *De recte formando theologiae studio* (Basel, 1556). Hyperius began preparing this work in 1546 (Olivier Fatio, 'Hyperius plagié par Flacius: la destinée d'une méthode exégétique' in *Histoire de l'exégèse au XVIe siècle*, ed. Olivier Fatio and Pierre Fraenkel [Geneva: Droz, 1978], 364.)

theological study (*cum de ratione studii theologicae commentaremur*),[6] now it seems good to make public some things[7] about the popular (*populari*) interpretation, that is, about preparing sermons for the people (*ad populum*), since many have demanded this of us much and often.[8]

The full title of this homiletic work, *De formandis concionibus sacris, seu de interpretatione scripturarum populari, libri II*, indicates that Hyperius considered sermon making to be popular interpretation of the Scriptures. Thus this work appears to be a counterpart to his *De recte formando theologiae studio*, which explains how theological studies are to be conducted in the schools, in other words, how a scholastic treatment of theology is to be done.

In the first chapter of *De formandis* Hyperius explained the popular approach by carefully distinguishing between scholastic and popular ways of interpretation. 'Interpreting' here refers to different ways of explaining the meaning of Scripture, not different ways of understanding it.

> No one is unaware that two ways of interpreting the Scriptures are used in the churches,[9] the one scholastic (*scholasticam*), the other popular (*popularem*). The former is appropriate in the assemblies of learned men and young students who have advanced to some extent in scholarship; the latter is provided entirely to instruct the common people, most of whom are ignorant, uneducated, and illiterate. The former is exercised within the narrow walls of the school; the latter takes place in spacious sanctuaries. The former is concise and compact, smelling of philosophical solitude and rigour; the latter is expanded, free in expression, and diffuse, and indeed delights in the light and forum, as it were, of oratory. In the former most things are examined by the standard of dialectical brevity and simplicity; in the latter rhetorical abundance and copiousness garner the most favour.[10]

At this point in his 1562 edition of *De formandis* Hyperius expanded his explanation of the scholastic-popular distinction:

> For this reason, if a passage from sacred literature is ever brought to the attention of a teacher in a school to be explained, he soon sticks to it

---

[6] In the expanded 1562 Marburg edition of *De formandis*, Hyperius added at this point: 'as much as the matter then required and allowed' (fol. 3v).

[7] Here the 1562 edition added: 'more extensively'.

[8] Andreas Hyperius, *De formandis concionibus sacris, seu de interpretatione scripturarum populari, libri II* (Marburg, 1553), fol. 4r. The preface is dated 22 September 1552. All translations are my own.

[9] The 1562 edition replaces 'in the churches' with 'by those skilled in divine matters'. This is more precise because for Hyperius only the popular approach is appropriate in the church context.

[10] *De formandis* (1553), fol. 3r.

completely, as though confined within a prison, circus or wrestling ring, and he meticulously discusses not only the things themselves in general and in all their parts, but also nearly every single word, considering it a terrible thing to omit anything or to digress even a little. But he who instructs the people searches for and selects only certain commonplaces from the proposed argument, those that he perceives to be more suited than others to the time, place, and persons. He devotes his speech to explaining these more extensively, and in order that a larger and freer scope may be opened to him in dealing with these commonplaces, he sometimes passes over some of the context of the sacred words, or he hastens only in passing over individual points as if treating another topic. Again, he who lectures in a school amasses proofs and supporting arguments with as much sound judgment and acumen as he can, and he is glad to use especially those that he perceives to be stronger and more vigorous. But he who decides to speak to the people is not as meticulous; he scrapes together arguments of any kind and supports himself with probable reasons, even such as are heard among ordinary common people, since he directs everything to the level of any listeners whatever. He who teaches in a school knowingly and willingly disregards whatever seeks to arouse good-will and moves the emotions, also digressions, extended descriptions, examples, amplifications, elaborate elegance of speaking style, numerous figures of speech; in short, all such embellishment and adornment of oratory. And indeed he does not try to appear to be devoted to brilliance in speaking, but he is content with a simple, yet plain and clear manner of speaking. On the other hand, he who devotes himself to the task of addressing the common people searches with admirable discretion for all such paraphernalia and equipment so far as is useful for teaching, refuting, exhorting, chastening, and comfort, and he considers nothing of more importance than to stir up and draw the minds of his listeners in the direction he wishes according to the nature of the matters being considered.[11]

Hyperius asserted that the scholastic-popular distinction can be easily observed in many biblical authors and Church Fathers, even though they did not explicitly draw this distinction. 'It would not be difficult to bring forth examples in which the same subjects or themes from the Scriptures were treated one way by the scholastic manner of interpreting, another way by the popular.'[12] Hyperius saw the popular manner of explaining in most of the speeches of the prophets and Christ, as well as in many of Paul's exhortations and words of chastisement and consolation. Also popular were the homilies, sermons, and orations of the Church Fathers:

---

[11] *De formandis* (1562), fols. 1v–2v.
[12] Ibid. fol. 2v.

Origen, Chrysostom, Basil, Nazianzus, Augustine, Maximus and Leo, and of the later writers Gregory the Great, Bede, and Bernard of Clairvaux. Some of Augustine's commentary on John's Gospel and on the Psalms also belongs to this category.[13]

On the other hand, Hyperius found the scholastic approach in some of Paul's weightier and more precise arguments about justification in Romans and Galatians, and about other subjects in First Corinthians. He noted, however, that in Romans Paul from time to time freely moves from a scholastic style to popular exhortation and consolation.[14] He also identified scholastic treatment in Hebrews' discussion of the two natures of Christ and of the abrogation of the Levitical priesthood. Among the Church Fathers the scholastic approach is evident in Jerome's commentaries on the prophets, in Ambrose's commentaries on Paul's epistles, as well as in the letters and polemical writings of Augustine.[15] Here he made no mention of the medieval scholastics as examples of this approach.

De formandis itself was a manual on preaching in which Hyperius explained how sermons should be prepared with the aid of rhetorical tools.[16] A couple of examples may suffice to show his emphasis on the popular character of sermons. He was convinced that preaching must be profitable to the congregation for doctrine, refuting, correcting, instructing, and consoling. From these practical functions of preaching, drawn from 2 Timothy 3:16 and Romans 15:4, Hyperius identified five kinds of sermons,[17] a new classification that had considerable influence on later Lutheran and Reformed homiletics. Hyperius also emphasized that preaching must be applicable to the needs of the congregation and be appropriate to the 'persons, time, and place'. For him application was not a part of a sermon distinct from the exegetical, but rather characterized the whole sermon as a way of interpreting Scripture for the present situation.[18]

In 1556 when Hyperius published his book on the way to study theology, titled *De recte formando theologiae studio*, he again focused on the distinction between scholastic and popular especially in the chapter 'How Carefully Interpreters Use a Method of Teaching'. Here Hyperius not

---

13   *De formandis* (1553) fol. 3v.
14   Ibid. (1562) fol. 3r.
15   Ibid. (1553) fols. 3v–4r.
16   Hyperius' homiletics have been carefully analyzed by P. Biesterveld, *Andreas Hyperius, voornamelijk als Homileet* (Kampen: Zalsman, 1895); Martin Schian, 'Die Homiletik des Andreas Hyperius', *Zeitschrift für praktische Theologie* 18 (1896), 289–324; 19 (1897), 27–66, 120–49; Peter Kawerau, 'Die Homiletik des Andreas Hyperius', *Zeitschrift für Kirchengeschichte* 71 (1960), 66–81; Meyer, *The First Protestant Handbook*.
17   *De formandis* (1553), Book II, ch. 1.
18   Meyer, *First Protestant Handbook*, 254.

only explained the distinction, but also described in detail how the scholastic way of teaching the Scriptures should be done:

> I will show the way and method that all the most outstanding interpreters of sacred literature are accustomed to use. There are two ways of treating the Scriptures, the one popular (*popularis*), the other scholastic (*scholastica*). The former way is used mostly for the ordinary common people in the sanctuaries and in good measure smells of the workshops of the rhetoricians; the latter is suited for the assembly of students staying in numerous schools and colleges, and savours of something philosophical since it is bound more to dialectical brevity and simplicity (*ad dialecticam brevitatem simplicitatemque*). Yet we recognize that the former has also been brought by some into the academic arena.[19]

He then elaborated on the popular way of treating the Scriptures, before focusing on the scholastic approach:

> Therefore in the popular treatment the teacher acts far more freely. It is enough that in explaining a subject — whether it be a whole book, or some portion of a book, or some question to be discussed in view of the event and circumstances — he begins by first giving the natural and evident meaning in a few words and impressing it simply on the hearts of his listeners.

Then he selects some primary commonplaces (*locos*) on which he dwells longer and explains them well. He does this in such a way that he applies everything to the present state of the churches; yet he especially labours to impress on people's minds the dogmas of our religion that it is necessary to know, and then to condemn the corrupt conduct of people and to lead them to purity of life and true holiness. Therefore he diffusely addresses the commonplaces (*locis communibus*) about faith, true calling upon God's name, love, obedience, kindness, prayer, fasting, patience, and cross-bearing; then he speaks long and often against superstitions, luxury, intoxication or drunkenness, and any other recently arising vices that, in his judgment, are in need of public reproof and are able to be corrected.

Now in all these things he uses frequent examples from the Scriptures. He also sets forth clear consequences, rewards as well as punishments.

[19] Andreas Hyperius, *De recte formando theologiae studio, libri IIII* (Basel, 1556), 368. The title of the second and later editions was changed to *De theologo, seu de ratione studii theologici libri IIII* (Basel, 1559). This work has been called the first Protestant encyclopedia of theology. Summaries of its contents may be found in Abraham Kuyper, *Encyclopaedie der Heilige Godgeleerdheid* (Kampen: Kok, 1908), I:155–68; Robert Preus, *The Theology of Post-Reformation Lutheranism* 1 (St Louis: Concordia, 1970), 82–8; and Fatio, 'Hyperius Plagié' par Flacius: la destinée d'une méthode exégétique' in *Histoire de l'exégèse au XVIe siècle*.

Now and then he brings together analogies from daily life. He then produces diverse proofs and persuasive supporting arguments. From time to time he intersperses things drawn from the humbler disciplines such as dialectic and rhetoric or from the ordinary common people, sometimes things astutely stated by the philosophers or other famous people, such as emblematic mottoes.

He does not pass over those things that embellish a speech and make it eloquent and beautiful. He is also an eager collector of examples and amplifications. Finally, he laboriously collects anything that he thinks may serve to stir the emotions:

> In sum, he omits nothing that in any way has the power to persuade and impress minds. Since this is his intention, his whole effort aims to entice all people to acknowledge their sins, believe, devoutly call upon God and correct their lives, and if possible, to transform them into entirely new people.[20]

On the other hand, the scholastic treatment of the Scriptures is much more laborious; here 'individual things, and indeed the most minute, are considered by being investigated precisely', so that the intended meaning of a passage may be very clear. Yet he did not insist that the method be rigidly followed without variation since that only produces boredom in students. He admitted that in commenting on Scripture he always began the same way, but sometimes changed his approach when the nature of the passage under consideration required it.[21]

THE SHAPE OF HYPERIUS' SCHOLASTIC METHOD

He went on to describe in detail the precise procedure by which a scholastic method would handle continuous exposition (i.e. exegesis); and then a scholastic method of explaining commonplaces (i.e. dogmatics). He did not claim originality in developing such a method, but only described a sort of 'common method' (*communem methodum*)[22] that he had noticed various theologians actually using:

> I will bring together and present a certain form of method, not indeed prescribed to us by any one teacher, but which I have observed in diverse authors both ancient and modern, as well as in the most distinguished interpreters of celebrated schools, whom I happened at some time to hear

---

[20] *De recte formando*, 368–70; cf. 474–5, where he described the popular way of explaining commonplaces.
[21] Ibid. 370–1.
[22] Ibid. 391.

in France, Germany, Britain, or elsewhere, and which I noted as far as was allowed in good faith.[23]

Elaborating on his scholastic method for exegesis, he first described the procedure for explaining a whole book. Before delving into the work itself, a number of preliminary topics need to be addressed.[24] First one focuses on the author of the book as well as the recipients or people about whom the work was written. Concerning the author it is fitting to focus on the author's situation, vocation, way of life, teachings, and way of speaking. Concerning the recipients or subjects of the work, one should explain where they live, what kind of people they are, their character, and their customs. Second, one deals with the occasion for the writing. Here the interpreter examines the state of the church or nation, whether any faults, perils, changes, or errors have affected it, how it arrived at that state, and what factor most moved the author to write. Here the purpose of the writer should be explained. Third, one goes on to explain the main point or theme of the whole book. Fourth, one identifies the major sections of the book. Fifth, one then identifies the parts into which each of the major sections is divided, noting, for example, a section's introduction, theme, supporting arguments, refutation of errors, and conclusion. Each of these individual parts is then summarized briefly. Sixth, a teacher should show how much use these things have publicly for the church and privately for the conscience. This may be appropriately done by examining the chief passages that are presently of service for doctrine, reproof, instruction, correction, and consolation. In these five areas, Hyperius asserted, the usefulness of biblical knowledge is especially evident.

If a teacher seeks to explain only part of a biblical book, it is not necessary to investigate all the preliminary points that are addressed when examining a whole book. Then it is sufficient to indicate briefly the occasion of the book, the author's intention, the main point of the section, and its use. After dealing with these preliminaries, a teacher goes on to explain the work itself. To do this one first examines the content (*res ipsae*) of the book before focusing on the author's words or language. Hyperius identified nine points to be covered in investigating the work itself.[25]

First, one needs to focus on the appropriate Bible version to be used. A teacher diligently compares the most faithful Latin version with the original Hebrew or Greek and if he finds anything deficient, he provides

---

[23] Ibid. 371; cf. 383. These locations indicate that Hyperius' 'common method' was based in part on professors he had observed during his studies in Paris, his travels to Cologne, Marburg, Erfurt, Leipzig, and Wittenberg, and his visits to Cambridge and Oxford. Krause, *Andreas Gerhard Hyperius*, 16–21.

[24] Ibid. 371–4.

[25] Ibid. 375–83.

a better translation and gives the reason. Second, one then explains the content of the work. To do this one first reviews the whole section being considered and briefly explains its content. Then, after reading a verse, one explains its meaning thoroughly. This is done sometimes by an *ecphrasis*, the simplest rendering of the meaning, sometimes by a paraphrase, and sometimes by way of annotation based on the arts of dialectic and rhetoric. In such annotation the causes (material, formal, efficient, and final) or the circumstances (who, what, where, how often, why, how, when) or the antecedents and consequents, or the form and force of individual arguments are considered, sometimes by analysis, sometimes by questions, sometimes by analogies. These are only some of the interpretative techniques that may be appropriate.[26]

Third, once the meaning has been precisely explained in this way the teacher examines the significance of the author's words. One should explain how much significance a whole verse has and then the significance of its individual parts. Fourth, sometimes a confirmation of the verse or of its interpretation is added. In the fifth place, if appropriate, one may take note of comments of other interpreters on the passage, indicating what is rightly or wrongly stated. Sixth, if another passage does not outwardly appear to agree with the one under consideration, one seeks to harmonize (*consiliet*) them.

Seventh, after explaining the content, one carefully examines the author's words. Here one observes (1) whether any word is ambiguous and in what sense it is used in the present passage; (2) whether a term is used in some figurative sense; (3) whether any phrase is worthy of note; (4) whether there is any allusion to another passage of Scripture or to something else; (5) whether there is any emphasis or subtlety; and (6) whether any word or phrase contains anything that may serve doctrine or exhortation. Eighth, a scholastic interpreter observes what in a passage may be useful for the present time. Following Paul he shows if anything is of service for doctrine, reproof, instruction, correction, or consolation. Ninth, after all the previous items have been treated, it is sometimes useful to examine some important question (*quaestio*) or appropriate commonplace that may arise in the passage. These should be examined with great care, following the procedure for investigating commonplaces outlined below.

This is the procedure that a scholastic interpreter (*scholasticus interpres*) uses for biblical exegesis. Hyperius, however, did not insist that such a method be rigidly followed in every detail. The more briefly and clearly

---

[26]   At this point Hyperius digressed and attempted to justify the use of dialectic and rhetoric in theological interpretation. For example, he asserted that the liberal arts are gifts of the Holy Spirit, and even the prophets, apostles, and Christ himself used syllogisms, enthymemes, and inductions. Ibid. 376–8.

such scholastic exposition is done, the better it is for the students. It is not necessary to move their emotions. The main virtue of a good teacher is clarity and fluency in expression. Prolixity only leads to boredom. Moreover, it would be ridiculous for a teacher always to follow precisely the same procedure. If this is done, such teaching will leave the impression of producing an overwhelming pile of details. Indeed, many things are not necessary and are not appropriate to teach to youth.[27]

Still, Hyperius considered it important for both students and teachers to be familiar with such procedures. He outlined them so that students might readily recognize what method a teacher was using and in what order topics were examined.

> Indeed, it is certain that whoever knows that there are two ways of interpreting the Scriptures, the one scholastic, the other popular, and can discern what characterizes each, will, once he has discovered which of the two a public interpreter is following, be a listener in all lectures not only with his mind but also with his eyes and ears; he will be more attentive to the instructor than he otherwise would be, and will also grasp everything said by the instructor much more quickly and easily than others do.[28]

For the teacher, following a sure prearranged method of instruction will much alleviate the burden of his task.

He went on to outline the 'scholastic method' (*methodum scholasticam*) of explaining commonplaces (*locos communes*) or serious questions (*quaestiones*).[29] He asserted that it would be silly to follow a procedure that treated every topic according to the rules of dialectic and only considered: whether it exists, what it is, what kind of thing it is, in what parts is it divided, what are its causes, what are its effects, what things are connected with it, and what are its opposites. He offered several reasons for not adhering rigidly to these rules. Even Aristotle did not everywhere observe the dialectical method that he prescribed. The nature of the commonplaces do not always allow it; for example, when a topic cannot be divided into smaller parts. For controversies sometimes only the causes and circumstances need to be considered when these are the heart of the issue. Finally, not only simple themes (e.g. faith, law, and similar concepts) but also compound themes (e.g. Christ is truly God and truly man) need to be investigated, and the dialectical procedure is not very useful for the latter.

Hence, especially for beginners, Hyperius proposed a procedure for <u>treating theological</u> commonplaces that was more appropriate to their

[27]　Ibid. 383–4.

[28]　Ibid. 384.

[29]　Hyperius later called this procedure the 'scholastic method' of treating commonplaces, ibid. 471.

nature. This procedure was based partly on the questions of the dialecticians and partly on a consideration of causes and circumstances.

He first outlined a seven-step procedure for explaining simple themes,[30] and then turned to compound themes. For simple themes the interpreter first examines the definition of the term, in Latin as well as in Greek or Hebrew, and considers its different meanings. Then he proceeds to define the thing denoted by the term, drawing from Scripture, the Church Fathers, and medieval scholastics and canonists. He adds some proofs drawn from the Scriptures and the Fathers, and refutes any wrong definition. If there is some controversy about the definition he also surveys that. The second step is a division of the topic into its component parts. This again draws from Scripture, the Fathers, and the scholastics; proofs and refutation of any error regarding the division are added, and any controversy is considered. Third, its causes (efficient, material, formal, and final) or its effects are considered. These are proved and error is refuted again from Scripture and the best authors. In the fourth place the circumstances (who, what, when, etc.) are carefully considered. Fifth, any significant debates about the topic in the churches or schools are examined. Sixth, in an epilogue one repeats the main points that should be remembered. Seventh, it is fitting to note how much spiritual fruit can be gained from the commonplace, both publicly for the church and privately for the conscience.

As for compound themes, Hyperius argued that they must be examined with much more freedom than is done with simple themes, for several reasons. Sometimes both sides of such themes need to be examined. Sometimes such themes are best brought to light by discussing their causes and circumstances. Sometimes a theme requires only a brief treatment in a few theses confirmed by Scripture; sometimes it requires extensive treatment. Moreover, no writers have considered the commonplaces by exactly the same method. Even Paul, taught by the Holy Spirit, scarcely explained two topics in the same way.

For all these reasons and more, Hyperius noted, teachers may diverge from the method they usually follow in the schools. Many practical factors may cause a teacher to alter his procedure and not treat everything with equal attention.[31]

Hyperius concluded his discussion of method in *De recte formando* by noting that the dialecticians of his day contended that every way of teaching can be reduced to three methods: the analytic (or resolutive), which descends from the end to the causes and principles; the synthetic

---

[30]   Ibid. 385–7. Hyperius outlined the same procedure for a scholastic treatment of simple commonplaces again in Book III, 471–3.

[31]   Ibid. 387–9. In Book III, 474, he advised that for compound themes it would be adequate to follow a popular form of explanation.

(or compositive), which ascends from the principles and causes to the end; and the definitive (or horistic), which proceeds from the definition to an explanation of its individual parts.[32] He responded that all scholars concede that these methods of dialectics are more fitting for teaching the liberal arts and for writing philosophically about the human disciplines than for discussing passages and commonplaces of theology. Indeed they are least useful for continuous exposition of Scripture. Moreover, scholars in the higher disciplines, such as theology, want to treat their subjects more freely, rather than being bound to the canons of dialectics. Even the master of method, Aristotle, did so.

However, if one wished to relate Hyperius' procedures to these three methods, he conceded that for continuous interpretation (i.e. exegesis) of Scripture the resolutive method is recommended; for explaining individual theological commonplaces (i.e. dogmatics) sometimes the compositive and sometimes the definitive method has a place. Still, he noted that in books that systematically treat theological commonplaces, theologians declare that they themselves are the most skillful observers of method. Also, every discipline, including theology, has its own character that distinguishes it from others. And the nature of many commonplaces by no means allows the precise methodical treatment of dialectics. For these reasons, Hyperius offered an alternative — a sort of 'common method' based on the practice of distinguished interpreters, a method that was not philosophical but theological.[33]

THE DISTINCTION IN EARLY REFORMED ORTHODOXY

Hyperius' formulation of the scholastic-popular distinction directly influenced theologians of early Reformed orthodoxy. The distinction became

---

[32]   For the background of these three methods, which can be traced back to Galen and the medical tradition, see Neal Gilbert, *Renaissance Concepts of Method* (New York: Columbia University Press, 1960).

[33]   *De recte formando*, 389–91. In the second edition of this work (*De theologo* (1559), 421–2) Hyperius slightly revised this section on the three methods. The argument is essentially the same, but Hyperius was less reluctant to relate his approach to the three methods. He also explicitly mentioned Galen as one who did not completely follow his own methods. In his unfinished dogmatic work *Methodi theologiae, sive praecipuorum christianae religionis locorum communium libri tres* (Basel, 1567), Hyperius forthrightly identified the method of his system as the synthetic or compositive, proceeding from God's Word as the principle of theology to the end, the consummation (15). Later in Reformed orthodoxy the analytic and synthetic methods became common options in theological methodology. See G. Hartvelt, 'Over de Methode der Dogmatiek in de Eeuw der Reformatie', *Gereformeerd Theologisch Tijdschrift* 62 (1962), 97–149.

well known in this period, though sometimes the 'popular' approach became referred to as 'ecclesiastical', since its place was in the church.

This influence is most apparent in Reformed theologians like Georg Sohn and Wilhelm Zepper who had a connection with Marburg where Hyperius had earlier taught. Sohn had studied at Marburg and became a theology professor there and then at Heidelberg. His *De verbo Dei et eius tractatione libri duo* (Herborn, 1588) includes sections on scholastic interpretation and ecclesiastical interpretation:

> Interpretation therefore is twofold, the one scholastic (*scholastica*), the other ecclesiastical or popular (*ecclesiastica seu popularis*); and similarly, one interpreter is scholastic, the other ecclesiastical. The former is commonly called a professor and teacher; the latter a churchman, preacher, and minister of the Word. The scholastic kind of interpretation, devised especially for teaching, is what is treated briefly and plainly within the walls of the schools in the assembly of the educated. Therefore a scholastic interpreter or professor requires educated listeners for whom he will unravel and explain Scripture briefly and plainly according to their mental capacity, with the help of the languages and dialectic; and he will examine conflicting interpretations, but he will be engaged in confirming and refuting of dogmas more than in instructing about life and conduct. For he will only briefly point out passages of instruction or consolation and correction, which the preacher ought to treat more extensively at the popular level.

> The ecclesiastical kind of interpretation, devised for moving and changing the hearts of listeners, is what is treated prudently and ornately for the people in the sanctuary. Therefore it admits people of every rank and listeners of every kind, educated and uneducated, old and young, male and female. [The minister] explains Scripture to them prudently and ornately. For this the precepts of the rhetoricians provide some assistance.[34]

Wilhelm Zepper, a former student at Marburg and pastor at Herborn, was also influenced by Hyperius' formulations, but was critical of scholastic treatments of theology that did not serve the popular practice of the churches. In his *Politia ecclesiastica*, the first systematic Reformed treatment of church polity, Zepper blamed the unhappy state of the churches partly on academies where only the theory of theology was taught while practice was neglected. For him scholastic theory must be wedded to practice.[35]

---

[34] *Opera* 1 (Herborn, 1609), 35–6. As examples of such scholastic exegetical interpretation Sohn identified the Levites, certain commentaries of Origen, Basil, Jerome, Augustine, Ambrose and Lyra, and commentaries of Melanchthon, Calvin, Beza, Hyperius (on Isaiah and some Pauline epistles), Oecolampadius, Bucer, and Vermigli.

[35] *Politia ecclesiastica* (1595; Herborn, 1607²), 11, 29.

As one, the theological faculty constantly persists in continuous theory (*theoria*), namely in a scholastic (*scholastica*) treatment of the commonplaces and analysis and interpretation of the holy books. But about the way to apply the commonplaces and interpretation of Scripture ecclesiastically and popularly (*ecclesiastice and populariter*) to the true edifying of ignorant people in faith and godliness there is the greatest silence in the theological schools.[36]

In his homiletics Zepper noted that in the disposition or organizing of a sermon 'the popular (*popularis*) pastor of a church delights in a freer course of action and is not confined within the bounds of the art of logic as precisely as a scholastic teacher (*doctor scholasticus*) is, but more often employs the method of prudence in his sermons'.[37] His discussion of the difference between a teacher and a pastor depended, even in his choice of phrases, on Hyperius' distinction in *De formandis*:

> There is, however, a great difference between a school teacher (*doctorem scholasticum*) and a church pastor (*pastorem ecclesiasticum*). The former, in any theological passage presented for consideration, unravels, investigates, and explains every single thing precisely word for word, and with as much sound judgment and acumen as possible searches for verifying arguments, in such a way, however, that confined within the narrow walls of the schools and absolutely concisely he explains everything by the standard of dialectical brevity and simplicity, wholly disregarding embellishment, profuseness, and digressions. The latter, however, as one who knows that he has to deal with a crowd of ignorant and uneducated common people and who focuses all his energy on edifying the church, with singular discretion selects from the proposed subject, however broad and large it may be, only those things that he considers to be most appropriate to the present persons, time, place, and state of things, also to the present works of God, that is, his blessings and judgments.[38]

Herborn theologian Matthias Martinius' dogmatic work *Methodus S.S. theologiae* contains two chapters 'on the calling of ministers to teach popularly (*populariter*)' and 'on the calling of ministers to teach scholastically (*scholastice*)'.[39]

In a Dutch polemical tract in the Arminian controversy, Johannes Uitenbogaert argued: 'That Calvin said Luther had written about these things [predestination] scholastically (*scholastijckelijck*), Melanchthon more

---

[36]   Ibid. 12–14.

[37]   Zepper, *Ars habendi et audiendi conciones sacras* (Siegen, 1598), 7.

[38]   Ibid. 65.

[39]   *Methodus S.S. theologiae* (Herborn, 1603), 102–5, 516–17.

popularly (*gemeynsamer*), was also not the case; the difference was not in the method, but in the content.'[40]

At the Synod of Dort in 1618 British delegate Joseph Hall warned in a sermon that the church should not meddle with the subtleties of the schools:

> There are, to be sure, two sorts of theology, the one scholastic (*scholastica*), the other popular (*popularis*). The latter seems to view the foundation of religion; the former looks at the form and decoration of its exterior. Knowledge of the latter makes a Christian; knowledge of the former makes a debater.[41]

Before drafting the Canons of Dort, the synod discussed how they should be drawn up. The president, Johannes Bogerman, advised:

> The order and style of these Canons ought to be adapted to the instruction of these churches. Let everything be presented plainly and simply, and at the same time not too meagerly, so that the Canons may not be scholastic or academic but ecclesiastical (*scholastici seu academici sed ecclesiastici*).

Bishop George Carleton of the English delegation also advised that 'the style of the Canons be popular, not scholastic (*popularis non scholasticus*)'.[42]

Herborn professor Johann Heinrich Alsted also used the distinction to describe his 'scholastic theology':

> Scholastic theology is so called because it is accustomed to be set forth and explained by the method which is appropriate for the schools and, besides, is more precise than the popular (*popularis*) method which prevails in the church among the people, since it is not the method of prudence, which is called exoteric and popular, that flourishes in the schools but rather the method of wisdom, which is called acroamatic and scholastic.[43]

These few examples suggest a rather wide acceptance of the scholastic-popular distinction in early Reformed orthodoxy.

CONCLUSIONS

Several conclusions can be drawn from Hyperius' reflections. He did not claim originality for his scholastic method, but rather drew up a 'common

---

[40] *Noodighe Antwoordt op der Contra-Remonstranten Tegen-Vertooch* (The Hague, 1617), 134.
[41] *Acta synodi nationalis Dordrechti habitae* (Leiden, 1620), I:43.
[42] As reported in the journal of delegate Caspar Sibelius. See my 'Reformed Scholasticism', 496.
[43] *Theologia scholastica didactica, exhibens locos communes theologicos methodo scholastica* (Hanover, 1618), preface.

method' based on procedures that he had noticed in earlier writers and in the teaching practices of professors he had observed. He clearly saw himself in continuity with an ongoing scholastic tradition in sixteenth-century universities. Yet his attempt to formulate a common method appears to be the first time that a theologian in the Reformed tradition offered developed reflection on theological methodology, including the difference between a scholastic and popular way of doing theology.

For Hyperius the scholastic approach was only a method or way of explaining the content of theology, not a set of doctrines. 'Scholastic' for him referred to teaching procedures that belong in the schools; this sense of the term was intimately related to its original sense referring to 'school' matters. As he saw it, the scholastic method simply meant a very thorough and precise analysis of a biblical passage or theological topic; for example, a careful examination of all aspects of the context of a biblical book. The tools of dialectic could well be used or adapted for such analysis, but only when allowed by the nature of the topic. Theologians should not simply adopt dialectical procedures, since theology requires its own method appropriate to exegesis and dogmatics. It is clear that with Hyperius the scholastic approach did not yet heavily rely on philosophical categories. A further step in that direction would be taken by Antoine de Chandieu, for whom the scholastic method meant an analytical treatment of theology using Aristotelian logic.[44]

Hyperius' distinction between scholastic and popular generally reflected the difference between the scholastic and humanist traditions. His idea of a popular explanation of theology was marked by rhetorical eloquence, a fundamental emphasis of Renaissance humanism; his homiletics is even characterized by its application of rhetorical tools to preaching. In a sixteenth-century context where humanists heavily criticized the scholastic tradition, and where the early Reformers strongly reflected the humanist tendency, Hyperius tended to balance scholastic and humanist concerns, since for him both the scholastic and the popular approaches were legitimate.[45] By thus legitimizing the scholastic approach in theology, Hyperius' scholastic-popular distinction may be considered a significant factor in the emergence of Reformed scholasticism.

Recognition of the scholastic-popular distinction also helps us to discern the limits of Reformed scholasticism. If both scholastic and popular treatments of theology are legitimate, both may be used by the

---

[44] See my 'Antoine de Chandieu's Call for a Scholastic Reformed Theology (1580)' in *Later Calvinism: International Perspectives*, ed. W. Fred Graham, Sixteenth Century Essays and Studies 22 (Kirksville, Mo.: Sixteenth Century Journal, 1994), 159–90.

[45] Erika Rummel *The Humanist-Scholastic Debate in the Renaissance and Reformation* (Cambridge, Mass.: Harvard University Press, 1995).

same person. Which approach is used depends on the social context and audience. Thus in a university setting a theologian may present a very scholastic treatment of theology, but in preaching or in devotional writing the same theologian may use a very popular style. And behind a popular explanation of a topic may lie a very scholastic analysis. If some writings of a theologian are scholastic and others are popular, this does not warrant the conclusion that that person is a transitional figure between the Reformation and Protestant scholasticism.

Though sometimes the scholastic approach spilled over into popular contexts, the scholastic-popular distinction was generally recognized in later Reformed orthodoxy and helped to prevent extreme scholasticizing of theology in inappropriate contexts. Indeed, Hyperius' emphasis that a scholastic analysis must always note the use of a passage or theme for the church helped promote the idea that a scholastic approach must ultimately serve the people.

PART 3
THE BRITISH CONNECTION

1

Protestant 'Scholasticism' at Elizabethan Cambridge:
William Perkins and a Reformed Theology of the Heart

Paul R. Schaefer

'Theology is the science of living blessedly forever. Blessed life ariseth from the knowledge of God and therefore it ariseth from the knowledge of ourselves, because we know God by looking into ourselves.'[1] In this famous quotation from the outset of his best known work, 'A

---

[1] William Perkins, 'A Golden Chaine', I:11. All Perkins references in this essay, unless noted otherwise, will be from William Perkins, *Workes* 3 vols. (Cambridge, 1608–9).

Note: Volume III of Perkins' *Workes* is divided into three parts. Any reference to Volume III will therefore have a '1' or a '2' follow the volume number and precede the page number to show from which part the reference is taken.

While this essay hopes to place Perkins in historical context, the focus has more to do with theology than biography. This, along with space constraints, precludes a detailing of his life. For an overall summary of Perkins' life, see Ian Breward, 'Introduction', *The Work of William Perkins*, ed. I. Breward (Appleford: Courtenay, 1970), 1–100. For some of the scholarly discussions about his theology, see Joel R. Beeke, *Assurance of Faith: Calvin, English Puritanism and the Dutch Second Reformation* (New York: Peter Lang, 1991); Richard A. Muller, *Christ and the Decree* (repr. Grand Rapids: Baker, 1988); Charles Robert Munson, 'William Perkins: Theologian of Transition' (PhD diss., Case Western Reserve University, 1971); V.L. Priebe, 'The Covenant Theology of William Perkins' (PhD diss., Drew University, 1967); Mark Randolph Shaw, 'The Marrow of Practical Divinity: A Study in the Theology of William Perkins' (ThD diss., Westminster Theological Seminary, 1981); F.E. Stoeffler, *The Rise of Evangelical Pietism* (Leiden: E.J. Brill, 1965); Andrew Woolsey, 'Unity and Continuity in Covenantal Thought: A Study in the Reformed Tradition to the Westminster Assembly' (PhD diss., Glasgow University, 1988).

Golden Chaine', William Perkins, one of the most prolific English
Reformed theologians of the Elizabethan period, showed twin concerns that marked his understanding of the theological enterprise. In
calling theology a 'science', he declared his affinity with a tradition
which viewed theology as a branch of scholarly pursuit. In admonish-
ing that its concern was for 'living blessedly forever', he declared that
when it left the academy, it concerned itself with matters that affected
the deepest recesses of the heart.

Such a merging of the life of the mind and the life of daily piety leads
to at least two difficult questions confronted by modern scholars as they
try to assess both the style and the content of the theology of this thinker
often called a 'Puritan',[2] especially as it relates to the Reformed theology
of the earlier sixteenth century: (1) was Perkins (and indeed were his
compatriots in the tradition called by Haller 'the spiritual brotherhood')[3]
a 'scholastic', a 'pietist' (*avant la lettre*), a 'primitivist', a 'humanist', or
rather something else when it came to viewing the theological task; and
(2) even given the label by which scholars might designate Perkins'
theological method and/or concerns, did his 'theology . . . of the blessed
life' differ markedly from that of his predecessors in the Reformed
tradition, in particular John Calvin, as they pondered the Christian life?

---

[2]   Ever since William Haller, *The Rise of Puritanism* (New York: Columbia
University Press, 1938), M.M. Knappen, *Tudor Puritanism* (Chicago: University of
Chicago Press, 1938), and Perry Miller, *The New England Mind in the Seventeenth
Century* (Cambridge, Mass.: Harvard University Press, 1939), scholars have debated
what constitutes a 'Puritan'. Some of the most important works over the last four
decades which have entered into this conversation include the following: Theodore
Dwight Bozeman, *To Live Ancient Lives* (Chapel Hill: University of North Carolina
Press, 1988); Stephen Brachlow, *The Communion of Saints* (Oxford: Oxford Univer-
sity Press, 1988); Patrick Collinson, *The Elizabethan Puritan Movement* (Oxford:
Clarendon Press, 1967); C.H. and K. George, *The Protestant Mind of the English
Reformation* (Princeton: Princeton University Press, 1961); Basil Hall, 'Puritanism:
The Problem of Definition' in *Studies in Church History* 2, ed. G.J. Cuming (London:
Nelson, 1965), 283–96; Christopher Hill, *Society and Puritanism in Pre-Revolutionary
England* (London: Secker and Warburg, 1964); Peter Lake, *Moderate Puritans and the
Elizabethan Church* (Cambridge: Cambridge University Press, 1982); John Morgan,
Godly Learning (Cambridge: Cambridge University Press, 1986); J.F.H. New,
Puritans and Anglicans: The Basis of Their Opposition (Stanford: Stanford University
Press, 1964); H.C. Porter, *Reformation and Reaction in Tudor Cambridge* (Cambridge:
Cambridge University Press, 1958); Margo Todd, *Christian Humanism and the Puritan
Social Order* (Cambridge: Cambridge University Press, 1987); John Von Rohr, *The
Covenant of Grace in Puritan Thought* (Atlanta: Scholars, 1986); Dewey Wallace,
Puritans and Predestination (Chapel Hill, N.C.: University of North Carolina Press,
1982); and Michael Walzer, *The Revolution of the Saints* (Cambridge, Mass.: Harvard
University Press, 1965).
[3]   See Haller, *Rise of Puritanism*, 15ff.

This second question has become all the more pressing since the publication of R.T. Kendall's *Calvin and English Calvinism to 1649.*[4] In that work, Kendall asserts that the tradition from England called 'Calvinism', which had as one of its primary architects William Perkins and was codified in the Confession and Catechisms of the Westminster Assembly, hardly deserves the rubric 'Calvinistic' since the thinkers within it modified Calvin's Christ-centred theology of grace in favour of a more anthropocentric model which they learned from thinkers like Beza. Due to the restrictions of space, a full examination of Perkins in comparison with Calvin is not possible. Instead, this essay will hope to show that such a thesis misses the mark by failing to deal sensitively with the differences between Calvin's and Perkins' contexts and by failing to note Perkins' Christ-centredness even within his very forthright call to holiness.

THE EDUCATIONAL AND SOCIAL CONTEXT

Although 'Puritans' are often characterized by their intense loyalty to Scripture[5] (hence their so-called 'preciseness'), the mainstream Puritans

---

[4]   R.T. Kendall, *Calvin and English Calvinism to 1649* (Oxford: Oxford University Press, 1979). For two other works which argue in a similar vein see: Holmes Rolston III, *John Calvin versus the Westminster Confession* (Richmond, Va.: John Knox, 1972); and William Chalker, 'Calvin and Some Seventeenth Century English Calvinists' (PhD diss., Duke University, 1961). For some of the works which criticize the discontinuity thesis see: Beeke, *Assurance of Faith*; Mark Dever, 'Richard Sibbes and "The Truly Evangelicall Church of England": A Study in Reformed Divinity and Early Stuart Conformity' (PhD diss., University of Cambridge, 1992); Paul Helm, *Calvin and the Calvinists* (Edinburgh: Banner of Truth, 1982); George Marsden, 'Perry Miller's Rehabilitation of the Puritans: A Critique', *Church History* 39 (1970), 91–105; Jonathan Rainbow, *The Will of God and the Cross: An Historical and Theological Study of John Calvin's Doctrine of Limited Redemption* (Allison Park, Pa.: Pickwick, 1990); W. Stanford Reid, 'Review: R.T. Kendall's *Calvin and English Calvinism to 1649*', *Westminster Theological Journal* 43 (1980) 155–64; Shaw, *Marrow of Practical Divinity*; Von Rohr, *The Covenant of Grace.*

[5]   Hence, Bozeman sees the Puritan vision as a 'primitivist' vision, one which leaned towards 'the standards of the Great Time [i.e. the world of the Bible]'. While he himself admits that Puritan views 'should not be confused with the Protestant anti-intellectualism of then or later times', his choice of primitivism, if used to describe educational concerns or epistemological foundations, would seem unfortunate. The revelation of God in Scripture had primacy in matters of both faith and reason, but the 'Cambridge spiritual brothers' never devalued 'humane learning', exchanging it for some 'Bible only' ideology. While the 'Puritans' had an extremely high regard for biblical authority, even at times seemingly making their 'precisenesse' overshadow the value they found in the liberal arts or even the traditions of the

hardly disregarded educational pursuits and indeed valued the educational practices of the day. Indeed, the seventeenth-century historian, Thomas Fuller, wrote that Perkins sought to transmit the teaching of the schools to his wider audience: 'our Perkins brought the schools into the pulpit, and, unshelling their controversies out of their hard school terms, made thereof plain and wholesome meat for his people'.[6] Perkins himself, while pointing out the goal of the preaching of the word, 'let us remember the end we aim at is not humane or carnall: our purpose is to save souls . . .', nevertheless also advocated a learned ministry and repudiated what he called 'Anabaptisticall fancies' which favoured 'revelations of the Spirit' and 'contemne[d] humane learning and the studie of Scripture'.[7]

Just what, however, was taught in the schools? In many ways the Cambridge which Perkins entered as a student appeared similar to the university as it had been since medieval times. The basic scholastic structure of the curriculum remained intact.[8] To earn a degree, Cambridge required students to know and use all the 'scholastic forms' such as disputation and declamation. Aristotle and the medieval reading of Aristotle remained a primary source of educational nourishment.[9] Nevertheless, subtle changes, possibly unnoticeable to many of the educators themselves, appeared as cracks in the medieval educational edifice.

The statutory curriculum itself, while scholastic and rather traditional, deviated from the standards of the Middle Ages. In keeping with

---

patristic period, they in fact never denied the usefulness of learning in the arts or the need to show that they stood in continuity with the Church Fathers. In fact, along with the positive statements quoted from Perkins on the liberal arts found in this chapter, one should also consult two treatises by Perkins where he unpacked the differences between Roman Catholicism and the Reformed faith, one with the intriguing title 'The Reformed Catholicke' and the other a defence of Reformed religion by showing its continuity with the Fathers entitled 'A Demonstration of the Forged Catholicism'. See Bozeman, *Ancient Lives*, 70, and Perkins, 'The Reformed Catholicke', I:549–618, and 'A Demonstration of the Forged Catholicism', II:486–600.

[6]   Thomas Fuller, *The Holy State and The Profane State* (London: J. Nichols, 1841), 81.

[7]   Perkins, 'On the Calling of the Ministrie,' III:2:431, 442.

[8]   For the statutes governing the Cambridge curriculum, see '*Statuta Reg. Eliza., c.*' and 'Interpretation of the Statutes' in *The Privileges of the University of Cambridge*, ed. George Dyer (London, 1824), I:164–206 and 277–99 respectively. Also consult Harris Francis Fletcher, *The Intellectual Development of John Milton*, 2 (Urbana: Illinois University Press, 1961), esp. ch. 1, and Mark Curtis, *Oxford and Cambridge in Transition, 1558–1640* (Oxford: Clarendon, 1959), 89–94.

[9]   See William Costello, *The Scholastic Curriculum in Early Seventeenth Century Cambridge* (Cambridge, Mass.: Harvard University Press, 1959), 35–8, 146–50.

humanist concerns, rhetoric was given more emphasis and moved from the later years to the first year of the BA. Logic, nevertheless, retained its high profile and was taught in the second and third years.[10] And, while, as Morgan contends, 'Aristotelianism proved a hardy plant',[11] the Aristotelianism learned by Cambridge undergraduates had undergone a facelift. The increased concern of Renaissance thinkers for textual studies found its way to Tudor Cambridge and brought with it a new reading of Aristotle in light of his own ancient context and in light of other classical authors.[12]

There is also, of course, the issue of Ramism. For some thinkers (but not all) often denominated 'Puritan', especially those such as Perkins and William Ames, Ramism as an alternative to medieval scholastic Aristotelianism provided a different way of framing the structure of their thought. Yet some caution is necessary here. Ever since Perry Miller first brought the importance of Ramist thought as a source for the Cambridge brotherhood's thought to the attention of the scholarly community,[13] scholars have differed widely over Ramism's relative importance when discussing the doctrines espoused even by Ramist advocates like Perkins and Ames. Indeed the general view held today is that Ramism, while certainly an important influence, should *not* be viewed as providing *the* blueprint for these divines' theological discourse.[14] Even McKim, who wrote the definitive work on Perkins and Ramism, states: 'The philosophy of Ramus provided [for Perkins and Ames] definitions for and grounded theology's centring focus on God. This was where Puritans who followed Calvin believed the proper emphasis should be. Ramism as adapted by the Puritans did not give specific content to theology as

---

[10] See Curtis, *Oxford and Cambridge*, 85–93.

[11] Morgan, *Godly Learning*, 106.

[12] See Todd, *Christian Humanism*, 61–3, 80–1. She writes on page 62, largely in criticism of Costello who believes that the statutory requirements show the continued indebtedness of Tudor and Jacobean Cambridge educators to medieval views: 'the medieval structure . . . was maintained by the statutes, as were the medieval pedagogical methods . . . But the way in which such integral parts of the medieval curriculum were presented to the undergraduates had changed dramatically.' Also note Curtis on page 93: 'Too often historians of education have mistaken rules and regulations for evidence of practice.' Finally, see Morgan, 226–8.

[13] See Miller, *The New England Mind*, chapters 5–7.

[14] See Bozeman, 67–8, Curtis, 93–5, Morgan, 110–12, Todd, 67–8, and Richard Muller, *God, Creation, and Providence in the Thought of Jacob Arminius* (Grand Rapids: Baker, 1991), 16–20. Muller writes on page 16: 'It would be a mistake to view Ramus as either an adversary to all things Aristotelian or as a humanistic liberator of theology from "scholastic subtleties". Ramus' thought is better understood as a modified Aristotelianism in the tradition of the late medieval logician Rudolf Agricola . . . [S]ome of [Ramus'] best arguments were drawn directly from Aristotle.'

such. The sources of theology for the English Puritans were more from Calvin's Geneva [than] from Ramus' Paris.'[15]

Perkins' extremely influential manual on homiletics and exegesis, 'The Arte of Prophesying',[16] showed this reception by the brotherhood of elements of the 'new learning'. Perkins advised the theological student not only to know the definitions, divisions, and properties of 'the substance of Divinity' (a somewhat 'scholastic' approach), but also told them to read diligently the Scriptures 'in this order: using gramaticall, rhetoricall, and logicall analysis, and the helpe of the rest of the arts . . .' (a somewhat 'humanist' approach).[17]

Since the 'aim' was 'to save souls', however, Perkins exhorted would-be preachers to 'conceal the arts' when delivering a message. He urged that 'plaine speech' should proceed from the pulpit, and warned against 'the least ostentation'. Preaching must be 'spiritual and gracious . . . simple and perspicuous', for the preacher's purpose in proclamation was the 'hiding of humane wisdome and the demonstration and showing of the Spirit'. Perkins nevertheless condemned 'barbarisme . . . in the pulpit' and extolled the 'arts, Philosophy, and a variety of reading whilest . . . framing the sermon' as not only laudatory but necessary.[18] A concern for a vigorous spiritual rhetoric combined with a concern for a vigorous piety of the heart ruled the day.

What probably should be inferred from all of this is that scholars must exercise caution when trying to determine the precise 'educational

---

[15] Donald K. McKim, *Ramism in William Perkins' Theology* (New York: Peter Lang, 1987), 167. For another sympathetic treatment of Ramist influence on the Cambridge brotherhood, see Keith Sprunger, *The Learned Doctor William Ames* (Urbana: University of Illinois Press, 1972). On Ramism in general, see Walter Ong, *Ramus: Method and the Decay of Dialogue* (Cambridge, Mass.: Harvard University Press, 1958).

[16] Perkins, 'The Arte of Prophesying', II:731–62. For a discussion of the importance of Perkins' 'The Arte of Prophesying', see Teresa Toulouse, *The Art of Prophesying: New England Sermons and the Shaping of Belief* (Athens, Ga.: University of Georgia Press, 1987), 14–23.

[17] Ibid. II:756–7. It is interesting to compare this statement with the description of an earlier Cambridge student 'conference' which included Laurence Chaderton, Perkins' tutor at Christ's College, Cambridge: 'At their meetings they had constant Exercises: first, They began with prayer, and then applied themselves to the Study of the Scriptures; one was for the Originall Languages, another's for the true sense and meaning of the Text; another gathered the Doctrines; and thus they carried on their several imployments, til at last they went out, like Apollos, eloquent men, and mighty in the Scriptures . . .' From Samuel Clarke, *The Lives of Thirty-Two Eminent Divines* (London, 1677), 133. Collinson remarks that this 'conference' had affinities with 'the method of biblical study perfected by Protestant humanists in Zurich and widely employed in the continental Reformed churches', *Elizabethan Puritan Movement*, 126.

[18] Ibid. 756–62.

school' to which one like Perkins belonged. Costello's declaration that the Cambridge tradition was 'Protestant and scholastic', even to the point of not only 'understanding' but also 'holding with' some Roman Catholic neo-scholastics,[19] cannot be regarded as adequate. Todd writes: ' "Understood", yes, but "held with"? . . . [T]here is considerable evidence that [Puritan] students and their tutors viewed the reading of neo-scholastics as a necessary evil and many students questioned how necessary it was.'[20]

For 'Protestants of the hotter sort', the Scriptures themselves of course stood as *the* bellweather by which to evaluate all doctrinal and practical concerns. Perkins wrote that since the Bible was 'canonical', it and it alone was 'where the truth is first to be found out and also afterwards to be examined'. Thus, all questions of 'doctrine and worship' must appeal to it for 'the supreme and absolute determination and judgment'.[21] So, while he argued on the one hand that 'Religione hindereth not humane learning as some fondly think; but it is a furthereance and helpe, or rather a perfection of humane learning',[22] Perkins also warned university theologians:

> Now [in the university] we have many occasions to be puft up in self-conceit: we see ourselves grow in time, in degree, in learning, in honour, in name and estimation: . . . what can all of these be but so many baits to allure us to pride and vaine opinions of our own worth?[23]

Thus, although 'Puritans' like Perkins recognized great value in 'humane learning', such learning had its limits. Of course, when Perkins and the Cambridge brothers set limits on the value of education and reason, such limits arose in conjunction with their view of 'natural' human nature as fallen.[24] Perkins, in 'A Golden Chaine', spoke in quite unflattering terms of the human mind apart from grace: 'Men's minds received from Adam: ignorance, namely a want, or rather a deprivation of knowledge in the things of God . . .; impotence, whereby the mind of itself is unable to understand spiritual things, though they be taught; vanity, in that the mind thinketh falsehood truth and truth falsehood.'[25] The result: '[Humane] wisdome is not to be glorified in';[26] rather, the mind must be regenerated.

---

19 Costello, *Scholastic Curriculum*, 121.
20 Todd, *Christian Humanism*, 73.
21 Perkins, 'The Arte of Prophesying', II:731.
22 Perkins, 'A Cloude of Witnesses Leading to Heavenly Canaan', III:2:9.
23 Ibid. 442.
24 Even Todd in her favourable comparison of Puritan and humanist social practices recognizes that they parted company on many theological points. See Todd, *Christian Humanism*, 95.
25 Perkins, 'A Golden Chaine', I:20.
26 Perkins, 'A Commentarie Upon the Epistle to the Galatians', II:416.

Before looking briefly at Perkins' understanding of grace and how grace affected the mind (and the will), some mention should also be made of Perkins' social context as a critic of the established church. The importance of this cannot be down-played given the criticism that Perkins, with his focus on the need for introspection, went beyond Calvin's Christ-centred assurance theology (part of Kendall's claim). Consideration of the 'social context' seems to soften somewhat this criticism. Calvin worked for much of his career in Geneva in a situation where one of the greatest dangers appeared to be new incursions by Rome and its perceived theology of merit. Perkins, on the other hand, worked in Cambridge amongst a people deemed 'Protestant' at least in principle.

Perkins forthrightly accepted the established church of 1559 as a true church of Christ.[27] Thus, the Church of England had been 'reformed according to the Word' for almost a generation by the time he wrote and preached. Yet, amidst this 'Reformed people', Perkins noticed a remarkable lack of true godliness. Thus, he rebuked this Protestant people. The 'complaint literature' produced by Perkins and the Cambridge divines who followed in his wake accorded well with tracts and treatises produced elsewhere against the settlement and society in general.[28]

In chastizing members within the church, Perkins focused not so much on matters of liturgical rites or polity but on this lack of godliness. In 'Galatians', first preached in 1599, he lamented that while reformed religion had been established for 'fortie years' (i.e. since the 1559 settlement), the majority of the people were more interested in 'gaming, drinking, and apparel' than in godly living.[29] In 'Zephaniah', first preached in 1593 and one of Perkins' most revivalistic-style sermons, he proclaimed that for 'five and thirtie' years God's word had been faithfully taught yet ignored by the vast majority of English people: 'But now England, how hast thou requited this kindeness of the Lord. Certainly even with a greater measure of unkindness, that is with more and greater sins than ever Israel did . . . If any man make doubt of this and therefore think I speak too harshly of our church, I will then deal plainly and particularly and rip up the sores of our nation that so they may be healed to the bottom.' Perkins included among these 'common sins of England' the problems of 'ignorance of God's will and worship, . . . contempt of the Christian religion, . . . blasphemy many ways, . . . profanation of the Sabbath, [and] unjust dealing in bargaining betwixt man and man'.

---

[27] For a discussion of Perkins' brand of 'conforming', see Paul R. Schaefer, 'The Spiritual Brotherhood on the Habits of the Heart: Cambridge Protestants and the Doctrine of Sanctification from William Perkins to Thomas Shepard' (DPhil diss., University of Oxford, 1992), 23–9.

[28] See Patrick Collinson, *The Religion of Protestants* (Oxford: Clarendon, 1982), 199–205, 220–5.

[29] Perkins, 'Galatians', II:372.

Perkins maintained that 'without a visible reformation', God's judgment against the nation 'shall certainly be executed'. The answer for 'visible reformation' lay not in separating from the Church of England as the 'blind and besotted Brownists [English separatists]' wanted, however, for 'our church doubtless is God's cornfield'. Amongst this 'corn', nevertheless, grew much 'chaff'. Indeed, since the visible church was 'so full of chaff' and the 'pure wheat'[30] was so 'thin[ly] . . . scattered', he continued, 'England . . . must look to be winnowed'. Such winnowing did not truly take place in separating from the established church since the 'searching' needed 'must not be of other men's hearts and lives, but of our own'.[31]

Although the question of 'voluntarism' as it relates to faith will be treated more below, the preceding note of Perkins as a reformer, and even revivalist,[32] within the established church raises an important point. Perkins spoke to a society in which every member, unless excommunicated, was deemed a member of the covenant people of God. He preached to a nation in which everyone was, at least outwardly, considered a Christian, one within the compass of God's merciful calling to Christ through the preaching of the word. Thus, the charge (primarily by Kendall) that he and those who followed him were 'voluntarists' must be placed within this cultural context — a context which produced what Collinson terms 'secondary voluntarism'.[33] In other words, one should expect these non-separating nonconforming revival-minded Protestants critical of the status quo to appeal to both the will *and* the mind along with the expectation of response as God moved in the heart.[34] Preaching as a means of grace and for response was viewed as the primary way in which God brought 'visible reformation'.

---

[30] Perkins mixed his metaphors from agriculture here.

[31] Perkins, 'A Faithfull and Plaine Exposition Upon the Two First Verses of the Second Chapter of Zephaniah', III:2:423.

[32] This is the kind of language for 'conforming Puritans' like Perkins favoured by O'Day. She says that the 'Puritans' were 'revivalist Protestants [who differed] not in doctrine from the men who support[ed] the settlement, but in attitude. [The Puritans'] spirit [was] essentially critical, revivalist, and outspoken'. Rosemary O'Day, *The English Clergy: The Emergence and Consolidation of a Profession, 1558–1642* (Leicester: Leicester University Press, 1979), xii.

[33] Collinson, *Religion of Protestants*, 247–64.

[34] Of course, such is the nature of preaching as a form of persuasive discourse. Even those who wish to argue discontinuity between these English Reformed divines and earlier Reformed thinkers need to recognize that Reformed thinkers such as Calvin also preached with the expectation of response. For a discussion of how Calvin used persuasive rhetoric, see T.H.L. Parker, *Calvin's Preaching* (Edinburgh: T. & T. Clark, 1992), 114–28. In this same regard, note what Dever says of Sibbes' preaching (which would seem true for Perkins as well): Dever, *Truly Evangelical Church*, 117.

PERKINS (IN BRIEF) ON GRACE, FAITH, AND WORKS

As one reads Perkins' treatises themselves, one notices, that he indeed had been deeply influenced by the Reformed writings of the sixteenth century. For example, the statement from 'A Golden Chaine' quoted at the beginning of this chapter bears a striking resemblance to Calvin's initial remarks in the *Institutes*.[35] One point of disjuncture arises within the similarity, however. Whereas Calvin left in abeyance whether knowledge of God or knowledge of ourselves came first, Perkins forthrightly allowed the interiorizing turn — we know God by looking within. Such a move, while not necessarily constituting a major theological discontinuity, certainly shows Perkins' insistence on a deeply personal and introspective piety; a piety, moreover, which Calvin might have wanted tempered with more objective features. As we shall see, this did not mean, however, that Perkins minimized or curtailed the absolute sovereignty of grace, or that his piety was so self-focused that it lacked the dimension of one looking beyond oneself to Christ in word and sacrament for growth in grace, comfort, and assurance.[36]

While it is true that Perkins stressed the 'inward look', he rejected a type of moral conjecture which told one to look within at one's obedience without at the same time recognizing that only the obedience of Christ provided one's justification before God:

> . . . in that we are justified by an obedience out of ourselves, we are taught utterly to deny ourselves, and go out of ourselves, as having nothing in us whereby we may be saved . . . the obedience of Christ must be unto us the foundation of our obedience: for he performed all righteousness for us, that we might be servants not of sinne, but servants of righteousnesse in all duties of obedience . . . [T]he obedience of Christ must be the foundation of our comfort. In all dangers and temptations, we that beleeve are to oppose the obedience of Christ against the fierce wrath of God, against hel, deth, and condemnation . . . Christ, in respect of his obedience, is our hiding place . . . Let us therefore by our faith, flie to this our hiding

---

[35] 'Nearly all the wisdom we possess, that is to say, true sound wisdom, consists in two parts: the knowledge of God and the knowledge of ourselves. But while joined with many bonds, which one precedes and brings forth the other is not easy to discern. In the first place, no one can look upon himself without immediately turning his thoughts to the contemplation of God, in whom he "lives and moves".' John Calvin, *The Institutes of the Christian Religion* (1559), ed. John T. McNeill and trans. Ford Lewis Battles, Library of Christian Classics, vols. 20-1 (Philadelphia: Westminster, 1960) I:i:1, 35.

[36] For an intriguing article on Perkins' Christocentricity, especially as it compares with Beza's, see Richard Muller, 'Perkins' *A Golden Chaine*: Predestinarian System or Schematized *Ordo Salutis*?', *Sixteenth Century Journal* 9 (1978), 69–81.

it came in the midst of a polemic for the faculty of understanding as the 'seat' of faith against those who wished to place the seat of faith 'partly in the mind, partly in the will'. Why the defence of a type of intellectualism, then? The answer could be because Perkins wanted to ground faith in the promise, the sure word of God in Christ. True faith, therefore, had to be knowledge, because an implicit faith, a faith which merely trusted in the word of the Church without knowledge, failed.

It also could be that Perkins wanted believers to avoid the danger of making love the form of faith. Such a view of love would allow human responses in works of pious affection towards God to play a part in justification before God. To equate faith with love would be to make it part of the fountain of grace. Perkins contended against such notions:

> . . . love is an effect which proceedeth from faith . . . And in nature, they differ greatly. Christ is the fountaine of the water of life. Faith in the heart is as the pipes and leads that *receive in*, and hold the water: and love in some part is as the cocke of the conduit, *that lets out* the water to every commer. The propertie of the hand is to hold, and of it selfe it cannot cutte: yet by a knife or other instrument put in the hand, it cuts: the hand of the soule is faith, and his propertie is to apprehend Christ with all his benefits: and by it selfe it can do nothing else: yet joine love unto it, and it will bee effectuall in all good duties.

Love and faith then had to joined together, but not in a way that would make works of love part of the way in which true faith was wrought in the heart. That prerogative belonged to God alone as the word was preached to the ear and as the Holy Spirit attended the heart.[44]

---

[44] All references in this paragraph are from ibid., I:125 emphasises this. Perkins followed this discussion by noting that the Holy Spirit 'wrought faith' by 'two principall actions': 'First, the enlightening of the mind: the second, the mooving of the will. For the first, the Holy Ghost enlightens mans mindes with further knowledge of the law, than nature can afford, and thereby makes them to see the sinnes of their hearts and lives and the uglinesse thereof. . . . Afterward, the same Spirit opens the eye to understand and consider seriously of righteousnesse and life eternall promised in Christ. This done, then comes the second worke of the Holy Ghost, which is the inflaming of the will, that a man having considered his fearfull estate by reason of sinne and the benefits of Christs death, might hunger after Christ. . . . And when he hath stirred up a man to desire reconciliation with God in Christ, then withal he gives him grace to pray not onely for life eternall, but especially for the free remission and pardon of all his sinnes. . . . After which he sends his Spirit into the same heart, that desireth reconciliation with God, and remission of sinnes in Christ: and doth seale up the same in his heart by a lively and plentifull assurance thereof.'
Perkins discussed the question of how much humiliation a person needed to apprehend the mercy of God in Christ in 'Whether a Man', I:383: 'A true saing it

As Perkins reflected on the nature of the Christian life, moreover, he asserted that Christ stood behind all of the 'degrees of God's love', his term in 'A Golden Chaine' for the application of redemption (effectual calling-justification-sanctification-glorification) by the Holy Spirit. As to sanctification, that very important concern of his, Perkins contended that Christ, through his death and resurrection, accomplished it for believers as its 'material' cause and the Holy Spirit applied the power of Christ's work to believers for their sanctification as its 'efficient' cause. Christ and the Spirit worked in the elect the desire to be renewed, leading them to forsake sin and pursue holiness: '[B]y the ... power [of Christ's death] he . . . abolished the corruption of sin in us his members. . . . By the power of Christ's resurrection . . . he causeth in [his members] an endeavour and purpose to live according to the will of God. The efficient cause of both [this abolition and this living] is the Holy Ghost who doth by his divine power convey himself into the believers' hearts and in them, by applying the power of Christ . . . createth holiness'.[45]

Describing the relation between the believer and Christ as a 'mystical union', Perkins contended that all benefits of such a spiritual relationship, including the sanctification in which the believer was so intimately involved, sprang from the merit of Christ's blood and could only be applied by the sovereign work of the Spirit. Indeed, this union arose before the first faltering steps of sanctification appeared and was absolutely

is, that the right way to go unto heaven is to saile by hell, and there is no man living that feeles the power and vertue of Christ, which first hath not felt the paines of hell. But yet in these pains there is a difference: and it is the will of God, that his children in their conversion shal some of them feel more, and some lesse. . . . [I]n the Scriptures we finde examples of men converted unto the Lorde without any vehement sorrow of their sinnes. . . . I say in preparing us to bee the Temples of his holy Spirit to dwell in, and the store houses to hoord up his heavenly graces in, doth other whiles use a milde and gentle remedie, and maketh the Law to looke upon us, though with no loving and gentle, yet with no fearful countenance; and other whiles in some he setteth a sharpe edge unto the Law, and maketh it wound the heart very deepe. . . . Wherefore if God by his Spirit have wrought in you sorrow for sinne in any small measure, though not in as great a measure as you desire, you have no cause to complaine: and in that you are grieved with a godly sorrow for your sins, it is a good token of the grace of God in you'. Also see Shaw, *Marrow of Practical Divinity*, 133.

For a discussion of the problem of 'intellectualism/voluntarism' as it relates to the thought of John Calvin (and the Puritans), see the following: my dissertation, 'Spiritual Brotherhood', 100–2, 141–5; Richard Muller, '*Fides* and *Cognitio* in Relation to the Problem of Intellect and Will in the Theology of John Calvin', *Calvin Theological Journal* 25 (1990), 207–24; and Arvin Vos, *Aquinas, Calvin, and Contemporary Protestant Thought: A Critique of the Views of Thomas Aqinas* (Grand Rapids: Eerdmans, 1985).

[45]   Perkins, 'A Golden Chaine', I:83.

vital to any discussion of good works or piety of the heart: 'In the conversion of a sinner, there is a real donation of Christ, and all his benefits unto us: and there is a real union, whereby every believer is made one with Christ. And by vertue of this union, the crosse and passion of Christ is as verily made ours, as if we had been crucified in our own persons.'[46]

Christ united a sinner to himself in 'effectual calling' which brought with it the gift of faith. In effectual calling God the Father through the Holy Spirit 'bestoweth upon the sinful man to be saved . . . Christ and Christ again and most effectually upon that sinful man, so that he may boldly say . . . Christ . . . is mine and I for my benefit and use enjoy the same'.[47] The Trinity was intimately involved in this union — the Father called, the Son accomplished, and the Spirit applied all that was necessary.

Thus, even when granting that a very activist element existed in Perkins' reflections on the Christian life, such an admittance should, nevertheless, be tempered with judicious reflection on the historical and pastoral contexts. Since Perkins clearly repudiated any ability on the natural person's part to lay hold of Christ, such ability coming only by Christ's gracious work on the heart by the Spirit, the shift from a generally more passive language in one like Calvin to the more active rhetoric seen in one like Perkins seems to show more of an historical contextual shift than a theological change. Calvin's emphasis on passivity stemmed from his deep concerns about the dangers of Roman merit theology, and yet his thinking did not preclude strident calls for personal and corporate discipline in the church.[48] On the other hand, although Perkins' pleas for activity derived from his anxiety over the general lack of enthusiasm for true piety among a so-called Reformed people, such concerns arose in the context of a sovereign grace soteriology. Pastoral needs shaped the tone, not confessional discontinuity. Perkins refused to allow this Protestant people to stand secure in their confession if such confession failed to lead to alteration of life.

---

[46] Perkins, 'Galatians' (1617 edn.), 123–4.

[47] Perkins, 'A Golden Chaine', I:78.

[48] Indeed, one is reminded of Calvin's famous letter to the people of Geneva upon his return there in 1541 after his exile in 1538: 'If you desire to have me as your pastor, correct the disorder of your lives. If you have with sincerity recalled me from my exile, banish the crimes and debaucheries which prevail among you. . . . I cannot possibly live in a place so immoral. . . . I consider the chief enemies of the Gospel to be, not the pontiff of Rome, nor heretics, nor seducers, nor tyrants, but bad Christians. . . . I dread abundantly more those carnal covetousnesses, those debaucheries of the tavern. . . . Of what use is a dead faith without good works? Of what importance is even truth itself, where a wicked life belies it and actions make words blush? Either command me to abandon a second time your town . . . or let the severity of the laws reign in the church. Reestablish there pure discipline.' Theodore Beza, *The Life of John Calvin*, trans. Francis Gibson (Philadelphia, 1836), 25–6, n. 1.

A FINAL REMARK

The godly way was a serious way. To aid in the struggle against the flesh, Perkins advised believers to make 'bills' or 'catalogues' of known sins: 'After Paul's example [in Galatians 5:20–1], every man shall do well to make a catalogue of the sinnes of his whole life. By this means shall we better know ourselves and take a manifest view of our sinful condition.'[49] In 'Repentance', he even told his listeners that such cataloguing should be a 'large bill' of sins from 'cradle to the grave', for such was what 'the saints of God have always done'.[50] As he noted in the oft-quoted opening of 'A Golden Chaine', the 'blessed life' arose from 'knowledge of God' which in turn arose from a true introspective 'knowledge of ourselves'.[51] Did not such exhortations to focus within actually subvert the doctrine of *sola gratia* which Perkins so strongly maintained?

While the case can be made that Perkins' rhetoric of 'bill-keeping' was somewhat unfortunate, remarks like these pointed not so much to some undercurrent of legalism or an attempt to bring merit into the scheme through the back-door, as to the utter seriousness with which Perkins noted the responsibility of the believer under grace. Perkins argued that believers needed to make 'catalogues and bills of thine own sins, specially of those sins that have most dishonoured God and wounded thine own conscience' because of the danger of 'counterfeit' believers within the established church. Thus, this device served as an element towards the 'visible reformation' which a visible established church needed. This should not be confused with a desire to see such reformation proceed along purely moralistic or anthropocentric lines, however, in such a way that persons keeping these 'catalogues' thought they had achieved something because of their own inherent or intrinsic spirituality. Sensitive souls were surely responsible for responding to the preaching of the word with a conscious recognition of their failings; nevertheless, such an inward turn leading to outward repentance and external good works had a context. In 'Mustard Seed', for example, Perkins used the 'bill-keeping' motif as one way, but only one among others, to 'quicken the seeds and beginnings of grace'. In the midst of these directions, he also pointed his listeners to the true way of peace:

> Labour to see and feel thy spiritual poverty, that is to see the want of grace in thyself, specially those inward corruptions of unbelief, pride, self-love, etc. . . . Labour to feel that by reason of them thou standest in need of every drop of the blood of Christ to heal and cleanse thee from want of

---

[49]   Perkins, 'Galatians', II:383.
[50]   Perkins, 'Repentance', I:460.
[51]   Perkins, 'A Golden Chaine', I:11.

these wants. And let this practice take such place with thee, that if thou be demanded what in thine estimation is the vilest of the creatures upon earth, thine heart and conscience may answer with a loud voice, I, even I, by reason of mine own sins: and again, if thou be demanded what is the best thing in the world to thee, thy heart and conscience may answer with a loud and strong cry, One drop of the blood of Christ to wash away my sins.[52]

These christological reflections had ramifications for Perkins' under-standing of Christian assurance as well. Kendall (and others) have correctly noted that Perkins could equate assurance with a 'reflex act' whereby believers saw their new life in Christ through the window of their sanctification.[53] What these modern writers seem to miss, however, is that Perkins never forgot his christological moorings and so could also direct ← anxious saints away from such works and to the court of mercy in order to find peace for their troubled souls:

> A sinner in his humiliation and conversion hath by this doctrine [of justification by grace alone through faith alone] a libertie *without respect to his own works, or to his own fulfilling of the law, to rest on the mere mercie of God for the forgiveness of his sinnes*, and for the salvation of his soule, and to appeal from the throne of divine justice to the throne of divine grace, and oppose the merit of Christ against the wrath and judgment of God. *And this hath alwais been the helpe of the godly in their distress.*[54]

Sinners learned about this 'throne of mercy' through the preached word which spoke of the God of mercy as a God who made a covenant of grace in Christ with his people. In 'A Golden Chaine', Perkins defined this covenant of grace as 'that whereby God freely promising Christ and his benefits, exacts again of man that he would by faith receive Christ and repent of his sins. . . . In this covenant we do not so much offer or promise any great matter to God, as in a manner only receive.'[55] As the Spirit worked in the heart, the preached word concerning this covenant possessed a persuasiveness and efficacy to bring to fruition the faith by

---

[52] Perkins, 'A Graine of Mustard Seed', I:643.

[53] One place where Perkins defined assurance in this 'reflex act' way was in his short catechism 'The Foundation of the Christian Religion', I:6: 'How may a man know that he is justified before God? He need not ascend into heaven to search the secret counsel of God, but rather descend into his own heart to search whether he be sanctified or not.'

[54] Perkins, 'Galatians', II:356, emphasis mine. See the Baynes chapter of my disser-tation, 'Spiritual Brotherhood', 118–31, for a more detailed discussion about the variety which marked the Cambridge Puritan treatment of assurance. For more on Perkins himself and the assurance question, see Beeke, *Assurance of Faith*, 96–112.

[55] Perkins, 'A Golden Chaine', I:70.

which a person apprehended the mercy of Christ: 'The elect, having the Spirit of God, do first discern the voice of Christ speaking in the Scriptures. Moreover that voice which they do discern, they do approve and that which they do approve, they do believe. Lastly, believing they are, as it were, sealed with the seal of the Spirit'.[56]

In sum, while Perkins could direct the weak to strengthen their faith through long lists of 'rules of directions' which spoke to his belief that the elect were responsible agents to follow God in a life of faith, repentance, and obedience, Perkins balanced his 'list-making' tendencies with the call to keep Christ in focus:

> Faith doth not justifie in respect of itself, because it is an action or virtue; or because it is strong, lively, and perfect, but in respect of the object thereof, namely Christ crucified, whom faith apprehendeth as he is set forth unto us in the word and sacraments. It is Christ that is the author and matter of our justice and it is he that applieth the same to us. As for faith in us, it is but an instrument to apprehend and receive that which Christ for his part offereth and giveth. . . . Though our apprehension be necessary, yet our salvation stands rather in this, that God apprehends us for his own, than that we apprehend him for ours; and rather in this, that we are known of him, than that we know him.[57]

---

[56]   Perkins, 'The Arte of Prophesying', II:735.
[57]   Perkins, 'Mustard Seed', I:641.

2

John Hales' Good-Night to John Calvin

W. Robert Godfrey

In the last twenty years a major scholarly reappraisal of the character and content of Protestant orthodoxy has taken place. Caricatures and unsubstantiated generalizations are yielding to careful examination of late sixteenth- and seventeenth-century texts. The scholars contributing to this volume have done invaluable work showing the vitality and sophistication of the scholastic theology of this period. Still much work remains to be done to overcome the perception of orthodoxy as dead and deadening.

This essay is an inquiry into aspects of the life and thought of John Hales and his relation to Reformed orthodoxy, especially as he experienced it at the Synod of Dort (1618–19). Hales' fame (very limited to be sure) rests primarily on certain phrases associated with his name. When his collected works were published after his death, the title of those works referred to him as the 'ever memorable' and his writings were called his *Golden Remains*. Those effective phrases probably made John Hales much more memorable than he would otherwise have been. A statement attributed to Hales also contributed to his fame and made him something of a symbol for the way in which cultivated, reflective thinkers of the seventeenth century came to be alienated from Calvinist orthodoxy. Hales has often been quoted as having said 'good-night' to John Calvin at the Synod of Dort. This essay will reexamine the life and thought of John Hales with a view to understanding what this 'good-night' really meant.

The Synod of Dort marked a uniquely important point in the development of Reformed orthodoxy. Dort was a rare international gathering of Reformed theologians in an ecclesiastical assembly to address a major theological challenge to Calvinist theology. It produced a large confessional document — the Canons of Dort — which was revered by Reformed churches throughout Europe. Its specific rejection of Arminianism represented a new stage in the clarification of Reformed orthodoxy.

A key source in any study of the Synod of Dort is the letters of John Hales, rightly described as 'shrewd and witty reports',[1] sent from the synod to the English ambassador to the Netherlands, Dudley Carleton. Carleton had sent John Hales to the synod as an informant so that the keen interest of King James I in the progress of the synod could be readily satisfied. When most of the synod's work shifted to private sessions, Hales' assignment passed to Walter Balcanqual who, as a delegate to the synod from Great Britain, had first-hand access to closed deliberations. Nonetheless the letters of Hales offer a unique insight into the daily workings of the synod and the theologies and personalities of the delegates.

The letters of John Hales have been the subject of keen interest since the days of the synod. Historians sympathetic to the Remonstrants (or Arminians), whose theology was condemned by the synod, have seen in Hales' letters evidence of the injustice of the synod and have reckoned Hales a sensible and sophisticated man who was alienated by both the actions and theology of the synod. Hales for many has become a symbol of 'modern' reaction to the 'rigid' Calvinism of Dort. For example:

> To see the Synod of Dort as Calvinism incarnate was to love Calvinism less and Arminianism more. Arminianism in England, for example, flourished all the more after the synod. John Hales lost his Calvinist theology at Dort and there bade John Calvin 'good-night', and like him went a good part of the non-Puritan English church.[2]

---

[1] John Platt, 'Eirenical Anglicans at the synod of Dort' in *Reform and Reformation: England and the Continent c.1500–c.1750*, ed. D. Baker (Oxford: Blackwell, 1979), 232.

[2] Keith L. Sprunger, *The Learned Doctor William Ames* (Urbana: University of Illinois Press, 1972), 64. Other historians have taken a similar position: Gerard (Geeraert) Brandt, *The History of the Reformation and Other Ecclesiastical Transactions in and about the Low Countries*, trans. J. Chamberlayne, 4 vols. (London, 1720), 3:26; Pierre DesMaizeaux, *An Historical and Critical Account of the Life and Writings of the Ever-Memorable Mr. John Hales* (London, 1719), 72–3, 'These Letters have been received with great applause by the Arminians, in Holland, who are of the opinion that they discover the partiality and injustice of the Synod against them. Fifteen of Mr. Balcanqual's Letters, and seven of Mr. Hale's, were translated into Latin, and inserted in the second edition of the *praestantium ac eruditorum virorum Epistolae Ecclesiasticae et Theologicae*, etc., published at Amsterdam in 1684, by Mr. Limborch . . .'; James Hinsdale Elson, *John Hales of Eton* (New York: Kings Crown Press, 1948), *passim*; Robert Peters, 'John Hales and the Synod of Dort' in *Studies in Church History* 7, *Councils and Assemblies*, ed. G.J. Cuming and L.G.D. Baker (Cambridge: Cambridge University Press, 1971), 277–88, *passim*.

The ease with which both older and more recent historians have characterized Hales as sympathetic to the Remonstrant cause rests on several facts. First, later in his life Hales was a friend of William Chillingworth (1602–44) and Edward Stillingfleet (1635–99) — both Latitudinarian divines. Hales' own writings at points seem to tend in a Latitudinarian direction. He took little note of the Puritan-Anglican controversies of his own day and stressed the importance of the individual reaching his own conclusions in religion. Second, after Hales' death certain Socinian works which were falsely attributed to him influenced many observers in the late seventeenth century to regard him as a rationalistic divine.[3] Last, and perhaps most important, was the famous statement attributed to him about the Synod of Dort, 'There I bid John Calvin good-night.'[4] Robert Peters has recently analyzed Hales' letters from Dort with the aim of showing Hales' progressive alienation from Calvinism, and dating Hales' final break with Calvinism at the synod.[5] The thesis of this essay is that the character of the letters and theology of John Hales has been consistently misunderstood and misrepresented and that a careful study of his work will reveal quite a different picture from the one that now exists of the 'ever memorable Mr. John Hales'.

The outline of John Hales' life is simple. He was born at Bath on 19 April 1584 and educated at Corpus Christi College, Oxford. He was elected Fellow of Merton in 1605 and of Eton in 1613. In 1618 he became chaplain to Dudley Carleton in the Netherlands. In 1619 he returned to Eton where he remained until he was dispossessed in 1649. He died at Eton on 19 May 1656. He was known as the 'ever memorable' to his friends and his *Golden Remains* was first published in 1659.

Only two works of Hales were written before he went to Dort. The first was his funeral oration for Thomas Bodley in 1613[6] which gives little evidence of his theology. He did, however, mention the many great men that the world had recently lost: William Whitaker (1546–95), Theodore Beza (1519–1605), Hieronymus Zanchius (1516–90), John Rainolds (1549–1607), Franciscus Junius (1545–1602), Joseph Justus Scaliger (1540–1609) and Justus Lipsius (1547–1606).[7] All of these except the last were noted Calvinists. He also mentioned that Bodley had learned holy and venerable theology from Calvin and Beza.[8]

---

[3]   Elson, *John Hales of Eton*, 118.

[4]   John Hales, *Golden Remains of the Ever Memorable Mr. John Hales* (London, 1673[2]), ix.

[5]   Peters, 'John Hales and the Synod of Dort', 285.

[6]   John Hales, *The Works of the Ever Memorable Mr. John Hales of Eton*, 3 vols. (Glasgow, 1765), I.207–33.

[7]   Ibid. I.208.

[8]   Ibid. I.213.

Hales' only other work which predates the Synod of Dort was a sermon preached in 1617, entitled 'Abuses of Hard Places of Scripture'.[9] This sermon was a balanced and temperate consideration of how to deal with the obscure passages of the Bible and the danger of building too much or too certainly upon them. 'That we be not too peremptory in our positions, where express text of Scripture fails us; that we lay not our own collections and conclusions with too much precipitancy.'[10] In those matters where Scripture is silent or unclear, Hales recommended: 'It shall well befit our Christian modesty to participate somewhat of the Sceptic, and to use their withholding of judgment, till the remainder of our knowledge be supplied by Christ . . .'[11]

Hales offered only one contemporary Protestant example of excess in investigating the meaning of the Bible: interpreting the Book of the Revelation. He warned that the ancients were wiser in admiring the book rather than trying to expound it. He acknowledged that it was very probable that the book prophesied against the Church of Rome. Yet he advised that Protestants argue against Rome with the abundant plain texts of Scripture lest it appear that they could do no better than rest upon obscure ones.[12]

Hales' concern did not lead him to criticize modern interpreters generally, however. Indeed for one who quoted antiquity at such length and to good effect, it is remarkable to hear him observe:

> For the most partial for antiquity cannot chuse but see and confess thus much, that for the literal sense the interpreters of our own times, because of their skill in the original languages, their care of pressing the circumstances and coherence of the text, of comparing the like places of scripture with like, have generally surpast the best of the antients. Which I speak not to discountenance antiquity, but that all ages, all persons may have their due.[13]

He noted particularly the harm done to the Roman church by the Reformers in pressing the literal sense of the Scripture. He mentioned especially 'the great credit of Calvin's writings in that kind'.[14] Calvin was the only Protestant exegete mentioned by name in the sermon.

There was little in the sermon that related directly to Calvinist theology. Yet he did refer to predestination at one point as 'one of the deepest mysteries of our profession'.[15] In referring to questions that

---

[9]   Ibid. II.1–46.
[10] Ibid. I.35.
[11] Ibid. I.45.
[12] Ibid. I.33–4.
[13] Ibid. I.40.
[14] Ibid I.38.
[15] Ibid. I.10.

Christians cannot answer, he said: 'Is it not St. Paul's own practice, when having brought in a question concerning God's justice in predestination, he gives no other answer but this, "O man, who art thou that disputest against God?" Rom. ix.20.'[16] He also seemed to teach a sovereign work of God in regeneration.[17]

These two works written before Dort probably could not justify Peters' claim that Hales was 'an ardent Calvinist' before Dort.[18] Perhaps J.H. Elson is closer to the truth when he observes 'one can assume that his Calvinism, like that of many of his contemporaries not of the Puritan party, consisted in a more or less conventional acceptance of the Calvinistic doctrine of predestination'.[19] Yet Elson, wanting to find even in this early period an anticipation of what he calls Hales' support of 'a loosely defined rational religion',[20] goes too far in saying, 'there is underlying the whole a skeptical attitude, which eventually would be destructive of the certainty necessary for even a formal acceptance of Calvinian doctrine.'[21] Hales seems to have a genuine admiration for Calvin and various other Reformed divines. He may never have identified strongly with any of the religious 'parties' within the Church of England, but only a careful analysis of his later writings can show accurately his mature attitudes to the Calvinist doctrine of predestination.

Elson and Peters are both convinced that the Synod of Dort made a deep and lasting impression on the theology of John Hales.[22] Both contend that the second major speech of Simon Episcopius, the leader of the Remonstrants at Dort, aroused Hales' sympathy for the Remonstrant cause.[23] Both argue that between the harsh dismissal of the Remonstrants from the floor of the synod by President Bogerman on 14 January 1619 and Hales' last letter from the synod on 7 February 1619, John Hales said good-night to John Calvin.[24]

The character of the evidence that they present to support their scenario, however, when carefully examined, is found to be seriously flawed. In both cases the 'decisive' pieces of evidence cited to show Hales' alienation from Calvinism are not from Hales at all. Elson cites

---

[16]   Ibid. I.44.
[17]   Ibid. I.29
[18]   Peters, 'John Hales and the Synod of Dort', 279.
[19]   Elson, *John Hales of Eton*, 40.
[20]   Hales *Works*, I.84.
[21]   Ibid. *Works*, I.41.
[22]   Peters, 'John Hales and the Synod of Dort', 278–9; Elson, *John Hales of Eton*, 65, 74.
[23]   Peters, 'John Hales and the Synod of Dort', 283; Elson, *John Hales of Eton*, 77.
[24]   Peters, 'John Hales and the Synod of Dort', 284–5; Elson, *John Hales of Eton*, 81–2.

a section from Hales' letter of 12/22 January about the dismissal of the Remonstrants which reads in part:

> The errors of public actions (if they be not very gross) are with less inconvenience tolerated than amended. For the danger of alteration, of disgracing and disabling authority, makes that the fortune of such proceedings admits no regress, but being once howsoever well or ill done, they must for ever after be upheld. The most partial spectator of our synodal acts cannot but confess, that in the late dismission of the Remonstrants, with so much choler and heat, there was a great oversight committed . . . The synod therefore, to whom it is not now *in integro* to look back and rectify what is amiss, without disparagement, must now go forward and leave events to God, and for the countenance of their action do the best they may.[25]

Elson does not indicate that these are not Hales' own words but that Hales is quoting some statement, apparently an official one, made to the synod.[26] Hales expressed no unhappiness with this declaration. Indeed after recounting another official statement justifying the procedures of the synod in regard to the Remonstrants, he observed: 'I was very glad to hear that admonition, and it gives me hope that our synod shall have an end not long after Easter, at the farthest.'[27] Far from being very critical of the dismissal, he seemed sympathetic to it.

Peters cites a different letter, 13 February 1619, to support his claim that Hales reacted negatively to the dismissal of the Remonstrants. Peters quotes in part the statement:

> they were called in and dismist with such a powdering speech as I doubt not but your Lordship hath heard with grief enough. I protest I am much afflicted when I think of it. For if the Remonstrants should write, that the President pronounced a sentence, which was not the sentence of the synod, they should not lie.[28]

Peters goes on to quote part of the same passage cited by Elson and then observes: 'It is clear that by now Hales had effectively bade John Calvin "good-night".'[29] Not only has Peters repeated Elson's error, but

---

25   Elson, *John Hales of Eton*, 81, citing the letter of Hales, *Works*, III.B.134–5.
26   In Hales, *Golden Remains* (1673), Appendix, 84–5, this letter is printed with the entire section quoted by Elson in quotation marks, indicating that Hales was quoting someone else. The 1765 *Works*, III.B, have erroneously omitted the quotation marks.
27   Hales, *Works*, III.B.135–6.
28   Hales, *Golden Remains*, Appendix, 73–4.
29   Peters, 'John Hales and the Synod of Dort', 285.

the 13 February letter that he cites to show Hales' affliction was not written by Hales at all, but by Walter Balcanqual.[30] And Balcanqual remained a good Calvinist all his days.

The letters of John Hales simply do not show a progressive alienation from Calvinism. That should not be surprising. Even if Dort and its Calvinism had offended him, it is unlikely that he would have revealed it in detail to the Calvinist ambassador for whom he was reporting. Rather the letters reveal the integrity of an observer who is trying to be objective. He only occasionally offered a personal opinion in the midst of his detailed reporting. At times he was critical, at times wry, and at times complimentary. In his 4 January 1619 letter he could speak of the wise patience of the synod in dealing with the Remonstrants.[31] In his 21/31 January letter he commended an excellent discourse on reprobation by Altingius (a very strange reaction for one supposedly alienated from Calvinism).[32] He did criticize the synod on some matters of procedure.[33] His reactions to Franciscus Gomarus varied with the situation, at times commending his discretion and insight[34] and at others seeing his weaknesses.[35] When Gomarus challenged Martinius to a duel on the floor of synod, Hales remarked wryly: 'Martinius who goes in aequipace with Gomarus in learning, and a little before him in discretion, easily digested this affront.'[36]

Hales' reactions to Episcopius and to the dismissal of the Remonstrants were particularly revealing of his attitudes. His response to Episcopius' first speech was not positive, calling it 'a long and tedious speech of two hours at the least'.[37] He added, 'When they had well and thoroughly wearied their auditory, they did that which we much desired, they made an end.'[38] Hales summarized Episcopius' second speech at some length for Carleton.[39] His only comment was that 'this and much more, for an hour's space, he delivered with great grace of speech and oratorical gesture'.[40] Elson feels that because it was reported

---

[30]   Hales, *Golden Remains*, Appendix, contains both the letters of Hales and the letters of Balcanqual. This 13 February letter of Balcanqual was erroneously printed with the Hales letters, but is clearly signed by Balcanqual. This letter is not printed in Hales, *Works*, III.B, which does not include the letters of Balcanqual.

[31]   Hales, *Works*, III.B.106.

[32]   Ibid. I.142.

[33]   Ibid. I.107, 149, 151.

[34]   Ibid. I.38, 133, 150.

[35]   Ibid. I.96.

[36]   Ibid. I.138–9.

[37]   Ibid. I.58.

[38]   Ibid. I.59.

[39]   Ibid. I.69–74.

[40]   Ibid. I.74.

at such length, it made a singular impact on Hales.[41] Yet it is clear that Hales regularly summarized significant statements and usually tried to send complete copies of speeches and resolutions to Carleton.[42] There was nothing unusual in his treatment of Episcopius. Later when Episcopius was refused a copy of an order from the synod, Hales remarked:

> This at first seemed to me somewhat hard: but when I considered, that these were the men which heretofore had, in prejudice of the church so extremely flattered the civil magistrate, I could not but think this usage a fit reward for such a service; and that by a just judgment of God, themselves had the first experience of those inconveniences, which naturally arise out of their doctrine in that behalf.[43]

When Hales first described the dismissal of the Remonstrants to Carleton in his letter of 5/15 January 1619 he expressed no reaction at all.[44] In his letter the next day he referred to the 'rough handling' of the Remonstrants[45] and 'passionate speeches' of the president.[46] Hales, like many of the foreign delegates, seemed to feel that the president's actions were unwise and excessive, but Hales no more than the others seemed permanently alienated from Calvinism.

On 7 February 1619 Hales wrote his last letter from Dort. Elson speaks of his 'disillusionment'[47] as the cause of his leaving. Peters speaks of his evident 'relief' at leaving his 'unpleasant task'.[48] Both cite the opening words of his last letter from Dort:

> Our synod goes on like a watch, the main wheels upon which the whole business turns are least in sight; for all things of moment are acted in private sessions; what is done in public is only for shew and entertainment.[49]

These words of Hales, however, do not indicate his alienation from his task as an observer, but only the impossibility now of fulfilling it. Hales could not gain access to the private sessions of the synod and felt that someone else who was a delegate could now better undertake his responsibilities. Walter Balcanqual did in fact replace him permanently. Yet Hales declared before leaving: 'it will be long ere the synod will come

---

[41]   Elson, *John Hales of Eton*, 77.
[42]   See e.g. Hales, *Works*, III.B.78.
[43]   Ibid. I.90.
[44]   Ibid. I.124.
[45]   Ibid. I.125.
[46]   Ibid. I.126.
[47]   Elson, *John Hales of Eton*, 82.
[48]   Peters, 'John Hales and the Synod of Dort', 287.
[49]   Hales, *Works*, III.B.148.

to determine anything, and about that time, if your honour shall be so pleased, I shall be ready to come back to Dort.'[50]

The letters of John Hales from the Synod of Dort simply do not show any signs that Hales has been alienated from Calvinism. The truest guide to Hales' reactions to Dort and Calvin after he left the synod must be sought in his later writings. This task is complicated by the fact that there are no explicit references to Dort in his later writings and that the exact dates of the composition of most of these later writings are unknown.

As one indication of Hales' negative reaction to Dort, Peters and Elson have both pointed to a rather critical attitude towards councils and synods expressed in Hales' later writings.[51] In his work 'Of Enquiry and Private Judgment in Religion', Hales stated:

> An infallibility therefore there must be; but men have marvelously wearied themselves in seeking to find out where it is. Some have sought it in general councils, and have conceived that if it be not there to be found, it is for certainty fled out of the world.[52]

He later added:

> Fourthly, councils, and synods, and consent of churches, they are taken to be the strongest weapons which the church had fought with; yet this is still human authority after another fashion; let me add one thing, that the truth hath not been more relieved by these than it hath been distressed.[53]

Even more pointedly Hales declared in 'A Tract on the Sacrament of the Lord's Supper; and Concerning the Church's Mistaking Itself about Fundamentals':

> I must for mine own part confess, that councils and synods not only may and have erred, but considering the means how they are managed, it were a great marvel if they did not err: for what men are they of whom those great meetings do consist? Are they the best, the most learned, the most virtuous, and the most likely to walk uprightly? No, the greatest, the most ambitious, and many times men neither of judgment nor learning; such are they of whom these bodies do consist. And are these men in common equity likely to determine for truth? . . . Again, when such persons are thus met, their way to proceed to conclusion, is not by weight of reason, but by multitude of votes and suffrages, as if it were a maxim in nature that the greater part must needs be the better.[54]

---

50 Ibid. I.147.
51 Peters, 'John Hales and the Synod of Dort', 288; Elson, *John Hales of Eton*, 83, 90.
52 Hales, *Works*, III.A.149.
53 Ibid. I.165.
54 Ibid. I.65–6.

Peters, with reference to this last quotation, states, 'Only experience could produce so deep a sense of disillusion: Hales gained that experience at Dort.'[55] This, however, seems to be an overstatement. Hales' critique of councils was primarily directed to the tendency to vest absolute authority in them, and he characteristically illustrated his contentions with reference to ancient rather than more contemporary councils. More importantly, he expressed his reservations about councils before he ever went to Dort. In his sermon of 1617 he stated:

> For infallibility either in judgment, or interpretation, or whatsoever, is annext neither to the see of any bishop, nor to the fathers, nor to the councils, nor to the church, nor to any created power whatsoever.[56]

Later he noted:

> For it is not depth of knowledge, nor knowledge of antiquity, or sharpness of wit, nor authority of councils, nor the name of the church, can settle the restless conceits that possess the minds of many doubtful Christians: only to ground for faith on the plain uncontroversable text of Scripture, and for the rest, to expect and pray for the coming of our Elias, this shall compose our waverings, and give final rest unto our souls.[57]

Hales had quite limited confidence in councils before he ever went to Dort.

A more likely effect of his attendance at the Synod of Dort may be his sermon 'Of Duels'. This sermon was preached at The Hague around the time of the synod and may have been sparked in part by Gomarus' challenge to Martinius issued on the floor of the synod. He noted that the chief cause for duels is the 'over-promptness in many young men, who desire to be counted men of valour and resolution' and noted that this 'is the special cause indeed that moved me to speak in this argument'.[58] Near the conclusion of his attack on duelling, he declared:

> How many have been censured for schismatics and heretics, only because by probable consequence, and afar off, they seemed to overthrow some Christian principle? But here are men, who walk in our streets and come to our churches, who openly oppose that great point of Christianity, which concerns our patience, and yet for their restraint, no synod is called, no magistrate stirs, no church-censure is pronounced.[59]

---

55   Peters, 'John Hales and the Synod of Dort', 288.
56   Hales, *Works*, II.37.
57   Ibid. I.45.
58   Ibid. II.110.
59   Ibid. I.140–1.

This negative reaction to an event at the synod did not, however, reflect a critique of Calvinist theology.

In the later writings of Hales there are several explicit references to John Calvin. On the Lord's Supper, Hales argued for a radical Zwinglian understanding of the sacrament. He blamed Martin Bucer for the doctrine of the real presence in Reformed churches, adding 'and from him it descended into the writings of Calvin and Beza, whose authority have well-near spread it over the face of the Reformed churches'.[60] In 'A Tract Concerning the Sin Against the Holy Ghost' he sharply attacked Calvin for his definition of this sin: 'I shall chiefly apply myself to Mr. Calvin's definition, because his judgment hath gained the greatest reputation among the multitude'. However, as if to allay any notion of a personal attack on Calvin or his thought, he quickly added, 'Arminius also useth Mr. Calvin's words.'[61] Finally, in two letters, dated 1638 and 1640, there were references to Calvin on the subject of usury:

> for John Calvin was the first good man, from the beginning of the world, that maintained the use to be lawful; and I have often wished, that whatsoever his conceit was, that he had been pleased to conceal it, for he hath done much hurt: and howsoever he means and tempers his conclusions with sundry constraints, and equitable and pious considerations, (so that he which practiseth use with Calvin's limits, shall do by it little hurt) yet I know not how, *multos invenit sententiae fautores, pietatis nullos.*[62]

All of these quotations mark places where Hales differed, at times sharply, with Calvin. Yet none of these issues were discussed at the Synod of Dort, and none of these differences seem to have affected Hales' basic conviction that Calvin was 'a good man'. He rather reacted to having Calvin function as an authority for men who would follow him uncritically.

There are references in Hales' later works to some of the issues specifically discussed at Dort. He wrote of 'that late famous controversy in Holland, *De Praedestinatione et auxiliis*' in his tract on schism, but made no personal evaluation of any kind.[63] He did write explicitly of predestination in his sermon 'Of Dealing With Erring Christians', which Elson supposes was preached in the late 1630s.[64] Hales noted:

> I will give you one instance, in which, at this day, our churches are at variance; the will of God, and his manner of proceeding in predestination, is undiscernible, and shall so remain until that day, wherein all knowledge

60   Ibid. I.60.
61   Ibid. I.43.
62   Ibid. I.200.
63   Ibid. I.117.
64   Elson, *John Hales of Eton*, 26.

shall be made perfect; yet some there are, who, with probability of scripture, teach, that the true cause of the final miscarriage of them that perish, is that original corruption that befel them at the beginning, increased though (sic) the neglect or refusal of grace offered. Others, with no less favorable countenance of Scripture, make the cause of reprobation only the will of God, determining freely of his own work, as himself pleases, without respect of any second cause whatsoever. Were we not ambitiously minded, every one to be lord of a sect, each of these tenets might be profitably taught and heard, and matter of singular exhortation drawn from either; for on the one part, doubtless it is a pious and religious intent, to endeavor to free God from all imputation of unnecessary rigour, and his justice from seeming injustice and incongruity: and on the other side it is a noble resolution, so to humble ourselves under the hand of Almighty God, as that we can with patience hear, yea, think it an honour, that so base creatures as ourselves should become the instruments of the glory of so great a Majesty, whether it be by eternal life, or by eternal death, though for no other reason but for God's good will and pleasure's sake.[65]

The first opinion which Hales described is ambiguous. No doubt the Arminians at Dort could have embraced it. Yet the orthodox infralapsarians at Dort might also have approved of it. The Canons of Dort on reprobation read:

God . . . has decreed to leave [them] in the common misery into which they have willfully plunged themselves, and not to bestow upon them saving faith and the grace of conversion; but, permitting them in His just judgment to follow their own ways, at last, for the declaration of His justice, to condemn and punish them forever, not only on account of their unbelief, but also for all their sins.[66]

Indeed the stress upon the vindication of God's justice and condemnation for all sin in Hales' statement accords better with the Canons of Dort than with Arminianism.

The second opinion to which Hales referred is not ambiguous. It is clearly supralapsarian. Not only did Hales cite it as a tolerable point of view, but commended it for the glory it gave to God. An Erasmian Hales, or one who rejected Calvinism at Dort, would have been unlikely to make this favourable reference to so strong an expression of Calvinism.

Hales' discussion of predestination was not limited to this one sermon. In his sermon 'Of St. Peter's Fall' he returned to the subject at greater length.[67] His purpose was not to discuss predestination *per se*, the truth of

[65]   Hales, *Works*, II.94–5.
[66]   Canons of Dort, I.15.
[67]   Hales, *Works*, II.206–13 out of the total sermon, 189–229.

which he took for granted. Rather he focused on one question related to it: whether the elect can for a time in their lives fall from grace. He noted that grace can be used in two ways:

> But the grace of God signifies two things: either the purpose of God's election, the grace and favour inherent in the person of God, which he still casts upon those that are his, notwithstanding their manifold backslidings; or else it signifies the habit of sanctifying qualities, inherent in the regenerate man, those good graces of God, by which he walks holy and unblameable.[68]

One can fall from the latter grace, but not from the former:

> So then you seek that into the state of damnation as it signifies something inherent in us, a man may fall, and yet not fall from the state of grace as it signifies God's purpose of election; for both these are compatible for a time.[69]

Hales showed how these two themes were compatible when he argued:

> . . . for the purposes of God, though impossible to be defeated, yet lay not upon things any violent necessity, they exempt not from the use of ordinary means, they infringe not our liberty, they stand very well with common causality; yea, these things are the very means by which his decrees are brought about.[70]

This approach allowed Hales to stress the importance of faithfulness in the Christian life:

> It is faith indeed that gives the tincture, the die, the relish unto our actions; yet, the only means to examine our faith is by our works. . . . To reason thus, I am of the elect, I therefore have saving faith, and the rest of the sanctifying qualities, therefore that which I do is good; thus, I say, to reason is very preposterous: we must go a quite contrary course, and thus reason; My life is good, and through the mercies of God in Jesus Christ, shall stand with God's justice: I therefore have the gifts of sanctification, and therefore am of God's elect.[71]

Hales' doctrine of predestination in this sermon was entirely Calvinistic. His doctrine of falling from grace was somewhat novel. It differed from the Canons of Dort which stated: 'But God . . . does not wholly withdraw the Holy Spirit from His own people even in their grievous falls; nor

---

[68] Ibid. I.207.
[69] Ibid. I.208.
[70] Ibid. I.211.
[71] Ibid. I.212.

suffers them to proceed so far as to lose the grace of adoption and forfeit the state of justification'.[72] Yet the canons echoed Hales' concerns at this point: 'By such enormous sins, however, they very highly offend God, incur a deadly guilt, grieve the Holy Spirit, interrupt the exercise of faith, very grievously wound their consciences, and sometimes for a while lose the sense of God's favor.'[73]

In summary, all the later works of Hales reveal no sharp criticism of Dort or its theology. The explicit differences with Calvin are on areas not discussed at Dort. On the key matter of predestination, one must conclude that Hales continued to be at least a moderate Calvinist.

If the evidence of his later works shows no significant alienation of Hales from Calvinism on the matter of predestination, what was the origin of Hales' famous 'good-night' to John Calvin? The famous statement does not actually occur in the works of John Hales. It was recalled by Hales' good friend Anthony Farindon in a letter that he wrote 17 September 1657, subsequently printed as part of the introduction to the 1659 *Golden Remains*. Farindon wrote:

> But I am very glad to hear you have gained *those letters* into your hands written from the *Synod of Dort*. You may please take notice, that in his younger days he was a *Calvinist*, and even then when he was employed at that Synod, and at the well pressing *S Joh.* iii.16. by *Episcopius* — 'There, I bid John Calvin good-night', as he has often told me.[74]

Two problems immediately surface in evaluating this recollection by Farindon. The first is that apparently Farindon did not meet Hales until 1639, some twenty years after the Synod of Dort,[75] and so at the earliest would have heard Hales' recollections twenty years after the fact. The second is that Episcopius did not seem to have impressed Hales particularly and there is no evidence that Episcopius ever spoke on John 3:16 at Dort.[76]

Peters has suggested that perhaps Martinius rather than Episcopius influenced Hales.[77] Hales did say in his letter of 19/29 January 1619:

---

[72]   Canons of Dort, V. 6. It also differs from article 5 of the Lambeth Articles (1595) which stated: 'A true, living and justifying faith, and the Spirit of God justifying [sanctifying], is not extinguished, falleth not away; it vanisheth not away in the elect either finally or totally', cited in Philip Schaff, *The Creeds of Christendom*, 3 vols. (Grand Rapids: Baker, 1977), 3.523–4.

[73]   Canons of Dort, V.5.

[74]   Hales, *Golden Remains*, ix.

[75]   Alexander Gordon, 'Farindon, Anthony (1598–1658)', *Dictonary of National Biography* 6, ed. Sir Leslie Stephen et al., 66 vols. (Oxford: Oxford University Press), 6.1069.

[76]   Hales, *Works*, I.285.

[77]   Peters, 'John Hales and the Synod of Dort', 286. Platt, *Eirenical Anglicans*, 237 has also made that suggestion.

My Lord Bishop of late hath taken some pains with Martinius of Breme, to bring him from his opinion of universal grace. By chance I came to see his letter written to Martinius, in which he expounded that place in the third of John, 'So God loved the world, that he gave his only begotten Son, etc.' Which is the strongest ground upon which Martinius rests himself.[78]

This letter, however, does not indicate that in fact Hales was influenced by Martinius.

Yet Farindon's contention, as a good friend, that Hales had 'often' spoken of bidding Calvin good-night, cannot be ignored. Perhaps it was on the doctrine of the limited atonement, the point of theology about which John 3:16 was most often cited, that Hales parted company with other Calvinists. This point of doctrine was debated extensively at the synod and posed some problems for orthodox delegates Martinius, Samuel Ward and John Davenant.[79] But there is no evidence in Hales' writings about his conclusions on the extent of the atonement.

Elson has offered another possibility as to what might have offended Hales at Dort:

In the observation of the actions of the ContraRemonstrants, he became perhaps for the first time, acutely aware of the implications of the full and complete programme of orthodox Calvinism. . . . Seeing in the Gomarist party such authoritarian threats as those offered by a rigid church government, a strict confessionalism, and a violent intolerance of diverse opinion, Hales undoubtedly became aware of similar threats in even a modified Calvinism such as existed among English Puritans.[80]

Hales' stress on the importance of individual judgment in religion may lend some credence to Elson's contention. But in Hales' writing there was no explicit attack on Calvinist ecclesiology, nor did Hales link ecclesiology with theology in the way Elson has done.

Perhaps the statement of Farindon must remain something of a mystery. Still it is clear that the interpretation so often placed on Hales' bidding Calvin good-night cannot be defended. Hales never rejected a Calvinist view of predestination, the central concern of the Synod of Dort and one of the touchstones of Calvinism.

The misinterpretation of Hales by subsequent generations of historians is unfortunate because it distorts his thought so that he becomes a

---

[78]   Hales, *Works*, III.B.145–6.
[79]   For a detailed analysis of this problem, see W. Robert Godfrey, 'Tensions Within International Calvinism: The Debate on the Atonement at the Synod of Dort, 1618–1619' (PhD diss., Stanford University, 1974).
[80]   Elson, *John Hales of Eton*, 83.

'modern' man in conflict with Protestant 'scholastics'. This misjudgment reflects and encourages a basically erroneous assessment of early seventeenth-century Calvinism as a rigid and monolithic theology. Such a perspective cannot be supported by the writings of John Hales. At Dort Hales endeavored to report faithfully and fairly what he observed. The 'ever memorable' John Hales deserves the same treatment at the hands of his interpreters.

A Small Step Towards Rationalism:
The Impact of the Metaphysics of Tommaso
Campanella on the Theology of Richard Baxter

Carl R. Trueman

THE 'PROBLEM' OF METAPHYSICS AND ARISTOTELIANISM

One of the most significant aspects of the older school of scholarship surrounding Protestant orthodoxy was the attention which it drew to the appropriation of Aristotle, Aristotelianism, and metaphysics by the generations of Protestant theologians subsequent to the Reformation.[1] More recently, Brian Armstrong's classic definition of Protestant scholasticism has made explicit the notion that Reformed orthodoxy's increasing use of Aristotelian and metaphysical language led to a fundamental deviation from the Reformation thought of theologians such as Calvin and to an increasingly rationalistic theology whereby human reason provided the ultimate criteria for the theological task. His view has exerted such a profound influence on the scholarly world that his definition now enjoys near-canonical status and is apparently considered so self-evident that it is cited in textbooks without any defence of its accuracy or even a reference to its origin.[2] Nevertheless, there are very good grounds for

---

[1] See P. Althaus, *Die Prinzipien der deutschen reformierten Dogmatik im Zeitalter der aristotelischen Scholastik* (Leipzig: Deichertsche, 1914 Darmstadt: Wissenschaftliche Buchgesellschaft, 1967²); W. Kickel, *Vernunft und Offenbarung bei Theodore Beza* (Neukirchen: Neukirchener, 1967), esp. 61–8; H.-E. Weber, *Reformation, Orthodoxie, und Rationalismus*, 3 parts (Gütersloh: Bertelsmann, 1937-51 Darmstatdt: Wissenschaftliche Buchgesellschaft, 1966).

[2] For Armstrong's definition, see his *Calvinism and the Amyraut Heresy: Protestant Scholasticism and Humanism in Seventeenth-Century France* (Madison: University of Wisconsin Press, 1969), 31–2; for its elevation to text book status, see A.E. McGrath, *Reformation Thought: An Introduction* (Oxford: Blackwell, 1993²), 129.

raising serious questions about the adequacy of a model of interpretation which is based upon such general concepts as 'Aristotelianism' and 'metaphysics'. Indeed, arguments about the use of Aristotelianism in Reformed orthodoxy often seem to be built upon a view of language which commits the so-called 'root fallacy', where little or no account is taken of the different ways in which words and linguistic concepts can be used over time, and where language itself is assumed to carry with it a certain metaphysical content.[3] A classic example of this error is the argument that the language of causality in Reformed theology inevitably carries with it a deterministic world-view — an argument difficult to square with its use by theologians as vigorously opposed to determinism as Jacob Arminius.[4] In fact, the basic weakness with the approach epitomized by Armstrong's definition is that it fails to take full account of the pluriform nature of Aristotelianism and metaphysics in the sixteenth and seventeenth centuries, a weakness which has unfortunately been reinforced by the apparent failure of many students of post-Reformation Reformed orthodoxy to take any account of the findings of those scholars who have worked in detail on the development of Aristotelianism during the Renaissance.

The findings of two Renaissance scholars in particular come to mind at this point, those of Paul Kristeller and Charles Schmitt. Kristeller's work is important for several reasons: first, he has pointed to the fact that humanism and scholasticism must be seen not as mutually exclusive categories, but as two separate spheres of activity, the one primarily literary and cultural, the other philosophical and methodological.[5] Thus attempts to drive a wedge

---

[3]   E.g. A.C. Clifford, *Atonement and Justification: English Evangelical Theology 1640–1790, an Evaluation* (Oxford: Clarendon, 1990), 95–110, where the author constantly leaps from Aristotle to Owen without reference to the pluriform nature of Renaissance Aristotelianism, apparently assuming that Owen's language of means and ends automatically reflects the teaching of Aristotle: see Clifford's equation of Owen, scholasticism, and Aristotle on p. 107 n. 11. For a brilliant discussion of the root fallacy, see J. Barr, *The Semantics of Biblical Language* (Oxford: Oxford University Press, 1961), 100–6; for its relevance to Reformed orthodoxy, see Richard A. Muller, 'Calvin and the "Calvinists": Assessing Continuities and Discontinuities between the Reformation and Orthodoxy', *Calvin Theological Journal* 31 (1996), 125–60, esp. 150–1.

[4]   A good example of this kind of argument is provided by P.C. Holtrop, *The Bolsec Controversy on Predestination, from 1551 to 1555* 1 (Lewiston: Edwin Mellen, 1993). The presupposition that causal language is deterministic by its very nature runs throughout this work, but is especially clear in the discussion of Beza on 842–59. On Arminius' use of causal language, see Richard A. Muller, *God, Creation, and Providence in the Thought of Jacob Arminius* (Grand Rapids: Baker, 1991), 99.

[5]   *Renaissance Thought: The Classical, Scholastic, and Humanist Strains* (London: Harper Torchbooks, 1961), 22, 113.

between theologians on the basis that some exhibit humanist tendencies while others show scholastic inclinations are simply based on a category mistake. More importantly, however, Kristeller has also drawn attention to the fact that, while peripatetic philosophy continued to dominate university education, Renaissance thinkers did not simply preserve Aristotle's thought in academic formaldehyde, but subjected it to constant revision and modification in the light of their own views on rhetoric, grammar, etc.[6] The result was that there came into existence a wide variety of philosophical models, all of which took the Aristotelian corpus as their starting point, and can therefore be classified as Aristotelian, but each of which exhibited its own significant distinctives in terms of both form and content. This is where the work of Charles Schmitt is of such significance. In a series of extremely important articles and books, Schmitt has decisively demonstrated that the pluriformity of Renaissance Aristotelian systems is such that the classification of any given thinker as 'Aristotelian' allows us to draw few, if any, conclusions about the content of his thought prior to a detailed engagement with the relevant primary texts.[7]

In the light of the work of Kristeller and Schmitt, one would think that it should no longer be possible to make sweeping *a priori* judgments about the impact of Aristotelian thought and metaphysical argumentation upon theologians who were educated within an academic world shaped by the Renaissance, and who read widely in the various Aristotelian traditions then available. Yet such sweeping judgments continue to the present day in the writings of those who conduct their research in isolation from the relevant findings of those working in related fields.[8] The task for historians of Protestant scholasticism who wish to map out the impact of Aristotelianism and metaphysics on the tradition is unfortunately not as simple as many have sought to make it:[9] what is needed is not an *a priori*

---

[6] Ibid. 34, 43.

[7] For Schmitt's arguments, see the articles collected in *The Aristotelian Tradition and Renaissance Universities* (London: Variorum, 1984).

[8] E.g. Clifford, *Atonement and Justification*, 95–110; Holtrop, *Bolsec Controversy*, *passim*; M. Jinkins, 'Theodore Beza: Continuity and Regression in the Reformed Tradition', *Evangelical Quarterly* 64 (1992), 131–54; A.E. McGrath, *A Life of John Calvin* (Oxford; Blackwell, 1990), 212ff.; J.B. Torrance, 'The Incarnation and "Limited Atonement" ', *Evangelical Quarterly* 55 (1982), 83–94.

[9] In an important article, the full significance of which has yet, it would seem, to be appreciated, Lynne C. Boughton has decisively demonstrated that the use of metaphysical argumentation in Reformed theology often had the opposite effect to that which many scholars have alleged. In fact, as she has shown, it was the exclusion of metaphysics from theological argumentation which led to the development of supralapsarian systems: see 'Supralapsarianism and the Role of Metaphysics in Sixteenth-Century Reformed Theology', *Westminster Theological Journal* 48 (1986), 63–96.

model of interpretation into which the evidence must somehow be forced to fit, but a careful examination of the content of the various Aristotelian and metaphysical strands which are evident in any given theologian's work; only then will it be possible to establish what specific kind of philosophical sources and ideas are being used, and what distinctive impact, if any, they have on a particular individual's work.

A TEST CASE: RICHARD BAXTER

A good example of the fruitfulness, and, indeed, the necessity, of this approach is provided by the theology of Richard Baxter. Baxter is particularly interesting because of the extent to which philosophical metaphysics impacts upon his thought, and also because of the uniqueness of his theology. Indeed, his theology defies simple classification in terms of the usual categories of seventeenth-century Protestantism, involving as it does elements from such disparate sources as the Reformed orthodox tradition, Grotius, and the Amyraldian school of Saumur.[10] In addition to these post-Reformation Protestant sources, there is extensive evidence of his deep reading of medieval and Renaissance scholastic works on nearly every page of his writings, the practical almost as much as the dogmatic. For a man who never attended university and was almost entirely self-taught, Baxter's knowledge of scholasticism is remarkable, possibly second to no other Protestant in the seventeenth century. In his early days, he found the scholastic authors particularly appealing for their precision and subtlety, and, despite his later realization that such approaches were not always appropriate, his work continued to reflect his profound reading of scholasticism.[11] References to Thomas, Scotus,

[10]   For a brief but helpful note on the difficulties of defining Baxter's theology, see H. Boersma, *A Hot Peppercorn: Richard Baxter's Doctrine of Justification in Its Seventeenth-Century Context of Controversy* (Zoetermeer: Boekencentrum, 1993), 25–7. On Baxter's life, see F.J. Powicke, *A Life of the Reverend Richard Baxter 1615–1691* (New York: Houghton Mifflin, n.d.); and G.F. Nuttall, *Richard Baxter* (London: Nelson, 1965). Other useful studies of Baxter's thought include G.P. Fisher, 'The Theology of Richard Baxter' and 'The Writings of Richard Baxter', *Bibliotheca Sacra and American Biblical Repository* 9 (1852), 135–69 and 300–29 respectively; the anonymous 'Richard Baxter's "End of Controversy" ', *Bibliotheca Sacra and American Biblical Repository* 12 (1855), 348–85; J.I. Packer, 'The Redemption and Restoration of Man in the Thought of Richard Baxter' (DPhil thesis, University of Oxford, 1954); Gavin J. McGrath, 'Puritans and the Human Will: Voluntarism within Mid-Seventeenth Century Puritanism as Seen in the Thought of Richard Baxter and John Owen' (PhD thesis, University of Durham, 1989).

[11]   See *The Autobiography of Richard Baxter* (Mobile: RE Publications, n.d.), 9–10. No one who has ever glanced at Baxter's *Methodus Theologiae* (London, 1681) could have any doubts that the same concern for method and distinctions remained with him throughout his career.

Durandus, Suarez, etc. abound, and many of his discussions, for example that concerning language, logic and futurity in his *Catholick Theologie*, clearly reflect a positive appropriation of medieval nominalist argumentation.[12]

It is therefore all the more surprising that this area of his thought has been left virtually untouched by recent studies of his theology.[13] This is almost certainly the combined result of the lack of knowledge of medieval theology and philosophy among students of the seventeenth century, and the traditional misconception that scholasticism and piety are mutually exclusive — a position usually maintained, one might add, by Protestant scholars of either pietistic or neo-orthodox leanings who seem never to have read widely in the scholastic literature of either medieval Catholicism or post-Reformation Protestantism, where, in the works of a Thomas Aquinas or a Wilhelmus à Brakel, a remarkable synthesis of doctrine and piety was frequently achieved.[14] As regards Baxter, this tendency has been reinforced by the unfortunate decision of his early editors to separate out and republish only his so-called 'practical works', with the result that he came to be known to posterity only as one who wrote works of popular piety and not as a scholastic theologian. Thus, while there was a strongly pietistic tradition in the eighteenth century which looked back to Baxter for inspiration, this group tended to draw exclusively on his practical works, and not on the dogmatic treatises by which Baxter himself wished to be remembered.[15] The Baxter of popular reputation is therefore the author of *The Reformed Pastor*, *The Saint's Everlasting Rest*, and *The Christian Directory*, the one who 'constantly writes out of experience and from his heart', and not the sophisticated metaphysician of the *Methodus Theologiae*.[16] In fact, however, even when seen solely through the lens of the practical works, such a picture of Baxter is

---

[12]   *Catholick Theologie* (London, 1675), 1.5.64–87.

[13]   The most significant recent study of Baxter, Boersma's *Hot Peppercorn*, makes only an occasional passing reference to the impact of scholastic thought on the Puritan's theology. Another writer on Baxter, Alan Clifford, attempts to drive a wedge between Baxter and Owen on the basis that the latter is scholastic while the former is not. This represents a basic misunderstanding of scholasticism as content not method, and also takes no account of the extensive positive use of scholastic texts, language, method, and argumentation throughout virtually everything Baxter wrote: see Clifford, *Atonement and Justification; passim*.

[14]   See, for example, Aquinas' discussion of prayer in the *Summa Theologiae* 2a2ae.83; also, Wilhelmus à Brakel, *The Christian's Reasonable Service*, trans. B. Elshout (Ligonier: Soli Deo Gloria, 1992-5).

[15]   Fisher, 'Theology of Richard Baxter', 135–6; G.F. Nuttall, *Richard Baxter and Philip Doddridge: A Study in Tradition* (London: Oxford University Press, 1951). Doddridge confessed to finding Baxter's *Methodus Theologiae* 'unintelligible' (17–18).

[16]   Nuttall, *Richard Baxter and Philip Doddridge*, 13.

decidedly one-sided, for in those writings where he is most warm, practical, and pious, there is still distinct evidence of a highly technical scholastic method and an underlying metaphysical interest which point clearly towards the concerns of his more purely doctrinal works and which provide a unity to his corpus that is eclipsed by the separation of the 'practical' works from the rest. For example, in *The Saint's Everlasting Rest*, the central concept of 'rest', around which the whole treatise was structured, was not defined in some pious or mystical way, but in a decidedly metaphysical and Aristotelian manner: 'Rest is the end and perfection of motion.'[17] Nevertheless, this metaphysical foundation, couched in scholastic language, did not prevent the work from enjoying the status of a devotional classic, replete with piety.

That the basic orientation of his metaphysics is broadly Aristotelian is beyond dispute and should be no surprise, given the contemporary Aristotelian dominance of higher learning and the seventeenth century Reformed suspicion that Platonism provided the philosophical background to Arminianism.[18] The important question, then, is not about whether he was an Aristotelian, but about what kind of Aristotelian he was.

The answer is not difficult to discover if one follows the right clues. Baxter's writings exhibit one methodological characteristic which makes them quite distinctive in terms of seventeenth-century Reformed systems: a threefold division of topics, rather than the more typical twofold division or bifurcation that one finds, for example, in the writings of William Perkins and William Ames.[19] Such bifurcation was commonplace among Puritans influenced by Ramist logic, but was not restricted to Ramists as it had been part of the rhetorical theory of the Agricolan school.[20] Several times in his writings, Baxter expressed his dissatisfaction with this approach, most dramatically perhaps in a passage in the *Reliquiae Baxterianae*:

> Having long (upon the suspension of my *Aphorisms*) been purposing to draw up a method of theology, I now began it. I never yet saw a scheme or method of physics or theology which gave any satisfaction to my reason. . . . I had been twenty-six years convinced that dichotomising will not do

---

[17] *Practical Works* 3 (London, 1707), 10.

[18] See, for example, the comments on the Platonic and Plotinian origin of Thomas Jackson's view of the decrees in the prefatory letter to William Twisse's *A Discovery of D. Jacksons Vanitie* (London, 1631).

[19] See Perkins' *A Golden Chaine* in his *Workes* 1 (London, 1608), 9–118; William Ames, *The Marrow of Theology*, trans. J.D. Eusden (Durham: Labyrinth, 1983).

[20] See W.J. Ong, *Ramus: Method and the Decay of Dialogue* (Cambridge, Mass.: Harvard University Press, 1958), 127–8.

it, but that the Divine Trinity in Unity hath expressed itself in the whole frame of nature and morality.[21]

The passage is interesting because it draws attention to the apparent theological ground for rejecting bifurcation: it is inadequate because it fails to do justice to the trinitarian nature of the revelation which Baxter perceives in the created realm, the threefold nature of being itself. If this were all he had to say on the matter, it would be quite reasonable to interpret the thinking behind this statement as similar to Augustine's references to the vestiges of the Trinity in the created realm in *On the Trinity*, Book 9. As such, it would appear as a somewhat idiosyncratic position in the seventeenth-century Reformed context, but would give no insight into the contemporary sources of Baxter's metaphysics. Fortunately, however, it is not all that he had to say on this issue: in the preface to the *Methodus Theologiae*, the work referred to in the autobiographical quotation, he gave far more detailed reasons for his belief in the need for trichotomizing.

In this work, there is a paragraph in which Baxter outlined his pilgrimage from being convinced of the methodological correctness of bifurcation to that of trichotomizing. The breakthrough came, he said, when he realized that God had impressed his trinitarian nature on all of his higher [*nobiliora*] works; what is significant is that he states that he came to this conviction not by reading the Bible, or even Augustine, the most obvious extra-biblical source, but by reading the *Metaphysics* of Tommaso Campanella.[22] The reference is extremely important to any understanding of Baxter's thought because it identifies the source both of one of his major methodological distinctives, and also of a considerable amount of his own metaphysical convictions.

Tommaso Campanella (1568–1639) was a Renaissance figure whose radical scientific and philosophical views meant that he was constantly under suspicion by the authorities and spent a considerable amount of his life suffering imprisonment and torture.[23] Most famous perhaps for his

---

[21]   *Autobiography*, 212.

[22]   'Ex lectione Campanellae (praecipue ejus Metaphysices) lucis nonnihil mihi emicuit.' *Methodus Theologiae*, Praefatio, 5 (no page numbering in original); also 'Quando vero a re subjecta sumenda est methodus olerumque Trichotomiam praeferendam sentio. *Trinitas* enim in *Unitate*, et *Unitas* in *Trinitate* a Deo ipso in omnia sua opera nobiliora activa clare impressa sunt. A rebus autem Methodus est. Hoc sicut Campanella, D. Glissonus et Scholasticorum plurimi ostendarunt' ibid., 6.

[23]   For a brief but accessible account of his life, see B.M. Bonansea, *Tommaso Campanella: Renaissance Pioneer of Modern Thought* (Washington: Catholic University of America Press, 1969), 23–32. The edition of Campanella which I have used for this article is the facsimile of the 1638 Paris edition, ed. Luigi Firpo (Turin: Bottega

defence of Galileo, he was also a philosopher of considerable acumen, who, despite his troubled life, still managed to write a considerable number of philosophical and theological works which sought to modify some of the traditional understanding of metaphysics and to overcome various problems left unresolved by the medieval scholastics.[24] In fact, at the heart of his philosophical agenda lay the desire to overthrow the broad Aristotelian world-view, particularly as represented by the Paduan Averroism of the time, and replace it with a new system which, while still empiricist in orientation, also embodied Platonic and even pre-Socratic elements, and which also took full account of the new scientific and geographical discoveries of the time.[25] There is, however, no evidence to suggest that it was Campanella's anti-Aristotelian polemic which commended his thought to Baxter. Indeed, the one point where Baxter is most influenced by the Italian philosopher is in a specific area of metaphysics where Campanella's work is more a revision of Aristotelianism than its outright rejection: his understanding of the nature of being. In his reconstruction of the concept of being, Campanella broke with the traditional Aristotelian approach of dividing it into two constituents, act and potency. This break with the tradition is not, however, precipitated by Campanella's total rejection of the appropriateness of applying these terms to existent reality, but by his belief that they should not be considered to be the most basic constituents of being. That place is reserved for the so-called primalities, of which there are three — power, wisdom, and love — which apply to all actual existents, primarily to God and analogically to creatures.[26]

Campanella defined these three primalities broadly as follows: power, the first primality, is fundamentally the power *to be*, to exist, to live, and as such logically precedes all other acts of power;[27] wisdom, the second primality, is the sensing of existence, primarily of the self, and as such points forward to the empiricist concerns of his scientific method;[28] and

---

d'Erasmo, 1961). His thought is discussed in the context of its times in J. Kvacala, *Thomas Campanella: Ein Reformer der Ausgehenden Renaissance* (Berlin: Trowitzsch, 1973).

[24] E.g. Bonansea, *Tomasso Campanella*, 139–40.

[25] On Campanella's desire to overthrow the authority of Aristotle and Aristotelianism, see the following: J.M. Headley, 'Tommaso Campanella and the end of the Renaissance', *Journal of Medieval and Renaissance Studies* 20 (1990), 157–74; idem, 'Tommaso Campanella and Jean de Launoy: The Controversy over Aristotle and his Reception in the West', *Renaissance Quarterly* 43 (1990), 529–50; M.-P. Lerner, 'Campanella, Juge d'Aristote', *Platon et Aristote à la Renaissance* (XVI Colloque International de Tours), ed. M. Gandillac (Paris: Librairie Philosophique J. Vrin, 1976), 335–57.

[26] See the title of *Metaphysics* 2.6.11.1.

[27] Ibid. 2.6.5.1.

[28] Ibid. 2.6.7.

love, the third primality, is the desire to exist, which is logically dependent upon both the power to exist and the knowledge of existence.[29] This last point is indicative of the hierarchical ordering of the primalities within Campanella's system: while he adamantly refused to ascribe chronological priority to any one of the primalities, arguing that they are all always simultaneous,[30] he did allow for the logical priority of power over wisdom, and of both of these over love. Thus, a procession of primalities is established where wisdom proceeds from power, and love proceeds from both.[31] (It is worth noting in passing the similarity between Campanella's understanding of the structure of being and Western understandings of the Trinity, with the emphasis on the *filioque* clause.)

This in turn leads to a second point: Campanella's metaphysics is directly related to his theology. God is the supreme being and the source of all other being and beings, and in creating he communicates his threefold nature to the creation: as far as anything can be said to exist, it must have been given that existence by God and must reflect the threefold nature of God's being.[32]

The impact of the Campanellan revision of Aristotelian metaphysics upon the thought of Richard Baxter is evident throughout his work, particularly in his two major systematic treatises, the *Catholick Theologie* and the *Methodus Theologiae*. The most obvious point at which the Campanellan scheme was used by Baxter as a tool for positive theological construction is in his doctrine of God, where he adopts the categories of power, wisdom, and love as defining the fundamental attributes of deity. Basic to God's immanent acts is that he lives, he understands, and he loves, and the same economic pattern is also followed in his external acts.[33] This whole scheme is given a specifically trinitarian reference by the ascription of one particular attribute to each person of the deity.[34] What is interesting is that this scheme was not confined to Baxter's two most scholastic works but also finds its way into the practical works as a principle both of organization and of piety. For example, in *The Life of Faith*, Baxter urged the believer to meditate upon the threefold image of God which he

---

29   Ibid. 2.6.10.1.
30   *Met.* 1.2.2.4.
31   Ibid. 1.2.2.4.
32   *Met.* 2.6.7.1.
33   *Methodus Theologiae* 1a.2, 37; *Catholick Theologie* 1.3.25.
34   'Certum habeo Deum tripliciter (inadaequate) a nobis concipiendum esse. 1. In esse Virtutis seu Potentiae Vitalis Activae Intellectivae, Volitivae; 2. In Actu triplici Immanente, vel ad se; 3. In Actione Transeunte ad extra, quatenus Agentis est. 9. Certum est in S. Literis, opera Potentiae saepissime quodammodo ascribi Patri, opera Sapientiae Filio, opera Amoris Spiritui Sancto.' *Methodus Theologiae* 1a.2.7; cf. *Catholick Theologie* 1a.3.26–7.

defines, in order, as wisdom, goodness or love, and power.[35] Here the scheme offers both a way in which to discuss God's attributes in relationship to salvation and a way for believers to organize their devotional meditation upon the work of God in Christ. There is, therefore, a clear connection at this point between Baxter's metaphysics, his methodology, his dogmatic works, and his practical piety. Indeed, the significance of his choice of these three attributes will be (and perhaps always has been) completely missed if his practical works are isolated from the wider theological and philosophical context in which they were written.

The threefold scheme also led Baxter to revise the traditional scholastic vocabulary for discussing the relationship of God's knowledge to his external acts. Medieval scholastics had developed an understanding of God's knowledge of the created world which used the twofold division of the knowledge of simple intelligence and the knowledge of vision. The object of the former was the set of all possibles which God knew simply by knowing himself, his own essence, while that of the latter was the set of all those things which God had willed to come to pass.[36] The distinction proved useful and was adopted by the Protestant scholastics of the seventeenth century. Thus, for example, we find Baxter's contemporary, John Owen, using it in his conflict with the Arminians.[37] Baxter, however, rejected this distinction as inadequate on the basis of his doctrine of God. God, he said, relates to his creation in three ways: omnipotence; knowledge; and will or love.[38] The three points of relation obviously correspond to the three fundamental attributes of God's being which Baxter derives from his reading of Campanella, and they provide the basis for his critique of the twofold scholastic distinction. Instead of arguing for a knowledge of simple intelligence and a knowledge of vision, Baxter preferred a knowledge of all things possible, a knowledge of all things congruous, and a knowledge of all things actually willed.[39]

If we did not know about Baxter's use of Campanellan metaphysics, then the move he makes here would seem to be of little significance, and we might be tempted to interpret it as a point of merely logical or organizational importance. The religious motivation behind it would seem, on the surface, to be a desire to avoid a radically voluntarist understanding of God by introducing the notion of congruity or fittingness between God's absolute and ordained power. God is bound, so to speak, to act in a manner that is fitting, and certain members of the set of all possibles can be ruled out from the start as being in themselves

---

[35] *Practical Works* 3, 540–7.
[36] See Aquinas, *Summa Theologiae* 1a.14.9.
[37] *The Works of John Owen* 10 (Edinburgh: T. & T. Clark, 1862), 23.
[38] *Catholick Theologie* 1.4.36.
[39] Ibid. 1.4.45–52.

incongruous. Thus the innovation safeguards the doctrine of God from any ambiguity which could have been attached to it. Such an interpretation is less than satisfactory, however, as the same result could easily have been achieved within the framework provided by the traditional twofold distinction. Indeed, the latter could sit quite happily with doctrines of God that were strongly intellectualist in orientation and which involved a distinctive emphasis upon the need for God to act in a fitting manner, as in the case of John Owen's arguments regarding the necessity of incarnation and atonement, where Owen argues that God's internal attributes demand that sin be punished in some way and thus prevent him from forgiving sinners by a mere act of his will.[40]

In fact, in the light of Baxter's adoption of Campanellan metaphysics, we can clearly see that Baxter's criticism of the traditional distinction concerning God's knowledge is more than a mere organizational or logical point: Baxter is actually drawing out the implications of his acceptance of Campanellan metaphysics for his understanding of God in order to strengthen and confirm his larger argument against any notion that God is the author of sin and, by inference, against a harshly deterministic worldview.[41] In Campanella's philosophy, Baxter found a metaphysics which could obviously be used to support his own theological agenda here, as all of God's external acts must be seen as the communication of the three primalities, and thus as involving not simply naked power but also wisdom and love. Therefore the specific issue in hand, the relationship of God's knowledge to what happens in the created realm, must also be defined at its most basic level in terms of a threefold act of power, wisdom, and will or love, a definition which is not simply a clarification of traditional ideas but which also points decisively to the distinctive contribution of Campanellan metaphysics to Baxter's theology. Indeed, precisely the same link between the rejection of traditional distinctions and a threefold metaphysics of being can be found in Campanella's own work, where the same dissatisfaction with the scholastic distinction between knowledge of simple intelligence and knowledge of vision is found, and where emphasis is placed upon the importance of God's immanent knowledge or wisdom as a controlling bridge between an almighty God and the realm of creation.[42] For both Campanella and Baxter, in theological terms, God's external works reflect his internal being, and so all of his activity within the created

---

[40] For Owen on the necessity of atonement, see his *Dissertation on Divine Justice* in *Works* 10, 481–624. On Owen's intellectualism, see Carl R. Trueman, 'John Owen's *Dissertation on Divine Justice*: An Exercise in Christocentric Scholasticism', *Calvin Theological Journal* (forthcoming); also *The Claims of Truth: John Owen's Trinitarian Theology* (Carlisle: Paternoster, 1997).

[41] This argument occupies most of the first part of *Catholick Theologie*.

[42] *Metaphysics* 2.8.4.6; cf. Bonansea, 214–15.

realm must be in accordance with his three basic attributes; and this is supported by a metaphysical framework which demands that God's act of creating and sustaining the external world involves the communication of the three primalities to that world. In light of this, the kind of revised distinctions in the knowledge of God which we find in Baxter and Campanella, while not absolutely necessary, are at least easily understandable and highly desirable, as the more traditional language fails entirely to draw attention to the threefold nature of being, and the implications of this for the God–creature relationship which depends upon it. More importantly, failure to appreciate the link between Campanella and Baxter effectively prevents the reader from fully understanding what Baxter is doing at this point.

This leads to the most radical way in which Campanellan metaphysics influenced the theology of Baxter: the revelation of the Trinity in creation. In the autobiographical quotation cited earlier, it was clear that Baxter regarded all of the created realm as reflecting God's trinitarian nature, and, as has become evident, he was able to do this on the basis of his assumption of the fundamental correctness of Campanella's three primalities of being, to which he himself gave a specifically trinitarian dimension. The implications of this move are little short of revolutionary within the world of seventeenth-century Reformed theology, as it lifts the doctrine of the Trinity out of the exclusive sphere of special revelation and places it within the framework of a generalized metaphysics of being, a natural theology. That this is so is not lost on Baxter himself:

> The Essential Immanent Acts of God are Three: 1. *SIBI VIVERE*, or to be Essential Active Life in Himself; 2. *SE INTELLIGERE*, to know Himself; 3. *SE AMARE*, or to be *amor sui*. . . . I have elsewhere shewed that many of them, and other divines, do take the last named Immanent Acts in God, to be the same with the Three Persons or Subsistences; Even the Three Divine Principles (*Potentia-Actus*, *Intellectus*, and *Voluntas*) as in Act thus Immanently; But of these great Mysteries elsewhere. All that I say here is, that seeing the Trinity of Divine Principles (or formal Essentialities) and the Threefold Act, are so certainly evident to Natural Reason itself, that no understanding person can deny them, we have no Reason to think the Trinity of Eternal Subsistences incredible, and a thing that the Christian faith is to be suspected for, but quite the contrary; though they are mysteries above our reach (as all of God is, as to a full or formal apprehension).[43]

The Campanellan language and metaphysics are obvious here, as is the purpose to which they are being put: a philosophical defence of the

---

[43]   *Catholick Theologie* 1.3.25, 27.

rationality of the doctrine of the Trinity. While we have to beware of interpreting Baxter's position here as leading him to a more explicitly radical theological position than was in fact the case, and also acknowledge that he does not go so far as to say outright that the doctrine of the Trinity can be proved simply on the basis of natural theology,[44] it must be pointed out that Baxter's position is somewhat different from the general Reformed tradition of the time which was highly sceptical of any use of natural analogies when discussing the Trinity.[45] Furthermore, there seems to be no reason why one could not use Campanellan metaphysics, as deployed by Baxter, as a basis for constructing a speculative doctrine of the Trinity on purely rational principles independent of special revelation, particularly when one bears in mind the parallel between the procession of primalities and the Western understanding of the procession of the persons.

The significance of Baxter's move here can be seen when comparison is made with the theology of his contemporary, and frequent opponent, John Owen. Owen's use of Aristotelian concepts has been documented, and his dependence at points upon metaphysics has also received attention.[46] Nevertheless, in all of Owen's writings, there are specific safety mechanisms built into his thinking which provide a defence against rationalism in the sense of an unrestrained use of human reason and logic as the primary criteria for doctrinal construction and evaluation. These mechanisms can be reduced to two basic points: general revelation, even in an objective sense, can give humans knowledge only of God the Creator, not God the Redeemer;[47] and the doctrine of the Trinity is available only within the sphere of God's special revelation and is in no way accessible via unaided human reason or natural theology.[48] Without a sound grasp of the Trinity, reason is useless in matters of theology, and thus its competence is radically subordinated to faith. There can be no true 'rationalism' within Owen's theology because reason can only operate within the context of faith, and it can only do this because the Trinity, the very foundation of Owen's whole theological scheme, is a doctrine which must be believed because it cannot be reached by reason alone.

---

[44]   See especially his comments in the *Methodus Theologiae*, 1a.2.7.
[45]   Cf. Calvin, *Institutes* 1.13.18; also the citations in *RD*, 105–6, where Heppe does, however, make the point that later, more rationalistically inclined theologians such as Keckermann did rehabilitate the more speculative approaches of Augustine and Melanchthon.
[46]   See Trueman, *Claims of Truth*; idem, 'John Owen's *Dissertation on Divine Justice*'.
[47]   *Works* 17, 54–5.
[48]   Ibid. 16, 340–1.

In contrast, then, to Owen, Baxter's speculative arguments about the Trinity based on Campanellan metaphysics represent a distinct move towards a more rationalistically oriented theology. Owen's doctrine of the Trinity has its own inner rationality where human reason seeks to understand that which faith presents to it, but it is not an example of rationalism because unaided human reason cannot aspire to an understanding of trinitarian doctrine by its own power. In Baxter's theology, by contrast, the very thing that prevents Owen from sliding into an unbridled use of human reason, the status of the Trinity as the exclusive property of special revelation, is potentially placed within humanity's grasp because of its relation to the general nature of being as a threefold, hierarchical phenomenon. Baxter's appropriation of the Campanellan critique of Aristotle thus opens the door for the development of a speculative doctrine of the Trinity, while Owen's more traditional Aristotelian metaphysics, with its twofold division of being into act and potency, has no such immediate point of contact with the doctrine and does not lend itself to such use.[49] One might almost say that, in comparison to that of Owen, Baxter's thinking at this point has certain affinities with the Socinian method: the Socinians used human reason as the criterion for determining what the Bible meant, which doctrines could be accepted, which rejected, etc.; Baxter, while not going that far, is still putting into place a metaphysical structure which broadens greatly the sphere of human reason's competence. While it might be provocative to some, it would not be entirely misleading to describe his thought on this issue as something of a halfway house between the more traditionally Reformed position of John Owen and the views of a Socinian such as John Biddle.[50]

CONCLUSION

A number of concluding observations immediately suggest themselves. First, as far as the broader scholarly picture is concerned, it is clear that the use of models of historical interpretation based upon generalized notions of the impact of 'Aristotelianism' or 'metaphysics' on the theology of the seventeenth century is not a tenable option for future scholarship. The seventeenth century world is simply too complex for such simplistic approaches ever to yield accurate and interesting results. 'Aristotelianism' is a pluriform phenomenon, as is evidenced by the variety of Aristotelian

---

[49]   For Owen's acceptance of the twofold nature of being, see, for example, *Works* 10, 19–20.

[50]   For Biddle on the Scripture principle, see his *A Twofold Catechism* (London, 1654), 1–6; on his life and theology in general, see H.J. McLachlan, *Socinianism in Seventeenth-Century England* (Oxford: Oxford University Press, 1951), 163–217.

schools in existence in the Renaissance and post-Renaissance world. Furthermore, the results of using 'metaphysics' are scarcely monolithic. No one disputes that both Baxter and Owen used metaphysics positively, but that in itself explains neither the differences in their methodologies nor the differences in their theologies. A more considered approach, based upon precise examination of primary texts and contemporary sources, is the only key to understanding why men such as Baxter thought and wrote the way they did.

Secondly, it is also clear that there is considerable work to be done on the sources of Baxter's thought. Whether dealing with his practical works or with his controversial writings, any approach which focuses solely upon the narrow seventeenth-century English, or even Protestant, context without reference to the wider Western tradition will simply not do justice to the content and structure of his theology. His use of medieval and Renaissance scholastic sources, and, one might add, the relationship between his practical and his doctrinal writings, needs to be explored in far greater depth than has hitherto been the case. Indeed, the 'Campanella connection' is an excellent example of the potential fruitfulness of such an approach, solving as it does a number of problems which should perplex anyone who reads Baxter, such as why he opts for trichotomizing rather than bifurcation, why he needs to revise the generally accepted scholastic vocabulary, and what is the underlying continuity between his doctrinal and his practical works — none of which can be answered on the basis of any Baxterian scholarhip to date. A brief paper such as this can, of course, only scratch the surface, merely hint at what potential there is in this field, but even so, it should by now be clear that Baxter's dependence upon a thinker such as Campanella for things as basic as general ontology and methodology makes it crucial that a full exploration of this aspect of his thought should now be undertaken in order to further our understanding of the dynamics of English Reformed thought in the mid-seventeenth century.

Finally, it is also clear that, in Baxter, we see hints of that truly rationalistic tendency within theology which was ultimately to bring about the collapse of Reformed orthodoxy in the following century. By making a small but decisive move towards placing the doctrine of the Trinity at the disposal of a general, naturalistic metaphysics, Baxter was in effect, and no doubt inadvertently, pointing towards the surrender of that most distinctive of Christian doctrines to the slings and arrows of autonomous human rationality. That Baxter was a writer of brilliant pastoral insight and piety, no one will deny; but it must not be forgotten that he was also a metaphysician of considerable acumen whose methodological and metaphysical innovations symbolized in a small but decisive way the movement towards a more rationalistic theology.

4

Scottish Reformed Scholasticism

P.G. Ryken

The aim of this essay is to draw Scottish Reformed scholasticism into the current discussion about Protestant scholasticism. That Scotland is usually omitted from that discussion is not surprising. As we shall see, the Scottish contribution to Protestant scholasticism was relatively small. Furthermore, Scottish ecclesiastical historiography has often been parochial, failing to locate Scotland within the wider context of international Calvinism.[1] There are exceptions to this insularity, of course. John Knox's inheritance from Luther, Calvin, and other reformers is well known,[2] as are the Scottish contributions to the writing of the Westminster Standards (1643–8).[3] Yet Scotland's place within the international Reformed community is often overlooked. The history of the Scottish church is usually told as its own story rather than as an episode in a wider narrative. The result has been that Scotland's participation in the incessant international interchange of post-Reformation thought rarely receives the sensitive treatment it deserves.

By its very nature, Scottish Reformed scholasticism demands to be placed within the broad narrative of Protestant orthodoxy. Yet on those rare occasions when Scottish ecclesiastical studies have given it any

---

[1] In his *Religious Life in Seventeenth-Century Scotland* (Cambridge: Cambridge University Press, 1937), G.D. Henderson attempted to remedy this deficiency (see especially 60–99), but few have followed his lead.

[2] See W. Stanford Reid, 'Reformation in France and Scotland: A Case Study in Sixteenth-Century Communication', *Later Calvinism: International Perspectives*, ed. W. Fred Graham, Sixteenth Century Essays and Studies 22 (Kirksville, Mo.: Sixteenth Century Journal, 1994), 195–214.

[3] See especially Wayne R. Spear, 'Covenanted Uniformity in Religion: The Influence of the Scottish Commissioners upon the Ecclesiology of the Westminster Assembly' (unpublished doctoral diss., University of Pittsburgh, 1976).

attention at all, scholasticism has been greeted with suspicion, even hostility. Its influence has often been considered pernicious. The nineteenth-century historian Henry Grey Graham spoke disparagingly of a Scottish clergy encumbered with '*Turretini Opera*, and many a work of Dutch Divinity, in Latin which was clumsy and ponderous as the barges on Dutch canals'.[4] A more recent study concludes that the theology of such works contributed to the 'excessive scholasticizing' or 'general scholasticizing of Reformed dogmatics' in Scotland.[5] Similarly, M. Charles Bell has described the history of Scottish Reformed theology in the seventeenth century as a long, slow decline 'from the vibrant, evangelical theology of Calvin to the more intellectualized scholasticism of the later Federal theologians'.[6] One is left with the vague impression that scholasticism is a 'bad thing' that invaded Scottish theology from the continent. But this is far from a settled conclusion, and there remains a need for a full scholarly investigation into the relationship between Protestant scholasticism and Scottish theology.

The present study cannot satisfy the need for that investigation, but it can at least suggest some areas worth investigating. In surveying the landscape of seventeenth- and early eighteenth-century Scottish Reformed orthodoxy, it advances four hypotheses about Scottish Reformed scholasticism:

1. The Scottish divines of the seventeenth and early eighteenth centuries had a keen appetite for Reformed scholastic theology.
2. The Scots made a contribution to Protestant scholasticism, but it was a small one, relatively speaking.
3. However dominant scholastic methods were in theological education in Scotland during this period, they were not prominent in Scottish homiletics. The elements of scholasticism that did appear in the pulpit — principally in the form of Ramism — were adapted to the spiritual needs of the average parishioner.

---

[4] Henry Grey Graham, *The Social Life of Scotland in the Eighteenth Century*, 2 vols. (London: Black, 1900), 1, 15.

[5] Donald J. Bruggink, 'The Theology of Thomas Boston, 1676–1732' (unpublished doctoral thesis, University of Edinburgh, 1956), 24, 28 (cf. 11, 121–3, 346). See also Stewart Mechie, 'The Theological Climate in Early Eighteenth Century Scotland' in *Reformation and Revolution*, ed. Duncan Shaw (Edinburgh: Saint Andrew Press, 1967), 258–72 (267); and Michael J. Crawford, *Seasons of Grace: Colonial New England's Revival Tradition in its British Context* (Oxford: Oxford University Press, 1991), 58.

[6] M. Charles Bell, *Calvin and Scottish Theology: The Doctrine of Assurance* (Edinburgh: Handsel Press, 1985), 84. Bell seems to be echoing the view espoused by Thomas F. Torrance in his introduction to *The School of Faith: The Catechisms of the Reformed Church* (London: Clarke, 1959).

4. The tools of scholasticism were sometimes mishandled in Scottish
    ecclesiastical controversies of the early eighteenth century, with
    the result that disputes were exacerbated rather than clarified.

It is important to recognize that the preceding propositions are hypotheses
rather than theses. The present study will provide enough evidence to
suggest their plausibility as the former without demonstrating their truth
as the latter. The propositions may turn out to require substantial
modification. They may even prove to be false. Yet they will at least serve
the purpose of drawing Scotland into the discussion about Protestant
scholasticism. And to the extent that the hypotheses are true, they serve
to illuminate the relationship between Scottish Presbyterianism and the
international Reformed community.

THE SCOTTISH APPETITE FOR SCHOLASTIC THEOLOGY

The first thing to be said about Scottish Reformed scholasticism is that
the Scots had a tremendous appetite for scholastic theology. The reception of scholastic theology in Scotland, particularly towards the end of
the seventeenth century, is a measure of the flourishing of Protestant
scholasticism in post-Reformation Europe.

One index of the Scottish appetite for Reformed scholasticism is the
frequency with which Scottish students ventured overseas for their
theological education. Those who aspired to pastoral ministry gravitated
towards the centres of Reformed orthodoxy in Germany, France, and
especially Holland.[7] Eighty Scottish students appeared on the matricula-
tion rolls at Leyden between 1620 and 1650,[8] and by 1700 one-third of
the students at the university were British (mostly Scottish). The reason
they were there, of course, was to study Reformed orthodoxy with
theologians like Johannes Marckius (1656–1713).[9] One result of this
interaction was that Dutch scholastic theology exercised a formative
influence over Scottish theology in the seventeenth century.[10]

---

[7]   Henderson, 62, 68, 71.

[8]   Ibid. 71.

[9]   Andrew L. Drummond, *The Kirk and the Continent* (Edinburgh: Saint Andrew,
1956), 137, 142.

[10] Keith L. Sprunger, *Dutch Puritanism: A History of English and Scottish Churches of
the Netherlands in the Sixteenth and Seventeenth Centuries*, Studies in the History of
Christian Thought, 31 (Leiden: E.J. Brill, 1982), 357. See also Henderson, 78, who
argues that the importance of Dutch influences 'in Scottish Church history is difficult
to exaggerate'.

University curricula provide another measure of the Scottish appetite for scholastic theology. In the eyes of one historian the seventeenth-century arts programme for Scottish undergraduates was 'pure scholasticism';[11] to another it seemed 'a decadent and eclectic scholasticism.'[12] In any case, it was a scholastic education. The same might well be said of the graduate programme for Scottish divinity students. By the 1690s, scholastic dogmatic theologies by Andreas Essenius (1618–77) and Leonardus Rijssenius (c. s1636–1700) comprised virtually the entire divinity curriculum at the University of Edinburgh.[13] Essenius' *Compendium Theologiae Dogmaticum* formed the basis for public lectures in the Divinity Hall,[14] while Rijssenius' *Summa Theologiae Elencticae* (which was actually an abridgment of Francis Turretin's *Institutio*) was used for private tutorials.[15] Each of these volumes was a comprehensive systematic theology, complete with full scholastic apparatus. The steady demand for such works in Scotland is highlighted by the fact that an edition of Rijssenius was published within the precincts of Edinburgh in 1692.

Scottish reliance on continental learning during the seventeenth century has sometimes been viewed as a sign of intellectual weakness, or even folly. Andrew L. Drummond writes of the 'intolerable boredom' that Scottish theology professors produced 'by echoing the opinions of the authorities they venerated'.[16] In a similar vein, Hugh Trevor-Roper speaks of a Scotland 'refreshed mainly by the stale waters of Calvinist bigotry fed to it through the narrow conduits of Utrecht and Sedan and Geneva'.[17] Scottish divinity students may well have been bored, but if they were, it was not because they were drinking from theological backwaters. The Scottish universities were getting their theology straight from the purest fountains of Reformed scholasticism on the continent.

Further evidence of the Scottish appetite for Reformed scholastic theology comes from the personal libraries of Scottish clergy. Scottish

---

[11] Ibid. 122 (cf. 198).

[12] Roger L. Emerson, 'Scottish Universities in the Eighteenth Century, 1690–1800', *Studies on Voltaire and the Eighteenth Century*, ed. James A. Leith, vol. 167 (Oxford: The Voltaire Foundation at the Taylor Institution, 1977), 453–74 (464).

[13] Thomas Boston, *The Complete Works of the Late Rev. Thomas Boston of Ettrick*, ed. Samuel McMillan, 12 vols. (London: Robert Tegg, 1853/Wheaton, Ill.: Richard Owen Roberts, 1980), XII, 21.

[14] Andreas Essenius, *Compendium Theologiae Dogmaticum* (Utrecht, 1685^2).

[15] Leonardus Rijssenius, *Summa Theologiae Elencticae* (Edinburgh, 1692); Francis Turretin, *Institutio Theologiae Elencticae*, 3 vols. (Geneva, 1688–9).

[16] Drummond, 144.

[17] Hugh Trevor-Roper, 'The Scottish Enlightenment' in *Studies on Voltaire and the Eighteenth Century*, ed. Theodore Besterman (Geneva: Institut et Musée Voltaire, 1967), 1635–58 (1643).

ministers did not leave scholasticism behind when they left the academy.
The example of Gabriel Wilson (*c*.1679–1750) is instructive. The citations
in his appendix to the *Answers* of the Marrow men read like a 'Who's
Who' of Protestant scholasticism: Ames, Bucanus, Daneau, Essenius,
Heidegger, Junius, Maresius, Melanchthon, Owen, Perkins, Polyander,
van Mastricht, Witsius, Wollebius, and others.[18] Even if Wilson's library
was of extraordinary quality,[19] it reveals the extent to which Protestant
scholasticism had penetrated Scotland by the end of the seventeenth
century.

Wilson's ministerial colleague, Thomas Boston (1676–1732), was not
nearly as fortunate. Indeed, he often lamented the impoverished condition of his personal library.[20] Yet Boston was able to imbibe liberal
quantities of Reformed scholasticism, and his works are sprinkled with
references to Protestant scholastics like Wolfgang Musculus, Theodore
Beza, Zacharias Ursinus, Girolamo Zanchi, Johannes Polyander, Marcus
Wendelinus, John Owen, Andreas Essenius, Herman Witsius, and especially Francis Turretin.[21] The fact that Wilson and Boston were rural
pastors rather than urban academics underscores the pervasiveness of
Protestant scholasticism in Scotland. Reformed scholastic theology was a
staple in the intellectual diet of the rural Scottish manse as well as the
Scottish college.

THE SCOTTISH CONTRIBUTION

Scottish ministers and theologians of the seventeenth century were eager
consumers of Reformed scholastic theology, but they were not major
producers. For the most part, the Scots were users rather than dealers of
Protestant scholasticism. Scholastic works flowed into Scotland from
elsewhere in Europe but Scottish works were not read widely on the
continent. In the international Reformed community, Scotland was on
the short end of the balance of scholastic trade.

That hypothesis is easier to disprove than to prove, and it is in need
of substantial qualification almost as soon as it is stated. Exceptions quickly
spring to mind. John Sharp (or Joannes Scharpius; *c*.1572–*c*.1647) is
perhaps the best exemplar of Scottish Reformed scholasticism. His *Cursus*

---

[18] In John Brown (of Whitburn), *Gospel Truth Accurately Stated and Illustrated*
(Glasgow, 1831[rev.]), 239–61.
[19] Thomas Boston, *Works*, XII, 333, refers to it as a 'great collection of books'.
[20] Boston, *Works*, XII, 102, 154–5.
[21] On the international scope of Boston's Calvinism, see my 'Thomas Boston
(1676–1732) as Preacher of the *Fourfold State*' (unpublished doctoral thesis, University of Oxford, 1995), 11–17.

theologicus is scholastic in at least three respects.[22] First, it is scholastic in its intellectual origin. Sharp frequently cites medieval sources for definition and critique, thereby entering into the theological disputes that exercised Peter Lombard, Duns Scotus, Thomas Aquinas, and other medieval scholastics. The *Cursus theologicus* is thus the best Scottish example of the repristination of medieval scholasticism in Reformed orthodoxy. Second, Sharp's 'theological course' is scholastic in its organization. Its division into the theses, queries, objections, and responses reflects the pedagogical necessities of life at Die University, where Sharp lectured as Professor of Theology. Third, it is scholastic in its polemical engagement with Roman Catholic theologians (especially Robert Bellarmine). The *Cursus theologicus* is scholastic in every sense of the word and represents the most comprehensive Scottish synthesis of Reformed scholastic dogmatics. Despite Sharp's scholastic credentials, however, it is worth noting that the *Cursus theologicus* was not written and published in Scotland, but on the continent. Sharp did his academic work in exile, and his scholastic achievement owes as much (or more) to France than it does to Scotland.

The same may be said of the scholastic achievement of John Cameron (*c.*1579–1625). Like Sharp, Cameron spent his most productive years in France and did his publishing on the continent. (Incidentally, these French connections confirm the value of viewing Scottish theology within its international context.) Cameron did not produce a complete body of divinity like Sharp did, but his *Opera* are no less scholastic.[23] For example, Cameron uses his explications of scriptural *loci* from Matthew as a vehicle for disputing Roman Catholic theology. By organizing his exposition into theses, proofs, distinctions, causes, arguments, responses, objections, refutations, and the like, Cameron is able to cover the full range of Protestant-Catholic polemics.

The academic career of Samuel Rutherford (1600–61) differs from those of Sharp and Cameron because — with the exception of a hiatus in London as a commissioner to the Westminster Assembly — it was confined to Scotland. Although Rutherford did not write a full-fledged Reformed dogmatics, several of his long theological treatises demonstrate his mastery of scholastic discourse. His occasional pejorative references to 'the School-men' did not prevent him from employing their methodology.[24] Rutherford's *Examen Arminianismi*, for example, was comprised of

---

[22]   John Sharp, *Cursus Theologicus, in quo Controversiae Omnes de Fidei Dogmatibus, hoc seculo Exagitatae inter nos et Pontificios, pertractantur; et ad Bellarmini argumenta respondetur*, corr. edn. (Geneva, 1628).

[23]   John Cameron, *Ioannis Cameronis Scoto-Britanni Theologi Eximii. [Ta sozomena]; sive, Opera Partim ab Auctore Ipso Edita, partim post eius obitum vulgata, partim nusquam hactenus publicata, vel e Gallico Idiomate nunc primum in Latinam linguam translata* (Geneva, 1642).

[24]   Samuel Rutherford, *Influences of the Life of Grace* (London, 1659).

lectures first delivered to students at St Andrews. Because these lectures made use of the Latin language and the dialectic method which Protestant scholasticism held in common throughout Europe, they were equally well-suited for use in divinity schools on the continent. It is not surprising that the *Examen Arminianismi* was published for the benefit of divinity students in Utrecht, or that it received the imprimatur of the Dutch Reformed scholastics Voetius and Essenius.[25] Rutherford had already given a scholastic response to Arminian theology in his *Exercitationes Apologeticae pro Divina Gratia*,[26] and the scholastic orientation of his *Disputatio Scholastica De Divina Providentia* is immediately evident from its title.[27] The latter work, especially, demonstrates Rutherford's analytic rigour and mastery of the theological tradition from the Fathers through the Reformers.

Other Scottish works of the seventeenth century are less thoroughly scholastic, but clearly find their origin in the scholastic *milieu*. Robert Boyd's (of Trochrigg, 1578–1627) massive exposition of the book of Ephesians is a good example.[28] Strictly speaking, the *Ephesios* is a biblical commentary. Yet Boyd frequently departs from discursive exegesis in order to probe systematic-theological concerns. Given his academic experience on the continent, especially at Saumur, this is not surprising.[29] In addition to a lengthy excursus, *De Praedestinatione*, Boyd makes hundreds of shorter forays into topics of dogmatic interest, forays which enable him to cover virtually every systematic *locus*. He interacts extensively with early church Fathers, medieval scholastic theologians, Roman Catholic contemporaries, and continental Reformed scholastics. When his attention turns to dogmatic theology, Boyd uses the tools of scholasticism to reformulate the theological tradition according to Reformation principles. The fact that both Cameron and Boyd employed scholastic techniques in the course of their exegetical work is striking because it shows that they considered scholasticism to have a legitimate role in biblical interpretation.

Further examples of Scottish Reformed scholasticism might be adduced. John Brown (of Wamphray; *c.*1610–79) is an important figure, even if his best work was done after he was banished to Holland in 1663.

---

[25]   Samuel Rutherford, *Examen Arminianismi* (Utrecht, 1668).

[26]   Samuel Rutherford, *Exercitationes Apologeticae pro Divina Gratia* (Amsterdam, 1636).

[27]   Samuel Rutherford, *Disputatio Scholastica De Divina Providentia* (Edinburgh, 1649).

[28]   Robert Boyd (of Trochrigg), *In Epistolam Pauli Apostoli ad Ephesios Praelectiones supra CC* (London, 1652).

[29]   See W.M. Campbell, 'Robert Boyd of Trochrigg', *Records of the Scottish Church History Society* 12 (1956), 220–34.

His *De Causa Dei contra Antisabbatarios* and *The Life of Justification Opened* (published posthumously) take their place among the more important Scottish theological works of the seventeenth century.[30] They are not systematic compendia, nor are they organized according to the exigencies of scholastic argumentation. Yet to one degree or another they reveal traits characteristic of Reformed scholasticism, such as careful definition of theological terms and a relentless engagement with Roman Catholic, Arminian, Socinian, and other theological interlocutors. Scholastic methods are also readily apparent in treatises on that most Scottish of theological disciplines: ecclesiology. The defences of Presbyterianism by David Calderwood (1575–1650), George Gillespie (1613–48), and Samuel Rutherford are structured and prosecuted in exhaustive detail, according to the canons of scholastic disputation.[31] Calderwood, Gillespie, and Rutherford both continue the ecclesiological discussions begun by the medieval scholastic theologians and carry them on against the entire backdrop of seventeenth-century European theology.

Together these examples demonstrate that the Scots did help to propagate Reformed scholastic theology in the seventeenth century. Yet they also serve to delimit the boundaries of that propagation. Few of the works we have mentioned exercised a substantial influence beyond the borders of Scotland. This is not to say that the work of these divines was without theological significance. Cameron and Rutherford, particularly, exercised an important influence over subsequent developments in the history of theology.[32] The Scots also made a unique contribution by introducing Presbyterian ecclesiology to Reformed orthodoxy. Yet no Scottish work in the field of dogmatic theology can withstand comparison to magisterial continental systems such as the *Opera* of Girolamo Zanchi or the *Institutio* of Francis Turretin, either in

---

[30] John Brown (of Wamphray), *De Causa Dei contra Antisabbatarios*, 2 vols. (Rotterdam, 1674–6); *The Life of Justification Opened* (Holland, 1695).

[31] David Calderwood, *Altare Damascenum; seu, Ecclesiae Anglicanae Politia, Ecclesiae Scoticanae obtrusa, a Formalista quodam delineata, Illustrata et Examinata* (Leyden, 1708); George Gillespie, *Aaron's Rod Blossoming; or, The Divine Ordinance of Church-Government Vindicated* (London, 1646); Samuel Rutherford, *The Due Right of Presbyteries; or, A Peaceable Plea for the Government of the Church of Scotland* (London, 1644). See also Rutherford's *Lex, Rex; or, The Law and the Prince; A Dispute for the Just Prerogative of King and People* (Edinburgh, 1644).

[32] For one interpretation of Cameron's influence on the rise of Amyraldianism see Brian G. Armstrong, *Calvinism and the Amyraut Heresy: Protestant Scholasticism and Humanism in Seventeenth-Century France* (Madison: University of Wisconsin Press, 1969). Rutherford has yet to receive the attention he deserves, especially for his contribution to the rise of constitutional democracy, but see R. Flinn, 'Samuel Rutherford and Puritan Political Theory', *Journal of Christian Reconstruction* 5 (1978–9), 49–74.

terms of scope or influence. The Scots knew quality orthodox scholastic theology when they read it, and they were able to write some of their own as the need arose, but they did not set the standard for Reformed scholasticism in the post-Reformation period.

Two further qualifications are in order. To suggest that the Scottish divines of the seventeenth century did not produce very many volumes of scholastic theology is not to offer criticism of those divines, implied or otherwise. For one thing, the need for scholastic works subsided after the Westminster Assembly had codified Presbyterian and Reformed orthodoxy for the Church of Scotland. Furthermore, the contribution of Scotland to Protestant scholasticism was proportional to the size and wealth of the country.[33] The Scottish population was small in the seventeenth century, and it was concentrated almost entirely in rural areas.[34] Economic factors may well have limited the production of scholastic works. The Scottish economy lagged behind that of its neighbours, particularly towards the end of the seventeenth century, and even the larger Scottish towns were not noted as centres of the book trade.[35] Scottish divines contributed to the scholastic enterprise insofar as their circumstances enabled them to do so.

SCOTTISH HOMILETICS

It is now properly recognized that scholasticism is more a methodology than a theology,[36] a recognition which has done much to rehabilitate its reputation. The standard criticisms of scholastic theology — that it is barren, unbiblical, impractical, speculative, reductionist, rationalistic, obscurantist — begin to dissolve once it is realized that scholasticism is a tool for doing academic work. Evaluating the utility of scholasticism is largely a question of genre. The scholastic method of disputation has a legitimate role in the presentation of dogmatic theology, a genre which demands propositional analysis, scientific reasoning, and logical differentiation.

Questions remain, however, about the intrusion of scholasticism into other theological genera. Even if scholasticism has its place at the lectern,

---

[33] I am indebted to David C. Lachman for this observation.

[34] Michael Flinn (ed.), *Scottish Population History from the 17th Century to the 1930s* (Cambridge: Cambridge University Press, 1977).

[35] Henderson, 60–1, has observed the connection between Scotland's poverty and its reliance on the continent for intellectual stimulation.

[36] See the excellent two-part summary by Richard A. Muller, 'Calvin and the "Calvinists": Assessing Continuities and Discontinuities between the Reformation and Orthodoxy', *Calvin Theological Journal* 30 (1995), 345–75 (especially 367–73), and 31 (1996), 125–60.

it does not necessarily belong in the pulpit. This suggests that one way to evaluate the contribution of Reformed scholasticism to the life of the church is to assess its impact on preaching. The study of Protestant scholasticism demands attention to homiletics as well as systematics. Indeed, preaching may be the best place to scrutinize the influence of scholasticism, since it is preaching that actually shapes the religious culture of a nation. This was especially the case in Scotland, where preaching had been the lifeblood of the kirk from the first days of the Reformation. Did Protestant preaching in the era of orthodoxy betray the vestiges of scholastic method? Did Reformed preachers feed scholasticism to their congregations undigested, bones and all?

The answer to these questions is 'No', at least in Scotland. Scottish preaching during the era of high orthodoxy was discursive rather than disputational. It made little or no use of scholastic discourse. The vast majority of the allusions, illustrations, themes and quotations employed by Reformed preachers in Scotland came either from the Bible or from nature, rather than from the authorities and traditions of academic theology. Further, the Scottish divines rarely disputed with particular theological opponents from the pulpit (although they did not refrain from criticizing central dogmas of Roman Catholicism). Instead, they concentrated on expounding a biblical text, stating its principal doctrines, and applying its message to the spiritual condition of their hearers.

This homiletical method was codified in the *Directory for the Publick Worship of God* prepared by the Westminster Assembly.[37] It was a method partly derived from the logic and rhetoric of Peter Ramus (1515–72). The influence of Ramism on English Puritan preaching has been observed and documented.[38] Its impact on Scottish preaching is usually overlooked, but the Scots were members of the same international Reformed community and they had a share in the Ramist inheritance. Although Ramism has been termed 'a revolt against scholastic logic',[39] it was itself a methodology from the schools.[40] To the extent that Scottish preaching

---

[37] *The Directory for the Publick Worship of God* in *The Confession of Faith* (Inverness: Publications Committee of the Free Presbyterian Church of Scotland, 1970), 369–94 (379–81).

[38] Perry Miller, *The New England Mind in the Seventeenth Century* (New York: Harvard University Press, 1939), 115–53, 312–62; Keith L. Sprunger, 'Ames, Ramus, and the Method of Puritan Theology', *Harvard Theological Review* 59 (1966), 133–51; John G. Rechtien, 'Logic in Puritan Sermons in the Late Sixteenth Century and Plain Style', *Style* 13 (1979), 237–58.

[39] Wilbur Samuel Howell, *Logic and Rhetoric in England, 1500–1700* (Princeton, N.J.: Princeton University Press, 1956), 7.

[40] On the influence of Ramism on early Reformed orthodoxy, see Richard A. Muller, *Post-Reformation Reformed Dogmatics*, 3 vols. (Grand Rapids: Baker, 1978–), I, 30.

was influenced by Ramism, therefore, it can be said to bear some of the
marks of scholasticism. However, the inherent passion of Ramism for
practical pedagogy and the utility of knowledge made it readily adaptable
for pulpit ministry. If Ramism was scholastic, it was the kind of scholasticism that could be popularized. Scottish sermons thus echoed Ramist
concerns for right thinking and right practice without themselves becoming scholastic treatises.

While a complete survey of seventeenth and early eighteenth century
Scottish preaching is far beyond the scope of this study, a few examples
serve to illustrate some of the foregoing observations. The sermons of
James Durham (1622–58) are typical of Scottish preaching in the middle
of the seventeenth century.[41] Durham invariably begins with a biblical
text, states and elucidates one or more doctrinal propositions, and then
applies the doctrine to the spiritual condition of his hearers. In other
words, his sermons satisfy the primary concerns of Ramism: they are
organized, orthodox, biblical, doctrinal, and practical. And to that extent
they share many of the concerns of Reformed scholasticism. But Durham's sermons are not scholastic in their methodology. They do not
demonstrate the exhaustive linguistic precision, metaphysical rigour, and
philosophical differentiation which characterized scholastic dogmatics.
However suitable such things may have been for school-theology,
Durham did not consider them desirable for pulpit practice, where plain
discourse is a pastoral virtue.

Another strain of seventeenth-century Scottish preaching was still
further removed from the scholastic method. One contemporary referred to it as the 'new guise of preaching which Mr. Hew Binning and
Robert Leighton began, contemning the ordinarie way of exposing and
dividing a text'.[42] What was different about Binning's (1627–53) sermons was that they were not divided and subdivided into 'doctrines'
and 'uses'.[43] His was a homiletic of simplicity. Although his sermons
were both doctrinal and practical, Binning eschewed the Ramist structure favored by most of his contemporaries. Robert Leighton (1611–84)
shared Binning's disdain for transparent organization.[44] His sermons,

---

[41]   James Durham, *The Great Corruption of Subtile Self, Discovered, and Driven from
it's Lurking-places and Starting-holes* (Edinburgh, 1686), *Christ Crucify'd: or, The Marrow
of the Gospel* (London, 1723); *The Unsearchable Riches of Christ, and of Grace and Glory
in and through HIM* (Edinburgh, 1729); *Heaven upon Earth* (Edinburgh, 1732).

[42]   Robert Baillie, *Letters and Journals*, ed. D. Laing, 3 vols. (Edinburgh, 1841–2),
III, 258.

[43]   Hugh Binning, *The Works of the Pious, Reverend, and Learn'd Mr. Hugh Binning,
Late Minister of the Gospel at Govan*, (Glasgow, 1768²).

[44]   Robert Leighton, *The Whole Works of the Most Reverend Father in God, Robert
Leighton, D.D., Archbishop of Glasgow*, 2 vols. (London, 1828).

too, were noted for their simplicity. Leighton did not distinguish between exposition and application when he preached, with the result that the style of his preaching was more reflective and meditative. Interestingly, he used much the same rhetorical style when he lectured as principal of the University of Edinburgh. Although his lectures were devoid of neither logic nor learning, they did not follow the format of the scholastic dialectic. Leighton lectured in the schools, but he was not a scholastic.

The preaching of James Renwick (1662–88) is representative of the field preaching which became necessary for Reformed ministers after the restoration of episcopacy in 1662.[45] The fields of Scotland were far removed from the schools of Edinburgh and Groningen where Renwick had received his training, and he adapted his preaching accordingly. His sermons follow closely the homiletic guidelines established in the Westminster *Directory*. They are not, in other words, scholastic. That is not to say that the sermons are deficient in exegetical rigour or theological substance, but only to say that Renwick accommodated his manner of presentation to the capacities of his hearers.

Thomas Boston accommodated his preaching in much the same way. Boston's substantial debt to Reformed scholastic theology has already been acknowledged. It was a debt that he himself did not hesitate to own — in the proper circumstances. In his lengthy notes on *The Marrow of Modern Divinity*, for example, Boston frequently quotes from and interacts with the Reformers, the continental Reformed scholastics, and the English Puritans.[46] An element of scholastic flair can be detected in the theological essays he wrote shortly after leaving the University of Edinburgh,[47] as well as in the exercises he prepared for his ministerial colleagues at presbytery.[48] It is regrettable that few presbyterial exercises from the seventeenth and early eighteenth centuries remain in existence. Were more available, they would undoubtedly confirm what Boston's example can only suggest: that there was a substantial difference in style and content between presbytery exercises and parish sermons. For a minister like Thomas Boston, the vestiges of the methodology of Reformed scholasticism largely disappeared at the steps to his own pulpit. Many of the issues

---

[45] James Renwick, *A Choice Collection of Very Valuable Prefaces, Lectures, and Sermons, Preached Upon the Mountains and Muirs of Scotland, in the hottest Time of the late Persecution*, (Glasgow, 1776³).

[46] Boston, *Works*, VII, 143–464.

[47] Boston, *Works*, VI, 11–240.

[48] Thomas Boston, 'MSS of Thomas Boston of Ettrick' in 'Sermons and related writings of Thomas Boston, James Fisher, John Brown and other members of the United Free Church of Scotland 1699–1851', Department of Special Collections and Archives, Aberdeen University Library, King's College, MS.3245/2, 62–8.

which dominated the Reformed systems which Boston read — to say nothing of the scholastic method for dealing with them — simply never appeared in his preaching. This was because the manner of discourse he valued at presbytery and elsewhere, he 'despised, and had a contempt of, as pedantic' for his own congregation.[49] His preaching was theologically informed. Yet his handling of theological issues offered no more than an occasional glimpse of the disputes that occupied scholastic attention. With proper sensitivity to the requirements of his genre of choice, Boston allowed his scholastic aptitude to remain concealed when he preached to his rural congregation.

Not all Scottish preaching was equally effective, of course, nor was it equally immune to scholastic influences. Samuel Rutherford's contribution to Reformed scholasticism has already been noted, yet his versatility extended well beyond systematic theology. Rutherford's *Letters* have long been valued for their personal intimacy, pastoral wisdom, and warmth of spiritual devotion.[50] This is a reminder — if such were needed — that scholasticism and piety are not mutually exclusive. Many of Rutherford's sermons share the devotional warmth of his letters. Yet some of them venture overmuch into polemical matters, offering what one of his editors calls 'necessary digressions, for the times, touching divers errors'.[51] These digressions usually arise from the biblical text, and they often deal with some aspect of the Christian life, such as repentance, faith, or sanctification. However, Rutherford sometimes fails to sustain the biblical and practical emphases which were the strengths of his preaching. In *Christ Dying, and Drawing Sinners to Himself*, for example, Rutherford disputes with Antinomianism or Arminianism on dozens of occasions, often interacting for pages with one or another of the English Antinomians.[52] Such extended polemics have their place, of course, but they rarely make for edifying preaching.

Rutherford's sermons are merely the exceptions that prove the rule. The majority of Scottish preachers — who were less thoroughly immersed in the academic environment than Rutherford was — were able to leave scholasticism to the schools. The preaching they offered their parishioners shared scholasticism's love for orthodox doctrine, but presented it in a manner suitable for the common parishioner.

---

[49] Boston, *Works*, XII, 153–4.

[50] Samuel Rutherford, *Mr. Rutherfoord's Letters, Now Divided into Three Parts*, (Edinburgh, 1761⁶).

[51] Samuel Rutherford, *Christ Dying, and Drawing Sinners to Himself* (London, 1647), title page.

[52] The same is true, to a lesser extent, of Rutherford's *Tryal and Triumph of Faith; or, An Exposition of the History of Christs dispossessing of the daughter of the woman of Canaan* (London, 1645).

SCHOLASTICISM AND CONTROVERSY

The influence of scholasticism on Scottish theology was more readily apparent when the church was troubled by internecine squabbles in the early eighteenth century. The same academic techniques that helped to distinguish Reformed theology from its rivals threatened to become disruptive — or even destructive — when they were mishandled within the kirk.

The best known of the eighteenth-century ecclesiastical conflicts, the Marrow Controversy (1718–23), generated a vast quantity of pamphlet literature.[53] Yet many of the short works produced during the controversy are deficient in theological erudition, a fact occasionally noted by the controversialists themselves.[54] Opponents are often quoted out of context, dubious constructions are placed on disputed terms, and unwarranted theological conclusions are deduced from valid premises. To put it another way, zeal for doctrinal orthodoxy often outstrips integrity of theological method. Many of the Marrow and anti-Marrow pamphlets attempt to employ scholastic techniques, but fail to do so effectively.

The Marrow Controversy reveals that scholastic method becomes pedantic when it is applied with universal thoroughness. It is noteworthy that several of the most important pamphlets and treatises written during the Marrow Controversy draw heavily from Samuel Rutherford's anti-Antinomian writings.[55] Rutherford thus helped to set the tone for early eighteenth-century Scottish polemics. Rutherford was a frequent critic of Antinomian and Arminian theology, and it is in some of his writings on these subjects that the effects of his scholasticism are least salutary. Polemics are partly a matter of taste, of course, and one's view of a particular polemicist largely depends upon which side of an argument one favours. Yet a lucid polemic will always be valued for the clarity it brings to a theological dispute, and on this score Rutherford cannot always be commended. His *Survey of the Spirituall Antichrist* is exhaustive in its rebuttal of Antinomian arguments, but it is often needlessly repetitive, failing to synthesize the issues or to appreciate the differences between various degrees of theological error.[56] Rutherford's *Survey* thus shows that

[53] The definitive treatment is David C. Lachman, *The Marrow Controversy*, Rutherford Studies in Historical Theology (Edinburgh: Rutherford House, 1988).

[54] See especially Robert Riccaltoun, *The Politick Disputant; or, Choice Instructions for quashing a Stubborn Adversary* (Edinburgh, 1722).

[55] See [James Bannatine], *An Essay upon Gospel and Legal Preaching* (Edinburgh, 1723); James Hadow, *The Antinomianism of the Marrow of Modern Divinity Detected* (Edinburgh, 1722); [James Hog], *The Controversie concerning the Marrow of Modern Divinity. Considered in several familiar Dialogues. Dialogue I* (Edinburgh, 1721), especially 80–105.

[56] Samuel Rutherford, *A Survey of the Spirituall Antichrist* (London, 1648).

scholasticism can become an encumbrance — as it subsequently became in the Marrow Controversy — when every point in a theological disagreement receives equally exhaustive treatment. The potential liabilities of scholasticism are also apparent in the extensive polemical writings against Professor John Simson (1667–1740). The confusion surrounding Simson's theology was partly due to his own lack of candour, but the treatises written against him also lack the sense of proportion which effective polemics require.[57]

CONCLUSION

These examples of the use and abuse of scholastic methodology in Scottish ecclesiastical disputes serve to show two things. First, they show the extent to which Scottish ministers and theologians of the seventeenth and eighteenth centuries had appropriated Reformed orthodoxy and were eager to defend it with scholastic rigour. They also show the susceptibility of scholasticism to being mishandled in the service of Protestant orthodoxy. But in that respect, scholasticism is no different from any other valuable tool.

---

[57] James Webster, *The Case of Mr. John Simson* (Edinburgh, 1715); John Flint, *Examen Doctrinae D: Johannis Simson, S.S.T. In Celebri Academia Glasguensi Professoris* (Edinburgh, 1717); John McClaren, *The New Scheme of Doctrine Contained in the Answers of Mr. John Simson, Professor of Divinity in the Colledge of Glasgow; to Mr. Webster's Libel, Considered and Examined* (Edinburgh, 1717).

PART 4
FROM HIGH ORTHODOXY TO ENLIGHTENMENT

1

The Denial of the Innate Idea of God in Dutch Remonstrant Theology:
From Episcopius to Van Limborch

John E. Platt

Throughout the seventeenth century the mainstream of Dutch Reformed theology continued to adduce the universality of the innate idea of God in man and the wonderful order observable in nature as the chief arguments for God's existence outside the sphere of scriptural revelation.[1] In so doing they could reasonably claim to be following Calvin's own example,[2] especially since they also continued to assert that the only outcome of such natural knowledge of God was to render men inexcusable before him for their failure to love, worship and obey. However, the practice, widespread among Dutch theologians of this period, of presenting more formal arguments for God's existence and the bulk of the actual arguments employed prove, on investigation, to originate from an altogether different source, namely Luther's greatest disciple, Philip Melanchthon.[3]

[1] See especially J. Platt, *Reformed Thought and Scholasticism: The Arguments for the Existence of God in Dutch Theology, 1575–1650* (Leiden: E.J. Brill, 1982).

[2] See J. Calvin, *Institutio Christianae Religionis*, Book I, Chapters 3–5. The best English translation is that by F.L. Battles, ed. J.T. McNeill, *Calvin: Institutes of the Christian Religion* (London: SCM, 1961), 43–69. The best modern discussions of Calvin's teaching in this area are E.A. Dowey, *The Knowledge of God in Calvin's Theology* (New York: Columbia University Press, 1952/Grand Rapids: Eerdmans, 1995³) and T.H.L. Parker, *Calvin's Doctrine of the Knowledge of God*, (Grand Rapids: Eerdmans, 1959²).

[3] There is a vast literature on Melanchthon (1497–1560). For the issue of our concern see Platt, *Reformed Thought*, 10–33; C. Bauer, 'Melanchthons Naturrechtslehre', *Archiv für Reformationsgeschichte* 4 (1951), 64–100; and F. Hübner, *Naturliche Theologie und theokratische Schwärmerei bei Melanchthon* (Gütersloh: Bertelsmann, 1936).

This is not the place to recount the story of how the latter's influence in this matter was brought to bear upon Dutch Reformed theology, principally by means of the immensely popular commentary on the Heidelberg Catechism of his former pupil, Zacharias Ursinus,[4] but it is important to note that this influence had almost imperceptibly glossed Calvin's views within the Reformed tradition.

The *locus classicus* in Scripture for the natural knowledge of God is Romans 1:18–21[5] and Calvin had largely based his teaching on this passage. As early as 1532, however, Melanchthon had taken the distinctive step of identifying the natural knowledge of God referred to in verse 18 with the law of nature and the arguments for God's existence which he then went on to present were marked by a strongly ethical strain.[6]

Bauer's excellent study of Melanchthon's teaching on natural law concludes:

> Melanchthon's development from the conception of natural law in the first version of the *Loci Communes* with its still critical and relatival character to the positive and systematic theory of natural law in the final version of the *Loci Communes* and in the *Ethicae doctrinae elementa* marks the way of a penetrating study of the works of Aristotle and Cicero in the second and third decades of the sixteenth century. Step by step a theory of natural law is developed in the commentaries on and annotations to Aristotle's *Ethics* and *Politics* and Cicero's *Officia* — which is then connected with the further development of Melanchthon's theology with its renewed assertion of the elements of natural knowledge of the divine.[7]

In the early decades of the century, Dutch Calvinist orthodoxy was greatly disturbed by the teaching of the Leiden professor, Arminius, and his

---

[4]   Ursinus (1534–83) was himself one of the authors of the Heidelberg Catechism. His commentary, a posthumous work based on his pupils' lecture notes, first appeared in 1584 and circulated in various forms. In 1591 his Heidelberg successor, David Pareus, edited the *Explicationes Catecheticae* and this went through at least twelve editions by 1651. The Dutch translation of this commentary by Festus Hommius, *Het Schat-Boeck der Christelycke Leere ofte Uytlegginghe over den Catechismus* (Leiden, 1602) was equally popular, appearing some nine times by 1650. See Platt, *Reformed Thought*, 49–103.

[5]   '18 For the wrath of God is revealed from heaven against all ungodliness and wickedness of men who by their wickedness suppress the truth. 19 For what can be known about God is plain to them, because God has shown it to them. 20 Ever since the creation of the world his invisible nature, namely, his eternal power and deity, has been clearly perceived in the things that have been made. So they are without excuse; 21 for although they knew God they did not honour him as God or give thanks to him, but they became futile in their thinking and their senseless minds were darkened' (RSV).

[6]   *Melanchthons Werke in Auswahl*, ed. G. Ebeling and R. Schäfer, vol. 5 (Gütersloh: Bertelsmann, 1965), 69–70.

[7]   C. Bauer, 'Naturrechtslehre', 99.

followers, who, shortly after the latter's death, became known as Remonstrants and whose condemnation was pronounced at the Synod of Dort in 1619.[8] Since the controversies centred on the doctrine of predestination, issues relating to natural theology were not to the fore. Nonetheless the Reformed majority were on the lookout for any signs of Remonstrant heterodoxy in any theological area and, while Arminius' own formal treatment of the arguments for the existence of God[9] had been a brief but impressively systematic presentation which was to meet with the approval of that doyen of Dutch Reformist orthodox, Gisbert Voetius,[10] it was not long before his followers were coming under attack over the matter of the natural knowledge of God; and this especially on account of alleged affinities with the works of an even deadlier foe.

For much of the seventeenth century the most dangerous external theological challenge to orthodox Protestantism, apart from the old enemy of Rome, would undoubtedly have been seen as Socinianism.[11] In 1609, the year of Arminius' death, Faustus Socinus' *Praelectiones theologicae* was published posthumously. In the second chapter of this work he launched an attack upon the entire notion of any human knowledge of God apart from revelation. The reverberations of this assault were to echo through discussions of the topic for the remainder of the century.

Socinus denied both of the sources of the natural knowledge of God to which, following Calvin, Reformed theology appealed. In place of the innate idea of God he substituted an original and continuing divine revelation, while the most powerful of the objections which he advanced against the concept was the evidence of individuals and entire peoples who possessed no belief in a deity.[12]

In 1611 the curators of Leiden University took the hazardous step of appointing as Arminius' successor, Conrad Vorstius,[13] a German

---

[8] See C. Bangs, *Arminius: A Study in the Dutch Reformation* (Nashville: Abingdon, 1971); and A.W. Harrison, *The Beginnings of Arminianism to the Synod of Dort* (London: University of London Press, 1926).

[9] 'De objecto christianae religionis, et primo de Deo primario ejus objectu, et quod Deus sit', 'Disputatio XIV' in *Disputationes magnam partem S. theologiae complectentes publicae et privatae* (Leiden, 1610), 23–5 (Leiden 1611[2]). Reprinted in Arminius, *Opera Theologica* (Leiden, 1629), 350–2. English trans. *The Works of James Arminius* 2 (London, 1828), 30–3.

[10] *Disputationes selectae theologicae,* vol. 1 (Utrecht, 1648), 170.

[11] See E.M. Wilbur, *A History of Unitarianism and its Antecedents* (Cambridge, Mass.: Harvard University Press, 1946). For Socinianism in relation to Dutch theology, see W.J. Kühler, *Het Socinianisme in Nederland* (Leiden: Sijthoff, 1912) and J.C. van Slee, *De Geschiedenis van het Socinianisme in de Nederlanden* (Haarlem: Bohn, 1914).

[12] F. Socinus, *Praelectiones theologicae* (Racow, 1609), 3–4.

[13] For Vorstius, see *Biografisch Lexicon voor de Geschiedenis van het Nederlandse Protestantisme* 1 (Kampen: Kok, 1978-), 407–10.

theologian who was already strongly suspected of Socinian sympathies, and the resultant furore prevented him from ever actually discharging his professorial office. As I have endeavoured to show elsewhere, for his disputation on the existence of God, Arminius drew upon a disputation of Vorstius' held at Steinfurt some six years earlier in 1598.[14] When the latter published his collection of ten 'De Deo' disputations in 1606 he added a series of notes to the first of these which far exceeded the original disputation in length.[15]

As it stands Vorstius' first disputation embodied the traditional Reformed appeal to the innate idea and to the order of nature and, indeed, showed signs of itself being indebted to one of the extremely influential disputations published by his own former mentor, Johannes Piscator, which were explicitly based on Calvin's *Institutes*.[16] However, in the period between the initial holding of the disputation and the appearance of the notes appended to it, Vorstius had modified his view and now asserted his rejection of the innate idea. In so doing he adduced the same evidence as Socinus of the discovery of the Brazilians and other such godless inhabitants of the new world.[17] Nonetheless, Vorstius went only halfway with Socinus and continued to allow that some natural knowledge of God was possible but that human reason must be put to proper use before this could be achieved.[18]

[14]   J. Platt, *Reformed Thought*, 149–56. The disputation in question was the first, 'De Deo nempe de existentia Dei: in qua demonstratur contra atheos, Deum esse'.

[15]   *Tractatus theologicus de Deo sive de nature et attributis Dei* (Steinfurt, 1606). The first appearance of the disputation in print would appear to have been an edition of 1602 no longer extant. See L.D. Petit, *Biographische lijst der werken van de Leidsche hoogleeraren 1575–1619* (Leiden: van Doersburgh, 1894), 93. A further edition in 1610 supplied notes to the remainder of the disputations, thus greatly increasing the size of the work.

[16]   See J. Platt, *Reformed Thought*, 35–46 and 205–6. For Piscator (1546–1625), who taught at Herborn from 1584 till his death and had Vorstius as his pupil from 1589 to 1594, see *Realencyklopädie für protestantische Theologie und Kirche*, 3rd edition, vol. 15 (Leipzig: J.C. Hinrichs'sche, 1904), 414–15. His *Aphorismi doctrinae Christianae maximam partem ex Institutione Calvini excerpti, sive Loci Communes theologici brevibus sententiis expositi* was first published at Herborn in 1589 and had been through no fewer than twelve editions by 1630. The disputation in question is the first, 'De cognitione Dei', *Tractus theologius de Dio*, 11–13.

[17]   'Non existimamus innatam esse nobis aliquem Dei notitiam; quum proprie loquendo nullius rei cognitio homini videatur innasci; . . . Nam alioqui firma divinitatis opinio fidei tribuitur, non naturae, Heb.11.6 . . . et etiamnum integras nationes inveniri quae nullam divinitatis opinionem habere videntur sicut de Brasilianis et quibusdam aliis novi orbis populis, scriptores rerum Indiarum aperte testantur' *Tractatus theologicus de Deo* (1606), 128.

[18]   'Restat igitur, ut eatenus tantum naturalis haec cognitio dicatur, quatenus homo naturalia in se et circum se praesidia habet quibus si recte utatur, eosque ratiocinando assurgere possit, ut Deum esse et sibi ipsi et aliis quantum satis est demonstrare, possit', ibid. 129.

Soon after his arrival in Holland, Vorstius published a defence of his earlier *Tractatus*, concluding his first chapter on the extent of the natural knowledge of God with the claim that the issue ought to be seen as philosophical rather than theological and referring to the second chapter of the fourth book of Clemens Timpler's *Metaphysicae*.[19] Timpler had been Vorstius' colleague as professor of philosophy at Steinfort from 1595 and it is evident that the appearance of the cited work, first published in 1604, was the main reason behind the latter's change of mind.[20]

As we saw above, much of the Reformed approach to the issue of the natural knowledge of God was based upon the synthesis effected by Melanchthon between Ciceronian Stoicism and Aristotelianism. Such a system, however, ran the constant risk of dissolution into its constituent parts, and on the matter of our concern this was particularly the case. Thus F.C. Copleston writes,

> A salient aspect of Melanchthon's teaching was his doctrine of innate principles, particularly moral principles, and of the innate character of the idea of God, both of which are intuited by means of the *lumen naturale*. This doctrine was opposed to the Aristotelian view of the mind as a *tabula rasa*.[21]

Thus it was that Timpler answered the question, 'whether the knowledge of God's existence is innate in man', in the negative with a direct appeal to the authority of Aristotle's dictum that all human knowledge has its first origin in the senses.[22] That he realized he was thus

---

[19] 'Atque haec de primo articulo sufficiant: qui sane philosophicus potius quam theologicus videri debet: quum de ipsis naturae humanae principiis deque naturali ordine et modo Deum cognoscendi ex ipsis physicae fundamentis non obscure disserat'. *Apologetica exegesis sive plenior declaratio locorum aliquot ex libro eiusdem de Deo . . . excerpta, eique pro erroneis imposita* (Leiden, 1611), 5.

[20] For Timpler (1567–1624), see M. Wundt, *Die Deutsche Schulmetaphysik des 17 Jahrhunderts* (Tübingen: Mohr, 1939), 72–8. The *Metaphysicae systema methodicum* enjoyed quite a vogue in its day, being reprinted no less than four times, the last in 1616. In 1615 we find Grotius recommending it in his suggested scheme of study for the French ambassador, du Maurier (*Briefwisseling van Hugo Grotius* 1 (The Hague: Nijhoff, 1929), 385).

[21] *A History of Philosophy*, vol. 3 (London: Burns, Oates and Washbourne, 1953), 227.

[22] 'Id enim proprie dicitur actu innatum esse homini quod simul ac homo in utero matris est genitus, cepit ipsi in esse. Iam autem tantum abest ut homo infans sive in utero matris adhuc conclusus; sive in lucem editus, statim actu cognoscat Deum esse, ut neque vocabulum ipsum quo Deus in sua lingua materna nominatur obrationis infirmitatem intelligat donec progressu aetatis usus rationis per naturam ipsi concedatur. Praeterea omnis intellectio et cognitio humana naturaliter primam suam originem ducit a sensu: quemadmodum id Aristoteles tum alibi, tum lib. 2 poster. analyt. cap. ultimo demonstrat', *Metaphysicae Systema Methodicum* (Steinfurt, 1604), 389.

challenging the Melanchthonian position is apparent, for the first objection which he proceeds to consider is the very point which lay at the heart of the latter's innatism, his understanding of natural law.[23] In response Timpler advances the claims of right reason as the essential factor in the operation of natural law in terms markedly reminiscent of the Thomist tradition.[24] Indeed, when he comes to rebut Socinus' rejection of any natural knowledge of God, Timpler does so with an overt appeal to Aquinas' axiom that faith presupposes natural knowledge as grace does nature.[25]

This Thomist view of the relation of grace to nature was also fully shared by Vorstius whose appendix to his original disputation on the existence of God had asserted the familiar dictum, 'grace does not destroy nature, but perfects and presupposes it'.[26] In view of the common ground shared by the two Steinfurt professors, it is hardly surprising that the theologians' reaction to Socinus should have taken the form that it did. It is worth underlining, however, that, for both men, the grounds for continuing to hold to the natural knowledge of God via the book of nature were essentially theological, whilst they rejected the innate idea not for theological reasons, as did Socinus, but because of their philosophical convictions.

Vorstius was never permitted to teach at Leiden and, while he stayed in Gouda writing replies to the numerous criticisms levelled at him, the young Remonstrant minister and former pupil of Arminius, Simon Episcopius,[27] was chosen to fill his place. Chief spokesman for the

---

[23] 'Quod lex naturae dictat eius cognitio nobis est innata. Atqui Deum esse lex naturae dictat. Ergo eius cognitio nobis est innata. Propositionis ratio est quia ut Paulus docet 2. capite Rom. v. 15. lex naturae omnium gentium cordibus est inscripta', ibid. 392.

[24] 'Lex enim naturae nihil aliud est quam recta ratio, aut jussum saltem rectae rationis. Recta autem ratio non habet locum in infantibus, quippe qui nondum capere ac intelligere possunt quid recta ratio dictitet. Propterea neque cognitio eius quam lex naturae dictitat in infantibus est innata', ibid. 393.

[25] 'Fieri enim potest ut unum et idem sit dogma fidei et dogma naturae et per consequens etiam naturaliter notam. Neque dissensio est inter librum naturae et scripturae, sed potius summa consensio. Hinc recte dicitur librum naturae deducere hominem ad librum scripturae. Et Thomas in summa Theolog. quaest. 2 art. 2 ait: fidem praesupponere cognitionem naturalem sicut gratia naturam', ibid. 394.

[26] 'Dogmata Christianae fidei rectae rationi contraria non sunt: licet illorum nonnulla captum istius naturalem excedant. Non enim gratia naturam destruit sed perficit ac praesupponit: nec divina revelatio lumen rationis extinguit, sed illustrat atque ex obscuro et exiguo clarum magnumque efficit', Vorstius, *Tractatus theologicus de Deo*, 8–9.

[27] For Episcopius, see *Biografisch Lexicon voor de Geschiedenis van het Nederlandse Protestantisme* 2 (Kampen: Kok, 1983), 191–5.

Remonstrants at the Synod of Dort, Episcopius was dismissed from his chair and banished in consequence of that synod's decision. He was one of the leaders of the group which set up the Remonstrant Brotherhood in 1619 and the author of its *Confessio* published in 1622. After several years' exile in France, he returned to Holland and eventually became the first professor of theology at the Brotherhood's seminary founded in Amsterdam in 1634, a position which he held until his death.

In this official Confession no attempt was made to demonstrate the existence of God and the first chapter, headed 'On Holy Scripture, and its authority, perfection and clarity', simply declared that supernatural revelation was quite sufficient to establish this.[28] Such a statement was guaranteed to draw orthodox fire and, when the four professors of theology at Leiden came to publish their *Censura* of the Confession, it is no surprise to encounter the charge that, by this silence on the issue of the natural knowledge of God, the Remonstrants were effectively So-cinian.[29]

Although Episcopius made some observations on this criticism in the course of his substantial rejoinder to the *Censura* in 1630,[30] it was not until the posthumous appearance of the *Institutiones Theologicae* in the first volume of his *Opera Theologica*[31] that we meet with a clear exposition of his views on this issue. The two questions which he addresses in the third chapter of the first book of his systematic work quickly reveal his thinking, for they are the same pair that Timpler had presented in the work that had so influenced Vorstius, 'I: Whether there is naturally in man and his mind an implanted or innate idea of the deity? II: Whether there are certain principles in nature from which man, with the help of right and natural reason, is able to deduce this conclusion, God exists?'.[32] Moreover he rejects the first of these for precisely the same reason as did Timpler

---

[28] *Confessio sive declaratio sententiae pastorum, qui in foederato Belgio Remonstrantes vocantur, super praecipius articulos religionis Christianae* (n.p., 1622), 1.

[29] J. Polyander, A. Rivet, A. Walaeus, A. Thysius, *Censura in Confessionem sive declarationem sententiae eorum qui in foederato Belgio Remonstrantes vocantur* (Leiden, 1626), 11.

[30] *Apologia pro Confessione . . . contra Censuram quatuor professorum Leidensium* (n.p., 1630), 25–6.

[31] Edited by Etienne de Courcelles (Curcellaeus), this first volume of Episcopius' *Opera Theologica* was published at Amsterdam in 1650. The second volume, edited by Philip van Limborch and Arnold Poelenburg, appeared at Rotterdam in 1665.

[32] 'Duo autem quaeri possunt, cum disputatur an sit Deus. I. Utrum homini ejusque animo naturaliter insita sive innata sit deitatis opinio? Utrum principia quaedum in natura sint, ex quibus homo rationis rectae et naturalis auxilio, conclusionem hanc deducere possit, quod sit Deus?' *Opera Theologica*, I, 6. Cf. 'Utrum cognitio de Dei existentia homini sit innata . . . utrum homini ex naturalibus principiis notum sit Deum esse', Timpler, *Metaphysicae*, 389.

with a specific appeal to the Aristotelian axiom of the neonate's mind as a 'tabula rasa'.[33]

It is clear that the constant allegations of Socinianism have made their impression for, immediately on turning to the second of the possible sources of natural knowledge of God, Episcopius considers the case of those who would deny this route also and claim that we can only know of God's existence by revelation. Having raised the issue here and presented the four objections advanced by Socinus in that notorious second chapter of the *Praelectiones Theologicae*, Episcopius later devotes a short chapter to the task of replying to them. From this latter it becomes apparent that he is arguing for the same position as Timpler and Vorstius, which is distinct from that of traditional Reformed theology on the one hand and of Socinus on the other.

Episcopius evidently sympathizes with the latter whose rejection of the natural knowledge of God he sees as a reaction to the Calvinist view that such must be ineradicably and irresistibly engraved on the human mind.[34] It is worth recalling once more that Calvin's presentation of the natural knowledge of God sought to establish precisely this point that, since no one could escape such knowledge, no one could plead ignorance as the excuse for their inevitable idolatry and disobedience.[35] Both the internal and external sources of this knowledge force themselves irresistibly upon human attention.

In Calvin there is no room for any positive natural theology and, as we have noted, it was to Melanchthon that the Reformed tradition owed more positive attempts to present arguments for God's existence. However, here it is important to grasp that Melanchthon always explicitly claimed that such arguments were for the confirmation of the right mind of the faithful and never addressed them to unbelievers.[36]

---

[33] 'Mihi id vix verisimile videtur. Quia credo istam esse conditionem animae humanae, ut non modo nulla ei notio naturaliter impressa sit, sed ut nullus etiam rationis usus in ea locum habere possit nisi per sermonem et institutionem: adeo ut hominis anima illis adminiculis destituta, veluti tabula rasa mansura sit, et non nisi sectura ductum naturae, bruti instar', *Opera Theologica*, I, 6.

[34] 'quia cognitionem illam Dei, volunt esse notionem naturalem, animo impressam, proinde, quae non potest non naturaliter inesse, atque inhaerere animo', ibid.

[35] Thus Calvin opens the third chapter of the first book of the *Institutes*, entitled, 'The Knowledge of God has been naturally implanted in the minds of men', 'There is within the human mind, and indeed by natural instinct, an awareness of divinity. This we take to be beyond controversy. To prevent anyone from taking refuge in the pretence of ignorance, God himself has implanted in all men a certain understanding of his divine majesty', Battles, 43.

[36] Thus in the second edition of his *Loci Communes* (1535), the arguments do not appear in their traditional scholastic setting in the 'De Deo' Locus as the prolegomena

Key

Vorstius, on the other hand, in the very title of his disputation on the existence of God, specifically asserted that he was directing his arguments against atheists.[37] Moreover, he recognized the consequent necessity of appealing to considerations outside of scriptural revelation since such people could not accept the latter.[38] With Episcopius, this apologetic motive is much more pronounced. Indeed, at the very outset of his discussion, he asserts that his reason for presenting such arguments for God's existence is to convince atheists of their error and further to win them over to the truth.[39]

A completely different anthropology underlies Episcopius' divergence from Calvin on this issue. For the latter, fallen mankind is trapped, helpless and condemned and the true knowledge of God is only granted to the chosen few, without regard to their merits, to be the objects of his saving revelation; all is of grace, nothing but condemnation is of nature. For Episcopius, on the contrary, the essential factor is the freely willed and rational human response. Against the Calvinist notion of an irresistible natural knowledge of God, he asserts that the willing use of right reason is required before the principles given in nature can yield knowledge of the deity.

> It is necessary to look for another response; namely that the knowledge of God is not so natural that by necessity it entirely inheres in man as flowing from the principles of nature, but is natural only in this way, *that if a man is willing only to use reason* he can find certain principles in nature through which, with the help of that right reason, he may arrive at the knowledge of God.[40]

---

to revelation, but later under the heading 'De Creatione'. 'Posteaquam autem mens confirmata est vera et recta sententia de Deo, de creatione, ex ipso verbo Dei; tunc et utile et iucundum est, etiam quaerere vestigia Dei in natura, et rationes colligere, quae testantur esse Deum', *Corpus Reformatorum*, 21, col. 369.

[37] 'De Deo nempe de existentia Dei: in qua demonstratur contra atheos, Deum esse', *Tractatus Theologicus de Deo* (Steinfurt, 1606), 1.

[38] 'Sed quoniam athei nec Scripturam sacram audiunt, nec Spiritus S. energiam sentiunt: re frustra videamur contra negantes principia disputare, ipsa rerum nature nobis hinc in subsidium vocanda est', ibid. 3.

[39] 'Sed tamen quia videmus esse mortales quosdam adeo aut vecordes aut profanos, ut non dubitare modo an Deus sit, sed aperte ac palam negare audeant Deum esse, qui propiissime Athei sunt, operae pretium esse puto ut ostendam, qua ratione non tantum muniti esse possitis contra tam capitalem errorem, sed etiam quibus argumentis eos convincere valeatis et ad saniorem mentem reducere', *Opera Theologica*, I, 6.

[40] 'Quare alia responsione opus est: videlicet cognitionem Dei, non esse sic naturalem, ut necessario omnino homini insit, eique non possit non inesse, tanquam ex naturae principiis fluens, sed sic tantum naturalem, *ut si homo velit ratione tantum uti*, principia quaedam reperire possit in nature, auxilio rationis istius rectae, per quae deveniat in Dei cognitionem', ibid. 16. My emphasis.

The virtue for Episcopius of such a view is that it allows a part for revelation to play in counteracting any weakness arising from defects in the necessary use of right reason.

> For even though it is possible, with the help of right reason, to attain to the knowledge of God, yet it can happen that a man is either so negligent and slothful as not to care about knowing God, or he does not apply his mind and right reason with judgment. . . . Hence revelation is useful, which strengthens a man, and faith is necessary which comes to the aid of that weakness and counteracts those faults.[41]

We noted earlier that Vorstius' objection to the innate idea of God was, following Timpler, essentially philosophical rather than theological, for Episcopius the reverse is true. For him man, even fallen man, must be in a position in which he is free to use his right reason and then, if he is willing, make his way to God. Thus Episcopius' very approach to the task of presenting arguments for God's existence to atheists is founded upon his assurance that they have the capacity to respond to such, 'if they are willing to be led in any way by right reason'.[42] This is a view which is not only totally at odds with that of Calvin but also goes far beyond that of Arminius in its assertion of human freedom.[43]

This emphasis of Episcopius' is especially apparent in his presentation of that argument for God's existence to which those who upheld the innate idea of God customarily appealed, 'that from universal consent'. Indeed we may reasonably suppose that this latter fact occasioned Episcopius' particular emphasis upon the role of reason and the will at this point. This is his fourth argument and for the first time in his presentation he draws directly and extensively from the famous work of his fellow Remonstrant, Hugo Grotius, incorporating verbatim many passages of the relevant section of the *De Veritate Religionis Christianae*. Although in this work the latter does not explicitly reject the innate idea of God, at least he never alludes to it[44] and instead advances two possible causes of the universal belief in a God:

---

[41] 'Nam etiamsi auxilio rationis rectae, ad cognitionem Dei perveniri potest, tamen fieri etiam potest, ut homo vel adeo socors et segnis sit, ut de cognoscendo Deo non laboret, sive animum et rectam rationem in consilium non adhibeat . . . Hinc patefactio utilis, quae hominem fulciat, et fides necessaria, quae infirmitati isti succurrat, et vitiis istis occurrat', ibid.

[42] 'si ullo modo ratione recta duci velint', ibid. 6.

[43] Cf. the latter's Public Disputation XI, 'De Libero hominis Arbitrio ejusque viribus', with its description of the condition of the mind and the will in fallen man in Theses VII–X, Arminius, *Opera Theologica* (1629), 263–4.

[44] However, there are grounds for concluding from additions made to later editions of Grotius' *De Jure Belli ac Pacis* (1631 and 1642) that he was moving towards some recognition of the innate idea.

No other cause at all can be given which extends to all the human race; which he cannot be anything else than the oracle of God himself or tradition . . .[45]

Episcopius adds to these in a way which significantly underlines that necessary use of reason and the will to which we have already referred.

No other cause for the agreement can be given other than either the oracle of God himself, or tradition or of the matter itself, or this evidence of reason and principles known from them; to the extent that these are like first notions which compel the mind to assent, *if anyone is willing to be led in any way by reason.*[46]

Although from the quotation just given Grotius appears to follow the standard view that belief in God is universal, his earlier statement, 'that there is some deity is assumed from the most obvious agreement of all peoples', is immediately qualified by the phrase, 'with whom reason and good custom have not been completely extinguished and induced to savagery'.[47] Episcopius' position does, of course, permit him to allow of exceptions to belief and he later takes up the suggestion of Grotius as to the nature of any such exceptions:

But let it be, granted even that some such peoples are to be found, yet nothing is proved other than that the idea of a deity is not naturally impressed on the minds of all, which we do not wish to deny. For thus that idea could not be extinguished or suffocated at all. But it can happen that men degenerate so far in this that they do not employ reason to help but carry on by the instinct of nature alone like the beasts and *they wish for insensibility.*[48]

---

[45] 'Omnino causam eius aliquam dari convenit, quae se ad omne genus humanum extendat: quae alia esse non potest, quam aut oraculum dei ipsius, aut traditio', *De Veritate Religionis Christianae* (Leiden, 1627), 5.

[46] 'Causa hujus tanti consensus alia dari non potest, quam aut oraculum Dei ipsius, aut traditio, aut rei ipsius, sive rationum et principiorum ex quibus id intelligitur evidentia; quatenus illa veluti primae notiones sunt, quae mentem cogent assentiri; *si quis ulla modo ratione duci velit*', *Opera Theologica*, I, 9. My emphasis.

[47] 'Numen esse aliquod sumitur a manifestissimo consensu omnium gentium . . . apud quas ratio et boni mores non plane extincta sunt inducta feritate' *De Veritate*, 5.

[48] 'Sed, esto; detur etiam nationes aliquas tales repiriri, nihil aliud tamen evincetur, quam notionem illam divinitatis none esse naturaliter impressam animis omnium; quod negare nos nolumus. Sic enim nullo modo extingui posset notio ista, nec suffocari. At fieri posse ut homines eo usque degenerent, ut rationem in consilium non adhibeant, sed solo naturae instinctu Brutorum instar ferantur, ac *ferri velint*, . . .' *Opera Theologica*, I, 10. My emphasis.

Again, we may note Episcopius' stress on the role of human free will in determining the matter of belief. Moreover, even in the extreme cases of nations, 'who have been reared in the midst of barbarity and only accustomed to brutish senses', his faith in their essential rationality is not overthrown, for, 'they are accustomed with those who lead them back to reason and those principles to assent to them with little difficulty, as if by this they were awakened from a deep sleep by the stimulus of nature'.[49]

On Episcopius' death in 1643, he was succeeded as professor of theology at Amsterdam by the man who was later to publish the first volume of the posthumous edition of his *Opera Theologica*, Etienne de Courcelles.[50] Born in 1585 at Geneva and educated there, he became a minister of the French Reformed Church in 1614 but by 1626 his sympathy for Arminian teaching had driven him from that church into that of the Remonstrants at Amsterdam. Apart from his position as a leading theologian of that Brotherhood, his claim to fame is as the friend of Descartes whose *Discours de la méthode* he translated for its first Latin publication at Amsterdam in 1644. Since this work contains one of the definitive statements of the great philosopher's concept of the innate idea of God in the human mind,[51] it is interesting to see if this had any influence upon Remonstrant teaching on this issue.

De Courcelles' principal work, the *Institutio religionis Christianae*, first appeared in the posthumous edition of his *Opera Theologica*, and he devotes the second chapter of its first book to the question of God's existence.[52] A comparison of this chapter with the equivalent section of Episcopius' *Institutiones Theologicae*, which we may recall was first published by de Courcelles, reveals great similarity between the two lists of arguments adduced for the existence of God. However, while the former had given some space to the task of rejecting the innate idea of God, the latter omits any reference to the issue. Are we to conclude that this reflects the influence of Descartes' championing of the notion? We can do no more than suspect this since de Courcelles' silence is complete and the arguments which he does present show no signs of Descartes' influence.

Even when de Courcelles turns to the phenomenon of universal consent to belief in God, which was traditionally explained by the

---

[49]   'Quae in media barbarie educatae et solis tantum sensibus brutorum instar adsuefactae . . . cum iis qui ad rationem et principiis ista eos reducant, haud gravate iis adsentiuntur, naturae quasi stimulo veluti ex profundo somno expergefacti', ibid.

[50]   For de Courcelles (Stephanus Curcellaeus), see J. Charite *Biographisch Woordenboek van Protestantische Godgeleerden in Nederland* 2 (The Hague: Nijhoff, n.d.), 337–40.

[51]   See 'Meditation III' in *The Philosophical Works of Descartes* 1, ed. E.S. Haldane and G.T. Ross (Cambridge: Cambridge University Press, 1970), 157–71.

[52]   *St. Curcellaeus opera theologica* (Amsterdam, 1675), 2–5.

innate idea, he does not raise the issue. Instead he is content to allow that such belief may have arisen either because God's existence is so manifestly a truth that no one of sound mind can deny it or that it arises from divinely revealed tradition, or, as is most probable, both together.[53] Here he is evidently following Episcopius' far more prolix account.

The last great name in this succession of the Remonstrant professors of theology at Amsterdam in the seventeenth century is that of Philipp van Limborch, Episcopius' great-nephew and de Courcelles' former pupil, who succeeded to this position in 1668 and retained it until his death in 1712.[54] A figure of note in the theological world of his day, his *Theologica Christiana* went through no fewer than seven editions in the half-century following its first appearance at Amsterdam in 1686.[55]

It was van Limborch who had published de Courcelles' *Opera Theologica*, but, when we place the former's chapter 'De Existentia Dei'[56] alongside the equivalent sections of the works of his predecessors, it immediately becomes clear that he is far closer to his great-uncle than to his former teacher. Whereas de Courcelles had set out arguments for God's existence quite similar to those of Episcopius', van Limborch reproduces the latter's list precisely.

Again, van Limborch prefaces his presentation with a brief discussion of the same possible sources of the knowledge of God considered at this point by Episcopius; the innate idea, natural principles requiring the use of right reason and divine revelation. When, however, once more in line with his model, he rejects the first of these, he does so in deliberately moderate tones.[57]

It has been suggested that van Limborch was also influenced by Descartes, and here it is interesting to note that, while remaining loyal to the Remonstrant denial of the innate idea, part of his reason for doing so is expressed in Cartesian terms. He claims that any notion we may possess of a deity is initially confused and requires the use of reason before it can

---

[53] 'Ea vera duplex esse potest; vel quod Deum esse tam manifestae sit veritatis, ut id nemo mentis compos negare aut in dubium vocare ausus fuerit; vel quod omnes ex constanti patrum suorum traditione acceperint Deum se olim hominibus patefecisse. Unumquodque autem istorum separatim, multoque magis ultrumque conjunctim, consensum istum non esse brutum evincit', ibid. 4.

[54] See P.J. Barnouw, *Philippus van Limborch* (The Hague: n.p., 1963).

[55] A Dutch translation appeared in Amsterdam in 1701 and an abridged English translation entitled *A Compleat System or Body of Divinity* in London in 1713.

[56] This is the second chapter of the first book, *Theologia Christiana* (Amsterdam, 1700[3]), 2–7.

[57] 'Quod primam sententiam attinet, nos ea acriter contendere nolumus: verisimilius tamen nobis est, nullam homini ideam esse innatam, sed intellectum ejus in nativitate tabulae esse instar rasae, nullamque nos rei notitiam aut perceptionem, nisi ministerio sensuum, ope institutionis, aut ratiocinationis, acquirere', ibid. 2–3.

attain the status of a clear and distinct idea.[58] Thus he rejects one of Descartes' positions on the grounds that it does not fulfil one of that philosopher's fundamental requirements.

Van Limborch was, of course, a thoroughly irenical character. The subtitle of his *Theologia Christiana* proclaimed its purpose, 'ad praxim pietatis ac promotionem pacis Christianae unice directa', but this alone does not account for the fact that the vehemence with which Episcopius had rejected the innate idea of God was now a thing of the past. The chief reason for this cooling is rather to be found in the changed theological climate. As we saw, Episcopius' motive for rejecting the innate idea arose from his concern to establish the essential role of human freedom and rationality in the attainment of any knowledge of God. In the Calvinist world of his day this had been a hard battle to fight but, by the time of his great-nephew, the victory had largely been won and the claims of right reason in theology were not merely recognized but even exalted and acclaimed.

---

[58] 'Inde est, quod in initio, ratiocinandi facultate nondum ad perfectionem sui perducta, ideas rerum admodum confusas formemus: accendente inquisitione et experientia sensim vis ratiocinandi perficiatur, et ideae magis distinctae concipiantur', ibid. 3.

2

Gisbertus Voetius:
Toward a Reformed Marriage of Knowledge and Piety

Joel R. Beeke

INTRODUCTION

Gisbertus Voetius (1589–1676) represents the mature fruit of the so-called Dutch *Nadere Reformatie* — a primarily seventeenth and early eighteenth century movement that paralleled English Puritanism in both time and substance. Voetius was to the *Nadere Reformatie* (usually translated as the Dutch Second Reformation) what John Owen was to English Puritanism.[1] Though largely unknown and ignored by English-speaking scholarship,[2] Voetius is nearly as well known to students of Dutch Post-Reformation orthodoxy as Owen is to students of English Puritanism.[3] Nonetheless, little

---

[1] For a summary of the *Nadere Reformatie* and a discussion of the term, *Nadere Reformatie*, see Joel R. Beeke, *Assurance of Faith: Calvin, English Puritanism, and the Dutch Second Reformation* (New York: Peter Lang, 1991), 383–413. Heartfelt appreciation is extended to Ray B. Lanning and Arthur Blok for translation assistance.

[2] Space does not permit a discussion of Voetius' life and labours. The only major work on Voetius in English is Thomas Arthur McGahagan, 'Cartesianism in the Netherlands, 1639–1676: The New Science and the Calvinist Counter-Reformation' (PhD diss., University of Pennsylvania, 1976). For articles on Voetius, see Johannes Van Oort, 'Augustine's Influence on the Preaching of Gisbertus Voetius' in *Collectanea Augustiniana* 2, ed. Bernard Bruning, Mathijs Lamberigts, J. van Houten (Louvain: Leuven University Press, 1990); Herman Hanko, 'Gijsbert Voetius: Defender of Orthodoxy', *Standard Bearer* 72 (15 February 1996), 229–32.

[3] Secondary Dutch and German sources on Voetius include: Arnold Cornelius Duker, *Gisbertus Voetius*, 3 vols. (Leiden: E.J. Brill, 1897–1914), which remains the definitive biography, though it is of limited value due to its datedness and its lack of

of Voetius' Latin corpus has been translated into Dutch, and even less into English.[4] This chapter aims to introduce Voetius to an English readership and to show how he wed a Reformed scholastic methodology to a heartfelt piety. Standing at the pinnacle of scholasticism immediately prior to its disintegration, Voetius illustrates how orthodox Reformed theologians used scholasticism as a methodology and challenges the old caricature of 'dead orthodoxy'.

Born at Heusden, the Netherlands, to a prominent family of West-phalian descent and Reformed persuasion, he pursued theological studies at the University of Leiden from 1604 to 1611, during the very years

---

extended analysis of Voetius' teachings; H.A. Van Andel, *De zendingsleer van Gisbertus Voetius* (Kampen: Kok, 1912); Jan Anthony Crame, *De theologische faculteit te Utrecht den tijde van Voetius* (Utrecht: Kemink, 1932); Marinus Bouwman, *Voetius over het gezag der Synoden* (Amsterdam: S.J.P. Bakker, 1937); C. Steenblok, *Voetius en de Sabbat* (Hoorn, 1941); idem, *Gisbertus Voetius: Zijn leven en werken* (Gouda: Gereformeerde, 1976[2]); L. Janse, *Gisbertus Voetius, 1589–1676* (Utrecht: De Banier, 1971); A. de Groot, *Gisbertus Voetius: Godzaligheid te verbinden met de wetenschap* (Kampen: Kok, 1978); idem, 'Gisbertus Voetius' in *Gestalten der Kirchengeschichte 7 Orthodoxie und Pietismus*, ed. Martin Greschat (Stuttgart: W. Kohlhammer, 1982), 149–62; Willem van't Spijker, 'Gisbertus Voetius (1589–1676)' in *De Nadere Reformatie: Beschrijving van haar voornaamste vertegenwoordigers* (The Hague: Boekencentrum, 1986), 49–84; F.A. Van Lieburg, *De Nadere Reformatie in Utrecht ten tijde van Voetius: Sporen in de Gereformeerde Kerkeraadsacta* (Rotterdam: Lindenberg, 1989); Johannes Van Oort, 'Augustinus, Voetius, und die Anfänge der Utrechter Universiteit' in *Signum Pietatis: Festgabe für Cornelius Petrus Mayer zum 60. Geburtstag*, ed. A. Zumkeller (Würzburg: Augustinus-Verlag, 1989); Johannes Van Oort et al., *De onbekende Voetius* (Kampen: Kok, 1989); W.J. van Asselt and E. Dekker (eds.), *De scholastieke Voetius: Een luisteroefening aan de hand van Voetius' 'Disputationes Selectae'* (Zoetermeer: Boekencentrum, 1995); Cornelis Adrianus de Niet, 'Voetius en de literatuur: Een korte verkenning', *Documentatieblad* 19 (1995), 27–36.

[4]   Voetius' major writings include: *Selectarum disputationum theologicarum*, 5 vols. (Amsterdam, 1648–69) — hereafter *SDT*; *Politicae ecclesiasticae*, 4 vols. (Amsterdam, 1663–76) — hereafter, *PE; Te asketika sive exercitia pietatis* (Gorinchem, 1654) — hereafter, *EP* — now available in Dutch, Cornelis Adrianus de Niet (ed.), as *De Praktijk der Godzaligheid met inleiding, vertaling en commentaar*, 2 vols. (Utrecht: De Banier, 1996). Additional Voetian treatises in Dutch include *Catechisatie over den catechismus der Remonstranten* (Utrecht, 1641); *Geestelijke Verlatingen* (Utrecht, 1646); *Proeve van de Kracht der Godzaligheydt* (Utrecht, 1656); and a few sermons, letters, and short polemical extracts from Latin works. The only Voetian material in English is a small portion of volume 3 of *SDT* in *Reformed Dogmatics: Seventeenth-Century Reformed Theology Through the Writings of Wollebius, Voetius, and Turretin*, ed. and trans. John W. Beardslee III (New York: Oxford University Press, 1965), 263–334.

when it was the focal point of the Arminian crisis. He was particularly influenced by the Calvinist lectures of Franciscus Gomarus. He also attended lectures of James Arminius and other professors whose ortho-doxy was called into question.[5] He later wrote, 'I shall be Gomarus' grateful disciple to the end of my life.'[6]

Appointed lecturer in logic while a student at Leiden, he defended orthodox Reformed theology in his teaching. In terms of methodology, he leaned on the new, humanistic Aristotelianism of Leiden rather than on Ramism, which insisted on the purely instrumental and non-autonomous role of philosophy. He was convinced that the new Aristotelianism had absorbed everything of value in Ramism and con-sequently regarded the Ramist controversy as superfluous.[7]

Already in his Leiden years, Voetius showed a keen interest in a more pietist form of theology. He read Thomas à Kempis' *The Imitation of Christ* with deep appreciation. From that time on two elements strove for pre-eminence in his life and work: an intellectual Reformed scho-lasticism and a piety resembling the *devotio moderna* spirit.[8]

The temporary victory of the Arminians in 1610 had far-reaching consequences for Voetius. His mentor, Gomarus, was forced from the faculty, Arminians were hired, and Voetius' own hopes for an academic career were dashed. For supporting Gomarus and opposing Arminius, he was put out of his dormitory and had to take up lodging with friends. After finishing his studies and returning to Heusden, he was not permitted to travel and accepted instead a pastoral call.

His hard work in combatting Romanism and Arminianism earned him an appointment to the international Synod of Dort (1618–19) despite his youth.[9] Two items of interest surface in connection to Dort: First, his most prominent action was his able defence of Johannes Maccovius, whose supralapsarian conception of predestination was of a more logically rigid nature than that of most other delegates. Voetius appealed to the authority of William Ames, who had expressed confi-dence in Maccovius' intentions, though he regretted some of his terminology. Interestingly, however, his later thought was marked by

---

[5]   McGahagan, 33–5.
[6]   *SDT*, 5:100.
[7]   *SDT*, 3:753.
[8]   Van't Spijker, 49.
[9]   Unfortunately the journal he kept during the synod has been lost. We do know that Voetius was disappointed by the results of the synod in several practical areas. Voetius would later comment that the more the church conceded to the govern-ment, the less it could hope for in the way of serious reform from the government (*PE*, 3:559).

an attempt to reconcile the experiential piety of Ames and the neo-Aristotelianism of Maccovius.[10] Second, he later wrote appreciatively of close friendships established with a number of English delegates noted for their emphasis on Puritan theology and practice.[11]

Later pamphlet wars against Roman Catholics and Arminians also raised his stature among the Reformed as a first-rate scholastic theologian. His work against the Arminian Daniel Tilenus influenced Grotius.[12] Even more importantly, his *Prove van de Cracht der Godsalichheydt* (1627; Proof of the Power of Godliness) and *Meditatie van de Ware Practijcke der Godsalicheydt of der goede Wercken* (1628; Meditation on the True Practice of Godliness or Good Works) established him as a writer of practical piety, who insisted on a converted life as the attestation of an orthodox faith. He was a vigorous controversialist. His debates with Samuel Maresius, concerning virtually every theological issue of the day, lasted four decades until the two theologians united to battle the emergence of Cartesianism in the late 1660s.[13] He was convinced that Cartesianism placed reason on a par with Scripture at the expense of faith, so that man becomes the measure of all things.[14]

He also opposed Johannes Cocceius, the Bremen-born theologian who taught at Franeker and Leiden, and whose covenant theology, in Voetius' opinion, overemphasized the historical and contextual character of specific ages. He believed that Cocceius' new approach to the Scriptures would undermine both Reformed dogmatics and practical Christianity.[15]

He resisted Jean de Labadie, whose preaching had been the source of spiritual revival in Swiss Reformed churches, for promoting notions

---

[10]   See John Hales, *Golden Remains of the Ever Memorable Mr. John Hales* (London, 1659), 159, and William Ames, *Opera* (Amsterdam, 1658), 9. See also Abraham Kuyper, *Johannes Maccovius* (Leiden: Donner, 1899), 82ff., 357ff.; Michael Bell, 'Propter Potestatem, Scientiam, Ac Beneplacitum Dei: The Doctrine of the Object of Predestination in the Theology of Johannes Maccovius' (ThD diss., Westminster Theological Seminary, 1986).

[11]   *SDT*, 2:408.

[12]   Hugo Grotius, *Briefwisseling van Hugo Grotius*, ed. B.L. Meulenbroek (The Hague: Nijhoff, 1940), 3:385–90.

[13]   Doede Nauta, *Samuel Maresius* (Amsterdam: H.J. Paris, 1935).

[14]   See McGahagan, *passim*. See also Theo Verbeek, 'From "Learned Ignorance" to Scepticism: Descartes and Calvinist Orthodoxy' in *Scepticism and Irreligion in the Seventeenth and Eighteenth Centuries*, ed. Richard H. Popkin and Ardo Vanderjagt (Leiden: E.J. Brill, 1993).

[15]   See H.B. Visser, *De Geschiedenis van den Sabbatstrijd onder de Gereformeerden in de Zeventiende Eeuw* (Utrecht: Kemink, 1939); Steenblok, *Voetius en de Sabbat;* Charles McCoy, 'The Covenant Theology of Johannes Cocceius' (PhD diss., Yale, 1957).

of mystical subjectivism and of separation from the instituted church.[16] He spoke out against the government when the rights of the church were at stake, rejecting Erastianism and demanding that the church be completely independent of the state and of all patronage.[17]

After an extensive pastoral ministry, he accepted a professorial post in the new Academy of Utrecht, where he taught for forty-two years until his death in 1676. His ideals were clearly set forth in his inaugural address, *De pietate cum scientia conjugenda* (On Piety Joined with Knowledge). Piety and knowledge are not to be separated. They are to promote each other's welfare, for they are wedded together. The mind must assist the heart and life, and the heart and daily living ought to reinforce the mind.[18] According to Voetius, any attempt to weaken the link between knowledge and piety by claiming an absolute autonomy of science and knowledge is unbridled libertinism. Therefore he regarded his task at Utrecht as to 'practically treat of the solid and orthodox science of theology, which is by its nature practical'.[19] He was appointed rector of the newly founded 'Illustrious School' at Utrecht in 1636. The title of his sermon preached in the Cathedral Church of Utrecht was *Sermoen van de nutticheyt der academiën en de scholen* (Sermon on the Usefulness of Academies and Schools). His goal was to integrate the Utrecht church with the academy. The church should send her youth to this academy, and live in love and unity with all who were linked with the academy. On the other hand, the faculty should not only promote learning, but also piety, both in the public lectures and in the private lives of the professors. All human sciences must remain subordinate to the study of theology for the sake of the church.

In his lectures, Voetius focused particularly on systematic theology, ethics, and church polity. He also taught logic, metaphysics, and the Semitic languages: Hebrew, Arabic, and Syriac. In his lectures on theology, he followed the Leiden *Synopsis purioris theologiae*, compiled by

---

Cf. Jonathan Neil Gerstner, *The Thousand Generation Covenant: Dutch Reformed Covenant Theology and Group Identity in Colonial South Africa, 1652–1814* (Leiden: E.J. Brill, 1991), 75–82; S.D. van Veen, 'Gisbertus Voetius' in *The New Schaff-Herzog Encyclopedia of Religious Knowledge*, vol. 12 (1912; Grand Rapids: Baker, 1977), 220–1.

[16] Cf. Cornelis Graafland, 'De Nadere Reformatie en het Labadisme' in *De Nadere Reformatie en het Gereformeerd Pietisme* (The Hague: Boekencentrum, 1989), 275–346.

[17] W. Robert Godfrey, 'Calvin and Calvinism in the Netherlands' in *John Calvin: His Influence in the Western World*, ed. W. Stanford Reid (Grand Rapids: Zondervan, 1982), 112–13.

[18] *EP*, 857.

[19] Ibid. 3.

Leiden professors (1625), together with the dogmatic works of Gomarus, Maccovius, Ames, and, of course, Calvin's *Institutes* and Thomas Aquinas' *Summa theologiae*.

In 1664 he published *Exercitia et bibliotheca studiosi theologae* (The Exercises and Library of a Studious Theologian), a comprehensive 700-page introduction to theological literature and a four-year programme of theological study. Its theme is one with his overall vision: theology must be known and practised. Voetius' most academic works were published over a twenty-two-year span in his five volumes of selections from his theological debates, *Selectarum disputationum theologicarum* (1648–69). These volumes are the outgrowth of his famous Saturday seminars. These seminars took the following form: Voetius himself composed theses, especially touching on the pressing issues of the day, and appointed debaters who were instructed on how to defend them. Other students sought to challenge the debaters. The five volumes of these debates, similar to medieval debate texts, do not contain verbatim reports, but the final redaction of the whole by Voetius himself. Reporting 358 debates, they are a prime example of the scholastic method of teaching practical Reformed orthodoxy.[20] In addition, Voetius published four volumes on church polity, *Politicae ecclesiasticae* (1663–76), which also grew out of the Saturday debates. He evidenced a working knowledge of all the literature on church government of his day, including polemical works and works dealing with the ancient creeds. More than any other major work, *Politicae ecclesiasticae* represents the ecclesiastical ideals of the Dutch Second Reformation. Together with these works, Voetius wrote his *Te asketika sive exercitia pietatis* (1654; 'Ascetica' or the Exercises of Godliness), a detailed manual of piety in theory and practice. In all these works, Voetius revealed himself as a scholastic, practical theologian who did not fear conflict.

By the time of his death on 1 November 1676, dedicated Voetians were to be found in every university and ecclesiastical province of the Netherlands. He was mourned by thousands, especially by the Utrecht circle, and was buried in what is now the Roman Catholic cathedral of Utrecht.

VOETIUS' THEOLOGY

Voetius experienced no tension between detailed scholastic analysis and experiential warmth. From his perspective, theology, both systematic and practical, consistently supports his inner conviction that the marriage

---

[20]   W.J. Van Asselt, *Vera philosophia cum sacra theologia nusquam pugnat: Een inleiding in de Gereformeerde Scholastiek* (Utrecht, 1995), 62.

between Reformed scholasticism and Reformed piety is a happy one.[21] Thus he cast all his theology and writing in a scholastic mould, intent on developing Reformed thought by careful analysis, detailed definition, thorough development of each theological concept, careful repudiation of every heresy, and logical organization which was intended to show the relations among all the truths of Scripture. In his *Disputatio de theologia scholastica*, he defined scholasticism simply as a method of doing theology — a method first found in the four volumes of Peter Lombard's *Sententiae* and subsequently developed in Thomas Aquinas' *Summa theologiae*.[22] Notwithstanding the reference to medieval scholastics in his initial definition, Voetius asserted that the true (i.e. Reformed) scholastic method vastly differs from their's in content though not in method. Echoing Renaissance objections, he charges the medieval scholastics with dwelling on 'useless, vain, dangerous, absurd, and even blasphemous questions and problems'. In line with Luther and Calvin, he argued that their knowledge of Scripture and theology was weak at best; consequently, their principles are based on human authority, which they often misread, be it Aristotle or the Fathers. They were too prone to mix theology and philosophy:

> Most are guilty of confusion of categories, and continually attempt to demonstrate the mysteries of faith by reason and natural light, or by philosophy and philosophical authority.[23]

All of these faults made the medieval scholastics seriously defective in *praxis*, both in the exercise of piety and in the care of the church. They were 'purely speculative doctors, men of the shadows', exalting reason at the expense of faith.[24]

He insisted on the superiority of faith over reason in order to protect the purity of faith. Reason has lost its purity in the fall. Though reason remains a critical instrumental faculty, even after it is liberated through regeneration it remains imperfect, so that we ought not let it act as an autonomous judge but only as the servant of faith.[25] If reason were to be the judge of faith, would not all distinction between nature and grace be erased, and the scriptural insistence on regeneration be rendered meaningless? The principle of objectivity in matters of faith is not reason but the Holy Scriptures. Together with Scripture, we need a subjective

---

[21]   H.A. Van Andel, *Zendingsleer*. For Voetius' approach to mission see idem, 'The Missiology of Gisbertus Voetius: The First Comprehensive Protestant Theology of Missions', *Calvin Theological Journal* 26 (1991), 79.

[22]   *SDT*, 1:13–4.

[23]   Ibid. 1:23–4.

[24]   Ibid. 1:24–6.

[25]   In heaven reason will finally be perfectly illuminated (ibid. 1:2).

principle to move us to receive the doctrines of faith, i.e. the illumination of the Spirit.[26] Also our reason needs to be illumined, for though faith is superior to reason, faith itself involves the intellect as well as the will. Reason is critical, not as the principle of doctrinal truth, but as that faculty which is instrumental in exegeting such truths from Scripture and casting them into propositional form.[27]

For Voetius, both theology and philosophy are to be continually subjected to the test of edification: Does whatever is being discussed contribute to the life of faith as revealed (1) in the Scriptures, (2) for the believer's salvation, and (3) for the welfare of the church? Both faith and reason must serve to promote genuine piety. He fully concurred with Calvin that all genuine knowledge of God is lacking where true piety is lacking.[28]

Despite Voetius' criticism of the content of medieval scholasticism, he was fully aware that he stood in the scholastic tradition. Scholasticism as a methodology is profitable, even necessary, he argued, in order adequately to defend 'hidden and divine things against those who oppose them'. In fact, the medieval scholastics themselves ought to be studied in order to defend the Reformed faith against Roman Catholicism, since 'in elenctic [polemical] theology adversaries must often be convinced by their own, domestic witnesses'.[29] Moreover, the practical and experiential dimensions of theology can be enhanced by scholasticism, for, in the words of Johannes Hoornbeeck, who expressed the Voetian position poignantly, 'There is no practice without theory'.[30] Theory and practice must be distinguished but never separated. Theory, whether theological or philosophical, is itself a practical issue.

Thus, scholasticism and philosophy can coexist well with true theology. If rightly subjected to Scripture, the demands of faith, and the light of the Spirit, then scholastic methodology and theology, despite their dangers, bear good fruit. In fact, according to Voetius, one cannot be an able and learned theologian without making use of scholastic methodology, for the content of Scripture is, from both a religious and ethical perspective, reasonable truth. That is not to say that reason becomes the basis, law, or norm of what we should believe. We do not come to know the Trinity, sin, the incarnation, and the atonement by reason or natural revelation. We must receive what Scripture says by faith — faith which has its origin in the illumination of the Spirit. The secret of faith lies

---

26   *SDT*, 1:4.
27   See McGahagan, 55–63.
28   *Institutes*, 1.2.1.
29   *SDT*, 1 [vi].
30   'Praxis nulla absque scientia est', *Theologiae practicae* (Utrecht, 1663), 1:85.

beyond the reach of reason.[31] Thus, notwithstanding considerable defer-
ence shown to reason and to quotations from medieval scholastics
throughout his corpus, Voetius' theology did not succumb to reason but
remained in its genius a theology of revelation.

A brief perusal of the Voetian corpus confirms that his first love was
for *theologia practica* — the practice or exercise of theology which procures
a personal piety that glorifies God. By 'practical theology', Voetius
intended what we would call a theology of Christian experience rather
than our current usage referring to the pastoral ministry of preaching,
counselling, and teaching. For Voetius, no division of theology can be
handled effectively without personal and practical application for daily
living, nor have the Reformed ever aimed to do so:

> Are Reformed theologians concerned over practical theology, and do they
> discuss it, or is their theology purely speculative?
> *Our reply*: Affirmative to the first, and negative to the second, against the
> calumnies of the Remonstrants and the papists. . . . The very light of the facts
> is enough to destroy this calumny, since the sermons of the more distinguished
> of our preachers and an almost infinite number of writings of the Reformers
> breathe pure practice [italics mine], so that our theologians, like Socrates, may
> be said to have brought theology from heaven down to earth, or, better, to
> have raised it to heaven from the earth and scholastic dust.[32]

All theology must be practical, being used to encourage the spiritual
exercise of divine graces — particularly the graces of repentance, faith,
hope, and love. All theology must be rooted in faith. Faith consists of
intellectual knowledge of truth, hearty assent to the truth, and childlike
trust in the truth.[33] Though faith is often mysterious and incomprehensible
in its operations, there is nothing uncertain about its sources or its effects.
Its sources are the objective truth of Scripture and the subjective illumination of the Spirit. Its effects are affirmation of the Scriptures, sanctification, assurance of salvation, and perseverance — all of which, together
with faith itself, are not conditions for salvation, but results of election.
Faith is the terminus and effect of regeneration, not the cause or internal
instrument of regeneration.[34]

---

[31] *SDT*, 1:3.
[32] Beardslee, 268–9.
[33] *SDT*, 2:516. Voetius viewed the element of knowledge in faith as intellectual,
historical faith that is not necessarily saving in its nature. In discounting the *saving*
nature of knowledge, Voetius parts ways with Calvin and Olevianus and follows in
the footsteps of Melanchthon and Ursinus (see Joel R. Beeke, 'Faith and Assurance
in the Heidelberg Catechism and Its Primary Composers: A Fresh Look at the
Kendall Thesis', *Calvin Theological Journal* 27 (1992), 45–7).
[34] *SDT*, 2:442.

Rooted in election, faith works itself out in the progress of the elect from rebirth to conversion, justification, sanctification, and perseverance, finding its terminus in glorification.[35] To this experiential process from rebirth to glorification, Voetius, in typical Puritan fashion, devoted a great deal of energy and attention. These steps of grace, involving inward experience wrought in the soul by the Holy Spirit which in turn will show itself outwardly in the believer's walk of life, form the heart of his *theologia practica*. His concern with the stages of inner experience, however, was never divorced from his more intellectual and scholastic understanding of faith. For Voetius, faith is both an explicit intellectual act and a supernaturally infused *habitus*. Faith is both intellectual and emotional, both dogmatic and personal, both a matter of mind and soul. His morphology of conversion was intended to conjoin the intellectual and emotional dimensions of faith; indeed, the concept of faith as intellectually dogmatic was reinforced, not annulled, by this morphology.[36]

Voetius' scholastic and theological agenda was set by his emphasis on *theologia practica*. This agenda was fleshed out in three major areas through his writings: ethics (treated in *Selectarum disputationum theologicarum*, all five volumes, but especially volumes 3 and 4), piety (treated in *Te asketika sive exercitia pietatis*), and church polity (treated in his four volumes of *Politicae ecclesasticae*, the work for which he became best known).

1. Ethics

In volumes 3 and 4 of *Selectarum disputationum theologicarum*, Voetius used the Decalogue as his framework for debating a wide variety of ethical questions. He provided a clear rationale for doing so, arguing that ethics is a critical science that ought not to detract from systematic theology or apologetics; rather, it ought to assist systematics and other subjects in focusing on the practical exercises of the life of faith. For support, he pointed to William Perkins, whom he called the Homer of *theologia practica*, as well as William Ames, Jean Taffin, and Willem Teellinck. Besides, Voetius noted, the Particular Synod of North Holland (1645) requested the Leiden faculty to devote more attention in their lectures to 'cases of conscience' (*casus conscientiae*), which included particular and practical applications of the Ten Commandments to various cases.[37]

---

[35] For Voetius' views on election, see Cornelis Graafland, *Van Calvijn tot Barth: Oorsprong en ontwikkeling van de leer der verkiezing in het Gereformeerd Protestantisme* (The Hague: Boekencentrum, 1987²), 223–31. Though a supralapsarian, Voetius fully supported the Canons of Dort which were largely set in an infralapsarian framework.

[36] See McGahagan, 66–9.

[37] On Voetius as an ethicist, see Steenblok, *Voetius en de Sabbat*, 9–46.

Voetius then raised and answered fifteen objections to focusing on *theologica practica* in an ethical setting.[38] He asserted that opposition is to be expected, for wherever Reformed ministers speak to the conscience and admonish against specific sins, such as Sabbath-profanation, drunkenness and carousing, theatre-attendance, mixed dancing, gambling, vain and immoral dress, illicit usury, worldly parties, etc., they will be charged with being pharisaical, legalistic, or anabaptistic.[39] These charges are altogether ungrounded, says Voetius, for wherever repentance and faith are dealt with scripturally and faithfully, practical guidelines for daily life and warnings against specific sins cannot be avoided. For preaching and teaching that does not touch on practical, daily living is not faithful to the primary doctrines of Scripture. Ethics is simply teaching people how to live out Reformed doctrine. When rightly presented, ethics is not a system of works-righteousness to earn salvation. It is a set of guidelines on how to live out of the righteousness of Christ — that righteousness which has saved and does save, but also compels a lifestyle of gratitude for so great a salvation. Reformed ethics calls the believer to live wholly unto God in every detail of life in order to glorify him for his gift of salvation.

In working out his system of ethics, Voetius naturally focused more on the law than the gospel. The gospel, however, is not neglected. Gospel means the good news of salvation in Christ alone; it is the joyful message of the New Covenant, but it comprehends the Old Testament as well. The conditions of the gospel are faith and repentance, but these conditions are fulfilled by God's grace in Christ for us and in us. Strictly speaking, the gospel and its promises are absolute and unconditional. Receiving eternal life, however, involves more than the gospel. Salvation by the gospel will be evidenced by the keeping of the law out of gratitude to God. Voetius quoted Augustine with approval: 'Our works do not precede us to justify us, but they follow our being justified'. Under 'law' Voetius comprehends all edifying doctrine revealed by God in the Old and New Testaments. Here Voetius, as a student of Hebrew, correctly interprets the full meaning of Torah as 'instruction' in living, a rule of life. Consequently, Psalms 1 and 119 speak of the law as *doctrina salutaris* — i.e. salutory, beneficial, edifying doctrine.

Voetius subsumed both law and gospel under the covenant of grace. Whereas Luther had taught law and gospel as standing in an *ordo salutis* relationship, i.e. first law and then gospel, both Bucer and Calvin, whom Voetius followed, carried this *ordo salutis* relationship a step further by developing the so-called third use of the law — hence, law, gospel, law. That is to say, the law drives me to Christ for salvation, and the gospel

---

38 Beardslee, 276–89.
39 *PE*, 4:680, 699.

drives me back to the law to foster a grateful and moral life of sanctification.[40] Thus, the believer lives practically and daily out of the covenant of grace, trusting in God's covenantal promise of grace, and acknowledging his covenantal demand for wholehearted obedience to his law.

Thus for Voetius, faith must become visible. The Christian must strive to please the Lord in every circumstance and detail of his life. He serves a holy and precise God. A key word in Voetius' vocabulary of the Christian life is 'precision'. Voetius offers this definition: 'We define "precision" as the exact or perfect human action conforming to the law of God as taught by God, and genuinely accepted, intended, and desired by believers.'[41] In other words, the believer desires to do nothing less or other than the will of God expressed in his law as a rule of life. Such 'precision' compels the believer to live carefully, and to obey God exactly; or, in Paul's phrase, 'to walk circumspectly' (Eph. 5:15). If this means being ridiculed with false labels, so be it. It is more important to please God than man:

> The labels of being a precisianist, a zealot, a pigheaded person have always been applied to Christians whenever they have refused to be lukewarm and compromising. . . . We must not pay much attention when devotion is decried as superstition, soberness as hypocrisy, tenderness of conscience as strictness, puritanicalness, obstinacy, etc., in order to try to make us seem ludicrous.[42]

Voetius does not deny that one can adhere to a precise form of piety out of legalism, hypocrisy, or superstition. All errant forms of precise living, however, should not detract from living in a biblically precise manner, being zealous for good works, with a heart that is earnestly devoted to the fear of God and a conscience that is intent on obeying His commandments. This kind of 'precisianism' God regards as a 'heroic excellence of virtue'. Voetius proceeded, in a scholastic manner, to explain what biblical precisianism is. He lists all the synonyms in Scripture that promote precise living, defines them carefully, and concludes that precisianism is the outworking of internal holiness. In the inner recesses of the soul, the believer makes decisions *coram Deo* — decisions which demonstrate themselves by an outward lifestyle that reflects heartfelt obedience to the law.

Voetius cited numerous Scriptures, Reformed doctrinal standards, and a large number of Reformers and Puritans to support his case for

---

[40] See Joel R. Beeke and Ray B. Lanning, 'Glad Obedience' in *Trust and Obey*, ed. J. Beeke (Morgan, Pa.: Soli Deo Gloria, 1996), for the Reformed development of the third use of the law.

[41] Beardslee, 317.

[42] Cited in Van't Spijker, 65; see ibid. 57–61.

precisianism. He concludes that Scripture and all sound Reformed confessions and divines 'speak in unison that the outcry against real [biblical] precisianism lacks all foundation entirely'.[43]

2. *Ascetics*

Voetius' stress on the inner life of grace did not bring him into sympathy with either the medieval mystics or the modern enthusiasts. Even in his handbook on the godly life, *Te asketica sive exercitia pietatis*, in which he emphasized the need for habitual meditation, he declined to separate the contemplative and the active life. He insisted even here that his concern was with the 'pragmatics' of the interior life.[44] Meditation, according to Voetius, did not lead to immediate knowledge nor to the experience of the essence of God; rather, mystic surrender is 'the road to delirium and enthusiasm'.[45] The knowledge of God we receive by meditation is not irrational; rather, reflexive knowledge is an essential component in spiritual knowledge. Though others regarded prayer and devotion as acts of the will, Voetius insisted that even in these devotional means the intellect was deeply, concurrently involved.[46]

Voetius understood 'ascetics' to be the systematizing of that part of theological doctrine which describes how genuine, biblical piety is to be experienced and practised. Hence much more than meditation is involved. Voetius deals with how to cultivate a continual life of prayer, repentance, faith, and conversion; how to approach and attend and reflect on the Lord's Supper; how to pray and give thanks, both at stated times and extemporaneously. He dwells in depth on several facets of conversion: contrition, reconciliation, and renewal. He discusses spiritual sorrow and joy, various difficulties in the life of faith, and a host of cases of conscience.[47]

In each branch and topic of 'ascetics', Voetius pursues a scholastic method. He provides definitions, arranges concepts in a positive and negative sense, answers objections, poses potential questions and provides detailed answers. Throughout he quotes a seemingly endless number of authors — including numerous medieval Roman Catholic mystics.[48]

---

[43] *SDT*, 4:771.

[44] *EP*, 68.

[45] Ibid. 73. Cf. Izaak Boot, *De Allegorische Uitlegging van Het Hooglied Voornamelijk in Neaderland* (Woerden: Zuijderduijn, 1971), 155–63.

[46] *EP*, 23.

[47] For an excellent overview of this work, see the introduction and detailed table of contents in Gisbertus Voetius, *De Praktijk der Godzaligheid*.

[48] E.g. de Niet's detailed table of contents of Voetius' work reveals sixty-four citations of various authors, and cites Bonventura more than any other author (five times); Augustine and Gerson are cited three times; Calvin only once.

Though one might now think that the thoroughness of his method dampens its liveliness, and perhaps even tends to reduce subjective experience to objective analyzable data, it appears that those in the Dutch Second Reformation found a great deal of help there for their spiritual pilgrimage.

3. Church Polity

Voetius' massive four-volume *Politicae ecclesiasticae*, edited from his Saturday debates on church government, is divided into three major sections: The first consists of debates relating to ecclesiastical matters and actions; the second section concentrates on persons in the church, including pastors, elders, deacons, church members, women, and martyrs; the final section deals with the duties of the church. Voetius delves deeply into the issue of Roman Catholic and Protestant unity, addressing the boundaries of tolerance and the freedom of prophecy.

For Voetius, as for Calvin, the authority of the church is not autonomous, but derived from Scripture:

> [Ecclesiastical authority] is *anypeuthunos*, but it is required to supply its reasons, in dogmatizing, in imposing laws, in polity. It does not immediately and directly oblige in conscience, but only hypothetically, that is to say, as much as and insofar as the act of its exercise agrees, either formally and explicitly or reductively and implicitly, with the prescriptions of the Sacred Word.[49]

Because the authority of the church is grounded in Scripture, Voetius felt justified, as did Calvin, in attributing to the institutional church a central role in the definition of dogma and in the exercise of Christian discipline. The power of the church, however, must be defined rightly:

> [The church is] ministerial, not dominating or autocratic. If it abuses its power, proposing belief or action outside of and against the word of God, it is to be treated in the manner of parents, heroes, teachers, kings and princes commanding such things. Read Acts 4 and 5, and Daniel 3 and 6, where the authority and order constituted by God are recognized, but their abuse is condemned.[50]

The source of the church's authority is not in itself, nor is its goal its own maintenance. Its goal is the glory of God and the salvation of its own members. In Voetian ecclesiology the church is not definable in terms of any of its institutions, but only as a gathering of believers for the purpose

---

[49] *PE*, 1:122.
[50] Ibid. 3:247–8.

of mutually edifying one another in matters pertaining to salvation.[51] Voetius followed Martin Bucer's emphasis that care for the church must be motivated by the moral ideal of the living church building itself up in love in order to glorify God.[52] His goal was to bring about a further reformation of the church and its members through bringing the Dutch nation under the biblically loving, firm, and practical discipline of the church — i.e. discipline not only through admonition and censure but also and especially through preaching.

For Voetius all ecclesiastical authority must be subservient to Christ. The litmus test of a church is whether Christ would be able to exercise his lordship through his Word. Consequently, we are not surprised to find embedded in Voetius' treatise on church government a compendium on homiletics, in which he detailed his thoughts about preaching.[53] Preaching should expound God's Word clearly and practically, taking into account the current needs of the congregation. Voetius supported the consecutive exposition of chapters and books of the Bible, but stopped short of prescribing one method of preaching as mandatory for all occasions. He criticized the lectionary system as falling short of declaring the whole counsel of God.

Even in dealing with church polity, Voetius' scholastic methodology and practical piety were consistently bound up. Throughout this massive work he used the scholastic method, amassing literally thousands of quotations from hundreds of sources to affirm his points. Christiaan Sepp has rightly noted that the wealth of knowledge contained in these volumes is almost limitless.

CONCLUSION

The life and work of Gisbertus Voetius affirms the thesis of Richard Muller that post-Reformation orthodoxy often disagreed with the content of medieval scholasticism, but advantageously used its organizational structure. As the seventeenth century wore on, many Reformed theologians, including Voetius, increasingly relied on scholastic methodology to sustain the vigorous polemics in which they were engaged against Roman Catholicism, Arminianism, and the new philosophical challenges of Cartesianism. Though Reformed scholastic orthodoxy stands in some methodological discontinuity with Calvin, it retains strong affinities with Reformation teaching; indeed, the Reformation is incomplete without

---

[51] 1:12.
[52] Van't Spijker, 75–6.
[53] *PE*, 1:598–631.

its confessional and theological codification.[54] It cannot be denied that Voetius and seventeenth-century Reformed scholasticism discussed issues which at times moved beyond the Reformation principle of *sola scriptura*,[55] yet it is a serious error, as Jonathan Gerstner has noted, to confuse this weakness 'with the broader Reformed effort to build a consistent theological system and thus miss the remarkable and real progress of seventeenth-century Reformed theology'.[56]

Voetius has been underestimated as a Reformed scholastic and experiential theologian in the Netherlands and throughout Europe, and even more so by British and North American scholarship. Though not a creator of a new theology, he was a competent systematizer who influenced thousands. His teaching also attracted many Presbyterian Scots and nonconformist English students.[57] To many of his students, his theology became a programme. His ideals were formulated into what became known (contrary to his wishes) as 'the Voetians' or 'the Voetian party'.[58] With their powerful combination of orthodox doctrine and vital piety, the Voetians were far more successful at reaching the common people than the Cocceians.[59]

Through his two important offices as professor and preacher, Voetius made Utrecht a stronghold of orthodoxy.[60] His writings disseminated his thought throughout and beyond the Netherlands. His influence was so widespread at the university that it was frequently called the *Academia Voetiana.*[61] Several factors, however, curtailed Voetius' influence on

---

[54]   R.A. Muller, *Christ and the Decree: Christology and Predestination in Reformed Theology from Calvin to Perkins* (Grand Rapids: Baker, 1988); idem, *Post-Reformation Reformed Dogmatics*, 3 vols. (Grand Rapids: Baker, 1986–). Cf. Martin I. Klauber, 'Continuity and Discontinuity in post-Reformation Reformed Theology: An Evaluation of the Muller Thesis', *Journal of the Evangelical Theological Society* 33 (1990) 467; Willem J. Van Asselt, 'Herwaardering van de gereformeerde scholastiek', *Kerktijd* 7 (1995), 1–12.

[55]   McGahagan, 56.

[56]   *Thousand Generation Covenant*, 70.

[57]   Keith Sprunger, *Dutch Puritanism*, 359.

[58]   This was fostered in part by Voetius' recommendation of *gezelshappen* — i.e. conventicles or organized group meetings of the godly for the purpose of cultivating personal faith and spiritual edification. Gradually, these gatherings, usually identified as Voetian, tended to become *ecclesiolae in ecclesia* — small churches within the territorial church (cf. Martin H. Prozesky, 'The Emergence of Dutch Pietism', *Journal of Ecclesiastical History* 28 (1977), 29–37; Beeke, *Assurance of Faith*, 407–8n).

[59]   See Gerstner, *Thousand Generation Covenant*, chaps. 2, 5, and 9 for how this was borne out in the Dutch South African colonists.

[60]   F.G.M. Broeyer, 'William III and the Church in Utrecht after the French Occupation', in *Church, Change and Revolution*, ed. J. Van den Berg and P.G. Hoftijzer (Leiden: E.J. Brill, 1991), 180.

[61]   Godfrey, 112.

succeeding generations, not the least of which were his wordy tomes and his often laborious Latin. Then too, his students often carried his ideals further than their teacher; their excesses contributed to the ultimate disintegration of both Reformed scholasticism and the Dutch Second Reformation. Furthermore, the increasing secularization of the Dutch people influenced the leading *Nadere Reformatie* divines of subsequent generations to abandon Voetius' vision for reforming all of society; instead, they focused largely on his emphasis on internal piety. By the eighteenth century, the Dutch Second Reformation had become reminiscent of the *Devotio Moderna* in its emphasis on thorough separation from the unredeemed world, though there were notable exceptions, such as Wilhelmus à Brakel — who, though primarily a Voetian theologian, sought to combine the best of Voetius, Cocceius, and Herman Witsius. Brakel's famous work, *De Redelijke Godsdienst*, recently translated into English as *The Christian's Reasonable Service*,[62] did much to keep alive in the Netherlands throughout the centuries that balance of systematic and experiential theology which John Murray has aptly called 'intelligent piety'.[63]

---

[62] 4 vols., trans. Bartel Elshout (Morgan, Pa.: Soli Deo Gloria, 1992–5).

[63] F. Ernest Stoeffler also notes Voetius' influence on F.A. Lampe and German Pietism, *The Rise of Evangelical Pietism* (Leiden: E.J. Brill, 1971), 170.

3

The Twilight of Scholasticism:
Francis Turretin at the Dawn of the Enlightenment

James T. Dennison, Jr.

Gilbert Burnet, future Latitudinarian bishop of Salisbury, visited Geneva, Switzerland in 1686 as part of a larger tour of the continent.[1] When pausing in the city of Calvin, he became a guest in the home of the current epigone, Francis Turretin.[2] Burnet's comments on the theological mood of the metropolis reflect the proclivities of late seventeenth-century progressives.[3] He reviewed some 'matters of very small consequence' on which factions had developed in the cantons with regard to three points of doctrine: the imputation of Adam's sin; the divine decrees; the vowel points in the Hebrew Bible. The arguments over this trinity 'are speculations so little certain, and so little essential to Religion, that a Diversity of Opinions ought not to be made the occasion of Heat or Faction'.[4] While Burnet acknowledged the stature and sincerity of the defenders of orthodoxy re the above propositions, he lamented: 'I wish they had larger and freer Souls'.[5]

---

[1]   Gilbert Burnet, *Some letters, containing an account of what seemed most remarkable in travelling through Switzerland, Italy, some parts of Germany, &c. in the years 1685 and 1686* (Rotterdam, 1687), 56–8.
[2]   On Turretin (1623–87), see my 'The Life and Career of Francis Turretin' in Francis Turretin, *Institutes of Elenctic Theology*, trans. George M. Giger and ed. James T. Dennison, Jr. (Phillipsburg, N.J.: P and R, 1992–6), 3, 639–58.
[3]   Cf. Eamon Duffy, '*Correspondence Fraternelle*; The SPCK, the SPG, and the Churches of Switzerland in the War of Spanish Succession' in *Reform and Reformation: England and the Continent c.1500–c.1750*, ed. Derek Baker (Oxford: Blackwell, 1979), 256–7.
[4]   Burnet, *Some letters*, 57.
[5]   Ibid. 58.

The orthodox zealots to whom Burnet was referring included his host, Francis Turretin,[6] Johann Henry Heidegger and the other defenders of the *Formula Consensus Helvetica*.[7] The *Consensus* had been adopted in Geneva, Berne and Zurich in order to guard against (further) invasion of Salmurian errors, i.e. the Amyraldianism originating in the French Academy at Saumur.[8] The theological triumvirate of the suspect Academy — Moïse Amyraut (Moses/Moyse Amyrald), Louis Cappel, Josué de la Place (Placaeus) — advanced doctrines specified for condemnation in the canons of the *Consensus*: 'universalism' or hypothetical redemptionism (Amyraut, Canons IV–IX and XIII–XXV); mediate imputation of Adamic transgression (de la Place, Canons X–XII); and the origin of the vowel points in the Hebrew Bible (Cappel, Canons I–III). Under the leadership of Francis Turretin, Geneva adopted the Formula (1678) to preserve the orthodoxy of the Synod of Dort (1619) in its Swiss fortress against the swelling tide of error washing in from the west. The victory was short-lived (actually less than thirty years). The tide threatening scholastic Reformed orthodoxy was more extensive than the theology of Saumur (though the French Academy contributed significantly to the demise of scholastic Calvinism in late seventeenth-century Geneva). Gilbert Burnet was prototypical of the change about to overwhelm Calvin's citadel.[9] Indeed, Burnet was prototypical of a change which would alter European civilization forever — a change which would offer 'larger and freer Souls'.

Paul Hazard's magisterial *The Crisis of the European Mind (1680–1715)* traced the paradigm shift which prepared Europe to be swept into the

---

[6] It was not coincidental that Turretin's son, Jean-Alphonse (1671–1737), was a guest in Burnet's home during his 1693 sojourn in England; cf. E. de Budé, *Vie de J.-A. Turrettini, théologien genevois 1671–1737* (Lausanne: Georges Bridel, 1880), 19–20. For Burnet's estimate of the father's character, see *Some letters*, 259–60.

[7] Martin I. Klauber, 'The Helvetic Formula Consensus: An Introduction and Translation', *Trinity Journal* 11 (1990), 103–23. On the specifically Genevan phase of the history of this document, see Donald D. Grohman, 'The Genevan Reaction to the Saumur Doctrine of Hypothetical Universalism: 1635–1685' (PhD diss. Knox College, Canada, 1971), 379–421.

[8] On Saumur and Amyraldianism, see Grohman, 'Geneva Reactions'; Roger Nicole, 'Moyse Amyraut (1596–1664) and the Controversy on Universal Grace First Phase (1634–1637)' (PhD diss. Harvard University, 1966); Brian Armstrong, *Calvinism and the Amyraut Heresy: Protestant Scholasticism and Humanism in Seventeenth-Century France* (Madison: University of Wisconsin Press, 1969); F.P. Van Stam, *The Controversy Over the Theology of Saumur, 1635–1650* (Amsterdam and Maarssen: APA-Holland University Press, 1988).

[9] 'The start of the Enlightenment would have been impossible without the repudiation of Geneva, and the moderate churchman were at the forefront of the anti-Calvinist assault', W.M. Spellman, *The Latitudinarians and the Church of England, 1660–1700* (Athens and London: University of Georgia Press, 1993), 55.

Enlightenment. *La crise de la conscience Européenne*, variously subsumed under the guise of 'rationalism', 'freedom', 'tolerance', 'secularism', changed all areas of Western thought and life. Prior to the end of the seventeenth century, mankind was everywhere in chains: in bondage to superstition (religion), ignorance (a prescientific world-view), absolutism (*jure divino* monarchy), and parochialism (localism and/or nationalism). Descartes, Cromwell, Newton, etc. combined to break these chains; at least that is the customary scholarly explanation. Yet each of these seventeenth-century trendsetters was a theist. Is it permissible to question the traditional scholarly explanation by posing the (apparently) simplistic question: how did theism undermine itself?[10] Or is asking the simplistic question to begin to doubt the scholarly consensus? The sundry scapegoats proffered to explain the shift from a precritical to an Enlightenment perspective seem woefully inadequate to account for the result. For instance, 'rationalism' has been suggested as the chief culprit, as if prior to 1660 men and women were irrational or reason was not an aspect of epistemology. Again, 'anti-clericalism' has been proposed to account for the new view of ecclesiastical privilege which emerged in the late seventeenth century, as if monarchs and parliaments had not been locked in an ongoing struggle to limit clerical power since the Middle Ages. And what of that favourite cliché, 'tolerance', redeemer of maturing pre-Enlightenment mankind, which is spoken of as if the late seventeenth century produced *de novo* a concept unknown prior to 1660;[11] as if the bloody seventeenth-century wars of religion had not made the ideal of *tolerantia* a practical necessity — the alternative being endless death and destruction?[12]

Optimists enamoured of the rationalism of the pre-Enlightenment era have overlooked the biting critique of 'mere reason' delivered by post-Enlightenment Romanticism. And was the late seventeenth century genuinely an era of clerical restriction and limitation of ecclesiastical privilege? Some would argue that the clergy adapted to the new era with

---

[10]   Richard Popkin has spent nearly a generation suggesting that it was scepticism, *not* theism which prepared the way to the Enlightenment; cf. 'Fideism, Quietism, and Unbelief: Skepticism For and Against Religion in the Seventeenth and Eighteenth Centuries' in *Faith, Reason, and Skepticism*, ed. Marcus Hester (Philadelphia: Temple University, 1992), 121–54.

[11]   Cf. for example Paul Kristeller, 'Humanism and Moral Philosophy' in *Renaissance Humanism: Foundations, Forms and Legacy* 3 *Humanism and the Disciplines*, ed. Albert Rabil, Jr. (Philadelphia: University of Pennsylvania Press, 1988), 304–5; Theodore K. Rabb, 'Religious Toleration During the Age of Reformation' in *Politics, Religion and Diplomacy in Early Modern Europe*, ed. Malcolm R. Thorp and Arthur J. Slavin (Kirksville, Mo.: Sixteenth Century Journal, 1994), 304–19.

[12]   The notion of 'reform' itself augurs tolerance to the degree that the 'new' is permitted to coexist with the 'old'.

an agenda dedicated to preserving their own position.[13] Finally, lest tolerance be too quickly embraced as the source of emancipation, consider the fate of Dissenters, Nonconformists, Huguenots and Pietists.

It cannot be denied that an era was passing away in the decades before 1700 — the twilight of scholasticism[14] was fading into the dawn of the Enlightenment. Cromwell's Ironsides and William's Glorious Revolution dramatically altered British history. The Revocation of the Edict of Nantes convulsed French society and pointed towards the Revolution. Publication of Descartes' *Discourse on Method* altered philosophical and theological discussion up until the time of Kant. But in Geneva, the catalyst for change was not Cartesianism (contra Michael Heyd); not Louis XIV's intolerance; not England's quasi-republicanism. In Geneva, the triumph of the theology of Saumur and the surging forces which accomplished the repudiation of the *Formula Consensus Helvetica* in 1706 marked the end of orthodox scholastic Calvinism in the master's citadel. The shifts are indisputable, the reasons for the shifts remain open to interpretation.

I am contending that the shift to Enlightenment Europe was the result of utilitarian, opportunistic, elitist and moralistic factors (i.e. the elements of modernity in late seventeenth century form); it was *not* the result of idealism (i.e. rationalism, freedom, tolerance, cosmopolitanism). What happened in the second half of the seventeenth century was the search for and triumph of self-interest — self-interest assembled into established elites. For Descartes, the consequence was a self-ish *a priori*. For Newton, the observing subject became the centre of the data paradigm. For Louis XIV, consummate egoism established state policy. For Gilbert Burnet, ecclesiastical supremacy was founded on a kinder and gentler elitism — eclectic ecumenism. Europe at the dawn of the eighteenth century was swept by modernistic moderatism.[15]

---

[13] Cf. J.A.I. Champion, *The Pillars of Priestcraft Shaken: The Church of England and Its Enemies, 1660–1730* (Cambridge and New York: Cambridge University Press, 1992).

[14] Richard Muller has spent much of his career exegeting Protestant scholasticism. His most recent survey appears in the *Calvin Theological Journal* 30 (1995), 345–75 and 31 (1996), 125–60. The bibliography available in his footnotes is a good guide to the relevant literature.

[15] The rupture between remnant pockets of fundamental orthodoxy and burgeoning moderatism manifested itself openly within the first decades of the eighteenth century in the Bangor Controversy (1717), the Salters Hall Conference (1719), the Belfast Society (1719), the Simson Affair (1726), the split between Harvard and Yale in New England (1701), the reduction of the subscription formula in Geneva to merely Scripture and the Geneva Catechism (1725). By mid-century, Voltaire and d'Alembert would observe that the Genevan clergy were indistinguishable from the Deists; cf. Geoffrey Adams, *The Huguenots and French Opinion 1685–1787: The Enlightenment Debate on Toleration* (Waterloo, Ontario: Wilfrid Laurier University Press, 1991), 50, 139. All over Europe, orthodoxy's bastions were being eroded by modernistic moderatism.

Francis Turretin discerned the ugly head of moderatism in the threat from the west — Amyraldianism. But resistance to this imported French anti-Dort evangelicalism would cease with his death. After 1687, the Venerable Company of Pastors would no longer resist 'universal grace', and its concomitants, and the Council would be increasingly secularized by practical concerns, such as how could Geneva present itself as an elegant cosmopolitan city to the watching world.

The megashift at the end of the seventeenth century was a contest for power, for control, for dominance of the socio-religio-political establishment.[16] This struggle for power was incarnated in the Turretin family. Dominating the theological (and, to some extent, the political) landscape of seventeenth-century Geneva was *la maison Turrettini*. Although the Diodati and Tronchin families were also influential theologically, the world recognized Geneva on account of Benedict and Francis Turretin.[17] Francis Turretin's *Institutes* was regarded by his contemporaries as perhaps the finest summary of scholastic Calvinism in the seventeenth century.[18] The last epigone was usually triumphant in conflicts with the political factions in Geneva, as is evident in his frequent clashes with the liberal, pro-Salmurian party. With his death, however, power passed to the emerging cosmopolitan elite.

The hagiographical funeral oration delivered by Benedict Pictet[19] glosses over the tensions generated by his uncle's high Calvinism. On

---

[16]   See the trenchant reflections of Richard Ashcraft, 'Latitudinarianism and Toleration: Historical Myth Versus Political History' in *Philosophy, Science and Religion in England 1640–1700*, ed. Richard Kroll, Richard Ashcraft, Perez Zagorin (Cambridge and New York: Cambridge University Press, 1992), 151–77; cf. also Margaret C. Jacob, 'The Crisis of the European Mind; Hazard Revisited' in *Politics and Culture in Early Modern Europe*, ed. Phyllis Mack and Margaret C. Jacob (London and New York: Cambridge University Press, 1987), 251–71.

[17]   Benedict Turretin (1588–1631) taught theology at the Academy from 1611–31. Francis' career as Professor of Theology spanned 1653–87. Both father and son were delegated by the Council to raise funds for the defence of the metropolis; cf. Dennison, 'Life and Career' in Turretin, *Institutes* 3, 642, 645; Pictet, 'Funeral Oration', ibid. 3:669–70. John Diodati was Professor of Theology from 1609–49, a delegate to the Synod of Dort and the teacher of Francis Turretin. Theodore Tronchin was Professor of Theology from 1615–57, also a delegate to the Synod of Dort, as well as a teacher of Francis Turretin. Louis Tronchin, son of Theodore, was Professor of Theology from 1662–1705, an advocate of the theology of Saumur and teacher of Francis Turretin's son Jean-Alphonse; Dennison, ibid. 642, 653 n. 50, 656 n. 98.

[18]   Gerrit Keizer, *Francois Turrettini sa vie et ses oeuvres et le Consensus* (Lausanne: Georges Bridel, 1900), 236.

[19]   See the English translation by David Lillegard in Turretin, *Institutes* 3, 659–76. For the Latin text, cf. 'Oratio funebris de vita atque obitu Francisci Turrettini; Habita die iii Novemb. an. M.DC.LXXXVII' in *Francisci Turrettini Opera* (New York: Robert Carter, 1847–8), I, xxix– xlviii.

hearing of Turretin's death, Daniel Chamier was less than lacrymose. 'If we had only heard the same news thirty years ago, our Church and your Academy would have been so happy!'[20]

While Francis Turretin had made friends with his doctrinal precision, he had also made enemies by defending scholastic Calvinism in the city, the church and the academy of Geneva. Turretin routinely locked horns with those pressuring the Venerable Company away from the Calvinism of the Synod of Dort. At the same time, he found himself combatting a subtle shift in the political orientation of the ruling class within the Council. As Geneva became more and more a cosmopolitan centre,[21] the Council increasingly directed its energies to promoting the image of the metropolis. Turretin ran afoul of this moderate and progressive agenda in clashes involving Charles Maurice (1669), Jean-Robert Chouet (1669), Louis Tronchin (1669), Phillipe Mestrezat (1669) and Pierre Mussard (1671). Lurking in the background of these controversies was *l'affaire Morus* (1649). The common thread of contention linking these cases was the Amyraldian theology of Saumur. While Turretin had visited Saumur in 1645 in order to hear for himself what the 'triumvirs' were teaching (the better to defend Dort-Geneva Calvinistic orthodoxy), Louis Tronchin and Jean-Robert Chouet had been educated at Saumur and returned as apologists for the Amyraldian modifications of Calvinism.[22] These progressives had the upper hand as the century advanced to the *siècle des lumières*. They controlled the avant-garde students, merchants and pastors. They were fresh, elegant, sophisticated advocates of the new wave of learning, polished orators, manipulative teachers, and effective bureaucrats. The polarization in theology between the 'conservative' Turretin and the 'liberal' Tronchin/Chouet/Mestrezat/Mussard was duplicated by a polarization between the ruling class and the artisans.[23] Moneyed

---

[20]   Letter to Louis Tronchin dated 24 Oct. 1687; cf. Martin I. Klauber, 'Jean-Alphonse Turrettini and the Abrogation of the Formula Consensus in Geneva', *Westminster Theological Journal* 53 (1991), 331.

[21]   Being prepared by the progressives for full membership in the coming Republic of Letters.

[22]   On Tronchin, see Martin I. Klauber, 'Reason, Revelation, and Cartesianism: Louis Tronchin and Enlightened Orthodoxy in Late Seventeenth Century Geneva', *Church History* 59 (1990), 326–39. For Chouet, consult the work of Michael Heyd, *Between Orthodoxy and Enlightenment: Jean-Robert Chouet and the Introduction of Cartesian Science in the Academy of Geneva* (The Hague: Martinus Nijhoff, 1982).

[23]   Cf. Andre-E. Sayous, 'La haute bourgeoisie de Genève entre le debut du XVIIᵉ et le milieu du XIXᵉ siècle', *Revue historique* 180 (1937), 43; also the study of Geneva's social and religious evolution by Roger Staufenegger, *Église et société Genève au XVIIᵉ siècle* (Genève: Droz, 1983), and Olivier Fatio, 'L'église de Genève et la révocation de l'édit de Nantes' in Olivier Reverdin et al., *Genève au temps de la révocation de l'édit de Nantes 1680–1705* (Genève: Droz, 1985), 161–96.

interests increasingly dominated Geneva politics in the twilight of the seventeenth century. Turretin's prestige and family reputation (as well as his family fortune) were sufficient to retard the slide from Dort Calvinism during his lifetime, but with his death the repudiation of his principles advanced rapidly as his son devoted the family wealth to a more progressive agenda.

Francis Turretin first publicly faced the agenda of the progressive party in 1669. Charles Maurice, a student at the Academy, received a call to a church in France. Mestrezat and Louis Tronchin argued that he should be exempted from subscribing to the 1649 Theses[24] since he was not called to a pastorate in Geneva. Turretin countered that since the Venerable Company was approving Maurice's candidacy, he was subject to Geneva's subscription requirement. Turretin prevailed, but Mestrezat and Tronchin revealed that their agenda differed significantly from that of the epigone.

Turretin continued to insist on subscription to the 1649 Theses. Tronchin was required to submit (1669); Chouet was exempted (1669). The compromise in the latter case was the first signal of a change in theological direction at Geneva. Chouet had been recruited by his uncle, Louis Tronchin. Uncle and nephew had been educated at Saumur; Chouet had even taught philosophy there (1664–9). Tronchin was joined by Mestrezat in urging Chouet to take the chair of philosophy at Geneva over the objections of the 'Cabale Italienne'.[25] The Italian opposition, Turretin and André Pictet, were rebuffed by the Venerable Company not only on Chouet, but on the distinction between *sic sentio* and *sic docebo* with respect to the 1649 Theses.[26] The hierarchy of the church and state in Geneva was being polarized by factions dedicated to their own self-interests.

Ambivalence characterizes the era and its protagonists. Chouet was a Cartesian, but the 'Italian cabal' did not apparently object to his philosphy.[27] What alarmed Turretin was his subtle advocacy of the Salmurian

---

[24]   For the background to this controversy, see Grohman, *Genevan reactions*, 258–333. Grohman provides an English translation of the Theses, 232–5.

[25]   Heyd, *Between Orthodoxy*, 44.

[26]   Heyd, ibid. 48; cf. Grohman, *Genevan reactions*, 334–48.

[27]   Gerrit Keizer, *Francois Turrettini sa vie et ses oeuvres et le Consensus*, (Lausanne: Georges Bridel, 1900), 194, lists a number of manuscripts in which Turretin appears supportive or neutral towards Cartesianism. The lone paragraph in the *Institutes* implicating Descartes finds Turretin essentially positive: a 'philosopher may be allowed to begin with doubt in order to a safer investigation of natural things', 1.13.14, 1, 47. This matches the ambivalence of continental Calvinism to Descartes: Gisbert Voetius was bitterly anti-Cartesian; Johannes Cocceius was a vigorous defender — cf. Theo Verbeek, *Descartes and the Dutch: Early Reactions to Cartesian Philosophy 1637–1650* (Carbondale and Edwardsville: Southern Illinois University Press, 1992) and Ernestine Van der Wall, 'Orthodoxy and Scepticism in the Early

modifications of Calvinism. Ironically the fifth column had been invited into the bastion of orthodoxy. Even more ironically, it was the 'sons of the fathers' who advanced the pro-Salmurian modifications. Tronchin was teaching theology and recruiting like-minded pro-Salmurian professors. Chouet quietly redirected philosophical-theological discussion in anti-scholastic directions, especially in his private lectures. Mestrezat commended the decisions of the French national synods as normative for Geneva.[28] The progressive agenda of the anti-Italian faction would gradually insinuate itself into the Academy, the Council and the Venerable Company.

The agenda of Tronchin, Chouet and Mestrezat was one of modification by way of separation: separation of theology and philosophy (Chouet); separation of Geneva's Calvinistic scholasticism from an emerging modern, cosmopolitan Protestantism (Tronchin); separation of Genevan culture and society from the 'ancien régime' in order to embrace the rising new bourgeois 'republic of letters' (Pierre Bayle).[29] It was not rationalism which set the new cabal over against the epigones. Though many have argued that the bridge to the Enlightenment goes by way of 'rational theology', it should be pointed out that the historic rational theology of Christian orthodoxy (Protestant and Roman Catholic alike) was the synthesis of reason and revelation, not the antithesis of rationalism to the exclusion of revelation or fideism to the exclusion of reason.[30] The liberal party in Geneva was not repudiating

---

Dutch Enlightenment' in *Scepticism and Irreligion in the Seventeenth and Eighteenth Centuries*, eds. Richard H. Popkin and Arjo Vanderjagt (New York: E.J. Brill, 1993), 121–41. For a review of parallel ambivalence in England and New England, see the 'Introduction', *Aristotelian and Cartesian Logic at Harvard*, ed. Rick Kennedy (Boston: The Colonial Society of Massachusetts, 1995), 1–138.

[28] The Synod of Alençon (1637) mildly censured Amyraut, but allowed him to continue to teach at Saumur. The Synod of Charenton (1644) ruled that Amyraut was not to be censured; the Synod of Loudun (1659) declared Amyraut orthodox and La Place's views acceptable; cf. Van Stam, *The Controversy*, 77–142, 203; Roger Nicole, *Moyse Amyraut: A Bibliography* (New York and London: Garland, 1981), 15–16.

[29] Bayle (1647–1706) was trained at Geneva by Chouet and Tronchin. His heterodoxy may be attributed, in part, to the ambivalence in the position of his respected mentors. On Bayle, see Elizabeth Labrousse, 'Reading Pierre Bayle in Paris' in *Anticipations of the Enlightenment in England, France, and Germany*, ed. A.C. Kors and P.J. Korshin (Philadelphia: University of Pennsylvania, 1987), 7–16, and her monograph *Bayle* (Oxford: Oxford University Press, 1983).

[30] Cf. Peter Gay, *The Enlightenment – An Interpretation: The Rise of Modern Paganism* (New York: Alfred A. Knopf, 1975), 227ff.; Richard H. Popkin, 'The Religious Background of Seventeenth-Century Philosophy' in *The Third Force in Seventeenth-Century Thought*, ed. Richard H. Popkin (New York: E.J. Brill, 1992), 276–7.

the historic synthesis.[31] It is true that there were those in the late
seventeenth century who preferred reason at the expense of revelation,
but we do not find them among Geneva's progressives, the Amyraldians
or the Latitudinarians — we find them among the sceptics, pantheists
and deists. If any use of reason in theology labels the user a 'rationalist',
then divines from Augustine to Thomas Aquinas to John Calvin to
Francis Turretin to Jonathan Edwards to Benjamin B. Warfield will
need to be branded 'rationalists'.[32]

Others have suggested that the bitter religious wars of the seventeenth
century spawned an atmosphere of tolerance — a thirst for freedom from
dogma, polemics, confessions and scholasticism. This canard is virtually
universal in the secondary literature which romanticizes the late seventeenth century as an era akin to the enlightened democracies of the
twentieth century. In fact, tolerance was a manipulative slogan for the
emerging elite of the late seventeenth century. They were imbued with
a bitter hatred of war and conflict — the legacy of the *ancien régime*. But
their own rigid absolutism[33] betrayed that 'liberty of conscience' and
'tolerance' were empty symbols. Tolerance was only permitted within
the limits prescribed by those who controlled the culture.

Francis Turretin was living through the end of the era of Protestant
scholasticism. But the erosion of Turretin's world did not occur from frontal
blows to fundamental premises. Rationalism was a Socinian error, rejected
by Turretin, Tronchin, Mestrezat and all other Geneva savants. Toleration
was available to Saumur, in Saumur; to Socinians, in Poland; to Roman
Catholics, in Italy and Spain. Geneva had the liberty to establish its own
doctrinal consensus. And Turretin's hand in adopting that *Consensus* was
the capstone of his campaign to resist the supreme threat to orthodoxy —
Amyraldianism. The opposition between Turretin and Tronchin, Chouet
and Mestrezat is reducible to anti- and pro-Salmurian sympathies.

---

[31] Martin Klauber can allege only the neglect of the 'internal witness of the Spirit'
between father and son, see his *Between Reformed Scholasticism and Pan-Protestantism:
Jean-Alphonse Turretin (1671–1737) and Enlightened Orthodoxy at the Academy of
Geneva*, (Sellingsgrove, Pa., Susquehanna University Press, 1994), 104. Yet having
accused Jean-Alphonse Turretin of repudiating the internal witness of the Holy Spirit
for 'rationalism', Klauber admits that the son did *not* deny what the father taught;
ibid. 141. Manufacturing non-existent distinctions unmasks a failure to make proper
distinctions!

[32] Rationalism is the conviction that truth derives from reason alone; revelation is
excluded. A rational approach to Christianity, on the other hand, endorses the use
of reason in apprehending the truth of the gospel, assent and trust in which arises
from the regenerative work of the Holy Spirit. On the classic synthesis of reason
and revelation, see Turretin, *Institutes*, 1, 23–34, 37–43, 64–5, 161–2.

[33] See especially Pierre Bayle; Myriam Yardeni, 'French Calvinist Political
Thought, 1534–1715' in *International Calvinism 1541–1715*, ed. Menna Prestwich
(Oxford: Oxford University Press, 1985), 315–37.

Descartes was not the threat in late seventeenth-century Geneva. Newton was not the threat in Turretin's Swiss fortress. Deism was not the threat in Geneva. Turretin's political involvement focused on one cardinal error — the theology of Saumur. If the bridge to the coming Enlightenment lay anywhere, it lay in the Academy of Amyraut, Cappel and de la Place. Orthodoxy could 'sanctify' Descartes. Orthodoxy could weigh Newtonian science and harvest the good. Orthodoxy could even pursue liberty of conscience and tolerance on the basis of fundamental articles.[34] But orthodoxy could not survive the anthropocentric focus of Amyraldianism.[35] Turretin's theology was theocentric (i.e. focused on the decrees of divine sovereignty) and Christocentric (i.e. focused on Christ as the mediator for *his* people): it was antipodal to the theology of Saumur. Tronchin, Chouet and Mestrezat had to moderate that theo- and Christocentric scholasticism before their progressive Amyraldian agenda could triumph. By reducing the anthropology of Geneva's Academy to the human subject, the pro-Salmurian party undermined the orthodox Augustinian-Calvinistic doctrine of total depravity. By redirecting the curriculum at the Academy,[36] the pro-Salmurian party gave expression to its revolutionary agenda: theology was no longer the queen of sciences, but the handmaid to philosophy; mankind was not sinful, 'dead in trespasses and sins', morally unable to cooperate with divine grace apart from the irresistible work of the Holy Spirit, but was handicapped, temporarily hindered by the moral indifferentism into which it has been cast by 'error'; predestination was not the 'horrible decree' of orthodox Calvinism, but the opinion of a God reduced to a domestic elitist whose whim is controlled by the agenda of the creature.

The Amyraldian humanization of God was the threat to orthodoxy most vigorously resisted by Francis Turretin. Humanizing Geneva's religio-political order would open the floodgates of subjectivism, reductionism and anthropocentrism. When Turretin died, his former enemies joined with his own son to open those floodgates. The progressive optimism of these proponents of modernity was not a newfound rationalism, scientism and toleration, it was an old cancer perennially threatening the foundation of orthodoxy — anthropocentrism.

Naturalism, secularism, subjectivism, scepticism — these were the forces which altered the orthodox citadels at the end of the seventeenth century.

---

[34] For Francis Turretin's discussion of fundamental articles, see *Institutes* 1, 48–54. Compare this with Jean-Alphonse Turretin, 'Discourse on Fundamental Articles in Religion' in *A Collection of Essays and Tracts in Theology from Various Authors with Biographical and Critical Notices*, Jared Sparks, vol. 1 (Boston: Oliver Everett, 1823), 7–91.

[35] For Francis Turretin, Amyraldianism was but a slight step from Arminianism, the supreme seventeenth-century Protestant liberalism.

[36] Cf. Heyd, *Between Orthodoxy*, *passim*.

For it was these forces which reduced God to the service of man. Naturalism reduced his Word to the service of the critic (cf. Cappel, Leclercq, Spinoza). Secularism reduced his aeon — transcendently other-worldly — to the service of the materialist. Subjectivism reduced his objective metaphysic to the service of an anthropocentric ego. Scepticism reduced his fidelity to the service of the doubter. Amyraldianism had no defences against these forces for in reality it sprang from the same source — the primacy of man.

The aftermath of the late seventeenth-century assault on orthodoxy was not only an increase in atheism, deism and scepticism, but a retreat into fideism. Alan Kors has argued that this fideism was a direct result of the polemics of the late seventeenth century.[37] In fact, he contends that the rational proofs for the existence of God and the fideistic rejoinder that one begins with faith (not reason) led to an increase in scepticism.[38] From this fideism would arise the pietism of the eighteenth century. The seventeenth century form of this incipient pietism was labeled 'fanaticism' and 'enthusiasm'.[39] The darker side of this fideism was the drift into rationalism and deism.[40]

Orthodoxy, consistently considered, was a rational Christianity supernaturally believed, with a theocentric stress on divine sovereignty and a Christocentric soteriology springing from a belief in anthropological depravity. Fideism retreated from the objective verifiability of the supernatural claiming the voice of the Spirit within. This de-emphasized sovereignty and Christocentrism, replacing them with a virtual monism of the Spirit. The result was an idealistic, if not mystical, optimism about man's spirit.

The Enlightenment was impossible apart from the repudiation of scholasticism. But Francis Turretin's scholastic Reformed Calvinism was not undone by rationalism, tolerance, experimental scientism, cosmopolitan ecumenism. It was undone by a subtle yet dramatic paradigm shift — the emergence of modernity. For such a threat, Turretin had only the traditional orthodox answers. But what he did

---

[37] Alan C. Kors, ' "A First Being, of Whom We Have No Proof": The Preamble of Atheism in Early-Modern France' in *Anticipations of the Enlightenment*, 22; cf. also his *Atheism in France, 1650–1729* 1 *The Orthodox Sources of Disbelief* (Princeton, N.J.: Princeton University Press, 1990). But note the critical remarks by Silvia Berti on Kors' thesis: 'At the Roots of Unbelief', *Journal of the History of Ideas* 56 (1995), 558f.
[38] Alan C. Kors, 'Skepticism and the Problem of Atheism in Early-Modern France' in *Scepticism and Irreligion*, ed. R.H. Popkin and A. Vanderjagt, 205.
[39] Cf. Michael Heyd, *'Be Sober and Reasonable': The Critique of Enthusiasm in the Seventeenth- and Early Eighteenth-Centuries* (Leiden and New York: E.J. Brill, 1995).
[40] Turretin had noted that the 'rationalist' Socinians were, in fact, irrational 'fideists' (my term) because they rejected the reasonable evidence for supernatural revelation on the grounds of self-authenticating reason, cf. *Institutes* 1, 23, 24, 28, 44, 161.

not know was that the emerging generation wanted no traditional answers; they wanted answers suited to a modern era — a republic of letters — a new age of man — a *novus ordo saeculorum*.

It was the twist which late seventeenth-century modernity placed on the paradigm of the old succeeded by the new that radically distinguished this age from all its predecessors. The classic Christian image of a defection from the pristine, a fall from paradise, was reversed by late seventeenth-century anthropocentrism. Modernity at the end of the scholastic era, the dawn of the Enlightenment, pulled the old switcheroo, the shell-game, the great con. Pre-Enlightenment modernity embraced the golden age of mankind as ahead, in front, in the future. The fall of man from innocence was reversed; man was on his way to innocence, ascending to perfection, not descending from it. Unbounded optimism for man's potential to bring in the 'heavenly city of the eighteenth century philosophers' (Carl Becker), the millennium, the age of pure reason — this was the mission of man come of age. Even the children of orthodoxy embraced the lie; they had become converts to their own self-importance, their own *suavitas* . They were sons and daughters of scholastic orthodoxy come of age — the future lay in the unbounded potential of man himself, not in the past history of God, the Bible, the Fall, Augustinian-Calvinistic predestination, salvation by Christ alone through grace alone, justification by Christ's imputed righteousness alone. They had embraced themselves and abandoned the dogmas of the scholastic past. They would genuflect appropriately at the names of the honored dead for the sake of image, publicity, politics; but the future belonged to them, not to the dead doctrines of mankind's infancy.

The crowd which attended Benedict Pictet's funeral oration on the death of his uncle, 3 November 1687, was civil, tolerant, respectful, political. In fact, many in that audience had already moved beyond the objective orthodox imagery of that oration. They were present to celebrate the passing of an era. And with the last rhetorical intonation of Turretin's eulogist, the task of reconstructing Protestantism would be undertaken by the ambitious, the smoothies, the con artists of the evangelical empire. As they left the church, they knew that they walked into an altogether different future — a future *sans* Francis Turretin, a future destined to end in *éclaircissement*. The agenda of the future was theirs at last! Behind them, with the corpse of Francis Turretin, they left the chains of scholasticism, orthodoxy, confessionalism. They were at last free to put themselves at the centre of the universe. A kinder and gentler Europe was about to be born; or as Bishop Burnet had hoped, a Europe fraught with 'larger and freer Souls'. It is ever the same: Francis Turretin was too orthodox, too Calvinistic, too precise for the smooth-talkers of that, or any other, era.

4

Theological Transition in Geneva
From Jean-Alphonse Turretin to Jacob Vernet

Martin I. Klauber

The period from the late seventeenth to the early eighteenth century has been the subject of much scholarly interest in recent decades. From Paul Hazard to Michael Heyd, historians have observed the gradual development of enlightened thought and the simultaneous move away from the traditional doctrines of the Christian faith.[1] The Academy of Geneva, founded by Calvin himself, was one of the most important Protestant theological centres in Europe and was at the forefront of such intellectual developments. During this period in Geneva, reason began to gain mastery over divine revelation and many of the cardinal doctrines of the faith fell from the forefront of theological discussion. Deism and atheism, rather than the challenges of the Counter-Reformation, were becoming the major threats to Reformed belief and the Genevan theologians attempted to defend the faith while placing it on more rational footing. Their extensive use of reason was a marked departure from the traditional Reformed approach to apologetics and radically transformed the very nature of Reformed Protestantism.

By the mid- to late eighteenth century, the Enlightenment was in full bloom and the traditional Reformed scholastic approach to theology had waned. In its place stood a new approach, commonly referred to as enlightened orthodoxy, that emphasized the practical nature of the faith devoid of the speculative aspects of scholasticism. Enlightened orthodox theologians attempted to maintain only those aspects of the faith that squared with reason.

---

[1] See Michael Heyd, *Between Orthodoxy and the Enlightenment: Jean-Robert Chouet and the Introduction of Cartesian Science at the Academy of Geneva* (The Hague: Martinus Nijhoff, 1982).

During this period, Genevan society was torn between the old, Calvinist traditions and the French Enlightenment. Jean-Jacques Rousseau and Voltaire, two of the most famous of the *philosophes*, spent considerable time in Geneva. According to John Roney, the opinion of 'the demise of orthodoxy in Geneva remained throughout the nineteenth century as well. In 1862, the conservative historian Hermann de Goltz claimed that by the late eighteenth century the traditional designation of "la Rome protestante" had been changed to "petit Paris." '[2]

The theology faculty remained vitally important to the Academy in the midst of this era of secularization. The most influential members of the department during the eighteenth century were Jean-Alphonse Turretin (1671–1737)[3] and his successor, Jacob Vernet (1698–1789).[4]

Jean-Alphonse Turretin was the last of the line of theology professors from his family at the Academy of Geneva, following his grandfather Benedict (1588–1631) and his father Francis (1623–87), the famed Reformed scholastic theologian. Jean-Alphonse started his theological

---

[2] John B. Roney, ' "La Rome protestante" as a New Model of Christian Commonwealth', (unpublished paper), 3.

[3] The only complete biography on Jean-Alphonse Turretin is Eugène de Budé, *Vie de J.-A. Turrettini, théologien genevois (1671–1737)* (Lausanne: Georges Bridel, 1880). Budé also edited three volumes of Turretin's correspondence, *Lettres inédites adressés de 1686–1737 à J.A. Turrettini, théologien genevois*, 3 vols. (Geneva: Jules Carey, 1887). Budé wrote several other biographies that touch on Jean-Alphonse Turretin; among them is his treatment of Benedict Pictet, Turretin's cousin and colleague on the theological faculty, *Vie de Bénédict Pictet, théologien genevois (1655–1724)* (Lausanne: Georges Bridel, 1874). For a discussion of Turretin's position on natural theology see Michael Heyd, 'Un rôle nouveau pour la science: Jean-Alphonse Turrettini et les débuts de la théologie naturelle à Genève,' *Revue de théologie et philosophie* 112 (1982), 25–42. Theological analyses include John W. Beardslee, 'Theological developments at Geneva under Francis and Jean-Alphonse Turretin' (PhD diss., Yale University, 1956); Martin I. Klauber, *Between Reformed Scholasticism and Pan-Protestantism: Jean-Alphonse Turretin (1671–1737) and Enlightened Orthodoxy at the Academy of Geneva* (Selingsgrove, Pa.: Susquehanna University Press, 1994). See also Martin I. Klauber and Glenn S. Sunshine, 'Jean-Alphonse Turrettini in Biblical Accommodation: Calvinist or Socinian?', *Calvin Theological Journal* (April, 1990), 7–27. Maria C. Pitassi, 'L'Apologétique Raisonnable de Jean-Alphonse Turrettini' in *Apologétique 1680–1740: Sauvetage ou naufrage de la théologie*, eds. Olivier Fatio and Maria C. Pitassi (Geneva: Publications de la Faculté de Théologie de l'Université de Genève, 1990), 180–212; Pitassi, 'Un Manuscrit Genevois du XVIIIe Siècle: La Réfutation du Système de Spinosa par Mr. Turrettini', *Nederlands Archief voor Kerkgeschiedenis* 68 (1988), 180–212.

[4] On Vernet see: Eugène de Budé, *Vie de Jacob Vernet, théologien genevois (1698–1789)* (Lausanne, 1893), and Graham Gargett, *Jacob Vernet, Geneva and the Philosophes* (Oxford: Voltaire Foundation, 1995).

career as the pastor of the Italian congregation in Geneva in 1693; he
was named professor of church history at the Academy in 1697, rector
in 1701 and finally professor of theology in 1705. Although his father
was one of the principal architects of the Helvetic Formula Consensus
(1675),[5] Jean-Alphonse led the movement towards eliminating such
credal religion through the abrogation of the Formula in 1706.[6]

Jacob Vernet represented one of the last vestiges of Reformed
orthodoxy at the Academy of Geneva. Of Provençal origin, Vernet was
the son of a second-generation member of the bourgeoisie. Serving as
professor of belles lettres from 1739–55 and professor of theology from
1756 until his death, Vernet came into contact with the major leaders
of the Enlightenment. According to Charles Borgeaud, Vernet was the
true successor of Turretin.[7] As his most prized student and successor to
the chair of theology, Vernet dominated the theological faculty at the
Academy during the second half of the eighteenth century and maintained close ties to the Turretin family throughout his life. Not only was
Jean-Alphonse his mentor, but when Vernet married Marie Butini, the
daughter of one of the local pastors, in 1733 the ceremony took place
at the Turretin household and Jean-Alphonse's son, Marc, was married
at the same time. It was Vernet who accompanied Marc on the
conventional tour of Europe following studies at the Academy and

---

[5] The Helvetic Formula Consensus was initiated in 1675 primarily by three Swiss
Reformed theologians, Lucas Gernler, Johann Heinrich Heidegger and Francis
Turrettin, in response to the modified position of the Academy of Saumur to the
canons of the Synod of Dort. The most notable of the Saumur theologians was Moise
Amyraut (1596–1664) who proposed a concept called 'hypothetical universalism'
that moderated, in theory, the Reformed doctrine of limited atonement as defined
at the Synod of Dort. He maintained that God's redemptive plan includes all men,
but cannot be fulfilled unless men believe. Since they cannot believe without the
power of the Holy Spirit, a second, limited election is necessary for the elect. The
basis for such an election is hidden in the counsel of God. Since his concept of
hypothetical universalism provided for the salvation of the elect alone, Amyraut
believed that his theory would bridge the gap between Reformed and Remonstrant
positions on the atonement. The majority of Reformed theologians, however,
rejected his system as the first step towards Arminianism. See Donald D. Grohman,
'The Genevan Reaction to the Saumur Doctrine of Hypothetical Universalism:
1635–1685' (PhD diss., Knox College, Toronto, 1971); Martin I. Klauber, 'The
Helvetic Formula Consensus: An Introduction and Translation', *Trinity Journal* 11
(1990), 103–23.
[6] See Martin I. Klauber, 'Jean-Alphonse Turrettini and the Abrogation of the
Formula Consensus in Geneva', *Westminster Theological Journal* 53 (1991), 325–38.
[7] Charles Borgeaud, *Histoire de l'université de Genève: L'Académie de Calvin, 1559–
1798* (Geneva: George, 1900), 550.

Vernet who introduced him to scholars in Zurich, Basel, Holland, London, and Paris.

Although Jean-Alphonse Turretin maintained an emphasis upon the mysteries of the faith, such as the Trinity and the Incarnation, by the era of Vernet there was some question as to whether or not these mysteries needed to be maintained. It is not surprising that many suspected that those holding to enlightened orthodoxy were unorthodox. It is the purpose of this study to show that the specific challenges of this era provided the theological faculty at the Academy of Geneva with the predisposition to employ a rationalistic approach to the faith. I will also indicate important aspects of transition between the theologies of Turretin and Vernet.

Jean-Alphonse Turretin used external arguments based on reason to support the truth of Scripture and rejected Calvin's argument that the internal witness of the Holy Spirit confirms the divine origin and truth of Scripture. Turretin was reacting against what he considered to be the overly-defined nature of Reformed, scholastic theology because of its divisiveness and lack of concern for personal piety. He preferred to return to Calvin's pastoral emphasis, as well as to the salvific nature of Scripture. Absent from Turretin's theological system was any systematic treatment of the doctrine of predestination, of the specific nature of divine decrees, and of the use of specific theological creeds to which ordinands were required to subscribe. He built a theological system that highlighted the clear doctrines that Christ himself taught. His theological system was primarily practical.[8]

Turretin's theology was, indeed, salvific in focus, but it was not a return to Calvin's. It more closely resembled the Socinian-Remonstrant tradition than orthodox Calvinism. By elevating reason as the primary arbiter

---

[8]   The primary sources for Turretin's theological system are found in the *Opera* (1776) and in the *Dilucidationes philosophico-theologico-morales* (1748). Both works contain Turretin's *Theses de theologia naturali*, the primary source for his views on natural theology, and his *De Veritate religionis Judaicae et Christianae*, in which he discusses his beliefs about special revelation. Both editions also include a series of Turretin's academic orations, his treatise on the essence of Christian belief, *De Articulis fundamentalibus*, and his *De Pyrrhonismo pontifico*, which is a critique of the French Bishop Jacques Bénigne Bossuet's polemics against Protestant theology. The Franeker edition contains Turretin's commentaries on Romans and Thessalonians. In addition, the *Bibliothèque publique et universitaire de Genève* houses several unpublished treatises of Turretin, including his commentary on the Sermon on the Mount, various collections of his sermon notes and part of his personal correspondence. See Jean-Alphonse Turretin, *Dilucidationes philosophico-theologico-morales, quibus praecipua capita tam theologiae naturalis, quam revelatae demonstrantur ad praxin christianam commendantur accedunt*, 3 vols. (Basel: J.R. Imhoff, 1748); *Opera omnia theologica, philosophica et philologica*, 3 vols. (Franeker: H.A. de Chalmot et D. Romar, 1774–6).

in theological inquiry, he virtually eliminated the need for the mysteries of the faith that were central to New Testament theology, e.g. the Trinity and the Incarnation of Christ. Turretin accepted these by faith without attempting to explain them, and his successors among the theological faculty at Geneva, led by Vernet, refused to speculate at all concerning biblical mysteries and would not even use the language of the early ecumenical councils in their discussions of the nature of Christ. As a result, it is not surprising that the Genevan theologians were accused of advocating a Socinian position on the Trinity.[9]

Turretin set the stage for this development with his new theological system and his reliance on rational investigation. His system of natural theology was far more extensive than that of his scholastic predecessors since he attempted to prove as much about God through reason as possible. Concerning special revelation, he used external arguments that relied upon rational proofs to establish the divine origin of Scripture and virtually abandoned the fideistic defence of the witness of the Holy Spirit. By doing so, he rationalized the process of salvation and reduced the faith to intellectual assent to the fundamental doctrines. He wrote: 'The Holy Spirit does not work in us blindly, but through reasons presented in the mind. . . . Without this our faith would be mere enthusiasm.'[10]

As a result of the enlarged role of natural theology, special revelation was less important to him than to any of his scholastic predecessors in Geneva. Although he viewed the Bible as coming from God, he limited the extent to which it could regulate Christian doctrine. One could not insist upon explicit definitions of predestination, for example, because the Bible does not clearly teach its technical aspects. One should only maintain those doctrines that are clear and necessary for salvation. The result was that Turretin failed to insist upon most of the doctrines that made Reformed theology distinct from other forms of Protestant thought. This did not alarm Turretin, however, because he believed that the scholastic insistence upon minute definitions of dogma only served to cause schism and discord between the various Protestant sects.

One should not view Jean-Alphonse Turretin's form of enlightened orthodoxy as a rejection of scholasticism in favour of a return to the purity of Calvin. Turretin did not make use of Calvin's primary defence of the

---

[9]   James I. Good, *History of the Swiss Reformed Church Since the Reformation* (Philadelphia: Publication and Sunday School Board, 1913), 282–301. One should employ the term 'Socinian' with extreme caution. It was often used as a mere epithet to mean heretic. It could also be used to refer to the theological system of Socinus, namely the excessive use of reason in scriptural interpretation to the point of denying theological mystery such as the Trinity and the Incarnation of Christ. The latter is the meaning here.

[10]   Jean-Alphonse Turretin, *Dilucidationes*, 2.3.13.

divine authority of Scripture, the interior witness of the Holy Spirit; he limited the role of the Spirit in regeneration to the point where salvation was virtually equivalent to intellectual assent to a few fundamental doctrines. To prove these truths, Turretin did not rely upon the self-authenticating nature of Scripture, but used the external marks of its authority to construct a rational defence of biblical historicity.[11]

Turretin was not a harbinger of Enlightenment thought. He was the author of an enlightened orthodoxy that attempted to square the Christian faith with the methodology of the Enlightenment. Although this enlightened orthodoxy rejected many of the distinctive elements of the Reformed faith, Turretin would never have countenanced the rejection of a core of essential Christian doctrines such as the Trinity and the Incarnation. His emphasis, however, upon a faith based on reason led eventually to the destruction of many of the very fundamentals of Christian belief that he had so ardently argued to preserve.

Vernet continued the trend towards the rationalization of the Christian faith and held to a strong form of personal piety.[12] He was disenchanted with the increasing emphasis on personal wealth and luxury in Genevan culture during the mid-eighteenth century. In 1769 he wrote *Réflexions sur les moeurs, sur la religion et sur le culte* in which he attacked the growing materialism of Genevan society, stating that it was resulting in a decline in morality. This work was the continuation of a discourse that Vernet gave before the Consistory in an attempt to stem the tide of irreligion and immorality. He argued that both temporal and religious interests would benefit from the maintenance of religious principles.[13] Luxury and vice went hand in hand, and Genevans were spending too much of their energies pursuing pleasure and were falling into unbelief. Public worship, he argued, would make Genevans better citizens and would result in a more orderly society.[14] According to Linda Kirk:

> Like Antoine Maurice and Charles Chais he [Vernet] explicitly disavowed the loose charms of deism. Men were reducing God to a speculative proposition or an axiom in physics which had no bearing on morality, and staying away from sermons just because they found them dull. He

---

[11] Ibid. 2.3.2–2.3.7; 2.7.17.

[12] Vernet studied theology under Benedict Pictet at the Academy of Geneva. Pictet was tireless in his pastoral support of French refugees and Vernet was undoubtedly strongly influenced by this level of social concern. See Martin I. Klauber, 'Reformed Scholasticism in Transition: Benedict Pictet and Enlightened Orthodoxy at the Academy of Geneva' in *Later Calvinism: International Perspectives*, ed. W. Fred Graham, Sixteenth Century Essays and Studies 22 (Kirkville, Mo.: Sixteenth Century Journal, 1994).

[13] Jacob Vernet, *Réflexions sur les moeurs, sur la religion et sur le culte* (Geneva, 1769).

[14] Ibid. 110–13.

dismissed Rousseau's *Profession of Faith* — which sceptics found fulsome
in its unfocused piety — by saying that the odd circumstances of his
upbringing had prevented Rousseau from knowing real Christianity.[15]

In this work, Vernet defined true religion as the relationship between
God and man in which we are obligated to honour and obey, to fear
divine justice and to depend on God's grace. It is interesting to note that
Vernet emphasized the aspects of Christianity that would not be objectionable to the deist or atheist. After all, who could be opposed to public
order and proper morality? In addition, Vernet emphasized the importance of natural theology as a proof for the veracity and reasonableness of
the faith, again establishing common ground with unbelievers. He made
a cryptic attack on the *philosophes* when he stated that many of the
Genevans who were falling into unbelief were those who had spent
considerable time in Paris.[16]

There is no mention in the *Réflexions* of any of the traditional Calvinist
doctrines such as predestination or the internal witness of the Holy Spirit.
Support for the veracity of the Christian faith was based primarily on
biblical miracles and fulfilled prophecy. According to Kirk:

> Vernet's *Reflections* mark an interesting moment of transition. Here he used
> Montesquieu's logic to promote piety and public order in Geneva: as a
> republic the city had to rest on the constitutive principle of virtue. Calvin
> had meant his city to be a model of piety but here the emphasis seems to
> have been reversed. Once Genevans had to lead godly lives to show they
> were saved; now it seemed that being saved only lent weight to the
> self-evident utilitarian case for cleanliness, decency and sobriety.

In other words the mark of a true Genevan by this time meant to be a
proper, moral citizen.[17]

Vernet's lifelong project was his translation of Turretin's Latin theses
entitled *Traité de la vérité de la religion chrétienne*.[18] Vernet translated
Turretin's *Traité* in several editions beginning in 1730 and, by the time
the last edition was published in 1788, it was more Vernet's work than
Turretin's. As the protégé of Jean-Alphonse Turretin, Vernet carried on
his teacher's tradition of harmonizing biblical revelation with rationalism.

The order of the book follows Turretin's traditional argument for the
truths of the Christian religion. One of its main objectives is to convince

---

[15]   Linda Kirk, 'Eighteenth-Century Geneva and a Changing Calvinism' in Stuart
Mews, ed. *Religion and National Identity* (Oxford: Blackwell, 1982), 371.

[16]   Vernet, *Réflexions*, 36–9.

[17]   Kirk, 'Eighteenth-Century Geneva', 379.

[18]   Jacob Vernet, *Traité de la vérité de la religion chrétienne. Tiré du latin de Mr. J.
Alphonse Turretin* (Geneva: M.M. Bousquet, 1730–47).

unbelievers of the reasonableness of Christianity. Vernet argued that revelation does not contradict reason, but is in accord with it. In his section on biblical revelation, Vernet changed Turretin's title from 'The Necessity of Revelation' to 'The Usefulness of Revelation' in the second edition of the *Traité*. The major reason for this change was to indicate the importance of natural theology. The 'heathen in Africa' who had never heard the gospel could potentially be saved without a specific knowledge of Christ if they responded favourably to the revelation that God had given them in nature and in conscience.[19]

Vernet contended that true revelation has five characteristics: First, revelation must never contradict reason, although Vernet does allow some room for biblical mysteries that go beyond the scope of reason. Second, revelation should not contradict itself and shows the reasonableness of the Christian faith. Third, revelation perfects natural theology and fourth it provides a specific knowledge of Christ and thus hope for eternal life. Fifth, true revelation is authenticated by signs such as biblical miracles and fulfilled prophecy. Revelation is thus superior to philosophy which tells us nothing specific about the origin of the world or the life to come.[20]

As for the proofs of Christianity, Vernet followed Turretin's traditional distinction between internal proofs based on sentiment and external proofs based on fact. In his discussion of internal proofs, Vernet 'emphasized that true Christianity had become overlaid with additions and accretions and that it must be restored to its original simplicity'.[21] Noble and reasonable simplicity leading to practical application is the best aspect of the faith. On the relationship between faith and reason, Vernet wrote: 'These are two torches that God has given to us, and it is necessary to carry one in one hand and the other in the other hand.'[22]

In his discussion of the external proofs for the veracity of the Christian faith, Vernet argued that Christianity

> is not a sort of natural science, that carries its own evidence in itself; the question is, concerning a doctrine taught upon the authority of divine revelation, and founded in part upon facts. It is therefore very important to see, whether in the character and life of those who announce this doctrine, and who attest these facts, there be such a thing which belies the sanctity of such a communion, and weakens the force of such a testimony; or whether on the contrary we do not find in both, materials to justify and prove the authority they assume.[23]

---

[19] Gargett, *Vernet*, 350.

[20] Budé, *Vie de Jacob Vernet*, 74.

[21] Gargett, *Vernet*, 55.

[22] Vernet, *Traité de la vérité*, xvi. See also, Gargett, *Vernet*, 56.

[23] Vernet, *An Argument Concerning the Christian Religion Drawn from the Character of the Founders* (London, 1800), 2.

Vernet went on to follow Turretin's listing of four types of proofs: the first proof was based on the impeccable character of Christ and the Apostles — they were not the type of people who were likely to lie concerning their beliefs; second, biblical miracles were well-attested by eyewitnesses in the New Testament era — Vernet was so confident in the validity of these miracles, he called them 'palpable facts';[24] third, Christ clearly fulfilled Old Testament prophecy; and last, the propagation of the gospel was itself a major miracle. The message of Christ could not possibly have survived amid such opposition if God had not been behind it. Miracles were of special importance to Vernet as authenticating the ministry of Christ and the Apostles.[25] As a result of these proofs, Vernet arrived at a level of confidence in the truths of the Christian faith that he labelled 'moral certainty'. This certainty is based on 'certain rules which good sense and constant experience dictate, in order to judge of human actions'.[26]

Vernet went further by arguing against post-biblical miracles, criticizing the Jansenists for their belief in contemporary miracles. This was undoubtedly a reflection of his criticism of Enthusiasm, a movement that Turretin had similarly denounced. As early as 1726, when Vernet composed his first treatise, *Deux Lettres à Monsieur l'abbé ****, Vernet had denied the validity of contemporary miracles as contrary to the rational order of the universe. At that time he became embroiled in a theological dispute with M. Hocquiné, a parish priest and Roman Catholic apologist, who chided Vernet over the inconsistencies of his rationalism.[27] Hocquiné argued that rationalism would lead not just to a denial of transubstantiation, but also to a denial of the Trinity and would lead straight to Socinianism. Vernet's response to Hocquiné is worth mentioning because it reveals his early penchant for rationalism and his complete disregard for the internal witness of the Holy Spirit. He wrote: 'You seem surprised by our reliance on natural light, we who have always made profession of the word of God as the unique rule of the faith . . . We derive our Articles of Faith solely from the Scriptures, but we make use of both Scripture and Reason in order to combat error.'[28]

One of the most interesting aspects of Vernet's career was his series of conflicts with the French *philosophes*. His contact with the *philosophes* began when he became the tutor for the children of a wealthy Parisian family in 1722. In all, he spent nine years away from Geneva in this

---

24   Ibid. 30.
25   Gargett, *Vernet*, 58–9.
26   Vernet, *Argument*, 117.
27   Vernet, *Deux Lettres à Monsieur l'abbé ****, Chanoine de Notre Dame de Paris* (Geneva, 1725). See also Gargett, *Vernet*, 8–9.
28   Vernet, *Défense des Deux Lettres Adressés à Mr. ***, Chanoine de Notre Dame* (Geneva, 1727). See also Gargett, *Vernet*, 15.

capacity, except for brief returns for examinations and for his ordination. In Paris, Vernet was able to mingle freely with the intellectual elite including many of the *philosophes*. Although he was initially friendly with both Voltaire and Rousseau, he later entered into a series of disagreements with them. These conflicts are admirably documented in Graham Gargett's masterful work, *Jacob Vernet, Geneva, and the philosophes.*[29] Gargett argues that Vernet attempted to portray himself as orthodox to his more conservative Reformed colleagues while currying favor with the *philosophes* to enhance his reputation within the republic of letters. Vernet desired to rid traditional Calvinism of its dogmatic trappings and return to a purer form of biblical theology. Voltaire saw this methodology as leading straight to deism.[30] Ultimately Voltaire exposed what he considered to be Vernet's hypocrisy and, although Vernet's biographers have

---

[29] The major secondary works on Vernet assume different perspectives on the Genevan theologian's conflicts with the *philosophes*. The first work on Vernet was written by his grandson, Michel-Jean-Louis Saladin, *Memoire historique sur la vie les ouvrages de Jacob Vernet, ministre de l'Eglise, accompagné de l'Invocation aux Muses', de Montisquieu, et de plusieurs lettres J.-J.- Rousseau et Voltaire, qui n'ont pas encore été publiées* (Paris, 1790). This was followed by Jean Gaberel's work *Voltaire et les Genevois* (1857) and his article 'Jacob Vernet et ses relations contemporaines', *Etrennes religieuses*, xxxiv (1883), 120–41 and finally by Eugène de Budé's biography of Vernet. The most recent work is Graham Gargett's *Jacob Vernet, Geneva and the philosophes* (Oxford: Voltaire Foundation, 1995), an exhaustive and definitive work which makes excellent use of both printed sources and archival materials to uncover significant holes in previous research. Gargett is extremely critical of Gaberel and of Budé for including many embellishments without adequate historical evidence. These works added unfounded stories to make Vernet seem the innocent victim of Voltaire's egregious attacks. For example, both Gaberel and Budé tell the story that when Vernet was incensed over Voltaire's *Lettre curieuse de M. Robert Covelle*, he decided to see Voltaire personally at Fernex, rather than compose a formal refutation. Voltaire received him warmly, seemed genuinely repentant for what he had said about Vernet and invited him to his house for dinner. Vernet refused, but did accept a ride back to Geneva in Voltaire's carriage. Vernet, however, did not want a ride to the centre of town where he would be seen publicly with Voltaire, and asked to be let out. Voltaire refused, brought him to the centre of town and let him out in front of the large crowd that typically gathered when Voltaire arrived in town. Although the people were quite surprised to see such rivals in the same carriage, Vernet took the occasion to say that Voltaire had recognized the error of his ways and had apologized for what he had written about Vernet. This story is typical of the older biographies which portrayed Voltaire as the real villain in the conflict with Vernet. Rather than provide a hagiography of Vernet's brilliance, Gargett portrays him as an above-average teacher and theologian who was a poor preacher. In addition, he speculates that Vernet suffered from psychosomatic illnesses which eventually led to his withdrawal from his preaching duties. Gargett writes: 'The case of Budé is particularly infuriating. His book is a mish-mash of plagiarism, banality and often, one suspects, invention.' Gargett, *Vernet*, xv.

[30] Gargett, *Vernet*, 40.

typically portrayed Voltaire as the villain, Gargett lays the blame squarely on Vernet's own character flaws. The author provides a blow by blow description of the conflicts between Vernet and the major figures of the Enlightenment.

The conflict between Vernet and Voltaire centred on the latter's desire to bring the theatre into Geneva. Interestingly enough, Vernet opposed the move primarily on practical, rather than theological, grounds. Their theological clashes became bitterly personal and were openly debated in print. Voltaire had moved to Délices, near Geneva, in 1755 and wrote the *Essai sur l'histoire universelle* which included a section on Geneva and Calvin. D'Alembert later met with Voltaire and the next year published his own scathing attack on Geneva and Calvin in the *Encyclopédie*.[31]

The Genevan theologians and politicians also came into conflict with Rousseau who had been quite supportive in the controversy with Voltaire. Rousseau was a native of Geneva and was quite friendly with some of the pastors and theologians there, including Vernet. In 1762, the Genevan Council ordered that Rousseau's *Emile* be publicly burned because they considered some of its contents objectionable. Although the work affirmed a belief in God, the immortality of the soul and the moral authority of Christ, it denied many of the specifically supernatural elements of Scripture, including miracles.[32]

A third major skirmish resulted from d'Alembert's article on Geneva in the *Encyclopédie* in which the author lambasted Calvin for the execution of Servetus and accused the eighteenth-century theologians of Geneva of advocating a Socinian Christology. Furthermore,

> respect for Jesus Christ and for the Scriptures is perhaps all that distinguishes the Christianity of Geneva from pure deism. Many pastors do not believe in the divinity of Jesus Christ . . . Their religion is a perfect Socinianism, rejecting all the mysteries of revelation. They imagine that the principle of true religion is to propose nothing to believe that goes against reason.[33]

This statement greatly angered the Company of Pastors in Geneva who met later in the year to name a commission to compose a formal response. The commission met for six seeks to write a concise response. Ironically, Rousseau joined the fray on the side of the pastors and asked d'Alembert to come up with his sources for the charges of Socinianism. D'Alembert at first responded that he could not compromise personal confidences and refused to divulge the information.[34]

---

[31]   Borgeaud, *Histoire de l'université de Geneva*, 551.

[32]   Gargett, *Vernet*, 336–60.

[33]   Jean Pierre Gaberel, *Histoire de l'Eglise de Genève depuis le commencement de la réformation jusqu'à nos jours* (Geneva; J. Cherbuliez, 1855–62), 196.

[34]   Ibid. 196–200.

Vernet wrote to d'Alembert on behalf of his colleagues and asked him to name the source. After all, they were the only individuals who could have provided the material for the essay. He also said that none of the Genevan theologians could possibly have authorized such a work. D'Alembert replied that he could not recall exact conversations but that, according to the French bishop Jacques Bénigne Bossuet, the Genevans denied the tradition of the Roman Church and were therefore Socinian.[35]

Such a weak response obviously angered Vernet and his colleagues, so they formally published a reply on 10 February 1758, written primarily by Vernet, containing several anti-Socinian statements. These comments affirmed belief in the divine inspiration of Scripture and the divinity of Christ, and of the Holy Spirit. They also stated that, although reason is important, it is subservient to the Word of God through which we can gain a saving knowledge of Christ. They also defended their use of philosophy and natural theology, arguing that these disciplines in no way contradict special revelation. Furthermore, they admitted the presence of biblical mystery that surpasses reason, but claimed that such mysteries cannot be absurd, that is contradictory to reason.[36]

This reply was published throughout Europe and the Genevans received widespread support, except from some of the old adherents of the Helvetic Formula Consensus who felt that the statement did not go far enough. They wanted a clearer statement of the Trinity, including specific statements that the Son was consubstantial with and equal to the Father, and that the Father and the Son are one and the same God in different persons. They also criticized the Genevan clergy for not making specific comments supporting the Helvetic Confession.[37]

Such criticisms were not out of line. The statement of the Genevan clergy was more revealing for what it did not include than for what it contained. Clearly a very general statement about the nature of the Trinity would be less objectionable to the standards of reason than a full-fledged adherence to the historic doctrine as defined by Scripture and the early ecumenical councils.

Vernet published his own response anonymously under the title *Lettres critiques d'un voyageur anglais (1759)* which went thought three editions.[38] In this work, Vernet clearly blamed Voltaire for influencing d'Alembert and providing some of the misinformation that ultimately appeared in the Geneva article. Furthermore, he called for d'Alembert to retract his

---

35   Ibid. 197.
36   Ibid. 198.
37   Ibid. 199.
38   Jacob Vernet, *Lettres Critiques d'un Voyageur Anglais sur l'Article Genève du Dictionaire Encyclopedique; & sur La Lettre de Mr. d'Alembert à Mr. Rousseau* (Utrecht, J.C. Ten Bosch, 1759).

allegations of Socinianism among the Genevan pastors. Vernet defended the Genevan Christology, arguing that they were using scriptural terms on difficult issues and clearly preached the Incarnation of the Son of God, the efficacy of Christ's death for our sins, and the necessity of divine grace. What is interesting about Vernet's statements is that he in no way argues in favour of the use of the theological term 'Trinity'. Vernet's desire was to rid theology of its scholastic trappings and to return to the pure language of the New Testament. What Vernet lost, however, was the precision of scholastic definition and the resultant lack of clarity opened up the possibility of charges of heterodoxy.[39]

In his *Instruction chrétienne* written in 1756, Vernet called Jesus of Nazareth the unique Son of God based upon his virgin birth, his godly character and his intimate union with God. Furthermore, Vernet described Jesus as the unique third person of the Trinity and clearly affirmed his divinity. Vernet refused to speculate as to how the human and divine natures of Christ were united, saying that this is a mystery that it is neither necessary nor possible to solve. Since Scripture teaches the divinity of Christ, we should accept it, but when the Bible does not explain how Christ could be both God and man, we should not go any further in our attempts to understand. It is enough to say that scriptural teaching on the nature of Christ is neither self-contradictory nor impossible.[40]

Vernet refused to accept the authority of the early ecumenical councils in their statements about the person of Christ. He would not countenance the pronouncement of the Council of Nicaea which stated that the Son was consubstantial with the Father, arguing that this language was not used in Scripture. Vernet asserted that the councils represented merely the opinions of the principal bishops rather than the views of individual churches or the church at large.[41] Ironically, this was the same argument used by the Socinians against the doctrine of the 'Trinity'.

In his defence of the Genevan pastors against d'Alembert's accusation of Socinianism, Vernet went into a long diatribe on the differences between Socinians and Arians. Gargett concludes that Vernet's convoluted response shows that Vernet recognized that there was some truth in d'Alembert's charges, however exaggerated they might have been.[42] Furthermore, Vernet expressed his rationalism in his description of the crucifixion as distasteful: a nude, disfigured and bloody corpse is not pleasing to the sight.[43]

non sequitor

---

[39] Vernet, *Lettres Critiques*, ii.

[40] Vernet, *Instruction chrétienne*, 5 vols. (Geneva: Henri-Albert Gosse, 1756), ii, 240–5.

[41] Gargett, *Vernet*, 288; cf. Vernet, *Instruction chrétienne*, ii, 371.

[42] Gargett, *Vernet*, 290.

[43] Ibid. 296–7; cf. Vernet, *Instruction chrétienne*, ii. 19–20.

In the *Traité de la vérité de la religion chrétienne*, Vernet argued that Scripture does emphasize the unity of God as the creator of the world and he attributed to Christ all the fullness of deity. The Holy Spirit, however, is only a divine principle and is not referred to specifically as a person. Vernet admitted that, although the precise relationships between the three persons of the Trinity are not thoroughly explained in the Bible, the doctrine of the Trinity does not contain any logical contradictions.[44] Vernet's successors went even further in moving away from trinitarian theology and, by 1814, the revised Genevan catechism ignored the doctrines of redemption and the divinity of Christ, preferring to label Jesus as the first-born of all creation who should be honoured but certainly not worshipped.

In the second edition of the *Lettres critiques*, Vernet defended the pastors of Geneva against their alleged lack of belief in a literal hell by stating that they stuck to the language of the Bible rather than to the theological formulas of the early church. Hell was no longer a principal doctrine among the Genevan theologians and he pointed out that there had been various options on the subject within the early church, including that of Origen. Vernet went on to say that the pastors no longer strictly held to the doctrine of predestination but that such biblical mysteries were not necessarily contrary to reason. They were merely beyond its scope. Gargett argues that it is very difficult to decipher Vernet's true beliefs in the *Lettres critiques* because the author was so careful to avoid committing himself decisively to any single position on a controversial theological issue. Therefore, instead of defending himself and the Genevan pastors against d'Alembert's accusations, Vernet raised more questions concerning his orthodoxy.[45]

Vernet went on in his *Instruction chrétienne* to elaborate on the nature of the last judgment. Vernet first stressed the equity of God in separating the sheep from the goats. He refused to speculate about the precise nature of hell, or the flames of torment, preferring to say that whatever punishment one may experience, it is necessarily in proportion to one's deeds in this life. He argued that we are not in a good position to ascertain the degree or nature of punishment, but must trust that God is so just and wise that he is the only one who can properly judge one's deeds and determine one's eternal destiny. Vernet left open the possibility that hell might be merely the recognition that one has been excluded from eternal bliss and speculates that the concept of eternal separation from God might simply refer to a lengthy but indefinite period of time. God might even grant a pardon if he so desires to someone who had endured such hardship. Above all, Vernet argued that God is fair and impartial in his evaluation

---

[44]   Gargett, *Vernet*, 56.
[45]   Ibid. 281–2.

of our lives. It is interesting that he included absolutely no mention of predestination or of reprobation in his discussion of the final judgment.[46]

Vernet also pointed out the positive benefits of eternal judgment to society at large. The promise of eternal happiness naturally motivates citizens to upright, moral behaviour. Those who suffer in this life can look forward to eternal rewards. The lack of such a judgment naturally leads to crime and impiety. This evaluation points out the positive value of God's judgment. Any rational individual should recognize these benefits.[47]

Vernet's rationalism developed to such an extent that it dominated his entire theological system. It is not surprising, given his denigration of the ecumenical councils, biblical mysteries and contemporary miracles, and his weak statements on the deity of Christ, that many still believed him to be unorthodox. Vernet's theological system was freed from the rigours of scholastic methodology and did not include the precision that the scholastic framework provided. As a result, his statements on the Trinity were unclear and left open the possibility of charges of Socinianism.

Even though the term 'Socinian' was typically a pejorative expression, d'Alembert's accusation was not far off the mark. The theological faculty at the Academy had returned to biblical simplicity to describe the cardinal doctrines of the Incarnation and the Trinity and had refused to speculate any further. This move represented a rejection of Reformed scholasticism as well as the traditions of the early church. Turretin's successors at the Academy were not, therefore, advocates of the Enlightenment philosophy of Voltaire. They had, however, accepted Turretin's methodology of open theological inquiry and his secular view of education to the point that they adopted the same presuppositions as their atheistic and deistic opponents, namely that religion should be subject to reason and that ethical concerns were the most beneficial results of theological study. They had clearly moved in the direction of deism by shedding the objectionable aspects of traditional Calvinism, a trend that Turretin himself had begun a generation earlier.

---

[46] Vernet, *Instruction chrétienne*, ii, 135–9.
[47] Ibid. ii, 140–1.

PART 5
THE RISE OF LUTHERAN ORTHODOXY

1

Melanchthon's Relation to Scholasticism

Lowell C. Green

INTRODUCTION

It was the fate of Philip Melanchthon, often called the *Praeceptor Germaniae*, that his life's work fell into two resonance chambers: his primary call was to teach in the liberal arts (including philosophy), and later his 'job description' was expanded to include also theology.[1] At times he has been blamed for the dual character of his career. Nevertheless, his real contribution to the Reformation consisted in the synthesis which he achieved between these two academic fields, and the influence of his work went far beyond the boundaries of Germany or of the Lutheran confession.[2]

[1] The following common abbreviations for standard works are used in this article: MELANCHTHON: *CR* = *Corpus Reformatorum*, vols. 1–28, *Philippi Melanthonis Opera quae Supersunt Omnia*, ed. Karl Gottlieb Bretschneider and Heinrich Bindseil (Halle: Schwetschke, 1834–); *SA* = *Melanchthons Werke in Auswahl*, Studienausgabe, 8 vols., ed. Robert Stupperich (Gütersloh: Bertelsmann, 1951–); *MBW* = *Melanchthons Briefwechsel. Kritische und kommentierte Gesamtausgabe*, eds. Heinz Scheible et al. 8 vols. (Stuttgart–Bad Cannstatt: Frommann-Holzboog, 1977).
LUTHER: *WA* = *D. Martin Luthers Werke. Kritische Gesamtausgabe* (Weimar: Böhlau, 1883ff.) *WABr* = *Briefwechsel* (Correspondence); *WAtr* = *Tischreden* (Table talk).
OTHER: *RE* = *Realencyklopädie für protestantische Theologie und Kirche*, ed. Albert Hauck, 24 vols. (Leipzig: Hinrichs, 1896–1913[3]) *ELC* = *Encyclopedia of the Lutheran Church*, ed. Julius Bodensieck for the Lutheran World Federation, 3 vols. (Minneapolis: Augsburg, 1965).
[2] On Melanchthon's contribution to education, see my essay, 'The Reformation and Education in the Sixteenth Century' *Faculty Publications. Bulletin of Appalachian State University* 67 (May 1970), 34–49. See also my 'Philip Melanchthon', *ELC*, 2:1517–27. Against Gerald Strauss, *Luther's House of Learning* (Baltimore: Johns

As a theologian, he combined the insights of biblical humanism with the principles of the Protestant Reformation in such a way that he exerted profound influence on both Lutheran and Reformed theology. Pupils of Melanchthon in the Lutheran tradition included Flacius, Wigand,[3] Chytraeus, Chemnitz, and Heerbrand. His direct pupils who favoured Reformed theology included Krafft (Crato)[4] and Ursinus,[5] and, in the following generations, such leading lights in theology as Keckermann and Alsted were strongly influenced by Melanchthon.[6]

Our assignment is to discuss Melanchthon's relation to scholasticism. Like Luther, he was decidedly opposed to medieval scholasticism. There is, however, a meaning to that term according to which 'scholasticism' might be rehabilitated and applied not only to seventeenth-century orthodoxy, but also to the theological work of Melanchthon and even of Luther. Our thesis is that Lutheran orthodoxy was marked by two characteristics: (1) the use of classical dialectic and rhetoric; and (2) an emphasis upon the need for a 'practical' theology, i.e. one related to the spiritual needs of the people. We shall find that the first characteristic is found very much in Melanchthon and less in Luther, and that the second is found very much in Melanchthon and even more prominently in Luther.

Hopkins University Press, 1978), see James Kittelson in his essay, 'Successes and Failures in the German Reformation: The Report from Strasbourg', *Archive for Reformation History* 73 (1982), 153–74. Similar to Strauss is the presentation of his pupil, Susan C. Karant-Nunn, 'The Reality of Early Lutheran Education: The Electoral District of Saxony – a Case Study', *Luther-Jahrbuch* 57 (1990), 128–46. The opinions of Strauss and Nunn are partially refuted by the facts and statistics given in my essay 'The Education of Women in the Reformation', *History of Education Quarterly* 19 (Spring 1979), 93–116; although this essay focuses upon female education, it presents the general picture as well.

[3] On the indebtedness to Melanchthon of Wigand and other Gnesio-Lutherans see Robert Kolb, 'The Advance of Dialectic in Lutheran Theology: The Role of Johannes Wigand (1523–1587)' in *Regnum, Religio et Ratio: Essays Presented to Robert M. Kingdon*, ed. Jerome Friedman, Sixteenth Century Essays and Studies 8 (Kirksville, Mo.: Sixteenth Century Journal, 1987), 93–192.

[4] On Johann Krafft or Crato, see Howard Louthan, *Johannis Crato and the Austrian Habsburgs: Reforming a Counter-Reform Court*, Studies in Reformed Theology and History (Princeton: Princeton Theological Seminary, 1994).

[5] On Ursinus, see Derk Visser, *Zacharius Ursinus, the Reluctant Reformer: His Life and Times* (New York: United Church, 1983).

[6] The relation of Melanchthon to Reformed as well as Lutheran theology is discussed by Paul Althaus, *Die Prinzipien der deutschen reformierten Dogmatik im Zeitalter der aristotelischen Scholastik* (Leipzig: Deichertsche, 1914/Darmstadt: Wissenschaftliche Buchgesellschaft, 1967[2]).

HUMANISM IN THE SERVICE OF THE REFORMATION

It has been common in the past to interpret Melanchthon's use of rhetoric and dialectic as lapses from true theology into humanism or even philosophy. Scholars like to discuss whether Melanchthon was a humanist or a theologian, as though his being a humanist was incompatible with his being a theologian. Even Wilhelm Maurer, in his penetrating study of the early Melanchthon entitled the first volume 'The Humanist', and the second 'The Theologian'. Although such a division is difficult to avoid, the true Melanchthon can be discovered only when his work in the arts and in theology is taken together. Such a fusion was achieved by Elert more than by most others.[7]

Philip Melanchthon came to Wittenberg in 1518 as professor of the liberal arts, or, specifically, of Greek grammar. Simultaneous admiration immediately began between Melanchthon and Luther. Luther seized the opportunity to improve his limited knowledge of Greek by studying it under the new grammarian. Luther, of course, had been acquainted with humanism before he met Melanchthon, and had been well educated in dialectic and rhetoric as well as in other subjects dealt with in the writings of Aristotle. But, as we shall see, he learned, like Melanchthon, to adapt a limited and purified 'philosophy' to the teaching of Christian doctrine.

Before coming to Wittenberg, the early Melanchthon, as a biblical humanist, had been deeply interested in, and well informed on, theological issues. He had used many biblical passages as illustrations in his early publications on Greek grammar and rhetoric. A valuable example of his early thinking is given in his notable inaugural address of 29 August 1518.[8] Melanchthon became so interested in Luther's cause during his

---

[7]   This criticism is not intended to obscure the value of Maurer's work. See Wilhelm Maurer, *Der junge Melanchthon zwischen Humanismus und Reformation* 1, *Der Humanist* 2, *Der Theologe* (Göttingen: Vandenhoeck & Ruprecht, 1967–9). The tendency towards a bifurcation of Melanchthon is also present in many other writers, as in the classical essay by Paul Joachimsen, 'Loci communes. Eine Untersuchung zur Geistesgeschichte des Humanismus und der Reformation', *Luther Jahrbuch* 8 (1926), 27–97, and esp. 33. Few have united the two aspects of Melanchthon so successfully as Werner Elert, 'Humanität und Kirche. Zum 450. Geburtstag Melanchthons' (1947) in *Zwischen Gnade und Ungnade: Abwandlungen des Themas Gesetz und Evangelium* (Munich: Evangelischer Presseverband für Bayern, 1948), 92–113.

[8]   This important oration, *De corrigendis adolescentiae studiis*, is in CR 11:15–25 and SA 3:30–42. Composed in very difficult Latin, it seems never to have been published in full in English. For a partial translation in which I was assisted by Charles D. Froehlich, see my book, *Melanchthon in English. New Translations into English with a Registry of Previous Translations. A Memorial to William Hammer (1909–1976)*, Sixteenth Century Bibliography 22 (St Louis: Center for Reformation Research, 1982), 13–17. A detailed description of the contents of the oration is given by John R. Schneider, *Philip Melanchthon's Rhetorical Construal of Biblical Authority. Oratio Sacra*, Texts and Studies in Religion, 51 (Lewiston, N.Y.: Edwin Mellen, 1990), 51–63.

first year at Wittenberg that he turned to the formal study of theology; he worked through the Sentences of Peter Lombard in preparation for earning the degree of Bachelor of Theology (*Baccalaureus biblicus*). His degree work was completed with a formal disputation on 9 September 1519. Luther exclaimed in a letter to Staupitz:

> You saw the theses of Philip, or rather you see how daring they are, but how very true. He responded in such a way that it seemed to us that it was like a miracle. So Christ was honoured, he stood above many Martins, he stood as the most powerful opponent to the devil and scholastic theology. He examined their foolish teachings and simultaneously the Rock of Christ. Therefore, he will be very powerful. Amen.[9]

What was the content of the disputation which aroused so much admiration, even from Luther? Under Thesis 10, he made the following assertion: *Omnis iustitia nostra est gratuita Dei imputatio*, 'All our righteousness is the gracious imputation of God'. Melanchthon also claimed in Thesis 16: 'It is not necessary for a Catholic to believe any articles other than those which bear the attestation of the Scriptures'. And in Thesis 18 he asserted: 'It is not the sin of heresy not to believe the indelible character of priests, transubstantiation, and similar teachings'.[10] Thesis 10 was one of the first Reformational statements on forensic justification; it reappeared in a number of Melanchthon's 'philosophical' and theological works of the next five years. This was to grow into the concept of imputative righteousness which characterized forensic justification in later Protestant scholasticism. And the concept expressed in Thesis 16 would later be interpreted as *sola scriptura*. Earning his *Baccalaureus biblicus* enabled Melanchthon to teach theology as well as liberal arts. Several years later he received a formal call to teach theology at Wittenberg.

As a young scholar at Tübingen, he had been an avowed opponent of scholasticism in the theological enterprise. He recognized that Aristotle had been wrongly interpreted by the medieval schoolmen, and determined to purge Aristotle of the accretions of medieval scholastic interpretation and restore a true understanding of his work. The Second or Posterior Analytics of Aristotle must be interpreted under rhetoric.

His opposition to medieval scholasticism revolved around the intrusion of metaphysical philosophy into theology. The medieval school-

---

[9]   Luther in letter to Johann Staupitz, 3 Oct 1519. *WABr* 1: 514, 33–7 (No. 202).
[10]   The Baccalaureate Theses are published in *SA* 1:24–5; an English translation is included in Charles Leander Hill, *Melanchthon: Selected Writings*, ed. Elmer E. Flack and Lowell J. Satre (Minneapolis: Augsburg, 1962), 16–18.

men had failed because they had divorced dialectic from rhetoric. Melanchthon advocated bringing rhetoric and dialectic into a fruitful relationship. This new relationship yielded the *loci communes* concept and a methodology which was opposed to medieval scholasticism.

It becomes apparent that we are here dealing with two uses of the word philosophy: first, philosophy as synonymous with the liberal arts (grammar, rhetoric, and dialectic) applied to theology, without altering theological content, a practice which Melanchthon approved, and, second, philosophy as metaphysics applied to theology, a practice which corrupted its content and which he rejected. In the first instance, we are dealing with philosophy and theology in conjunction; in the latter case, with philosophy and theology in disjunction.

Philosophy and theology in conjunction

Philosophy as synonymous with the liberal arts comprised the *trivia* (grammar, dialectic, and rhetoric) and the *quadrivia* (arithmetic, geometry, astronomy, and music). Philosophy as metaphysics was sometimes treated by the humanists under Greek or Latin grammar, where it was studied in lections of writers such as Aristotle or Seneca. When 'philosophy' was placed in conjunction with theology, what was meant was the liberal arts.

Melanchthon strongly emphasized the importance of dialectic and rhetoric for the theologian and pastor.[11] Before moving from Tübingen to Wittenberg in 1518, he had already written his first book on rhetoric.[12] In its prefatory letter, addressed to his former pupil, Bernhard Maurus, he compared the two subjects as he stated that the task of dialectic was to teach (*docendum*) and the task of rhetoric was to move (*movendum*).[13] Some humanists had downgraded 'empty rhetoric'. In his celebrated 'Reply to Pico', Melanchthon took the famous Pico della Mirandola to task for downgrading rhetoric as empty elegance;[14] instead, he compared rhetoric or eloquence with painting, for as a

---

[11] Melanchthon later developed his views on rhetoric into the first system of Protestant homiletics. See Uwe Schnell, *Die homiletische Theorie Philipp Melanchthons*, Arbeiten zur Geschichte und Theologie des Luthertums 20 (Berlin: Lutherisches Verlagshaus, 1968).

[12] I used the following copy which is in the library of Concordia Seminary, St Louis: *Philippi Melanchthonis De Rhetorica Libri Tres* (Basel: Johannes Frobenius, May 1519).

[13] *CR*, 1:64–5.

[14] The reply of Melanchthon to Pico della Mirandola is in *CR*, 9:687–703. A fine translation of this difficult work and a helpful commentary are given in Quirinius Breen, *Christianity and Humanism: Studies in the History of Ideas* (Grand Rapids: Eerdmans, 1968), 39–68.

painter imitates a body, so speech paints and portrays the thoughts of the mind.[15] He added:

> We indeed call that man an orator who teaches men accurately, clearly, and with a certain dignity concerning good and necessary things: whom you [Pico] would call a philosopher I do not yet understand satisfactorily. As a matter of fact I call a philosopher one who, when he has learned and knows things good and useful for mankind, takes a theory (*doctrina*) out of academic obscurity and makes it practically useful in public affairs, and instructs men about natural phenomena, or religions, or about government.[16]

Wilhelm Maurer has traced the views of Melanchthon on dialectic and rhetoric from medieval learning. Whereas the medieval schoolmen had separated the two disciplines, in his book *De rhetorica* (1519) Melanchthon regarded rhetoric and dialectic as inseparable in practice and thereby made an important advance over medieval scholasticism. The young humanist criticized the medieval schoolmen who had turned dialectic into hair-splitting distinctions which he called 'barbaric wordiness', and who had too often neglected rhetoric. If dialectic without rhetoric became barbaric wordiness, rhetoric without dialectic became empty elegance; when dialectic and rhetoric were isolated from each other, the result was 'empty jabber'.[17] As we shall see, Melanchthon regarded rhetoric also as a heuristic device for establishing *loci communes* or commonplaces for examining correct propositions.

There was a natural relation between theology and the liberal arts (philosophy) in his writings. In teaching the arts, he used examples from the Bible or from theological statements, as may be seen in his early textbooks on rhetoric, dialectic, and grammar. In teaching theology, he used insights from the arts (dialectic and rhetoric) to organize his material. In teaching Greek grammar, he provided short selections from the Greek New Testament as printed texts for the use of his students; material from these philological studies reappeared in commentaries, short doctrinal statements, and, soon, in the first Protestant dogmatics, the *Loci communes seu hypotyposes theologicae* of 1521.[18]

---

[15] Breen, 57.

[16] *CR*, 1:692–3. Breen, 57–8.

[17] Maurer, *Der junge Melanchthon*, 1:193–4.

[18] On Melanchthon's use of the Bible in his arts courses see my essay, 'Form-geschichtliche und inhaltliche Probleme in den Werken des jungen Melanchthon. Ein neuer Zugang zu seinen Biberlarbeiten und Disputationsthesen', *Zeitschrift für Kirchengeschichte* (*ZKG*) 84 (1973), 30–48; this essay supersedes my earlier articles and corrects the work of other writers. John R. Schneider begs the question when he writes that 'Green's position . . . has not been acknowledged generally as a valid

Luther praised the first edition of the *Loci communes* and called the work worthy of canonization.[19] Although he was known at times to criticize 'the blind, heathen teacher', Aristotle,[20] Luther could also speak approvingly of him. In his 'Address to the Christian Nobility of the German Nation' (1520), he wrote:

> I should very much like to see us retain the books of Aristotle on logic, rhetoric, and poetics, or to have them brought into a shorter form useful for exercising the young people to speak and to preach well, but the commentaries and notes must be done away with, and likewise the rhetoric of Cicero without commentaries and notes, and so also the logic of Aristotle should be read in its original form and without the long commentaries.[21]

It was a mark of Melanchthon as humanist that he utilized the four 'causes' to impart clarity to his work. The reader is warned not to associate his thinking here too readily with the metaphysical usage of 'cause and effect'; a quick review of *causa* in a Latin dictionary will remind us that the word can mean 'reason, motive, inducement, interest (of the people), a (legal) case, a claim, a situation, a condition,

---

one, or as posing an important revision of textual criticism in the study of the young Melanchthon.' Schneider, *Rhetorical Construal*, note 19, 143–4. He overlooks the fact that those whom he cites wrote ten or fifteen years before my article appeared in 1973 and therefore could not have responded to it; furthermore, the validity of my proposition is not established by who accepts it but by the soundness of its documentation and argumentation. Schneider refers to scholars (especially Maurer) who rejected my textual criticism of the *Theologica Institutio*. Schneider gives the wrong reference; instead, see Maurer, *Der junge Melanchthon*, 2:104, where he claims that the *Theologica Institutio* was written in the hand of Melanchthon. Maurer and other critics were misled by Kolde, who had rejected Plitt's finding that the *Theological Instituto* were not in the hand of Melanchthon; they failed to consult the manuscript which is in the *Christaneum* in Hamburg. Examination of that text shows that it is definitely not in the handwriting of Melanchthon but in an unknown hand. Since the text is not in his hand, and since Melanchthon explicitly rejected the authenticity of the text, I categorized the *Theologica Institutio* as a text of 'third rank' (*von drittem Rang*); Schneider incorrectly translates this as 'third rate'. In my system, first rank texts are autographs of Melanchthon, second rank texts are published works or works in the handwriting of others which, although not extant in his hand, were approved by him; third rank are pirated texts of unknown origin which Melanchthon rejected. The *Theologica Institutio* was such a text. (Schneider's reference is to pages 35 to 37 in my above-mentioned article in *ZKG*).

[19] *WA* 18:601, 4–6.
[20] Ibid. 6:457, 34–5.
[21] Ibid. 6:458, 26–31.

or a subject of discussion'.[22] Melanchthon's usage of *causa* frequently means 'the subject under discussion'. He listed the four causes in his *Compendiaria dialectices ratio* of 1520 as follows:

> A cause is that from which another things follows. The efficient cause is a person or thing which effects something else, as the carpenter a house or the father a son. The material cause is that from which something is made, as, out of wood a table. The formal cause is the outward appearance of the material. The final cause is the use of a thing.[23]

As an example, the four causes might be applied to justification as follows: the *material* cause is the person who needs to be saved, the *efficient* cause is the One who justifies, the *formal* or formative cause is the means of grace by which God acts, and the *final* cause is the purpose of this action, which is man's salvation.[24] Luther also occasionally employed this language, which is traced back to Aristotle, but he advised caution in the use of terms such as *causa*. Melanchthon's pupils and their successors, however, later made such terminology dominant in their theologies.[25]

---

[22] *Cassell's New Latin Dictionary* (New York: Funk & Wagnall's, 1960), s.v. The medieval usage is even wider, as given in *Mittellateinisches Glossar*, ed. E. Habel (Paderborn: Ferdinand Schöningh, 1959): 'Sache, Ding; Gepäck, Hinderungsgrund, Schuld; Tatsache, Hergang; Rechtshandel, Prozeß; Nutzen, Gewinn; causam supplere, die Sache zu Ende bringen, causam regere, einen Prozeß führen; in causam, vor Gericht; in causam ponere, in Anklagezustand versetzen; in causa esse, schuld sein; in causa habere, als Grund angeben; sine causa, ohne Schuld; causa alicullus, auf jemand Veranlassung.' *causa*, s.v.

[23] *CR*, 20:759.

[24] Melanchthon's use of the four 'causes' led to a famous controversy when Melanchthon used three (really, four) causes to explain what he called 'conversion': the Word of God, the work of the Holy Spirit, and the willing consent of the believer. Here, the believer is the material, the Spirit is the effecting One, the Word is the form or direction to be taken, and the sanctified life of the converted person is the purpose or goal. In this case, Melanchthon drew criticism by saying that the person acted upon must be willing to undergo such sanctification; when he was criticized for saying that a person must give his willing consent, he said that he was referring not to the unregenerate but to the regenerate person, that is, the believer. See my article, 'The Three Causes of Conversion in Philipp Melanchthon, Martin Chemnitz, David Chytraeus, and the Formula of Concord', *Lutherjahrbuch* 47 (1980), 89–114.

[25] An example was the use of the 'causes' by his pupil, David Chytraeus, in his *Catechesis* (1554) in the discussion of the law. Johann Michael Reu, *Quellen zur Geschichte des kirchlichen Unterrichtes in der evangelischen Kirche Deutschlands zwischen 1530 und 1600*, 11 vols. or parts (Gütersloh: Bertelsmann, 1904–35), I.Teil, III.Band, 1.Abt., 3. Lieferung (1916), 293–4; edition of 1575, ibid. 325. The causes were also used in Chytraeus' discussion of good works, ibid. 306–7. In the seventeenth century, the writers not only borrowed Melanchthon's concept of *loci*

Some of these epigones even recast Luther's writings and conversations in the form of *loci communes*.[26]

Theology and philosophy in disjunction

We have seen that 'philosophy' in the sense of the liberal arts was regarded by both Luther and Melanchthon as an important auxiliary science at the service of the theologian; rightly used, it was the 'handmaiden' of theology. However, when we turn to philosophy in the sense of metaphysics, the situation changes. Luther warned against the corruption of theology by incursions of 'that heathen', Aristotle. Melanchthon joined Luther in rejecting the metaphysics and ethics of Aristotle.[27] He went so far as to write: 'Philosophy prostitutes, I repeat, it prostitutes the church, and we would contend that it does so with the unnatural appetites of Sodom.'[28] Melanchthon discussed at length the distinction between philosophy and theology, and warned against confounding the two, in his *Scholia in epistulam Pauli ad Colossenses* of 1527. He wrote that the gospel is the doctrine of spiritual life (*vitae spiritualis*), and philosophy is the doctrine of bodily life (*vitae corporalis*).[29] Confined to bodily matters, philosophy has its proper place. In relation to theology, philosophy must be only the handmaiden of theology and must not be allowed to alter its content.

---

communes but greatly expanded the system. In Johann Gerhard, the prince of the dogmaticians, the 'causes' are discussed in each article much more elaborately than by Melanchthon. This use of the dialectic and rhetoric of Aristotle and Cicero, as stamped into theological form by Melanchthon, continued in Lutheran dogmatics under such men as Calov and Quenstedt to the last of the Lutheran 'orthodox dogmaticians', David Hollaz, and made its way also into the dogmatics systems of Reformed theologians. Melanchthon's *loci* system also pervaded books in the other learned professions.

[26] Georg Rörer, the most reliable of the scribes of Luther, criticized one Joseph Hänel for recasting the Table Talk of Luther into *loci communes*. See introductory article in *WAtr* 5:xlii.

[27] In Melanchthon's treatise against Tommaso Rhadino of February 1521, *Didymi Faventini adversus Thomam Placentinum pro Martino Luthero theologo oratio*, *CR*, 1:301; *SA*, I:72, 16–31.

[28] Melanchthon wrote: 'Prostituit, inquam, prostituit Ecclesiam philosophia, ut cum infandis etiam Sodomae libidinibus certemus'. In his treatise against Rhadino, *Didymi Faventini*, *CR* 1:313; *SA* I:87, 1–3.

[29] *SA* 4:240–2. Cited in Hans Emil Weber, *Reformation, Orthodoxie und Rationalismus*, 3 parts (Gütersloh: Bertelsmann, 1937–51/Darmstadt: Wissenschaftliche Buchgesellschaft, 1966), cited hereafter as Weber, I/1:175.

The concept of loci communes[30]

Melanchthon's introduction of *loci communes* shaped the future of Protestant scholarship for several centuries to come. The concept was derived from both classical dialectic and rhetoric. *Loci communes* are common topics under which a teacher arranges his material in order to clarify what he wants to say. We might translate this into English as 'central topics', 'basic conceptions', or 'common places'. This method of selecting common topics under which to group material became standard not only for theology but for many other subject areas as well.

Let us trace the development of this concept in Melanchthon's works. He discussed *loci communes* in his first book on rhetoric, *De rhetorica* (1519), in a later work, the *Elementa rhetorices* of 1542,[31] in his first book on dialectic, the *Compendiaria dialectices ratio* of 1520,[32] and in the later *Erotemata dialectices* of 1547.[33] He also published a short tract, *De locis communibus ratio*,[34] in 1531.

In a letter to Johann Hess on 7 April 1520, he discussed the relation of the concept of *loci communes* to both rhetoric and dialectic, stating that he had learned this from the rhetoricians.[35]

> I have been equipped now for the obelisks and Paul's Romans. The work of the obelisks increases remarkably. They are not annotations, as when I began, but I am writing *loci communes* concerning laws, sin, grace, the sacraments, and other mysteries.[36]

Here, he was distinguishing between a commentary (annotations) on Romans and a dogmatics growing out of critical notes (obelisks) on the *Sentences* of Peter Lombard. The result was that celebrated book, the *Loci*

---

[30] On the concept of the *loci communes* see especially Paul Joachimsen, 'Loci communes'; Wilhelm Maurer, 'Zur Komposition der Loci Melanchthons von 1521'; *Lutherjahrbuch* 25 (1958), 146–80. ibid. 'Melanchthons Loci communes von 1521 als wissenschaftliche Programmschrift', *Lutherjahrbuch* 27 (1960), 1–50; Quirinius Breen, 'The Terms "Loci Communes" and "Loci" in Melanchthon' in idem, *Christianity and Humanism: Studies in the History of Ideas* (Grand Rapids: Eerdmans, 1968), 93–105; John R. Schneider, *Rhetorical Construal*, 205–62.

[31] *CR*, 13:451–4.

[32] Ibid., 20:748–50.

[33] Ibid., 13:641–752, and especially 659–63.

[34] Ibid., 20:693–4.

[35] Melanchthon wrote: 'Secutus sum Rhetorum consilium, qui locis communibus comprehendere artes iubent', *CR* 1:159; *MBW* 1:72–3. Cf. Paul Joachimsen, 'Loci communes', 30; in n. 7, Joachimsen erroneously ascribes this statement to *CR* 1:157.

[36] Letter of 27 Apr 1520. *CR* 1:158. Date correction from 17 Apr by *MBW* 1:72–3.

communes of 1521.[37] What did he mean by 'obelisks'? An obelisk or obelus was a printer's mark, resembling a tapered column of stone, which designated a spurious, corrupt, doubtful, or superfluous word or passage; later, a hyphen (–), an asterisk (★), or a dagger (†) was used.[38] Hence Melanchthon's 'obelisks' were critical notes on Lombard's *Sentences*. Later Melanchthon systematized these notes and thereby produced his commonplaces, which were the first Protestant dogmatics.

In *De rhetorica*, 1519, Melanchthon had written that the whole work of proof and refutation is drawn from such topics or *loci*, which are the 'seats of argument'. He then listed various kinds: *locus* of definition, *locus* of description, *locus* from etymology, *loci* of arguments from accidence, *locus* of opposites, *locus* of similar things, and *locus* of proportions. He added: 'Cicero has written most elegantly and Rudolf Agricola has written most copiously about the *loci*.'[39]

In a special section, *de locis communibus* (concerning commonplaces), Melanchthon wrote:

> I therefore call 'commonplaces' the forms of things which generally fall into the use of humane and literary matters, such as fortune, wealth, honour, life, death, virtue, prudence, righteousness, liberality, temperance; and their contraries, such as poverty, ignominy, exile, temerity, injustice, dirtiness, intemperance, or extravagance.[40]

He then gave the examples from Rudolph Agricola and Erasmus,[41] adding that such *loci communes* are useful in educating the young so that they can learn to perceive the true qualities of things.[42]

What was Melanchthon's relation to Aristotle and Cicero? Peter Petersen claimed that Melanchthon's concept of the *loci communes* was

---

[37] Joachimsen writes: 'We see . . . that Melanchthon's work grows out of his direct opposition to the theological summaries of scholasticism, especially to the most common one, the *Summa sententiarum* of Peter Lombard', 29–30.

[38] *Oxford English Dictionary* 12:11–12. I used *The Compact Edition of the Oxford English Dictionary* (New York: Oxford University Press, 1971), 1:1962.

[39] He wrote: 'Hoc autem confirmandi and confutandi artificium totum petitur a disciplina Topica, id est locorum. Illi enim sunt argumentorum sedes, and horum ratio proxime sequitur primam axiomatis compositionem, nempe per Hypotheticam propositionem', *De rhetorica*, 45.

[40] 'Voco igitur locos communes, formas rerum, quae fere in usum rerum humanarum and literarum cadunt, ut fortunam, opes, honores, vitam, mortem, virtutem, prudentiam, iustitiam, liberalitatem, temperantiam, and his contraria: Paupertatem, ignominiam, exilium, temeritatem, iniustitiam, sordes, intemperantiam, seu luxum'. *De rhetorica*, 69–70.

[41] Ibid. 70.

[42] Ibid. 71.

derived from the logic of Aristotle.[43] Quirinius Breen corrected this by pointing out that whereas Aristotle in his Second or Posterior Analytics (which dealt with logic) restricted certain knowledge to logic and relegated probable knowledge to dialectic, Melanchthon (like Cicero) ascribed certain knowledge to rhetoric and dialectic. Breen described Aristotle's position as follows: 'Thus logic deals with propositions whose premises are necessarily true, dialectics with those whose premises are probable. . . . One must be aware of the fundamental distinction between probability (and falsity) and certainty before entering upon the search for wisdom'.[44] Melanchthon rejected Aristotle and followed Cicero at this point.

Breen reminds us that Cicero did not believe in any certain knowledge, but only in probable statements. Therefore to him dialectics was important as a means of discovering knowledge. The chief tool of dialectic as a finder of knowledge was the topic or *locus*. The loci became in Cicero the *sedes argumentorum*, i.e. the veins within a subject matter in which one digs for knowledge of it, the pits from which one pulls up learning.[45] Breen comments regarding Rudolph Agricola and Erasmus:

> Both are concerned more deeply with knowledge found in the Ciceronian manner than in the Aristotelian. Through them Cicero's *loci* got a wide reception in Northern Europe. Agricola sought by the *loci* to reconstitute all knowledge; Erasmus (in addition to that) sought more particularly to reinterpret Christianity by *loci* belonging to Ethics.[46]

As Breen notes, Melanchthon was influenced by Agricola in his Heidelberg days (1509–12) and by Erasmus during the following years. However, he had become independent of both when he prepared the first edition of his *Loci communes* in theology. Melanchthon forsook the views of both Aristotle and Cicero: He firmly insisted that divine revelation is the source of not merely probable knowledge but of fully certain knowledge. Melanchthon wrote in the 1559 edition of the Loci:[47]

> For the doctrine of the church is not adduced from empirical demonstrations but from statements which God has given to the human race in certain and clear testimonies, through which in his great goodness he has made himself and his will known. . . . But in philosophy the things that

---

[43] Peter Petersen, *Geschichte der aristotelischen Philosophie im protestantischen Deutschland* (Leipzig: Felix Meiner, 1921), 93–5.

[44] Breen, *Christianity and Humanism*, 95.

[45] Ibid. 97.

[46] Ibid. 98.

[47] On Aristotle's position on probable and certain truth, and on demonstration, see his *Posterior Analytics*, Book 1, Chapter 2. Available in English translation in Richard McKeon, *Introduction to Aristotle* (New York: Modern Library, 1947), 11–12.

are certain are sought and are distinguished from uncertain things. And the causes of certainty are universal experience, principles and demonstrations. In this way in the doctrine of the church the cause of certainty is the revelation of God and it is necessary to consider which sentences have been delivered by God. . . . But the articles of faith are certain on account of revelation, which is confirmed by the certain and clear testimonies of God, such as the raising of the dead and many other miracles.[48]

Luther's Response to Melanchthon's 'Scholastic Terminology'

The relation between Luther and Melanchthon on the matter of 'scholasticism' is much more complex than is commonly recognized. Luther was not hostile to the liberal arts, nor was Melanchthon willing to sacrifice evangelical truth upon the altar of metaphysical philosophy. Moreover, the facile assumption that Melanchthon had no original ideas of his own but merely took Luther's teachings and pressed them into scholastic formulations is simply wrong. Both men worked independently. There were many facets in Melanchthon's teaching that were not borrowed from Luther, and many important insights of Luther failed to enter Melanchthon's writings; moreover, there were some significant theological divergencies between them. It proved to be the fate of Lutheran theology that Melanchthon's formulations, expressed in systematic form, were more easily transmitted to future generations than Luther's prophetic utterances. Seventeenth-century Lutheran orthodox theologians unconsciously followed Melanchthon more closely than Luther; in teaching the distinction between law and gospel, they lost its connection with the doctrine of God and with Christology in Luther's distinction of *Deus absconditus seu revelatus*. This important distinction became only one among many *loci theologici*, rather than the dynamic force in an integral theology which it had constituted under Luther.

Luther once wrote a short paper to guide his own son on dialectic and rhetoric; this treatise has only survived in a reference by Luther in the Table Talk.[49] There he compared the role of dialectic and rhetoric, instructed his son on the use of the four causes, and discussed kindred matters. Space restrictions prevent us from citing several other noteworthy examples where Luther discussed dialectic and rhetoric, or utilized such terms as the four kinds of *causa* or the term of *causa sine qua non* in order to make an important point. We must reserve these matters for a future publication, where we aim to bring a fuller account of Luther's use of scholastic concepts.

---

[48]   *Loci praecipua theologici* of 1559, *CR* 21:604; *SA* II/1:168, 11–20. 168, 27–169, 2. English translation by Jacob A.O. Preus, *Loci Communes 1543 Philip Melanchthon* (St Louis: Concordia, 1992), 16, A.

[49]   *WAtr* 4:647–9, Table Talk No. 5082b.

THE TWOFOLD APPROACH TO THEOLOGY

Already in Luther and Melanchthon we find the later distinction between a theoretic and a practical theology. The distinction is not between theory and practice so much as between scientific theology and kerygmatic or personal theology, to use today's terms. Melanchthon saw value in theoretic theology; however, more important was a theology of the heart; *vera cognitio* of theology comes only when one hears and believes the promises of God in spite of the grief and troubles of this present life. In his 1533 lectures on the *Loci communes* as recorded by Bugenhagen, Melanchthon pointed out that 'The human mind cannot grasp the nature of God by means of speculations', and added in words which placed him at the side of Luther: 'This methodology does not proceed *a priori*, i.e. from the hidden nature of God to the knowledge of the will of God, but rather from the knowledge of Christ and revealed mercy unto the knowledge of God. To exercise and confirm the minds by this knowledge is far better than to philosophize about the hidden nature of God'.[50]

Robert Scharlemann describes theoretic theology as 'a humanistic discipline . . . Its contents were taken from Scripture according to the rules of rhetoric and logic that applied everywhere'. He points out that Melanchthon thought that when there were controversies, they came from the neglect of these rules, and that controversy could therefore be settled by returning to the right rules of theoretic theology. Theoretic theology, however, did not go far enough. Only practical theology, which was formed by adversity, moved beyond theoretic theology and led to the true knowledge of God.[51]

It is a familiar fact that the theology of Luther was eminently practical. He described a 'practical theology' with his famous dictum regarding the three things which made a theologian: *oratio*, *meditatio*, and *tentatio*, i.e. prayer, meditation, and trials.[52] First, one must pray for guidance; second,

---

[50]   *CR* 21:256. On the comparison of theoretical and practical theology in Melanchthon, see Robert P. Scharlemann, *Thomas Aquinas and John Gerhard*, Yale Publications in Religion 7 (New Haven: Yale University Press, 1964), 25–6, and Weber, I/1:183. Scharlemann, in describing a 'dual concept' of theological method in Luther and Melanchthon, spoke of a theoretic and a practical or 'acoustic' concept, acoustic meaning one which resounded in the preached Word, 5, 22–8. Perhaps a better distinction would be between an objective and a personal meaning. The latter use, the 'true knowledge of the divine will', comes from afflictions and *calamitates*, 25. See also Weber, I/2:252–5.

[51]   Scharlemann writes: 'Its practical side is not ethics but the use of the audible Word as the vehicle for giving and receiving the new being, the power to live from the *adesse Dei* in faith', *Aquinas and Gerhard*, 27.

[52]   Luther, in Preface to the Wittenberg edition of his works, 1539. *WA* 50:659, 3–4.

one must continually remain in the Word; third, life's trials exercise the faith of the theologian and such experience leads the theologian back to the Word and to true wisdom. These three parts of theology were frequently taken up and expanded by later theologians.[53]

In his preface to Luther's 1519 Commentary on the Psalter, Melanchthon wrote:

> What good does it do to know that the world was created by God, as Genesis teaches, unless you adore the mercy and wisdom of the Creator? And what good does it do to know the mercy and wisdom of God, unless you take it into your own soul that to you he is merciful, to you he is righteous, to you he is wise? And that is truly to know God.[54]

Here we have the difference between a theoretical and a practical theology.

Martin Chemnitz, a pupil of Melanchthon, gave the preeminence to practical or experiential theology when, in a course on Melanchthon's *Loci*, he spoke as follows: 'Actually, the meaning is in accordance with the experience of the pious in the practice of doctrine, in repentance, in fear, in faith, in prayer, and in proper consolations.' And he added: 'It is truthfully said that theology consists more in feeling than in knowledge.'[55]

Robert Preus commented:

> And this desire to bring out the practical application of Christian doctrine is really only another legacy of Chemnitz and Luther. Chemnitz is always embarrassed when forced to enter any sort of technical discussion that might becloud the practical aim of his theology. . . . Chemnitz would contend that only when theology becomes practical can it be really known and understood at all.[56]

---

[53] See the expansion of this into *precatio, studium seu meditatio et diligentia in discendo*, and *experientia seu praxis*, including trials and suffering, in Chytraeus, *Catechesis* (1575), given by Reu, *Quellen zur Geschichte*, I. Teil, III, 2. Abt., 1. H. (1916), 317.
[54] *WA*, 5:26, 4–7.
[55] 'Sensus vero est experientia piorum in usu doctrinae, in poenitentia, timore, fide, invocatione, consolationibus propriis'. *Loci theologici Domini Martini Chemnitii, theologi longe celeberrimi, atque ecclesiae Brunsvicensis qvondam svperintendentis fidelissimi: quibus et loci communes Domini Philippi Melanchthonis perspicve explicantur, and quasi integrum Christianae doctrinae corpus, Ecclesiae Dei sincere proponitur*, ed. Polycarp Leyser (Frankfurt and Wittenberg: Tobias Mevius and Elerd Schumacher, 1653), fol.4, verso. 'Vere enim dictum est, Theologiam magis consistere in affectu quam in cognitione', 17.
[56] Preus, *Theology of Post-Reformation Lutheranism*, 2 vols. (St Louis: Concordia, 1970–72), I:204–5.

CONCLUSION

Melanchthon and Luther presaged the age of scholastic theology in two respects: first, as we have seen, in their use of dialectic and rhetoric to secure clarity of thought and fitting words, and second, in their concern that theology be 'practical': that it not remain academic and scientific, but that it be related to the life of the Christian believer. It must somehow connect with the doctrine of justification or with the goal of everlasting salvation.

Later Lutheran orthodoxy or scholasticism followed both reformers in these respects. It was built upon dialectic and rhetoric, and it tended to be 'practical' and to follow the analytic method, which recognized the salvation of the believer as its goal. The analytic method then worked back as it considered the other doctrines of the Christian faith from the aspect of soteriology.

2

Johann Gerhard's Doctrine of the Sacraments[1]

David P. Scaer

WORD AND SACRAMENTS

Sacraments in Johann Gerhard's theology are external confirmations of the word, that is the gospel, to create and confirm faith.[2] The word was both divine command and promise. As the word is directed to man's soul,

---

[1] Johann Gerhard (1582–1637) was, after Martin Luther and Martin Chemnitz, the most significant Lutheran theologian in classical Lutheranism and known as the 'archtheologian' of the seventeenth century. From 1616 he was professor at the University of Jena and his dogmatics, *Loci Communes,* was the standard dogmatics in post-Reformation Lutheranism. The writer expresses his gratitude to the Reverend James D. Heiser, Director of the Johann Gerhard Institute of Decatur, Illinois for reading through the manuscript and for his many helpful suggestions.

[2] Citations are taken from the fourth volume of John Gerhard, *Loci Theologici,* ed. Preuss (Berlin: Gustaf Schlawitz, 1866). This first appeared in 1657, twenty years after Gerhard had died in 1637, and was edited by his son. Editions continued during the period of Lutheran orthodoxy until 1767 when rationalism was becoming firmly entrenched. The Preuss edition appeared in 1866. An English translation was made by Richard J. Dinda with the title *The Theological Commonplaces of John Gerhard* and is available only in typescript and microfiche (St Louis, Miss.: Concordia, 1981). The Dinda translation provides a basis for most quotations from Gerhard in this essay. The Latin word *loci,* which appears in the title of Gerhard's work and is translated as 'commonplaces', refers to the separate categories or topic headings in which the various doctrines are presented. Gerhard's discussion on baptism was assigned to *locus* 18; circumcision and passover to 19; and the sacrament of baptism to 20. References to the fourth volume of Gerhard's *Loci* will be taken from the Preuss edition with numbers of locus and paragraphs following, for example '191 (18:2)'. References taken from other volumes will be preceded by the volume number, e.g., '1.5:32'.

the sacraments are intended for both soul and body, a view Gerhard credits to Chrysostom and Gregory Nazianzenus.[3] For example in the Lord's Supper there is a spiritual eating for the soul and a sacramental eating for the body.[4] What is proclaimed to the ears in preaching is held before the eyes in the sacraments, a principle characterizing God's revelation. The correlation between God's revelation as audible word and external sign and man's nature as body and soul supports Gerhard's contention that the sacraments belong to God's original creative purposes. Through sacraments spiritual mysteries deeper than those given in the divine image are revealed to man. While word and sacraments are two different operations of God, everything which belongs to the word is attributed to the sacraments, which on that account are called visible words. The word provides the sacraments with their authority, power and dignity.[5] Sacraments have particular workings which cannot be attributed to the word in general. Roman Catholics had distinguished the word consecrating the sacraments from the proclaimed word. Gerhard does not dispute the distinction but holds that the word consecrating the external elements as sacraments is also the word proclaiming salvation. Such elements, not through a change of substance, but through a union of earthly and heavenly things, no longer serve a secular but a sacred purpose.[6]

Both before and after the Fall sacraments bring man into a closer and permanent relation with God, but in the state of sin they confer forgiveness, their final cause. Man was created holy with a flawless knowledge of God, but certain divine mysteries were to be known to him only by his eating of the fruit of the tree of life.[7] The tree was Christ and the fruit was the sacrament, an argument borrowed from Augustine:

---

[3]   137 (18:2).

[4]   Following the lead of the Reformer, Lutherans have hesitated to use John 6 in their discussion of the eucharist, a point to which Bellarmine took exception. Gerhard's distinction between a sacramental eating and a spiritual one permitted him to deny that the former is discussed here, but he paradoxically held that John 6 'sets forth the spiritual eating and fruit of the Lord's Supper' (144 [18:17]). Perhaps the best explanation is that he was convinced exegetically of Bellarmine's argument, but Lutheran tradition did not allow him to accept it. Gerhard ate his cake and still had it.

[5]   169 (18:55).

[6]   163 (18:51).

[7]   Luther understands the tree of the knowledge of good and evil as a sacrament but I have not found where he says this of the tree of life. *Luther's Works*, American Edition, eds. J. Pelikan and H.T. Lehmann (St Louis: Concordia/Philadelphia: Fortress, 1955–), 1:95. Calvin sees the tree of life as a guarantee of immortality *Institutes* 4.14.18.

Therefore, in a certain way the tree of life was also Christ the Rock. God wanted man to live in paradise but without physically revealing the mysteries of spiritual things. Man therefore had food on the rest of the trees but a sacrament in that tree.[8]

The trees of the garden provided for man's physical needs, but in the tree of life, which was set aside by a promise, God intended to lead Adam into mysteries higher and deeper than those which were innately his by his special creation. Man's creation in God's image was the prelude to an even better life. The pattern for Gerhard's sacramental understanding is derived from Genesis 2, developed through the Old Testament and culminates in baptism and the Lord's Supper in the New Testament. This pattern becomes important in his debate with the Roman Catholic theologian Robert Bellarmine who denied that Old Testament rites were sacraments of grace. By contrast, Gerhard argued that sacraments in both testaments are not isolated rites but extensions of the presence of Christ from whom they receive their essence and efficacy. By eating the fruit of the tree of life, Adam would have shared in Christ himself. Hence sacraments are more than empty rituals or mechanistic magical forms. In the sacraments of both Old and New Testament, one deals directly with Christ but more intensely so in baptism and the Lord's Supper. 'So also the sacraments are not significative of the absence of Christ but exhibitive of His presence'.[9] God's presence in baptism and the Lord's Supper is intrinsically a christological one and so the church should not expect to find Christ anywhere except in the sacraments.

Deprived of the tree of life, man was provided with other sacramental avenues through which he and God could approach each other. Wherever God gave the Word, he provided signs as sacraments. Just as circumcision and the passover held the place of honour among the Old Testament sacraments, so baptism and the Lord's Supper hold this position now.[10] Each sacrament within a designated period of time has its particular signification, purpose and function, a view Gerhard took from Luther's *Lectures on Genesis*.[11] The sacraments of one era cannot be equated or interchanged with those of another time, though they share certain similarities. Baptism and circumcision are sacraments of initiation, the one a prerequisite for the passover and the other for the eucharist, but baptism does not make a distinction between male and female or Jews and Gentiles as circumcision did.[12] Circumcision signifies an internal circumcision of

---

[8]   137 (18:2).
[9]   141 (18:10).
[10]   176 (18:64), 'Ergo etiam sacramenta verbo promissionis addita tam in V. quam N.T. pertinent.'
[11]   177 (18:64); 164 (18:46).
[12]   160–1 (18:44)

the heart in infants and baptism an internal washing of sins.[13] As necessary as the sacraments are for forgiveness, the sacramental principle is set in place as part of the original creation and is not a divine afterthought or response to a fallen humanity. Sacraments are neither an exception to God's creative design nor originally intended as a divine condescension to sinners, but are the ordinary ways in which God approaches man.[14] Gerhard can speak of God addressing himself to human weakness in the sacraments.

Where Genesis chapter two provides the basis for living sacramentally with God, chapter three adds sacrifice to the definition of a sacrament. By providing skins as clothing for Adam and Eve, God showed that sacrifice of life, in this case the lives of animals, was necessary and so established sacrifice as a required ritual.[15] Before and after the institution of circumcision and passover as the authentic sacraments of the Old Testament, sacrifices served as sacraments.[16] The rite was as much a sacrifice in which man gave himself to God as it was a sacrament revealing mysteries to believers. God accepted Abel's sacrifices and showed his approval of other sacrifices, including those mandated in Leviticus, by sending fire from heaven to consume them.[17] Gerhard also understood the rainbow as sacramental, an external sign for the covenant God made with Noah, although it did not offer what baptism did. Both Old and New Testament sacraments conferred grace,[18] but these rites were not of equal value or interchangeable and did not have the same internal content or external signification. Old Testament sacraments were temporary and New Testament ones permanent.[19] The debate over whether Old Testament sacraments conferred grace did not come up with the Reformed theologians who consistently denied this benefit to any rite, but with the Roman Catholics. Bellarmine defended a view, put forward by the Council of Florence in 1439 and taken up by the Council of Trent (1545–60), that grace was given only in the New Testament rites.[20] Following Luther, Gerhard holds that 'these sacraments of the ancients … have the same use and purpose which the sacraments of the New

---

[13]   178 (18:64), 'Ergo circumcisio fuit salutare medium, per quod non solum praeputium carnis, sed etiam cordis in infantibus fuit ablatum.'
[14]   137 (18:2).
[15]   137 (18:2).
[16]   137 (18:2); 177 (18:64). Gerhard's consideration of the number of sacraments being limited to baptism and the Lord's Supper is part of his discussion of circumcision and passover as Old Testament sacraments (246–55 [19:53–68]).
[17]   137 (18:2).
[18]   182 (18:69), 'Ergo sacramenta V.T. itidem fuerunt efficacia media spiritualium beneficiorum credentibus collatorum.'
[19]   183 (18:70).
[20]   174 (18:60).

Testament have'.[21] Considering that Gerhard devoted one *locus* each to circumcision and passover, this was no small matter for him.[22] Lutherans, rather than Catholics, took a consistent sacramental approach to the Bible.

THE DEFINITION OF SACRAMENT

Gerhard notes that 'sacrament' is derived from the Latin *sacramentum* and acknowledges that its use for baptism, the Lord's Supper and other church rites goes beyond the biblical usage.[23] Andreas Carlstadt and Ulrich Zwingli suggested its removal from theological vocabulary, but Gerhard, like Luther, keeps the term. He then incorporates its original meaning into his definition of the New Testament rites which the church is bound to practise as Sacraments. Originally a sacrament was a legal term for a bond posted with a holy man by two opposing litigants before their civil case came to trial. The loser forfeited his deposit, the *sacramentum*, to the temple treasury and the victor had his bond returned. The prospect of losing a sizeable amount of money discouraged frivolous lawsuits and encouraged settlement before trial. Later the term meant only the promise without a bond. Litigants made a pledge, *sacramentum*, that they would supply the required cash if they lost. Later *sacramentum* was used for an oath soldiers swore to serve their full terms. In the Latin translation of the Bible *sacramentum* is the translation of *musterion* (Eph. 1:9; 5:32; 1 Tim. 3:16; Rev. 17:7), a mystery, that is, something which is beyond ordinary human experience, for example, God's plan of salvation, Christ's relationship to the church or the rule of evil in the world. Great mysteries are hidden within ordinary things and events. In church parlance *sacramentum* was applied to external signs pointing to sacred things or hidden mysteries concealed within them. Jerome said 'the sacraments of God were preaching, blessing and confirming [confirmation], distributing communion, visiting the sick [and] praying'.[24] Even the cross could be thought of as a sacrament pointing to the atonement. Gerhard grants this wider meaning with the provision that other rites not be placed on the same level as baptism and the Lord's Supper. Although Melanchthon and Luther accepted a wider definition of a sacrament, Gerhard's definition fitted only baptism and the Lord's Supper.[25] A sacrament was 'a solemn sacred action instituted by God in which the special promise of the gospel

---

[21] 176 (18:63).
[22] 187–95 (18:73–8).
[23] 138–9 (18:3–6).
[24] 138 (18:6).
[25] 139–49 (18:7). Luther speaks of three sacraments in the *Babylonian Captivity* (*Luther Works* 36:18).

is applied and sealed through an external, visible sign'.[26] Correspondingly, 'the only two properly called and specifically so-called and permanent Sacraments of the Old Testament are circumcision, Gen. 17, and the passover lamb, Ex. 12'.[27]

Old Testament sacraments were part of the discussion on the seven rites claimed as sacraments by the Council of Trent. Martin Chemnitz, Trent's most significant Lutheran critic, was answered by Bellarmine. Both agreed that the word plus the element constituted a sacrament, but in Gerhard's opinion, Bellarmine manipulated this definition to accommodate penance. At issue was not whether penance, confirmation, marriage, ordination, and extreme unction satisfied one or two of the three sacramental requirements of being God's command, giving grace and the Holy Spirit, and having an external sign, but whether any of the five fitted all three. Only baptism and the Lord's Supper were divinely commanded rites with external elements offering the forgiveness of sins.[28] Even Bellarmine recognized the validity of the Lutheran argument.[29]

For Gerhard sacraments were not the only signs in which God worked. Creation provided the external substance for the sacraments, but only those parts chosen by God to reveal himself are signs. From these signs he elevates only certain ones to sacraments.[30] Gerhard offers three classes of signs. (1) Some, such as the rainbow, the burning bush, and the opening of the Red Sea, confirm a truth of the divine word and guarantee its certainty. Jesus confirms his claim to divinity through miracles. (2) Other signs such as eclipses and comets confirm warnings about impending judgment. (3) Still other signs, to which the sacraments belong, are rituals which confirm previously made promises. A proclaimed word is corroborated by signs within rituals.[31]

---

[26]   138 (18:6).

[27]   183 (18:70).

[28]   139 (18:6).

[29]   147–8 (18:24), 'Chemnitz does not do a bad job of investigating in general the nature and character of the sacraments on the basis of baptism and eucharist which by common consent are the true sacraments.' So Bellarmine.

[30]   In Paul Tillich's sacramentology, all of creation is revelatory or sacramental, with some parts intrinsically possessing higher and lower levels of this potential. This was really only a form of pantheism or panentheism. For Gerhard, God made the choice of the elements through which he would reveal himself.

[31]   143 (18:16), Gerhard claims support here from Luther who saw sacraments in the ordinary signs of priestly rituals, vestments, vessels, and food, and in the extraordinary signs of the dew on Gideon's fleece and the backward motion of the shadow on Ahaz's sundial. See Luther's *Lectures on Genesis, Luther's Works* 1:309. 'Thus in the Old Testament faces of the Lord were the pillar of fire, the cloud, and the mercy seat; in the New Testament, baptism, the Lord's Supper, the ministry of the Word, and the like. Be means of these God shows us by a visible sign, that He is with us, takes care of us, and is favorably inclined towards us.'

Sacraments are the external signs confirming an invisible grace preached to believers. They follow rather than precede the preached Word. The invisibility of grace does not mean that the heavenly reality is absent. Rather the sacraments contain within themselves the grace which they symbolize. The sign contains and shares in the reality which it signifies, a definition distinguishing the Lutheran position from the Reformed. Signs resembling the sacraments in containing heavenly realities within themselves include the swaddling clothes in which the Christ Child was wrapped, the ark of the covenant, the burning bush and the pillar of fire. In these God was present. So also the Holy Spirit was in the dove.[32] Outward signs point to the greater realities contained in them. Sacraments exceed human expectations, but are typical of God's approaches to man.

Gerhard's attention to the Roman Catholic position did not distract him from refuting the Reformed position that the sacraments were signs pointing to absent realities. Article Thirteen of the Augsburg Confession (1530) defined sacraments as signs distinguishing the Christian community. They have value as rituals instilling moral virtues among believers and as allegories symbolizing the Christian experience of repentance and regeneration.[33] In his conflict with Reformed theologians in general, Gerhard showed that such descriptions were inadequate. Such symbolic interpretations were as far as Carlstadt, the Anabaptists and Zwingli were prepared to go, and remained characteristic of Reformed theologians who denied any real efficacy to the sacraments.[34] Calvin and Beza held that God had instituted the sacraments only as signs, but without heavenly realities within themselves.[35] Gerhard argues that a sign has no meaning without a reality which it signifies. 'No sign is its own signified thing'. Since in the Reformed definition of signs such realities are absent, their sacraments are not signs.[36] For Gerhard, signs point to the heavenly things which the signs contain but the heavenly things are greater than the signs.

---

[32] 140 (18:9).

[33] Luther in the *Small Catechism* taught that baptism signifies the daily drowning of the sinful self and its rising to a new life.

[34] 141–2 (18:12); 170–1 (18:56). These allegorical or symbolic interpretations of the sacraments characterized the rationalist theologians of the eighteenth-century Enlightenment, including Lutherans, and then Schleiermacher, all of whom doubted the divine institution of the sacraments. They were kept as traditional rites to instil moral values and give adhesion to the community. See Julius August Wegscheider, *Institutiones Theologiae Christianae Dogmaticae* 3 vols. (Halle: Gebauer, 1817³), 364–7 and Frederick Daniel Ernst Schleiermacher, *Der Christliche Glaube*, 3 vols. (Berlin: Reimer, 1836³), 2:280–4.

[35] 146 (18:22–3).

[36] 146 (18:23). Scholars recognize that just as Luther and Melanchthon did not have identical positions, neither did Reformed theologians. Gerhard provides citations from the Reformed fathers to show that they were agreed that sacraments

The necessary relationship between the sign and the thing signified is analogous to the relationship between father and son. A father is not the son, but he could not be a father without a son.[37] Gerhard notes an inconsistency in Beza who admits that in some cases 'the signification of which they [signs] are used is truly being given to us, just as in the blowing of the wind Christ was giving His disciples His Holy Spirit'.[38] The importance of the relationship between the sign and the reality is clear in what Gerhard says about circumcision. 'Thus, sacramental circumcision not only signifies but also effects, applies and seals spiritual circumcision by faith to those who use the sacrament'.[39] This was also true of infants. The same principle applies to baptism where the external washing corresponds to an internal one. Gerhard notes that Zwingli condemned Luther and Melanchthon's definition of the sacraments as signs strengthening faith because they 'wander very far from the truth'.[40] The Reformed doctrine of election cast doubt on whether they even understood sacraments as signs. Children were destined to heaven or perdition apart from the sign of baptism. So in Beza's theology the sign had no ultimate significance.[41]

The external signs of the sacraments correspond to the particular efficacy of each. Physical circumcision effected the spiritual circumcision it symbolized. Baptism as an outward washing with water effects an internal, spiritual washing.[42] It is proper to claim it saves us. The bread of the Lord's Supper is the actual communion of Christ's body. Signs contain the reality within themselves. 'Surely then the sacramental signs consist not only of signifying but also of conferring and applying'.[43] Essential to Gerhard's definition of sacraments was the inclusion of the external

---

as signs did not confer grace: Zwingli held, 'I believe — in fact, I know for certain — that all the Sacraments are so far removed from conferring grace that they not even offer or dispense it'; for Calvin 'A sacrament is nothing else but an external testimony of divine kindness towards us, a testimony which represents spiritual graces with a visible sign'; Beza answers his own question, 'From where does that efficacy of the Sacraments come? In sum, from the operation of the Holy Spirit, not from signs except insofar as our inner senses are moved by those external objects'.

[37]   146 (18:22–3).
[38]   173 (18:59).
[39]   146 (18:23).
[40]   170 (18:56).
[41]   172 (18:59).
[42]   146 (18:23).
[43]   146 (18:23). Gerhard notes that Beza recognized a necessary correlation between the sign and what it signified. Some signs 'bear witness to that which they are used to signify is truly given us'. Gerhard might have read too much into Beza's statement. He would have hardly intended that the Holy Spirit was actually given through and in the sign. Or did he?

element within a rite. The external thing by itself was not a sacrament. In circumcision the cutting of the foreskin is required, in the passover the slaying and eating of the lamb; in baptism the washing with water and in the Lord's Supper the eating of bread and drinking of wine. Elements by themselves do not constitute sacraments.[44] This argument was directed against the Roman Catholic position which saw saving significance in the elements apart from the rite. Reservation of the host was dependent on a transubstantiation of the elements. Gerhard maintained that 'nothing has the rationale of a sacrament outside of its divinely-instituted use'.[45] Apart from the rite or act there was no sacrament.

Seventeenth-century Lutheran, Roman Catholic and Reformed theologians agreed with Augustine's definition of sacraments from his Homily 80 on John: 'The word comes to an element and a sacrament is created'. If one or the other is absent, there is no sacrament.[46] Interpreting the commonly held definition was another matter. Martin Chemnitz, the moving force behind the *Formula of Concord* and the publication of the Lutheran Confessions in the *Book of Concord*, was the link between Luther and Melanchthon's Reformation and seventeenth-century Lutheran scholasticism. He set the tone for Gerhard's and most Lutheran interpretations of Augustine's 'word and element' definition by further delineating eight requirements for a specific rite to be considered a sacrament.[47] Chemnitz took baptism and the eucharist as the true sacraments and from them he deduced his principles by which others were judged. (1) The element must be part of a liturgical act. (2) The act had to be instituted by divine command. (3) It must be a New Testament rite. (4) It cannot be limited in regard to time. (5) A specific benefit has to be attached to the act. (6) This benefit must belong to the act by divine ordinance. (7) Specific benefits besides justification or forgiveness must be offered in the act itself. (8) Such benefits are not merely announced but actually given to believers. This delineation excluded Old Testament rituals and the five additional rites Rome claimed as sacraments. However, this did not restrict Gerhard's use of the term for Old Testament rituals and other church rites.[48] Bellarmine's

---

44 147–8 (18:24).
45 Ibid.
46 141 (18:11).
47 Ibid.
48 160 (18:44), Circumcision and passover play a fundamental part in Gerhard's argument that baptism and the Lord's Supper are the only authentic sacraments. It is not obvious why his definition for sacraments should be so formulated as to exclude rites which he consistently calls 'Old Testament Sacraments' (173 [18:60)]). He also recognizes with Bellarmine that ordination (holy orders) and marriage are necessary, not in the sense they benefit the individuals who receive them but as they benefit the church. Gerhard denies that these rites are *vere et proprie dicta sacramenta* but implies that they could be called sacraments in another sense (157 [18:63]).

response to Chemnitz provided an outline for Gerhard's exposition on the sacraments, as in the case of penance.

At issue was not whether penance (confession and absolution) was divinely instituted, but Bellarmine's distinction between proclamation and consecration, and his interpretation of the consecratory word as *the element* in Augustine's definition. Gerhard recognized the distinction between proclamation and consecration, but maintained that the consecration was also proclamation. More important, he insisted that an element by definition was visible and tangible: the audible word of consecration was for the ears while the elements of baptism and eucharist had to be visible to the eyes.[49]

Differences over the baptism of John brought the parties into dispute over the Lutheran principle that only New Testament rites qualified as sacraments. Bellarmine held that John was an Old Testament prophet whose baptism was nevertheless on a par with that of Jesus. So Gerhard's New Testament requirement was refuted. Gerhard devoted a separate *locus* to circumcision and passover as sacraments, but held they were not on a par with baptism and the eucharist.[50] He understood John's baptism as a full New Testament sacrament. Gerhard argued that what applied to the baptism of Jesus applied to that of John. In this case Bellarmine's arguments that John was an Old Testament figure and hence his baptism belonged to that era are the more convincing. Gerhard might have gone another route and conceded that John's baptism, like other Old Testament sacraments, offered forgiveness, a point he had already established against Bellarmine. Gerhard was right in equating John's baptism with the one offered by Jesus before his death. Both were superior to circumcision, but only anticipatory and limited in regard to time and hence inferior to the baptism Jesus established after his resurrection. Several jumps in logic cannot go unnoticed. Gerhard assumed that Jesus offered the same baptism before and after his resurrection. Since John's baptism was identical to that of Jesus before his death, all are of equal value.[51] Then Gerhard takes an excruciating route to show that John was both prophet and apostle and argues that his inclusion in the New Testament canon makes him a figure of the new era.[52] His view that John was an apostle hardly fits the evidence. John was 'that great Elijah' standing on the edge of the older age peering into the new era, but not participating in it.

---

[49]   142 (18:13).

[50]   220–55 (19:1–66).

[51]   This method also leads to the assumption that all the writers of the New Testament, including Mark and Luke, were apostles. The term 'Apostolic Scriptures' required that the apostles themselves were the authors.

[52]   143 (18:15).

SACRAMENTS AS MIRACLES AND ANTITYPES

Baptism and the Lord's Supper may also be called miracles, antitypes, mysteries, ceremonies and rites.[53] As miracles they exceed human comprehension in giving grace, but unlike Christ's miracles the sacraments experience no change of substance.[54] Water remains ordinary water and bread does not lose its substance in becoming Christ's body.[55] New Testament sacraments may also be called antitypes corresponding to Old Testament rituals and historical events which were types. Christ, whom the prophets knew through the Old Testament rituals, is actually made present for the church in the sacraments.

SACRAMENTS AS DIVINE AND HUMAN RECIPROCITY

Tertullian was the first to refer to the *sacramentum* of baptism and the Lord's Supper as promises or oaths made by believers. Gerhard took this original meaning into his own definition so that sacraments are believers' promises to God to carry out faith's obligations and satisfy the sacraments' requirements.[56] Thus Gerhard saw the sacraments as mutual obligations between God and man. Both of these aspects are found in Reformed theology, especially with Calvin. Zwingli saw sacraments as predominently man's obligation to God. For Gerhard, sacraments were not legally required pledges but faith's response.

> For just as that money was, as it were, pledged by which they were obliged to each other as if by some definite agreement, so those signs of the covenant added to the promise of grace not only make us certain about the will of God but also bind our faith to Him.[57]

The idea of reciprocity reappears in Gerhard's discussion of Old Testament sacrifices as sacraments. Before Abraham, sacrifices were the means through which God gave grace to his people. What the people sacrificed to God became the sacraments through which he gave good gifts to them.[58] So 'in a certain way sacraments and sacrifices fit

---

[53]   147 (18:24).
[54]   141 (18:10).
[55]   Gerhard does speak of a change taking place in the Lord's Supper. Between the 'symbolic shadow' of the Reformed and the 'essential mutation' of the Roman Catholics, he speaks of 'a sacramental mutation', *Loci* 5:153 (21:153). This was in response to Bellarmine's assertion that since the Lutherans did not believe in an essential mutation (transubstantiation), they did not attribute to the consecratory words the power for bread to become Christ's body.
[56]   139 (18:7).
[57]   149 (18:7).
[58]   177 (18:64).

together'.[59] Man's sacrifices to God became God's sacraments to man. In one sacramental/sacrificial act God and man approach one another.

ARISTOTLE'S CAUSES

Gerhard followed the Thomistic method in using Aristotle's causes. This was useful in his response to the Reformed accusation that the Lutherans attributed to the sacraments what rightfully belonged only to God and in refuting the Roman Catholic position that the sacraments' power was found in their substance.[60] Sacraments were not the formal cause of salvation but instrumental causes.[61] They were not autonomous rites with intrinsic power, but instruments of the benefits of Christ's death, which was the meritorious cause. Material causes of the sacraments were the heavenly elements — regeneration in baptism and Christ's body in the Eucharist.[62] Sacraments are instrumental causes in effecting believers' salvation. Justification or forgiveness is their final cause. Baptism as the instrumental cause was 'the medium of regeneration and thus also the medium for stirring and strengthening faith'.[63] The internal washing of regeneration, the heavenly thing, is baptism's material cause. The principal cause can be either God, Christ's death or the Holy Spirit, but not the sacraments themselves, as the Reformed charged that Lutherans believed. Gerhard's method is evident in his explanation of Titus 3:5: 'God (the principal cause) saved us (final cause or effect) through the washing of regeneration (through baptism which is the instrumental cause)'.[64] God is 'the efficient principal cause and author of the sacraments'.[65] Faith is also identified as an instrumental cause. 'God is the principal cause of justification, the suffering of Christ is the meritorious cause; the word and sacraments are the instrumental causes on the part of God, faith is the instrumental cause on our part'.[66] Understanding faith as a cause in any sense may suggest synergism to some, though Gerhard hardly intends this.

In Gerhard's sacramental theology, *material* can be used in two senses. Without a physical substance or *material*, a sacrament is not a sacrament.[67] To the external element or *material* comes the Word. Confusing as it may

---

59   184 (18:71).
60   171 (18:58).
61   195 (18:80).
62   147–8 (18:24).
63   144 (18:17).
64   169 (18:55).
65   148 (18:26).
66   197–8 (18:84).
67   147–8 (18:24).

sound, the *material* or *the material cause* of the sacrament is not the earthly or external thing like water or bread but the heavenly thing, regeneration or Christ's body. Causes belonged to Gerhard's method of refutation, but are not basic to presenting his own position. He is more the biblical than scholastic theologian as is evident in his 1610 publication, *Ausfuhrliche schriftmaszige Erklarung der beiden Artikel von der heiligen Taufe und dem heiligen Abendmahl.*[68] Ultimate proof comes from the apostolic words which are not mere opinion but infallible truth.[69]

SACRAMENTS AS DIVINELY COMMANDED

Gerhard's identification of God as 'the efficient principal cause of the Sacraments' is directed against the Council of Trent's assertion that the church in Christ's stead can institute sacraments.[70] Gerhard distinguishes between the institution of the sacraments and what he calls 'publication of their institution'. Baptism originates in Christ's death and is published in Matthew 28:16–20. He approvingly quotes Thomas Aquinas that 'the church of Christ is said to have been made through the sacraments which flowed from the side of Christ as he was hanging on the cross', but 'the publication of this event can be made by somebody else'.[71] Related to the origin of the sacraments in the death of Christ is the church's origin within these sacraments. The church is not constituted by believers coming together to form an assembly but by the sacraments.

AN OCCASION FOR CHRISTOLOGICAL CLARIFICATION

Where Lutherans gave the prominent place in the sacraments to Christ, the Reformed gave a larger role to the Holy Spirit. Specific christological differences surfaced over the relationship of Christ's divine and human natures in his institution of the sacraments. Reformed Christology, with its Nestorian-like separation of the two natures, would be consistent in assigning their institution only to Christ's divine nature and not the human. With their doctrine of the *genus maiestaticum*, Lutherans held that all Christ's divine attributes were given to the human nature and that one nature worked within the other, the *genus apotelesmaticum*. Participation of the human nature in the institution of the Sacrament was no problem for Lutherans, but it was an issue for the Reformed in the 1584 debate at

---

[68]   The original 1610 edition was republished (Berlin: Gustav Schlawitz, 1868).
[69]   173 (18:59).
[70]   148 (18:26).
[71]   Ibid.

Heidelberg. There Grynaeus conceded that both natures participated. This allowed Gerhard to show the inconsistency in Reformed Christology which otherwise did not assign divine attributes to the human nature.[72] For the Reformed the Holy Spirit, rather than the sacraments, bestows God's good things. The Lutherans did not deny a role to the Holy Spirit in the sacraments, even though their strong christological emphasis may have suggested such a denial. In his discussion of the minister's intention in celebrating the sacraments, Gerhard cites Cyprian that the word's power in making the sacrament is that of the Holy Spirit. 'The solemnity of the words, the invocation of the holy name and the signs assigned to the ministry of the priests by the institutions of the apostles celebrate the visible sacrament, but the Holy Spirit fashions and effects the thing itself '.[73]

MINISTERS OF THE SACRAMENTS

Bellarmine accused Luther of holding that lay persons could administer the Sacraments. In response Gerhard held that the institution of the sacraments required that their administrators be ministers as successors to the apostles. By addressing the words of sacramental consecration to the apostles, Christ recognized ministers as the legitimate administrators. 'In regard to baptism and the Lord's Supper, it is clear from the *sedes* of their institution that Christ committed the administration of these sacraments to the apostles and their successors'.[74] Establishing ministers as administrators of the sacraments was part of the institutions of baptism and the Lord's Supper. In the case of impending death a lay person can baptize, but under no circumstances can he administer the Lord's Supper. 'As far as Luther is concerned, he does not simply and absolutely grant to all baptized people the power to administer the Sacraments'.[75] Baptism had a necessity which the eucharist did not.

---

[72] 148–9 (18:27).

[73] 159 (18:40). The Lutheran fear of acceding to the Reformed role of the Spirit in the sacraments may account for the absence of an epiclesis, a prayer to the Spirit in baptism and particularly in the eucharist, which was a general custom in the east.

[74] 149 (18:28).

[75] 148 (18:29). Whether only a clergyman can administer Holy Communion has continued to be debated by Lutherans since the Reformation. Carl Ferdinand Wilhelm Walther (1811–87), the first president of the Missouri Synod of The Lutheran Church — and its most influential theologian, admittedly went against the majority opinion of Lutheran theologians and allowed for lay administration of Holy Communion in cases of emergency. To support his position, Walther cited Johann Gerhard among other theologians. See his *Pastoral Theology*, trans. John M. Drickamer (New Haven, Miss.: Lutheran News, 1995), 134–9. The citation used

As part of the same discussion, Gerhard disavows the Roman position that ordination gives to priests an indelible character which contributes to the validity or efficacy of the sacraments. Bellarmine went so far as to say that some perish everlastingly because they died before receiving priestly absolution.[76] Since the minister is only Christ's instrument, his faith, moral character, understanding and intent about the sacraments do not improve or diminish their efficacy.[77] Gerhard takes over Chrysostom's argument that what God does cannot be perfected by man. This is especially true of the words of Jesus, 'This is my body'.[78] Gerhard approvingly cites Augustine who recognized a baptism administered by Marcion or one secretly harbouring the Arian heresy.[79] Doubt about a minister's intent or faith would leave recipients in uncertainty. 'Christ did not institute a joking baptism nor a baptism of a parrot but a sacred and solemn act of the church. Therefore, because of the institution of Christ a baptism is true and complete if a minister establish this act to the use of the church although he provide not the true intent'.[80] What is determinative of sacramental validity is the church's intent and not that of those who administer or receive the rite.[81] A baptism performed jokingly was never intended as sacrament by those administering or receiving it.

RECIPIENTS OF THE SACRAMENTS

In reaction to placing the eucharist in the mouths of the dead, Gerhard sees only living people as the sacraments' recipients. More importantly he denied the eucharist to baptized children, a custom in place in the Eastern Church but not among Roman Catholics and Protestants. He notes that infant communion was practised by the ancient church, but cites Dionysius, Cyprian, Augustine and Innocent in support of his position in refusing them communion.[82] Gerhard is persuaded the New Testament requires recipients to examine themselves and so concludes children are excluded. Gerhard recognized a certain logic in the

---

by Walther is Gerhard's reference to Johannes Corvinus who argues that since lay persons can baptize they can also administer the Lord's Supper. Walther omits the next sentence in which Gerhard distances himself from Corvinus: *Loci* 5:11–12 (20:17). Lutherans attached a necessity to baptism as the initiating sacrament which they did not attach to the Lord's Supper as the confirming sacrament.

[76] 148 (18:29).
[77] 150–1 (18:30–1).
[78] 158–9 (18:40).
[79] 151 (18:31).
[80] 157–8 (18:38).
[81] 155–6 (18:36).
[82] 160–161 (18:44).

argument for infant communion based on the correlation between baptism and the eucharist and circumcision and the passover: if circumcision made children participants in the passover, they could presumably be given the Holy Communion. But in response he notes that girls were not circumcised, but participated in the passover. Old and New Testament sacraments do not necessarily correspond at each point. Only boys received the sacrament of initiation (circumcision), but both boys and girls received the sacrament of confirmation[83] (passover). So in the New Testament both receive the sacrament of initiation (baptism), but neither the sacrament of confirmation (Lord's Supper). His argument is clear, even if it is not convincing.

FAITH AND THE ESSENCE OF THE SACRAMENTS

As already noted, Gerhard denied that the minister's or the recipient's faith or lack of it adds to or detracts from the sacraments' essence or efficacy. In contrast the Reformed fathers Calvin and Beza incorporated the recipients' faith into their definition of the sacraments. Without faith the outward shells or the external forms of the sacraments remain, but they are no sacraments. Faith becomes a formal cause of the sacraments. For Gerhard faith receives what the sacrament offers, but does not belong to its essence. 'The sacraments do not benefit for righteousness and salvation without faith', but faith does not constitute the sacraments. He argues that if faith belonged to the definition of the sacraments, they could not create and confirm faith.[84]

NECESSITY OF THE SACRAMENTS

The question of the necessity of the sacraments came up in the Council of Trent's condemning what was alleged to be the Lutheran position that salvation was possible by faith alone without the sacraments. Gerhard denies this caricature fits the Lutheran position. Faith was necessary to receive the sacraments' benefits, but it did not belong to their definition and could not be substituted for them. Faith and the sacraments saved but in different ways. Their essences and functions were not interchangeable.

---

[83] By *sacramentum confirmationis* Gerhard means the Lord's Supper and not the rite of confirmation which is administered after baptism in the Eastern Orthodox churches and at puberty in Western churches.

[84] 162 (18:49). To demonstrate the Reformed inclusion of faith in the sacramental definition, he lists several of their theologians: Grynaeus, Piscator, Keckermann, Calvin and Beza.

Sacraments offered salvation, and faith received the salvation they offer. What the sacraments offered, faith received. In his reply to Chemnitz's critique of Trent, Bellarmine mitigated the council's position by asserting that 'no sacraments have an absolute necessity but every necessity for them depends on God's command and institution with a natural congruence connected therewith'.[85] Gerhard finds this acceptable with the understanding that God can work in people through the word. Even Catholic theologians allowed for salvation apart from the sacraments in the case of catechumens martyred before baptism. Gerhard adopts Jerome's position that the despising of baptism and not its lack condemns: 'When one despises the sacraments, he despises God Himself, who is their Creator'. Bernard is also cited. 'It is not the lack but the contempt of the sacraments which condemns'. Gerhard distinguishes between grace and faith, which is absolutely necessary, and the sacraments, which are ordinarily necessary. Unborn and unbaptized infants are among those whom God approaches with salvation apart from baptism. Such children can be sanctified by the name of the Trinity before birth. He also allows for God to work grace in those children who do not hear the gospel because they are savagely killed before birth or as infants.[86] Gerhard moved the discussion from the general necessity of the sacraments to the necessity of each rite. The Lord's Supper is necessary for adults but not for children, an argument not without flaws, as shown above. Baptism is necessary for children, but not in the sense that God is prevented from working salvation by the word in the unborn and those who die before baptism. He also allows this for children of non-practising Christians. Gerhard can speak of a necessity for other rites. He can agree with Bellarmine that ordination is necessary in providing the means of salvation through the ministry and benefits the entire church. A similar necessity can be argued for marriage, but not in the sense that all single persons must be married. Marriage and ordination are neither necessary nor sacraments in the sense that baptism and the Lord's Supper are.[87]

CONCLUSION

The point/counterpoint theological method of the age of Protestant scholasticism clarified differences and produced minimal ambiguity.

---

[85] 164 (18:53).

[86] 164–7 (18:53). Here Gerhard opens the way for a Lutheran response to the fate of aborted children which is an issue in our time.

[87] 167 (18:53). Luther could speak of marriage as a sacrament and put ministry on the same level of baptism and the Lord's Supper. *Luther Works* 1:309 and 53:115. Thus Gerhard is developing ideas intrinsic in Lutheran theology.

Gerhard painstakingly analyzed and answered his opponents' arguments. With Rome his major concern was whether all the rites claimed as sacraments were necessary.[88] Bellarmine conceded that baptism and the Lord's Supper were sacraments in a sense the other rites were not.[89] Gerhard challenged the Reformed view that sacraments were only signs. Paradoxically those who stood in Gerhard's tradition of a high sacramental theology developed a practice in which the sacraments played a minor role.

---

[88]   146 (18:21).
[89]   147 (18:24).

Select Bibliography

Primary Sources

Alsted, Johann Heinrich, *Theologia scholastica didactica, exhibens locos communes theologicos methodo scholastic* (Hanover, 1618)

Ames, William, *Opera* (Amsterdam, 1658)

—, *The Marrow of Theology*, J.D. Eusden (tr.) (Durham: Labyrinth 1983), Archivio Antico dell'Universita di Padova, MS. 651. fols. 29r–65r

Aquinas, Thomas, *Summa Theologiae*

Arminius, Jacob, *Disputationes magnam partem S. theologiae complectentes publicae et privatae* (Leiden, 1610, 1611^2)

—, *Opera Theologica* (Leiden, 1629) [*The Works of James Arminius*, 3 vols. (London, 1828)]

Baillie, Robert, *Letters and Journals*, D. Laing (ed.), 3 vols. (Edinburgh, 1841–2)

[Bannatine, James], *An Essay upon Gospel and Legal Preaching* (Edinburgh, 1723)

Baxter, Richard, *Catholick Theologie* (London, 1675)

—, *Methodus Theologiae* (London, 1681)

—, *Practical Works* 3 (London, 1707)

—, *The Autobiography of Richard Baxter* (Mobile: RE Publications, n.d.)

Beza, Theodore, *Summa totius christianismi, sive descriptio & distributio causarum salutis electorum & exitii reproborum, ex sacris literis collecta* [*Tabula praedestinationis*] (Geneva, 1555)

—, *Confession de la foy chrestienne, contenant la confirmation d'icelle, et la refutation des superstitions contraires* (Geneva, 1558; 1561^2); in modern French: *Confession de foi du chrétien*, Michel Réveillaud (ed. with an intro.) in *La Revue Réformée* VI/23–4 (March and April, 1955), 1–180

—, *De coena Domini, plana et perspicua tractatio. In qua Ioachimi Westphali calumniae postremum editae refelluntur* (Geneva, 1559)

—, *Correspondence de Théodore de Bèze* (Geneva: Droz, 1960–)

—, *Autre brieve confession de foy* (Geneva, 1561)

—, *Tractationes theologicae*, 3 vols. (Geneva, 1570–82)

—, *The Life of John Calvin*, Francis Gibson (tr.), (Philadelphia, 1836)

Biddle, John, *A Twofold Catechism* (London, 1654)

Biel, Gabriel, *Epithoma pariter et collectorium circa quattuor sententiarum libros* (Tübingen, 1501)

Binning, Hugh, *The Works of the Pious, Reverend, and Learn'd Mr. Hugh Binning, Late Minister of the Gospel at Govan* (Glasgow, 1768[2])

Boston, Thomas, *The Complete Works of the Late Rev. Thomas Boston of Ettrick*, Samuel McMillan (ed.), 12 vols. (London: Robert Tegg, 1853 / Wheaton, Ill.: Richard Owen Roberts, 1980)

—, 'MSS of Thomas Boston of Ettrick' in 'Sermons and related writings of Thomas Boston, James Fisher, John Brown and other members of the United Free Church of Scotland 1699–1851', Department of Special Collections and Archives, Aberdeen University Library, King's College, MS.3245/2, 62–8

Boyd, Robert (of Trochrigg), *In Epistolam Pauli Apostoli ad Ephesios Praelectiones supra CC* (London, 1652)

à Brakel, Wilhelmus, *De Redelijke Godsdienst* [The Christian's Reasonable Service], Bartel Elshout (tr.), 4 vols. (Morgan, Pa.: Soli Deo Gloria, 1992–5)

Brandt, Gerard (Geeraert), *The History of the Reformation and Other Ecclesiastical Transactions in and about the Low Countries*, J. Chamberlayne (tr.), 4 vols. (London, 1720)

Brown, John (of Wamphray), *De Causa Dei contra Antisabbatarios*, 2 vols. (Rotterdam, 1674–6)

—, *The Life of Justification Opened* (Holland, 1695)

Brown, John (of Whitburn), *Gospel Truth Accurately Stated and Illustrated* (Glasgow 1831[rev.])

Bullinger, H., *Studiorum ratio* (Zurich, 1527), 128–33

Burnet, Gilbert, *Some letters, containing an account of what seemed most remarkable in travelling through Switzerland, Italy, some parts of Germany, &c. in the years 1685 and 1686* (Rotterdam, 1687)

Calderwood, David, *Altare Damascenum; seu, Ecclesiae Anglicanae Politia, Ecclesiae Scoticanae obtrusa, a Formalista quodam delineata, Illustrata et Examinata* (Leyden, 1708)

Calvin, John, *Joannis Calvini Opera Quae Superunt Omnia*, G. Baum et al. (eds.), *Corpus Reformatorum*, vols. 29–87 (Braunschweig and Berlin, 1853–1900)

—, *Dilucida explicatio sanae doctrinae de vera participatione carnis et sanguinis Christi in sacra coena ad discutiendas Heshusii nebulas* (Geneva, 1561)

—, *Institutio Christianae Religionis* [*Calvin: Institutes of the Christian Religion*], J.T. McNeill (ed.), Ford Lewis Battles (tr.), Library of Christian Classics, vols 20–1 (Philadelphia: Westminster, 1960 / London: SCM, 1961)

—, *Calvin's New Testament Commentaries: Galatians, Ephesians, Philippians and Colossians*, D.W. Torrance and T.F. Torrance (eds.), T.H.L. Parker (tr.), (Grand Rapids: Eerdmans, 1965)

—, *Iohannis Calvini Commentarius in Epistolam Pauli ad Romanos*, T.H.L. Parker (ed.), (Leiden: E.J. Brill, 1981)

—, *Treatises Against the Anabaptists and Against the Libertines*, Benjamin Farley (tr. and ed.), (Grand Rapids: Baker, 1982)

—, *The Bondage and Liberation of the Will: A Defense of the Orthodox Doctrine of Human Choice against Pighius*, A.N.S. Lane (ed.), G.I. Davies (tr.), Texts and Studies in Reformation and Post-Reformation Thought 2 (Grand Rapids: Baker, 1996)

Cameron, John, *Ioannis Cameronis Scoto-Britanni Theologi Eximii. [Ta sozomena]; sive, Opera Partim ab Auctore Ipso Edita, partim post eius obitum vulgata, partim nusquam hactenus publicata, vel e Gallico Idiomate nunc primum in Latinam linguam translata* (Geneva, 1642)

Campanella, Tommaso, *Metaphysica*. Facsimile of the 1638 Paris edition [*Works*], Luigi Firpo (ed.), (Turin: Bottega d'Erasmo, 1961)

Chemnitz, Martin, *Loci theologici Domini Martini Chemnitii, theologi longe celeberrimi, atque ecclesiae Brunsvicensis quondam superintendentis fidelissimi: quibus et loci communes Domini Philippi Melanchthonis perspicue explicantur, & quasi integrum Christianae doctrinae corpus, Ecclesiae Dei sincere proponitur*, Polycarp Leyser (ed.), (Frankfurt and Wittenberg: Tobias Mevius and Elerd Schumacher, 1653)

Clarke, Samuel, *The Lives of Thirty-Two Eminent Divines* (London, 1677)

Constantius, M. Anton [Stephen Gardiner], *Confutatio cavillationum . . . a impiis Capernaitis* (Paris, 1552)

de Courcelles, Stephen (Courcellaeus), *St. Curcellaeus opera theologica* (Amsterdam, 1675)

Descartes, Renée, 'Meditation III' in idem, *The Philosophical Works of Descartes 1*, E.S. Haldane and G.T. Ross (eds.), (Cambridge: Cambridge University Press, 1970), 157–71

Durham, James, *The Great Corruption of Subtile Self, Discovered, and Driven from it's Lurking-places and Starting-holes* (Edinburgh, 1686)

—, *Christ Crucify'd: or, The Marrow of the Gospel* (London, 1723)

—, *The Unsearchable Riches of Christ, and of Grace and Glory in and through HIM* (Edinburgh, 1729)

—, *Heaven upon Earth* (Edinburgh, 1732)

Eck, Johann, *In primum librum Sententiarum annotatiumculae*, Walter Moore (ed.), (Leiden: Brill 1976)

Episcopius, Simon, *Confessio sive declaratio sententiae pastorum, qui in foederato Belgio Remonstrantes vocantur, super praecipuos articulos religionis Christianae* (n.p., 1622)

—, *Apologia pro Confessione . . . contra Censuram quatuor professorum Leidensium* (n.p., 1630)

—, *Opera Theologica*, 2 vols. (1: Etienne de Courcelles (Curcellaeus) (ed.), Amsterdam, 1650; 2: Philip van Limborch and Arnold Poelenburg (eds.), Rotterdam, 1665)

Essenius, Andreas, *Compendium Theologiae Dogmaticum* (Utrecht, 1685^2)

Flint, John, *Examen Doctrinae D: Johannis Simson, S.S.T. In Celebri Academia Glasguensi Professoris* (Edinburgh, 1717)

Fuller, Thomas, *The Holy State and The Profane State* (London: J. Nichols, 1841)

Gerhard, John, *Loci Theologici*, E. Preuss (ed.), (Berlin: Gustaf Schlawitz, 1866)

—, *The Theological Commonplaces of John Gerhard*, Richard J. Dinda (tr.), typescript and microfiche (St Louis, Miss.: Concordia, 1981)

Gillespie, George, *Aaron's Rod Blossoming; or, The Divine Ordinance of Church-Government Vindicated* (London, 1646)

Gregory of Rimini, *Gregorii Ariminesis, OESA Lectura Super Primum et Secundum Sententiarum*, Damasus Trapp and Venicio Marcolino (eds.), 7 vols. (Berlin 1979–87)

Grotius, Hugo, *De Veritate Religionis Christianae* (Leiden, 1627)

—, *De Jure Belli ac Pacis* (1631, 1642)

—, *Briefwisseling van Hugo Grotius* 1 (The Hague: Nijhoff, 1929)

—, *Briefwisseling van Hugo Grotius*, B.L. Meulenbroek (ed.), (The Hague: Nijhoff, 1940)

Hadow, James, *The Antinomianism of the Marrow of Modern Divinity Detected* (Edinburgh, 1722)

Hales, John, *Golden Remains of the Ever Memorable Mr. John Hales* (London, 1659; 1673[2])

—, *The Works of the Ever Memorable Mr. John Hales of Eton*, 3 vols. (Glasgow, 1765)

Hall, Joseph, *Acta synodi nationalis Dordrechti habitae* (Leiden, 1620)

[Hog, James], *The Controversie concerning the Marrow of Modern Divinity. Considered in several familiar Dialogues. Dialogue I* (Edinburgh, 1721), especially 80–105

Hoornbeeck, Joannes, *Theologiae practicae* (Utrecht, 1663)

Hyperius, Andreas, *De formandis concionibus sacris, seu de interpretatione scripturarum populari, libri II* (Marburg, 1553)

—, *De recte formando theologiae studio, libri IIII* (Basel, 1556)

—, *Methodi theologiae, sive praecipuorum christianae religionis locorum communium libri tres* (Basel 1567)

de La Faye, Antoine, *Theses Theologicae in schola Genevensi ab aliquot sacrarum literarum studiosis sub DD. Theod. Beza and Antonio Fayo S.S. theologiae professoribus propositae et disputatae. In quibus methodica locorum communium S.S. theologiae epitome continetur* (Geneva, 1586) [Propositions and Principles of Divinitie propounded and disputed in the universitie of Geneva, by certaine students of Divinitie there, under M. Theod. Beza, and M. Anthonie Faius, professors of Divinitie (Edinburgh, 1591)]

Leighton, Robert, *The Whole Works of the Most Reverend Father in God, Robert Leighton, D.D., Archbishop of Glasgow*, 2 vols. (London, 1828)

Lombard, Peter, *see* Peter Lombard

Luther, Martin, *D. Martin Luthers Werke: Kritische Gesamtausgabe*, J.C.F. Knaake (ed.), 58 vols. (Weimar: Böhlau, 1883–1948)

—, *D. Martin Luthers Werke: Kritische Gesamtausgabe: Tischreden*, 6 vols. (Weimar: Böhlau, 1912–21)

—, *D. Martin Luthers Werke: Kritische Gesamtausgabe: Briefwechsel*, 12 vols. (Weimar: Böhlau, 1930–67)

Martinius, Matthias, *Methodus S.S. theologiae* (Herborn, 1603)

McClaren, John, *The New Scheme of Doctrine Contained in the Answers of Mr. John Simson, Professor of Divinity in the College of Glasgow; to Mr. Webster's Libel, Considered and Examined* (Edinburgh, 1717)

Melanchthon, Philip, *Philippi Melanchthonis De Rhetorica Libri Tres* (Basel: Johannes Frobenius, May 1519)

—, *Loci Communes* (1535)

—, *Loci praecipua theologici* (1559) in Jacob A.O. Preus (tr.), *Loci Communes 1543 Philip Melanchthon* (St Louis: Concordia, 1992)

—, *Philippi Melanchthonis Opera quae Supersunt Omnia, Corpus Reformatorum*, Karl Gottlieb Bretschneider and Heinrich Bindseil (eds.), vols. 1–28 (Halle: Schwetschke, 1834–)

—, *Melanchthons Werke in Auswahl*, Studienausgabe, Robert Stupperich (ed.), 8 vols. (Gütersloh: Bertelsmann, 1951–)

—, *Melanchthons Werke in Auswahl*, G. Ebeling and R. Schafer (eds.), (Gütersloh: Bertelsmann, 1965)

—, *Melanchthons Briefwechsel. Kritische und kommentierte Gesamtausgabe*, Heinz Scheible et al. (eds.), 8 vols. (Stuttgart-Bad Cannstatt: Frommann-Holzboog, 1977)

Olevianus, Caspar, *Expositio symboli apostolici* (Frankfurt, 1576)

—, *A Firm Foundation: An Aid to Interpreting the Heidelberg Catechism*, L.D. Bierma (ed. and tr.), Texts and Studies in Reformation and Post-Reformation Thought 1 (Grand Rapids: Baker, 1995)

Owen, John, *The Works of John Owen*, 24 vols. (Edinburgh: T. & T. Clark, 1862)

Pareus, David, *Libri Duo: I. Calvinus Orthodoxus de Sacrosancta Trinitate: et de aeterna Christi Divinitate. II. Solida Expositio XXXIIX. Difficilimorum Scripturae Locorum et Oraculorum: et derecta ratione applicandi Oracula Prophetica ad Christum. Oppositi Pseudocalvino Iudaizanti nuper a quodam emisso* (Neustadt: Matthaeus Harnisch, 1595)

—, *Explicationes catecheseos* (1591–1608) in Reuter, *Ursini . . . opera theologica* 1 (Heidelberg, 1612)

—, *Corpus doctrinae orthodoxae* (1612, 1616)

—, *Corpus doctrinae Christianae* (Hannover, 1634) [The Commentary of Dr. Zacharias Ursinus on the Heidelberg Catechism], G.W. Williard (tr.), (1851; Grand Rapids: Eerdmans, 1954)

Perkins, William, *Workes*, 3 vols. (Cambridge, 1608–9)

Peter Lombard, *Magistri Petri Lombardi Sententiae in IV Libris Distinctae*, Ignatius Brady (ed.), Spicilegium Bonaventurianum 5 (Grottaferrata, 1981)

Peter Martyr Vermigli, *Loci communes*

—, *In selectissimam S. Pauli Priorem ad Corinth. Epistolam Commentarij . . .* (Zurich, 1551)

—, *In Epistolam S. Pauli Apostoli ad Romanos commentarii doctissimi* (Basel, 1558)

—, *Defensio Doctrinae veteris & Apostolicae de sacrosancto Eucharistiae Sacramento . . . adversus Stephani Gardineri . . . librum* (Zurich, 1559)

—, *In primum, secundum, et initium tertii libri Ethicorum Aristotelis ad Nichomachum . . . Commentarius doctissimus* (Zurich, 1563)

—, *Exhortatio ad iuventutem, in Loci Communes* (London, 1583)

—, *Dialogue on the Two Natures of Christ*, John Patrick Donnelly (tr.), Sixteenth Century Essays and Studies 31 (Kirksville, Mo.: Sixteenth Century Journal, 1995)

Pictet, Benedict, 'Oratio funebris de vita atque obitu Francisci Turrettini; Habita die iii Novemb. an. M.DC.LXXXVII' in *Francisci Turrettini Opera* 1 (New York: Robert Carter, 1847–8), xxix–xlviii

—, 'Funeral Oration', David Lillegard (tr.) in Francis Turretin, *Institutes* 3, 659–76

Pighius, Albertus, *De libero hominis arbitrio et divina gratia* (Cologne, 1542)

Piscator, Johannes, *Aphorismi doctrinae Christianae maximam partem ex Institutione Calvini excerpti, sive Loci Communes theologici brevibus sententiis expositi* (Herborn, 1589)

—, *Animadversiones . . . in Dialecticam P. Rami* (Frankfurt, 1582)

Polyander, J. et al., *Censura in Confessionem sive declarationem sententiae eorum qui in foederato Belgio Remonstrantes vocantur* (Leiden, 1626)

Riccaltoun, Robert, *The Politick Disputant; or, Choice Instructions for quashing a Stubborn Adversary* (Edinburgh, 1722)

Rijssenius, Leonardus, *Summa Theologiae Elencticae* (Edinburgh, 1692)

Rutherford, Samuel, *Exercitationes Apologeticae pro Divina Gratia* (Amsterdam, 1636)

—, *Due Right of Presbyteries; or, A Peaceable Plea for the Government of the Church of Scotland* (London, 1644)

—, *Lex, Rex; or, The Law and the Prince; A Dispute for the Just Prerogative of King and People* (Edinburgh, 1644)

—, *Tryal and Triumph of Faith; or, An Exposition of the History of Christs dispossessing of the daughter of the woman of Canaan* (London, 1645)

—, *Christ Dying, and Drawing Sinners to Himself* (London, 1647)

—, *A Survey of the Spirituall Antichrist* (London, 1648)

—, *Disputatio Scholastica De Divina Providentia* (Edinburgh, 1649)

—, *Influences of the Life of Grace* (London, 1659)

—, *Examen Arminianismi* (Utrecht, 1668)

—, *Mr. Rutherfoord's Letters, Now Divided into Three Parts* (Edinburgh, 1761[6])

Saladin, Michel-Jean-Louis, *Memoire historique sur la vie les ouvrages de Jacob Vernet, ministre de l'Eglise, accompagné de l'Invocation aux Muses', de Montisquieu, et de plusieurs lettres J.-J. Rousseau et Voltaire, qui n'ont pas encore été publiées* (Paris, 1790)

Schulting, Cornelius, *Bibliothecae catholicae et orthodoxae*

Sharp, John, *Cursus Theologicus, in quo Controversiae Omnes de Fidei Dogmatibus, hoc seculo Exagitatae inter nos et Pontificios, pertractantur; et ad Bellarmini argumenta respondetur*, corr. ed. (Geneva, 1628)

Simler, Josiah, *Oratio de vita et obitu viri optimi, praestantissimi Theologi D. Petri Martyris Vermilii . . .* (Zurich, 1562)

Socinus, F., *Praelectiones theologicae* (Racow, 1609)

Sohn, Georg, *Opera* (Herborn, 1609)

Timpler, Clemens, *Metaphysicae Systema Methodicum* (Steinfurt, 1604)

Turretin, Francis, *Institutio Theologiae Elencticae*, 3 vols. (Geneva, 1688–9)

—, *Institutes of Elenctic Theology*, James T Dennison Jr. (ed.), M. Giger George (tr.), (Phillipsburg, N.J.: P and R, 1992–6)

Turretin, Jean-Alphonse, *Dilucidationes philosophico-theologico-morales, quibus praecipua capita tam theologiae naturalis, quam revelatae demonstrantur ad praxin christianam commendantur accedunt*, 3 vols. (Basel: J.R. Imhoff, 1748)

—, *Opera omnia theologica, philosophica et philologica*, 3 vols. (Franeker: H.A. de Chalmot et D. Romar, 1774–6)

—, 'Discourse on Fundamental Articles in Religion' in Jared Sparks (ed.), *A Collection of Essays and Tracts in Theology from Various Authors with Biographical and Critical Notices* 1 (Boston: Oliver Everett, 1823), 7–91

Twisse, William, *A Discovery of D. Jacksons Vanitie* (London, 1631)

Uitenbogaert, Johannes, *Noodighe Antwoordt op der Contra-Remonstranten Tegen-Vertooch* (The Hague, 1617)

Ursinus, Zacharias, *Doctrinae Christianae Compendium* (Geneva, Leiden, 1584; Cambridge, 1585; London, 1586)

—, *Volumen Tractationum theologicarum* (1584; reprint, Neustadt: Harnisch, 1587)

—, *Explicationum catecheticarum* (Neustadt, 1585; Cambridge, 1587)

—, *Explicationes Catecheticae*, David Pareus (ed.), (1591) [Het Schat-Boeck der Christelycke Leere ofte Uytlegginghe over den Catechismus], Festus Hommius (tr.), (Leiden, 1602)

—, *Ursini . . . opera theologica* (Heidelberg, 1612)

—, *Corpus doctrinae orthodoxae* (Heildelberg, 1612, 1616)

—, *Corpus doctrinae Christianae* (Heildelberg, 1621, 1623, 1634, 1651)

Van Limborch, Philip, *Theologia Christiana* (Amsterdam 1700^3) [*A Compleat System or Body of Divinity*] (London, 1713)

Vermigli, Peter Martyr, *see* Peter Martyr Vermigli

Vernet, Jacob, *Deux Lettres à Monsieur l'abbé ****, Chanoine de Notre Dame de Paris* (Geneva, 1725)

—, *Défense des Deux Lettres Adressés à Mr. ***, Chanoine de Notre Dame* (Geneva, 1727)

—, *Traité de la vérité de la religion chrétienne. Tiré du latin de Mr. J. Alphonse Turretin* (Geneva: M.M. Bousquet, 1730–47)

—, *Instruction chrétienne*, 5 vols. (Geneva: Henri-Albert Gosse, 1756)

—, *Lettres Critiques d'un Voyageur Anglais sur l'Article Genève du Dictionaire Encyclopedique; & sur La Lettre de Mr. d'Alembert à Mr. Rousseau* (Utrecht: J.C. Ten Bosch, 1759)

—, *Réflexions sur les moeurs, sur la religion et sur le culte* (Geneva, 1769)

Voetius, Gisbert, *Catechisatie over den catechismus der Remonstranten* (Utrecht, 1641)

—, *Geestelijke Verlatingen* (Utrecht, 1646)

—, *Disputationes selectae theologicae* 1 (Utrecht, 1648)

—, *Selectarum disputationum theologicarum*, 5 vols. (Amsterdam, 1648–69)

—, *Te asketika sive exercitia pietatis* (Gorinchem, 1654) [De Praktijk der Godzaligheid met inleiding, vertaling en commentaar], Cornelis Adrianus de Niet (ed.), 2 vols. (Utrecht: De Banier, 1996)

—, *Proeve van de Kracht der Godzaligheydt* (Utrecht, 1656)

—, *Politicae ecclesiasticae*, 4 vols. (Amsterdam, 1663–76)

Vorstius, Conrad, *Tractatus theologicus de Deo sive de nature et attributis Dei* (Steinfurt, 1606)

—, *Apologetica exegesis sive plenior declaratio locorum aliquot ex libro eiusdem de Deo . . . excerpta, eique pro erroneis imposita* (Leiden, 1611)

Zanchius, H., *Operum Theologicorum*, 8 vols. (Geneva, 1617)

Zepper, Wilhelm, *Politia ecclesiastica* (1595; Herborn, 1607)

—, *Ars habendi et audiendi conciones sacras* (Siegen, 1598)

Secondary Sources

Adams, Geoffrey, *The Huguenots and French Opinion 1685–1787: The Enlightenment Debate on Toleration* (Waterloo: Wilfrid Laurier University Press, 1991)

Althaus, Paul, *Die Prinzipien der deutschen reformierten Dogmatik im Zeitalter der aristotelischen Scholastik* (Leipzig: Deichertsche, 1914; Darmstadt: Wissenschaftliche Buchgesellschaft, 1967[2])

van Andel, H.A., *De zendingsleer van Gisbertus Voetius* (Kampen: Kok, 1912)

Armstrong, Brian G., *Calvinism and the Amyraut Heresy: Protestant Scholasticism and Humanism in Seventeenth-Century France* (Madison: University of Wisconsin Press, 1969)

van Asselt, Willem J., 'Herwaardering van de gereformeerde scholastiek', *Kerktijd* 7 (1995), 1–12

—, *Vera philosophia cum sacra theologia nusquam pugnat: Een inleiding in de Gereformeerde Scholastiek* (Utrecht, 1995)

van Asselt, W.J. and E. Dekker (eds.), *De scholastieke Voetius: Een luisteroefening aan de hand van Voetius' 'Disputationes Selectae'* (Zoetermeer: Boekencentrum, 1995)

Bagchi, David V.N., *Luther's Earliest Opponents: Catholic Controversialists, 1518–1525* (Minneapolis: Fortress Press, 1991)

—, 'Diversity or Disunity? A Reformation Controversy Over Communion in Both Kinds' in R.N. Swanson (ed.), *Unity and Diversity in the Church*, Studies in Church History 32 (Oxford: Blackwell, 1996), 207–19

Baker, J. Wayne, *Heinrich Bullinger and the Covenant: The Other Reformed Tradition* (Athens, Ohio: Ohio University Press, 1980)

Bangs, C., *Arminius: A Study in the Dutch Reformation* (Nashville: Abingdon, 1971)

Barth, Karl, *Church Dogmatics*, 13 vols., G.W. Bromiley and T.F. Torrance (eds.), G.W. Bromiley (tr.), (Edinburgh: T. & T. Clark, 1956)

Bauer, C., 'Melanchthons Naturrechtslehre', *Archiv für Reformationsgeschichte* 4 (1951), 64–100

Bauer, Karl, *Die Wittenberger Universitätstheologie und die Anfänge der deutschen Reformation* (Tübingen: J.C.B. Mohr (Paul Siebeck), 1928)

Beardslee III, John W., 'Theological Developments at Geneva under Francis and Jean-Alphonse Turretin' (PhD diss., Yale University, 1956)

—, *Reformed Dogmatics: Seventeenth-Century Reformed Theology Through the Writings of Wollebius, Voetius, and Turretin,* (ed. and tr.), (New York: Oxford University Press, 1965)

Beeke, Joel R., *Assurance of Faith: Calvin, English Puritanism, and the Dutch Second Reformation* (New York: Peter Lang, 1991)

—, 'Faith and Reassurance in the Heidelberg Catechism and Its Primary Composers: A Fresh Look at the Kendall Thesis', *Calvin Theolgical Journal* 27 (1992), 45–7

Bell, Michael, 'Propter Potestatem, Scientiam, Ac Beneplacitum Dei: The Doctrine of the Object of Predestination in the Theology of Johannes Maccovius', (ThD diss., Westminster Theological Seminary, 1986)

Bell, M. Charles, *Calvin and Scottish Theology: The Doctrine of Assurance* (Edinburgh: Handsel Press, 1985)

Berti, Silvia, 'At the Roots of Unbelief', *Journal of the History of Ideas* 56 (1995), 558f.

Bierma, Lyle D., 'The Covenant Theology of Caspar Olevian', (PhD diss., Duke University, 1980)

—, 'Federal Theology in the Sixteenth Century: Two Traditions?', *Westminster Theological Journal* 45 (1983), 304–21

—, 'The Role of Covenant Theology in Early Reformed Orthodoxy', *Sixteenth Century Journal* 21 (1990), 458–9

—, *German Calvinism in the Confessional Age: The Covenant Theology of Caspar Olevianus* (Durham, N.C.: Labyrinth, 1996)

Biesterveld, P., *Andreas Hyperius, voornamelijk als Homileet* (Kampen: Zalsman, 1895)

Bizer, Ernst, *Frühorthodoxie und Rationalismus* (Zurich: EVZ, 1963)

Boehm, L., 'Humanistische Bildungsbewegungen und mittelalterliche Universitätsverfassung: Aspekte zur frühneuzeitlichen Reformgeschichte der deutschen Universitäten' in J. Ijsewijn (ed.), *The Universities of the Late Middle Ages* (Louvain: Leuven University Press, 1978)

Boersma, H., *A Hot Peppercorn: Richard Baxter's Doctrine of Justification in Its Seventeenth-Century Context of Controversy* (Zoetermeer: Boekencentrum, 1993)

Bonansea, B.M., *Tommaso Campanella: Renaissance Pioneer of Modern Thought* (Washington: Catholic University of America Press, 1969)

Boot, Izaak, *De Allegorische Uitlegging van Het Hooglied Voornamelijk in Nederland* (Woerden: Zuijderduijn, 1971)

Boughton, Lynne C., 'Supralapsarianism and the Role of Metaphysics in Sixteenth-Century Reformed Theology', *Westminster Theological Journal* 48 (1986), 63–96

Bouwman, Marinus, *Voetius over het gezag der Synoden* (Amsterdam: S.J.P. Bakker, 1937)

Bouwmeester, G., *Zacharias Ursinus en de Heidelbergse Catechismus* (The Hague: Willem de Zwijgerstichting, 1954)

Bouwsma, William J., 'The Two Faces of Humanism' in H.A. Oberman and T.A. Brady (eds.), *Itinerarium Italicum: The Profile of the Italian Renaissance in the Mirror of its European Transformations* (Leiden: E.J. Brill, 1975), 3–61

——, *John Calvin: A Sixteenth-Century Portrait* (New York: Oxford University Press, 1988)

Bozeman, Theodore Dwight, *To Live Ancient Lives* (Chapel Hill: University of North Carolina Press, 1988)

Brachlow, Stephen, *The Communion of Saints* (Oxford: Oxford University Press, 1988)

Breen, Quirinius, *Christianity and Humanism: Studies in the History of Ideas* (Grand Rapids: Eerdmans, 1968)

——, 'The Terms "Loci Communes" and "Loci" in Melanchthon' in idem, *Christianity and Humanism: Studies in the History of Ideas* (Grand Rapids: Eerdmans, 1968), 93–105

Broeyer, F.G.M., 'William III and the Church in Utrecht after the French Occupation' in J. van den Berg and P.G. Hoftijzer (eds.), *Church, Change and Revolution* (Leiden: E.J. Brill, 1991)

Bruggink, Donald J., 'The Theology of Thomas Boston, 1676–1732', (unpubl. doctoral thesis, University of Edinburgh, 1956)

de Budé, Eugène, *Vie de Bénédict Pictet, théologien genevois (1655–1724)* (Lausanne: Georges Bridel, 1874)

——, *Vie de J.A. Turrettini, théologien genevois (1671–1737)* (Lausanne: Georges Bridel, 1880)

——, *Lettres inédites adressés de 1686–1737 . . . J.A. Turrettini, théologien genevois*, 3 vols. (Geneva: Jules Carey, 1887)

——, *Vie de Jacob Vernet, théologien genevois (1698–1789)* (Lausanne, 1893)

Burchill, C.J., 'Girolamo Zanchi: Portrait of a Reformed Theologian and His Work', *Sixteenth Century Journal* 15 (1984), 185–207

——, 'On the Consolation of a Christian Scholar: Zacharias Ursinus (1534–83) and the Reformation in Heidelberg', *Journal of Ecclesiastical History* 37 (1986), 565–83

Champion, J.A.I., *The Pillars of Priestcraft Shaken: The Church of England and Its Enemies, 1660–1730* (Cambridge and New York: Cambridge University Press, 1992)

Clifford, A.C., *Atonement and Justification: English Evangelical Theology 1640–1790, an Evaluation* (Oxford: Clarendon Press, 1990)

Cobban, A.B., *The Medieval Universities: Their Development and Organization* (London: Methuen, 1975)

Collinson, Patrick, *The Elizabethan Puritan Movement* (Oxford: Clarendon Press, 1967)

——, *The Religion of Protestants* (Oxford: Clarendon Press, 1982)

Corda, Salvatore, *Veritas Sacramenti: A Study in Vermigli's Doctrine of the Lord's Supper* (Zurich: Theologischer, 1975)

Costello, William, *The Scholastic Curriculum in Early Seventeenth Century Cambridge* (Cambridge, Mass.: Harvard University Press, 1959)

Courtenay, William J., 'Covenant and Causality in Pierre d'Ailly', *Speculum* 46 (1971), 94–119

—, 'The King and the Leaden Coin: The Economic Background of Sine Qua Non Causality', *Traditio* 28 (1972), 185–209

Crame, Jan Anthony, *De theologische faculteit te Utrecht den tijde van Voetius* (Utrecht: Kemink, 1932)

Crawford, Michael J., *Seasons of Grace: Colonial New England's Revival Tradition in its British Context* (Oxford: Oxford University Press, 1991)

Curtis, Mark, *Oxford and Cambridge in Transition, 1558–1640* (Oxford: Clarendon Press, 1959)

Dantine, Johannes, 'Das christologische Problem in Rahmen der Prädestinationslehre von Theodor Beza', *Zeitschrift für Kirchengeschichte* LXXVII (1966), 81–96

—, 'Les Tabelles sur la doctrine de la prédestination par Théodore de Bèze', *Revue de théologie et de philosophie* XVI (1966), 365–77

Dekker, Eef, 'Jacobus Arminius and His Logic: Analysis of a Letter', *Journal of Theological Studies* 44 (1993), 118–42

Dever, Mark, 'Richard Sibbes and "The Truly Evangelicall Church of England": A Study in Reformed Divinity and Early Stuart Conformity', (PhD diss., University of Cambridge, 1992)

Diemer, N., *Het scheppingsverbond met Adam (het verbond der werken) bij de theologen der 16e, 17e en 18e eeuw in Zwitserland, Duitschland, Nederland en Engeland* (Kampen: J.H. Kok, 1935)

Dijk, K., *De Strijd over Infra- en Supralapsarisme in de Gereformeerde Kerken van Nederland* (Kampen: Kok, 1912)

Donnelly, John Patrick, *Calvinism and Scholasticism in Vermigli's Doctrine of Man and Grace* (Leiden: E.J. Brill, 1976)

—, 'Calvinist Thomism', *Viator* 7 (1976), 441–5

—, 'The Social and Ethical Thought of Peter Martyr Vermigli' in J.C. McLelland (ed.), *Peter Martyr and Italian Reform* (1980)

—, 'Immortality and Method in Ursinus' Theological Ambiance' in Derk Visser (ed.), *Controversy and Conciliation* (1986)

Dowey, Edward A., *The Knowledge of God in Calvin's Theology* (New York: Columbia University Press, 1952; Grand Rapids: Eerdmans, 1995[3])

Drummond, Andrew L., *The Kirk and the Continent* (Edinburgh: Saint Andrew Press, 1956)

Duffy, Eamon, 'Correspondence Fraternelle: The SPCK, the SPG, and the Churches of Switzerland in the War of Spanish Succession' in Derek Baker (ed.), *Reform and Reformation: England and the Continent c.1500–c.1750* (Oxford: Blackwell, 1979), 256–7

—, *The Stripping of the Altars: Traditional Religion in England 1400–1580* (New Haven and London: Yale University Press, 1992)

Duker, Arnold, Cornelius, *Gisbertus Voetius*, 3 vols. (Leiden: E.J. Brill, 1897–1914)

Ebeling, Gerhard, 'The Hermeneutical Locus of the Doctrine of God in Peter Lombard and Thomas Aquinas' in Ernst Käsemann et al., *Distinctive Protestant and Catholic Themes Reconsidered* (New York: Harper and Row, 1967)

Eckermann, W., 'Die Aristoteleskritik Luthers: Ihre Bedeutung für seine Theologie', *Catholica* 32 (1978), 114–30

Elert, Werner, 'Humanität und Kirche. Zum 450. Geburtstag Melanchthons' (1947) in *Zwischen Gnade und Ungnade: Abwandlungen des Themas Gesetz und Evangelium* (Munich: Evangelischer Presseverband für Bayern, 1948), 92–113

Elson, James Hinsdale, *John Hales of Eton* (New York: Kings Crown, 1948)

Emerson, Roger L., 'Scottish Universities in the Eighteenth Century, 1690–1800' in James A. Leith (ed.), *Studies on Voltaire and the Eighteenth Century* 167 (Oxford: The Voltaire Foundation at the Taylor Institution, 1977), 453–74

Farthing, John L., *Thomas Aquinas and Gabriel Biel: Interpretations of St Thomas Aquinas in German Nominalism on the Eve of the Reformation* (Durham, N.C.: Duke University Press, 1988)

—, '*De coniugio spirituali*: Jerome Zanchi on Ephesians 5:22–33', *Sixteenth Century Journal* 24 (1993), 621–52

—, 'Christ and the Eschaton: The Reformed Eschatology of Jerome Zanchi' in W.F. Graham (ed.), *Later Calvinism* (1994), 333–54

—, '*Foedus evangelicum*: Jerome Zanchi on the Covenant', *Calvin Theological Journal* 29 (1994), 149–67

—, 'Holy Harlotry: Jerome Zanchi and the Exegetical History of Gomer (Hosea 1–3)' in Muller and Thompson (eds.), *Biblical Interpretation in the Era of the Reformation*, 292–312

Fatio, Olivier, 'L'église de Genève et la révocation de l'édit de Nantes' in *Genève au temps de la révocation de l'édit de Nantes 1680–1705* (Geneva: Droz, 1985), 161–96

Fatio, Olivier and & Pierre Fraenkel (eds.), *Histoire de l'exégèse au XVIe siècle* (Geneva: Droz, 1978)

Fazy, Henri, *Procès de Jérôme Bolsec publié d'après les documents originaux* in *Mémoires de l'Institut nationale genevois* 10 (1865), 3–74

Fenlon, D., *Heresy and Obedience in Tridentine Italy: Cardinal Pole and the Counter-Reformation* (Cambridge: Cambridge University Press, 1972)

Fisher, G.P., 'The Theology of Richard Baxter' and 'The Writings of Richard Baxter', *Bibliotheca Sacra and American Biblical Repository* 9 (1852), 135–69, 300–29

Flinn, Michael (ed.), *Scottish Population History from the 17th Century to the 1930s* (Cambridge: Cambridge University Press, 1977)

Fraenkel, Pierre, *De l'Écriture à la dispute* (Lausanne: Revue de theologie et de philosophie, 1977)

Gaberel, Jean Pierre, *Histoire de l'Eglise de Genève depuis le commencement de la réformation jusqu'à nos jours* (Geneva: J. Cherbuliez, 1855–62)

—, *Voltaire et les Genevois* (1857)

—, 'Jacob Vernet et ses relations contemporaines', *Etrennes religieuses*, xxxiv (1883), 120–41

Gamble, Richard, 'Brevitas et facilitas: Toward an Understanding of Calvin's Hermeneutic', *Westminster Theological Journal* 47 (1985), 1–17

Ganoczy, Alexandre, *La Bibliothèque de l'Académie de Calvin* (Geneva: Droz, 1969)

—, *The Young Calvin*, David Foxgrover and Wade Provo (tr.), (Philadelphia: Westminster, 1987)

Gargett, Graham, *Jacob Vernet, Geneva and the Philosophes* (Oxford: Voltaire Foundation, 1995)

Gay, Peter, *The Enlightenment. An Interpretation: The Rise of Modern Paganism* (New York: Alfred A. Knopf, 1975)

Geizendorf, Paul F., *Théodore de Bèze* (Geneva, 1960)

George, C.H. & George, K., *The Protestant Mind of the English Reformation* (Princeton: Princeton University Press, 1961)

Gerstner, Jonathan Neil, *The Thousand Generation: Dutch Reformed Covenant Theology and Group Identity in Colonial South Africa, 1652–1814* (Leiden: E.J. Brill, 1991)

Gilbert, Neal, *Renaissance Concepts of Method* (New York: Columbia University Press, 1960)

Godfrey, W. Robert, 'Tensions Within International Calvinism: The Debate on the Atonement at the Synod of Dort, 1618–1619' (PhD diss., Stanford University, 1974)

—, 'Calvin and Calvinism in the Netherlands' in W. Stanford Reid (ed.), *John Calvin: His Influence in the Western World* (Grand Rapids: Zondervan, 1982), 112–13

Graafland, Cornelis, *Van Calvijn tot Barth: Oorsprong en ontwikkeling van de leer der verkiezing in het Gereformeerd Protestantisme* (The Hague: Boekencentrum, 1987[2])

—, 'De Nadere Reformatie en het Labadisme' in *De Nadere Reformatie en het Gereformeerd Pietisme* (The Hague: Boekencentrum, 1989), 275–346

—, *Van Calvijn tot Comrie: Oorsprong en ontwikkeling van de leer van het verbond in het Gereformeerd Protestantisme*, 2 vols. (Zoetermeer: Boekencentrum, 1994)

Grabmann, Martin, *Die Geschichte der scholastischen Methode* (Berlin: Akademie, 1957)

Graham, Henry Grey, *The Social Life of Scotland in the Eighteenth Century*, 2 vols (London: Black, 1900)

Graham, W. Fred (ed.), *Later Calvinism: International Perspectives*, Sixteenth Century Essays and Studies 22 (Kirksville, Mo.: Sixteenth Century Journal, 1994)

Grane, Leif, *Contra Gabrielem: Luthers Auseinandersetzung mit Gabriel Biel in der Disputatio contra scholasticam theologiam 1517* (Copenhagen: Gyldendal, 1962)

—, 'Luthers Kritik an Thomas von Aquin in De captivitate Babylonica', *Zeitschrift für Kirchengeschichte* 80 (1969), 1–13

—, 'Formgeschichtliche und inhaltliche Probleme in den Werken des jungen Melanchthon. Ein neuer Zugang zu seinen Biberlarbeiten und Disputationsthesen', *Zeitschrift für Kirchengeschichte (ZKG)*, 84 (1973), 30–48

—, *Modus loquendi theologicus: Luthers Kampf um die Erneuerung der Theologie (1515–18)*, Acta Theologica Danica, 12 (Leiden: E.J. Brill, 1975)

—, 'Lutherforschung und Geistesgeschichte: Auseinandersetzung mit Heiko A. Oberman', *Archiv für Reformationsgeschichte* 68 (1977), 56–109

—, 'The Education of Women in the Reformation', *History of Education Quarterly* 19 (Spring 1979), 93–116

—, 'The Three Causes of Conversion in Philipp Melanchthon, Martin Chemnitz, David Chytraeus, and the Formula of Concord', *Luther-Jahrbuch* 47 (1980), 89–114

—, *Melanchthon in English. New Translations into English with a Registry of Previous Translations. A Memorial to William Hammer (1909–1976)*, Sixteenth Century Bibliography 22 (St Louis: Center for Reformation Research, 1982)

—, 'Luther and scholasticism' in Marilyn J. Harran (ed.), *Luther and Learning* (Selinsgrove: Susquehanna University Press, 1985), 52–68

de Greef, W., *The Writings of John Calvin* (Grand Rapids: Baker, 1993)

Grohman, Donald D., 'The Genevan Reactions to the Saumur Doctrine of Hypothetical Universalism: 1635–1685', (PhD diss., Toronto School of Theology, Toronto, Canada, 1971)

de Groot, A., *Gisbertus Voetius: Godzaligheid te verbinden met de wetenschap* (Kampen: Kok, 1978)

—, 'Gisbertus Voetius' in Greschat, Martin (ed.), *Orthodoxie und Pietismus*, vol 7: *Gestalten der Kirchengeschichte* (Stuttgart: W. Kohlhammer, 1982), 149–62

Gründler, O., 'Thomism and Calvinism in the Theology of Girolamo Zanchi', (ThD thesis, Princeton Theological Seminary, 1961)

Hall, Basil, 'Calvin Against the Calvinists' in Duffield, Gervase (ed.), *John Calvin: A Collection of Distinguished Essays* (Grand Rapids: Eerdmans, 1966), 23–27

—, 'Puritanism: The Problem of Definition' in Cuming, G.J. (ed.), *Studies in Church History* 2 (London: Nelson, 1965), 283–96

Haller, William, *The Rise of Puritanism* (New York: Columbia University Press, 1938)

Hamm, B., *Frömmigkeitstheologie am Anfang des 16. Jahrhunderts: Studien zu Johannes von Paltz und seinem Umkreis* (Tübingen: J.C.B. Mohr (Paul Siebeck), 1982)

Häring, N., *Die Theologie des Erfurter Augustinre-Eremiten Bartholomäus Arnoldi von Usingen. Beitrag zur Dogmengeschichte der Reformationszeit* (Limburg: Pallotiner, 1939)

Harrison, A.W., *The Beginnings of Arminianism to the Synod of Dort* (London: University of London Press, 1926)

Hartvelt, G., 'Over de Methode der Dogmatiek in de Eeuw der Reformatie', *Gereformeerd Theologisch Tijdschrift* 62 (1962), 97–149

Headley, J.M., 'Tommaso Campanella and Jean de Launoy: The Controversy over Aristotle and his Reception in the West', *Renaissance Quarterly* 43 (1990), 529–50

—, 'Tommaso Campanella and the end of the Renaissance', *Journal of Medieval and Renaissance Studies* 20 (1990), 157–74

Helm, Paul, *Calvin and the Calvinists* (Edinburgh: Banner of Truth, 1982)

—, 'Calvin and the Covenant: Unity and Continuity', *Evangelical Quarterly* 55 (1983), 71–7

Henderson, G.D., *Religious Life in Seventeenth-Century Scotland* (Cambridge: Cambridge University Press, 1937)

Heppe, Heinrich, 'Der Charakter der deutsch-reformierten Kirche und das Verhältniss derselben zum Luthertum und zum Calvinismus', *Theologische Studien und Kritiken* 1850 (Heft 3), 672

—, *Geschichte des deutschen Protestantismus in den Jahren 1555–1581*, 8 vols. (Marburg, 1852–9)

—, *Dogmatik des deutschen Protestantismus im sechzehnten Jahrhundert*, 3 vols. (Gotha: Friedrich Andreas Perthes, 1857)

—, *Theodore Beza: Leben und ausgewählte Schriften* (Elberfeld, 1861)

—, *Reformed Dogmatics Set Out and Illustrated from the Sources*, Ernst Bizer (rev. and ed.), G.T. Thomson (tr.), with a foreword by Karl Barth, (London, 1950 / Grand Rapids: Baker, 1978)

Heyd, Michael, *Between Orthodoxy and Enlightenment: Jean-Robert Chouet and the Introduction of Cartesian Science in the Academy of Geneva* (The Hague: Martinus Nijhoff, 1982)

—, 'Un rôle nouveau pour la science: Jean-Alphonse Turrettini et les débuts de la théologie naturelle . . . Genève', *Revue de théologie et philosophie* 112 (1982), 25–42

—, *'Be Sober and Reasonable': The Critique of Enthusiasm in the Seventeenth- and Early Eighteenth-Centuries* (Leiden and New York: E.J. Brill, 1995)

Hill, Christopher, *Society and Puritanism in Pre-Revolutionary England* (London: Secker and Warburg, 1964)

Holtrop, Philip C., *The Bolsec Controversy on Predestination, from 1551 to 1555*, 2 vols. (Lewiston: Edwin Mellen, 1993)

Howell, Wilbur Samuel, *Logic and Rhetoric in England, 1500–1700* (Princeton, N.J.: Princeton University Press, 1956)

Hübner, F., *Naturliche Theologie und theokratische Schwärmerei bei Melanchthon* (Gütersloh: Bertelsmann, 1936)

Huelin, Gordon, 'Peter Martyr and the English Reformation', (PhD diss., University of London, 1954)

Jacob, Margaret C., 'The Crisis of the European Mind; Hazard Revisited' in Phyllis Mack and Margaret C. Jacob (eds.), *Politics and Culture in Early Modern Europe* (London and New York: Cambridge University Press, 1987), 251–71

James III, Frank A., 'Praedestinatio Dei: The Intellectual Origins of Peter Martyr Vermigli's Doctrine of Double Predestination', (DPhil diss., Oxford University, 1993)

—, *Peter Martyr Vermigli and Predestination: The Augustinian Inheritance of an Italian Reformer* (Oxford University Press, forthcoming)

— *Via Augustini: Augustine in the Later Middle Ages, Renaissance and Reformation*, (ed.), (Leiden: E.J. Brill, 1991), 157–88

Janse, L., *Gisbertus Voetius, 1589–1676* (Utrecht: De Banier, 1971)

Janz, Denis R., *Luther and Late Medieval Thomism: A Study in Theological Anthropology* (Waterloo, Ontario: Wilfrid Laurier University Press, 1983)

—, *Luther on Thomas Aquinas: The Angelic Doctor in the Thought of the Reformer* (Stuttgart: Franz Steiner, 1989)

Jensen, Kristian, 'Protestant Rivalry: Metaphysics and Rhetoric in Germany, c.1590–1620', *Journal of Ecclesiastical History* 41 (1990)

Jinkins, M., 'Theodore Beza: Continuity and Regression in the Reformed Tradition', *Evangelical Quarterly* 64 (1992), 131–54

Joachimsen, Paul, 'Loci communes. Eine Untersuchung zur Geistesgeschichte des Humanismus und der Reformation', *Luther-Jahrbuch* 8 (1926), 27–97

Kähler, Ernst, *Karlstadt und Augustin: Der Kommentar des Andreas Bodenstein von Karlstadt zu Augustins Schrift De spiritu et litera*, Hallische Monographien 19 (Halle: Niemeyer, 1952)

Karant-Nunn, Susan C., 'The Reality of Early Lutheran Education: The Electoral District of Saxony – a Case Study', *Luther-Jahrbuch* 57 (1990), 128–46

Kawerau, Peter, 'Die Homiletik des Andreas Hyperius', *Zeitschrift für Kirchengeschichte* 71 (1960), 66–81

Keizer, Gerrit, *Francois Turrettini sa vie et ses oeuvres et le Consensus* (Lausanne: Georges Bridel, 1900)

Kendall, R.T., *Calvin and English Calvinism to 1649* (Oxford: Oxford University Press, 1979/Carlisle: Paternoster, 1997)

Kevan, Ernest F., *The Grace of Law: A Study in Puritan Theology* (Grand Rapids: Baker, 1965)

Kickel, Walter, *Vernunft und Offenbarung bei Theodor Beza* (Neukirchen: Neukirchner, 1967)

Kingdon, R.M. & Bergier, J.-F. (eds.), *Registres de la Compagnie des Pasteurs de Genève au temps de Calvin*, 2 vols. (Geneva: Droz, 1962–4), in Philip E. Hughes (ed. and tr.), *The Register of the Company of Pastors of Geneva in the Time of Calvin* (Grand Rapids: Eerdmans, 1966)

Kirk, Linda, 'Eighteenth-Century Geneva and a Changing Calvinism' in Stuart Mews (ed.), *Religion and National Identity* (Oxford: Blackwell, 1982)

Kittelson, James, 'Successes and Failures in the German Reformation: The Report from Strasbourg', *Archive for Reformation History* (1982), 153–74

Klauber, Martin I., 'Helvetic Formula Consensus (1675): An Introduction and Translation', *Trinity Journal* 11 (1990), 103–23

—, 'Reason, Revelation, and Cartesianism: Louis Tronchin and Enlightened Orthodoxy in Late Seventeenth Century Geneva', *Church History* 59 (1990), 326–39

—, 'Jean-Alphonse Turrettini and the Abrogation of the Formula Consensus in Geneva', *Westminster Theological Journal* 53 (1991), 325–38

—, *Between Reformed Scholasticism and Pan-Protestantism: Jean-Alphonse Turretin (1671–1737) and Enlightened Orthodoxy at the Academy of Geneva* (London and

Toronto: Associated University Presses / Selinsgrove, P.A.: Susquehanna University Press, 1994)

—, 'Reformed Scholasticism in Transition: Benedict Pictet and Enlightened Orthodoxy at the Academy of Geneva' in W.F. Graham (ed.), *Later Calvinism* (1994)

Klauber, Martin I. and Glenn S. Sunshine, 'Jean-Alphonse Turrettini in Biblical Accommodation: Calvinist or Socinian?', *Calvin Theological Journal* (April 1990), 7–27

Kleineidam, E., 'Die Bedeutung der Augustinereremiten für die Universität Erfurt im Mittelalter und in der Reformationszeit' in C.P. Meyer and & W. Eckermann (eds.), *Scientia Augustiniana: Festschrift für Adolar Zumkeller* (Würzburg: Augustinus, 1975), 395–422

Knappen, M.M., *Tudor Puritanism* (Chicago: University of Chicago Press, 1938)

Kolb, Robert, 'The Advance of Dialectic in Lutheran Theology: The Role of Johannes Wigand (1523–1587)' in Jerome Friedman (ed.), *Regnum, Religio et Ratio: Essays Presented to Robert M. Kingdon*, Sixteenth Century Essays and Studies 8 (Kirksville Mo.: Sixteenth Century Journal, 1987), 93–192

Kors, Alan C., ' "A First Being, of Whom We Have No Proof": The Preamble of Atheism in Early-Modern France' in Kors and Korshin (eds.), *Anticipations of the Enlightenment* (1987)

—, *Atheism in France, 1650–1729*, 1: *The Orthodox Sources of Disbelief* (Princeton, N.J.: Princeton University Press, 1990)

—, 'Skepticism and the Problem of Atheism in Early-Modern France' in R.H. Popkin and A. Vanderjagt (eds.), *Scepticism and Irreligion* (1992), p. 205.

Kors, A.C. and P.J. Korshin (eds.), *Anticipations of the Enlightenment in England, France, and Germany* (Philadelphia: University of Pennsylvania Press, 1987)

Krause, Gerhard, 'Andreas Hyperius in der Forschung seit 1900', *Theologische Rundschau* 34 (1969), 262–341

—, *Andreas Gerhard Hyperius: Leben, Bilder, Schriften* (Tübingen: Mohr 1977)

Kristeller, Paul Oskar, *Renaissance Thought: The Classic, Scholastic and Humanist Strains* (New York: Harper and Row, 1955, 1961^2)

—, *Medieval Aspects of Renaissance Learning*, E.P. Mahoney (ed. and tr.), (Durham, N.C.: Duke University Press, 1974)

—, 'Humanism and Moral Philosophy' in Albert Rabil Jr. (ed.), *Renaissance Humanism: Foundations, Forms and Legacy*, 3: *Humanism and the Disciplines* (Philadelphia: University of Pennsylvania Press, 1988), 304–5

Kühler, W.J., *Het Socinianisme in Nederland* (Leiden: Sijthoff, 1912)

Kusukawa, Sachiko, *The Transformation of Natural Philosophy: The Case of Philip Melanchthon* (Cambridge: Cambridge University Press, 1995)

Kuyper, Abraham, *Johannes Maccovius* (Leiden: Donner, 1899)

Kvacala, J., *Thomas Campanella: Ein Reformer der Ausgehenden Renaissance* (Berlin: Trowitzsch, 1973)

Labrousse, Elizabeth, *Bayle* (Oxford: Oxford University Press, 1983)

—, 'Reading Pierre Bayle in Paris' in Kors and Korshin (eds.), *Anticipations of the Enlightenment*, 7–16

Lachman, David C., *The Marrow Controversy*, Rutherford Studies in Historical Theology (Edinburgh: Rutherford House, 1988)

Lake, Peter, *Moderate Puritans and the Elizabethan Church* (Cambridge: Cambridge University Press, 1982)

Lang, August, *Der Heidelberger Katechismus und vier verwandte Katechismen* (Leipzig: Deichert, 1907)

Leclercq, Jean, *The Love of Learning and The Desire for God: A Study of Monastic Culture* (New York: Fordham University Press, 1961)

Leff, Gordon, *Gregory of Rimini: Tradition and Innovation in Fourteenth Century Thought* (Manchester: Manchester University Press, 1961)

Lerner, M.-P., 'Campanella, Juge d'Aristote' in M. Gandillac (ed.), *Platon et Aristote à la Renaissance*, XVI Colloque International de Tours (Paris: Librairie Philosophique J. Vrin, 1976), 335–57

Letham, Robert, 'The *Foedus Operum*: Some Factors Accounting for Its Development', *Sixteenth Century Journal* 14 (1983), 459–61

van Lieburg, F.A., *De Nadere Reformatie in Utrecht ten tijde van Voetius: Sporen in de Gereformeerde Kerkeraadsacta* (Rotterdam: Lindenberg, 1989)

Lillback, Peter, 'Ursinus' Development of the Covenant of Creation: A Debt to Melanchthon or Calvin?', *Westminster Theological Journal* 43 (1981), 247–88

—, 'The Binding of God: Calvin's Role in the Development of Covenant Theology', (PhD diss., Westminster Theological Seminary, 1985

Link, Wilhelm, *Das Ringen Luthers um die Freiheit der Theologie von der Philosophie*, Ernst Wolf and Manfred Mezger (eds.), (Munich: C. Kaiser, 1955[2])

Louthan, Howard, *Johannis Crato and the Austrian Habsburgs: Reforming a Counter-Reform Court*, Studies in Reformed Theology and History (Princeton: Princeton Theological Seminary, 1994)

Lund, Eric, 'Second Age of Reformation: Lutheran and Reformed Spirituality, 1550–1700' in Louis Dupré and Don E. Saliers (eds.), *Christian Spirituality*, 3: *Post-Reformation and Modern* (New York: Crossroad, 1989), 213–39

Marsden, George, 'Perry Miller's Rehabilitation of the Puritans: A Critique', *Church History* 39 (1970), 91–105

Maurer, Wilhelm, 'Zur Komposition der Loci Melanchthons von 1521', *Luther-Jahrbuch* 25 (1958), 146–80

—, 'Melanchthons Loci communes von 1521 als wissenschaftliche Programmschrfit', *Luther-Jahrbuch* 27 (1960), 1–50

—, *Der junge Melanchthon zwischen Humanismus und Reformation*, 1: *Der Humanist*, 2: *Der Theologe* (Göttingen: Vandenhoeck & Ruprecht, 1967–9)

McCoy, Charles, 'The Covenant Theology of Johannes Cocceius', (PhD diss., Yale, 1957)

McDonnell, Killian, *John Calvin, the Church, and the Eucharist* (Princeton, Princeton University Press, 1967)

McGahagan, Thomas Arthur, 'Cartesianism in the Netherlands, 1639–1676: The New Science and the Calvinist Counter-Reformation' (PhD diss., University of Pennsylvania, 1976)

McGrath, Alister E., 'Augustinianism? A Critical Assessment of the So-Called "Medieval Augustinian Tradition" on Justification', *Augustinana* 31 (1981), 252–3

—, *Luther's Theology of the Cross: Martin Luther's Theological Breakthrough* (Oxford: Blackwell, 1985)

McGrath, Gavin J., 'Puritans and the Human Will: Voluntarism within Mid-Seventeenth Century Puritanism as Seen in the Thought of Richard Baxter and John Owen', (PhD thesis, University of Durham, 1989)

McKim, Donald K., *Ramism in William Perkins' Theology* (New York: Peter Lang, 1987)

McLachlan, H.J., *Socinianism in Seventeenth-Century England* (Oxford: Oxford University Press, 1951)

McLelland [McClelland], Joseph C., 'The Reformed Doctrine of Predestination according to Peter Martyr', *Scottish Journal of Theology* 8 (1955), 255–71

—, *Visible Words of God: A Study in the Theology of Peter Martyr* (Edinburgh: Oliver and Boyd / Grand Rapids: Eerdmans, 1957)

— *Peter Martyr and Italian Reform*, (ed.), (Waterloo, Ontario: Wilfred Laurier University Press, 1980)

McNair, Philip, *Peter Martyr in Italy* (Oxford: Oxford University Press, 1967)

—, 'Biographical Introduction: Peter Martyr Vermigli' in J.C. McLelland (ed.), *Early Writings: Creed, Scripture and Church*, Peter Martyr Library (Kirksville: Thomas Jefferson University Press and Sixteenth Century Journal, 1994)

McNeil, J.T., *The History and Character of Calvinsim* (New York, Oxford University Press, 1954)

McPhee, Ian, 'Conserver or Transformer of Calvin's Theology? A Study of the Origins and Development of Theodore Beza's Thought, 1550–1570', (PhD diss., Cambridge University, 1979)

McSorley, Harry J., *Luther: Right or Wrong? An Ecumenical-Theological Study of Luther's Major Work, The Bondage of the Will* (New York: Newman Press / Minneapolis: Augsburg Publishing House, 1969)

Mechie, Stewart, 'The Theological Climate in Early Eighteenth Century Scotland' in Duncan Shaw (ed.), *Reformation and Revolution* (Edinburgh: Saint Andrew Press, 1967), 258–72

Meyer, Edward Cecil, 'The First Protestant Handbook on Preaching: An Analysis of the *De formandis concionibus sacris seu de interpretatione scripturarum populari libri II* of Andreas Hyperius in Relation to Medieval Homiletical Manuals' (PhD diss., Boston University, 1967)

Miller, Perry, *The New England Mind. Seventeenth Century* (Cambridge, Mass.: Harvard University Press, 1939)

Moltmann, Jürgen, 'Zur Bedeutung des Petrus Ramus für Philosphie und Theologie im Calvinismus', *Zeitschrift für Kirchengeschichte* 68 (1957), 295–318

Morgan, John, *Godly Learning* (Cambridge: Cambridge University Press, 1986)

Mostert, Walter, 'Luthers Verhältnis zur theologischen und philosophischen Ueber-lieferung' in H. Junghans (ed.), *Leben und Werk Martin Luthers von 1526 bis 1546. Festgabe zu seinem 500. Geburtstag* 1 (Göttingen: Vandenhoeck & Ruprecht 1983), 347–68

Mozley, J.B., *A Treatise on the Augustinian Doctrine of Predestination* (New York, 1878²)

Muller, Richard A., 'Perkins' *A Golden Chaine*: Predestinarian System or Schematized *Ordo Salutis?*', *Sixteenth Century Journal* 9 (April 1978), 69–81

—, *Post-Reformation Reformed Dogmatics*, 3 vols. (Grand Rapids: Baker, 1978–)

—, '*Duplex Cognitio Dei* in the Theology of Early Reformed Orthodoxy', *Sixteenth Century Journal* 10 (1979), 51–61

—, 'The Federal Motif in Seventeenth Century Arminian Theology', *Nederlands Archief voor Kerkgeschiedenis* 62 (1982), 102–22

—, '*Vera philosophia cum sacra theologia nusquam pugnat*: Keckermann on Philosophy, Theology, and the Problem of Double Truth', *Sixteenth Century Journal* 15 (1984), 341–65

—, *Dictionary of Latin and Greek Theological Terms* (Grand Rapids: Baker, 1985)

—, 'Scholasticism Protestant and Catholic: Francis Turretin on the Object and Principles of Theology', *Church History* 55 (1986), 203–5

—, *Christ and the Decree: Christology and Predestination in Reformed Theology from Calvin to Perkins* (Durham, N.C.: Labyrinth, 1986 / Grand Rapids: Baker, 1988)

—, 'Arminius and the Scholastic Tradition', *Calvin Theological Journal* 24 (1989), 263–77

—, ' The Barth Legacy: New Athanasius or Origen Redivivus? A Response to T.F. Torrance', *Thomist* 54 (1990), 673–704

—, '*Fides* and *Cognitio* in Relation to the Problem of Intellect and Will in the Theology of John Calvin', *Calvin Theological Journal* 25 (1990), 207–24

—, *God, Creation and Providence in the Thought of Jacob Arminius* (Grand Rapids: Baker, 1991)

—, 'Covenant of Works and the Stability of Divine Law in Seventeenth-Century Orthodoxy: A Study in the Theology of Herman Witsius and Wilhelmus à Brakel', *Calvin Theological Journal* 29 (1994), 75–101

—, 'God, Predestination, and the Integrity of the Created Order: A Note on Patterns in Arminius' Theology' in W.F. Graham (ed.), *Later Calvinism* (1994)

—, 'Calvin and the "Calvinists": Assessing Continuities and Discontinuities between the Reformation and Orthodoxy', *Calvin Theological Journal* 30 (1995), 345–75, and 31 (1996), 125–60

—, *Scholasticism and Orthodoxy in the Reformed Tradition: An Attempt at Definition* (Grand Rapids: Calvin Theological Seminary, 1995)

—, 'Scholasticism in Calvin: A Question of Relation and Disjunction' in idem, *The Unaccommodated Calvin* (New York and Oxford: Oxford University Press, [forthcoming])

Muller, Richard A. and John L. Thompson (eds.), *Biblical Interpretation in the Era of the Reformation: Essays Presented to David C. Steinmetz in Honor of His Sixtieth Birthday* (Grand Rapids: Eerdmans, 1996)

Munson, Charles Robert, 'William Perkins: Theologian of Transition', (PhD diss., Case Western Reserve University, 1971)

Myers, W. David, *'Poor, Sinning Folk': Confession and Conscience in Counter-Reformation Germany* (Ithaca and London: Cornell University Press, 1996)

Nauert, Charles, 'The Clash of the Humanists and Scholastics: An Approach to Pre-Reformation Controversies', *Sixteenth Century Journal* 4 (1973), 2–5

—, *Humanism and the Culture of Renaissance Europe* (Cambridge, Mass.: Harvard University Press, 1995)

Nauta, Doede, *Samuel Maresius* (Amsterdam: H.J. Paris, 1935)

Neuser, Wilhelm H. (ed.), *Calvinus Sacrae Scripturae Professor: Calvin as Confessor of Holy Scripture* (Grand Rapids: Eerdmans, 1994)

New, J.F.H., *Puritans and Anglicans: The Basis of Their Opposition* (Stanford: Stanford University Press, 1964)

Nicole, Roger, 'Moyse Amyraut (1596–1664) and the Controversy on Universal Grace First Phase (1634–1637)', (PhD diss., Harvard University, 1966)

—, *Moyse Amyraut: A bibliography* (New York and London: Garland Publishing, 1981)

Niesel, W., *The Theology of John Calvin*, Harold Knight (tr.), (London: Lutterworth, 1956)

de Niet, Cornelis Adrianus, 'Voetius en de literatuur: Een korte verkenning', *Documentatieblad* 19 (1995), 27–36

Nösgen, K.T., *Symbolik oder Konfessionelle Prinzipienlehre* (Gütersloh, 1879)

Nuttall, G.F., *Richard Baxter and Philip Doddridge: A Study in Tradition* (London: Oxford University Press, 1951)

—, *Richard Baxter* (London: Nelson, 1965)

Oberman, Heiko, *Archbishop Thomas Bradwardine, a Fourteenth Century Augustinian: A Study of His Theology in its Historical Context* (Utrecht: Kemink, 1957)

—, *The Harvest of Medieval Theology: Gabriel Biel and Late Medieval Nominalism* (Grand Rapids: Eerdmans, 1967[rev])

—, 'Headwaters of the Reformation: *Initia Lutheri — Initia Reformationis*' in Heiko A. Oberman (ed.), *Luther and the Dawn of the Modern Era* (Leiden: E.J. Brill, 1974), 40–88

—, *Werden und Wertung der Reformation*, Spätscholastik und Reformation 2 (Tübingen: J.C.B. Mohr (Paul Siebeck), 1977)

—,' "Immo": Luthers reformatorische Entdeckungen im Spiegel der Rhetorik' in G. Hammer and K.-H. Zur Mühlen (eds.), *Lutheriana: Zum 500. Geburtstag*

Martin Luthers von den Mitarbeitern der Weimarer Ausgabe, Archiv zur Weimarer Ausgabe 5 (Cologne and Vienna: Böhlau, 1984), 17–38

—, *The Dawn of the Reformation* (Edinburgh: T. & T. Clark, 1986)

—, *Initia Calvini: The Matrix of Calvin's Reformation* (Amsterdam: Koninklijke Nederlandse Akademie van Wetenschappen, 1991)

O'Day, Rosemary, *The English Clergy: The Emergence and Consolidation of a Profession, 1558–1642* (Leicester: Leicester University Press, 1979)

Ong, Walter J., *Ramus: Method and the Decay of Dialogue* (Cambridge, Mass.: Harvard University Press, 1958)

van Oort, Johannes, 'Augustinus, Voetius, und die Anfänge der Utrechter Universiteit' in A. Zumkeller (ed.), *Signum Pietatis: Festgabe für Cornelius Petrus Mayer zum 60. Geburtstag* (Würzburg: Augustinus, 1989)

—, 'Augustine's Influence on the Preaching of Gisbertus Voetius' in Bernard Bruning et al. (eds.), *Collectanea Augustiniana* 2 (Louvain: Leuven University Press, 1990)

van Oort, Johannes et al., *De onbekende Voetius* (Kampen: Kok, 1989)

Overfield, James, *Humanism and Scholasticism in Late Medieval Germany* (Princeton: Princeton University Press, 1984)

Packer, J.I., 'The Redemption and Restoration of Man in the Thought of Richard Baxter', (DPhil thesis, University of Oxford, 1954)

Parker, T.H.L., *Calvin's Doctrine of the Knowledge of God* (Grand Rapids: Eerdmans, 1959[2])

—, *Calvin's Preaching* (Edinburgh: T. & T. Clark, 1992)

Paulus, N., *Der Augustiner Bartholomäus Arnoldi von Usingen, Luthers Lehrer und Gegner: Ein Lebensbild* (Freiburg: Herder, 1893)

Pesch, Otto H., *Martin Luther, Thomas von Aquin und die reformatorische Kritik an der Scholastik: Zur Geschichte und Wirkungsgeschichte eines Missverständnisses mit weltgeschichtlichen Folgen* (Göttingen: Vandenhoeck & Ruprecht, 1994)

Peters, Robert, 'John Hales and the Synod of Dort' in G.J. Cuming and L.G.D. Baker (eds.), *Studies in Church History* 7: *Councils and Assemblies* (Cambridge: Cambridge University Press, 1971)

Petersen, Peter, *Geschichte der aristotelischen Philosophie im protestantischen Deutschland* (Leipzig: Felix Meiner, 1921), 93–5

Petit, L.D., *Biographische lijst der werken van de Leidsche hoogleeraren 1575–1619* (Leiden: van Doersburgh, 1894)

Pitassi, Maria C., 'Un Manuscrit Genevois du XVIIIe Siècle: La Réfutation du Système de Spinosa par Mr. Turrettini', *Nederlands Archief voor Kerkgeschiedenis* 68 (1988), 180–212

—, 'L'Apologétique Raisonnable de Jean-Alphonse Turrettini' in Olivier Fatio and Maria C. Pitassi (eds.), *Apologétique 1680–1740: Sauvetage ou naufrage de la théologie* (Geneva, Publications de la Faculté de Théologie de l'Université de Genève, 1990), 180–212

Platt, John, 'Eirenical Anglicans at the synod of Dort' in D. Baker (ed.), *Reform and Reformation: England and the Continent c.1500–c.1750* (Oxford: Blackwell, 1979)

—, *Reformed Thought and Scholasticism: The Arguments for the Existence of God in Dutch Theology, 1575–1650* (Leiden: E.J. Brill, 1982)

Plitt, G., *Jodokus Trutfetter von Eisenach, der Lehrer Luthers in seinem Wirken geschildert* (Erlangen: Deichert, 1876)

Popkin, Richard H., 'Fideism, Quietism, and Unbelief: Skepticism For and Against Religion in the Seventeenth- and Eighteenth-Centuries' in Marcus Hester (ed.), *Faith, Reason, and Skepticism* (Philadelphia: Temple University, 1992), 121–54

—, 'Religious Background of Seventeenth-Century Philosophy' in idem (ed.) *The Third Force in Seventeenth-Century Thought* (New York: E.J. Brill, 1992), 276–7

Popkin, Richard H. and Arjo Vanderjagt (eds.), *Scepticism and Irreligion in the Seventeenth- and Eighteenth-centuries* (New York: E.J. Brill, 1993)

Poppi, Antonino, 'La Teologia nell' Universita e nelle Scuole' in idem (ed.), *Storia e Cultura al Santo di Padova: Fra Il XIII e Il XX Secola* 3 (Vicenza, 1976)

Porter, H.C., *Reformation and Reaction in Tudor Cambridge* (Cambridge: Cambridge University Press, 1958)

Powicke, F.J., *A Life of the Reverend Richard Baxter 1615–1691* (New York: Hought on Mifflin, n.d.)

Preus, Robert D., *The Theology of Post-Reformation Lutheranism*, 2 vols. (St Louis: Concordia, 1970–72)

Priebe, V.L., 'The Covenant Theology of William Perkins', (PhD diss., Drew University, 1967)

Prozesky, Martin H., 'The Emergence of Dutch Pietism', *Journal of Ecclesiastical History* 28 (1977), 29–37

Rabb, Theodore K., 'Religious Toleration During the Age of Reformation' in Malcolm R. Thorp and Arthur J. Slavin (eds.), *Politics, Religion and Diplomacy in Early Modern Europe* (Kirksville, Mo.: Sixteenth Century Journal, 1994), 304–19

Rainbow, Jonathan, *The Will of God and the Cross: An Historical and Theological Study of John Calvin's Doctrine of Limited Redemption* (Allison Park, Pa.: Pickwick, 1990)

Raitt, Jill, *The Eucharistic Theology of Theodore Beza* (Chambersburg: American Academy of Religion, 1972)

—, *The Colloquy of Montbéliard: Religion and Politics in the Sixteenth Century* (Oxford: Oxford University Press, 1993)

Rashdall, Hastings, *The Universities of Europe in the Middle Ages* (Oxford, 1895)

Rechtien, John G., 'Logic in Puritan Sermons in the Late Sixteenth Century and Plain Style', *Style* 13 (1979), 237–58

—, 'Reformation in France and Scotland: A Case Study in Sixteenth-Century Communication' in W.F. Graham (ed.), *Later Calvinism*, 195–214

Reu, Johann Michael, *Quellen zur Geschichte des kirchlichen Unterrichtes in der evangelischen Kirche Deutschlands zwischen 1530 und 1600*, 11 vols. or parts (Gütersloh: Bertelsmann, 1904–35)

Reuter, Karl, *Das Grundverständnis der Theologie Calvins* (Neukirchen, 1963)

—, 'Richard Baxter's "End of Controversy" ', *Bibliotheca Sacra and American Biblical Repository* 12 (1855), 348–85

Ritschl, Albrecht, *A Critical History of the Christian Doctrine of Justification and Reconciliation*, John S. Black (tr.), (Edinburgh: T. & T. Clark, 1872)

Ritschl, Otto, *Dogmengeschichte des Protestantismus 3: Die reformierte Theologie des 16. und des 17. Jahrhunderts in ihrer Entstehung und Entwicklung* (Göttingen: Vandenhoeck & Ruprecht, 1926)

von Rohr, John, *The Covenant of Grace in Puritan Thought* (Atlanta: Scholars, 1986)

Rolston III, Holmes, *John Calvin Versus the Westminster Confession* (Richmond, Va.: John Knox, 1972)

Rummel, Erika, *The Humanist-Scholastic Debate in the Renaissance and Reformation* (Cambridge, Mass.: Harvard University Press, 1995)

Ryken, P.G., 'Thomas Boston (1676–1732) as Preacher of the *Fourfold State*', (unpubl. doctoral thesis, University of Oxford, 1995)

Sambin, Paolo, 'Intorno a Nicoletto Vernia', *Rinascimento* 3 (1952)

—, 'La formazione quattrocentesca della Biblioteca di S. Giovanni di Verdara in Padova' in *Atti dell'Instituto Veneto di Scienze Lettere ed Arti*, Classe di scienze morali e lettere 114 (1955–6), 263–80.

Sayous, Andre-E., 'La haute bourgeoisie de Genève entre le debut duXVIIe et le milieu du XIXe siècle', *Revue historique* 180 (1937), 30–57

Schaefer, Paul R., 'The Spiritual Brotherhood on the Habits of the Heart: Cambridge Protestants and the Doctrine of Sanctification from William Perkins to Thomas Shepard', (DPhil diss., University of Oxford, 1992)

Scharlemann, Robert P., *Thomas Aquinas and John Gerhard*, Yale Publications in Religion 7 (New Haven: Yale University Press, 1964)

Schian, Martin, 'Die Homiletik des Andreas Hyperius', *Zeitschrift für praktische Theologie* 18 (1896), 289–324, 19 (1897), 27–66, 120–49

Schleiermacher, Frederick, Daniel Ernst, *Der Christliche Glaube*, 3 vols. (Berlin: Reimer, 18363)

Schmitt, Charles B., 'Towards a Reassessment of Renaissance Aristotelianism', *History of Science* XI (1973), 159–93

—, *Studies in Renaissance Philosophy and Science* (London: Variorum, 1981)

—, *The Aristotelian Tradition and Renaissance Universities* (London: Variorum, 1984)

Schell, Uwe, *Die Homiletische Theorie Philipp Melanchthons*, Arbeiten zur Geschichte und Theologie des Luthertums 20 (Berlin: Lutherisches Verlagshaus, 1968)

Schneider, John R., *Philip Melanchthon's Rhetorical Construal of Biblical Authority. Oratio Sacra*, Texts and Studies in Religion, 51 (Lewiston, N.Y., The Edwin Mellen Press 1990), 51–63

Schrenk, Gottlob, *Gottesreich und Bund im älteren Protestantismus, vornehmlich bei Johannes Cocceius* (Gütersloh: Bertelsmann, 1923)

Schüler, Martin, *Prädestination, Sünde und Freiheit bei Gregor von Rimini* (Stuttgart: W. Kohlhammer, 1934)

Schutte, Anne Jacobson, *Pier Paolo Vergerio: The Making of an Italian Reformer* (Geneva: Droz, 1977)

Shaw, Mark Randolph, 'The Marrow of Practical Divinity: A Study in the Theology of William Perkins', (ThD diss., Westminster Theological Seminary, 1981)

Shepherd, N., 'Zanchius on Saving Faith', *Westminster Theological Journal* 36 (1973), 31–47

Sinnema, Donald, 'Reformed Scholasticism and the Synod of Dort (1618–19)' in B.J. van der Walt, (ed.), *John Calvin's Institutes: His Opus Magnum* (Potchefstroom: Potchesfstroom University, 1986), 467–506

——, 'Antoine de Chandieu's Call for a Scholastic Reformed Theology (1580)' in W.F. Graham (ed.), *Later Calvinism* (1994), 159–90

——, 'The Issue of Reprobation at the Synod of Dort (1618–19) in the Light of the History of this Doctrine' (diss., Toronto, 1985)

van Slee, J.C., *De Geschiedenis van het Socinianisme in de Nederlanden* (Haarlem: Bohn, 1914)

Smid, T.D., 'Bibliographische Opmerkingen over de *Explicationes catecheticae* van Zacharias Ursinus', *Gereformeerd Theologisch Tijdschrift* 41 (1940)

Spear, Wayne R., 'Covenanted Uniformity in Religion: The Influence of the Scottish Commissioners upon the Ecclesiology of the Westminster Assembly', (unpubl. doctoral diss., University of Pittsburgh, 1976)

Spellman, W.M., *The Latitudinarians and the Church of England, 1660–1700* (Athens and London: University of Georgia Press, 1993)

van't Spijker, Willem, 'Gisbertus Voetius (1589–1676)' in *De Nadere Reformatie: Beschrijving van haar voornaamste vertegenwoordigers* (The Hague: Boekencentrum, 1986), 49–84

——, *Principe, Methode en Functie van de Theologie bij Andreas Hyperius* (Kampen: Kok, 1990)

Spitz, L., 'Humanism and the Protestant Reformation' in A. Rabil (ed.), *Renaissance Humanism* 3 (Philadelphia: University of Pennsylvania Press, 1988)

Sprunger, Keith L., 'Ames, Ramus, and the Method of Puritan Theology', *Harvard Theological Review* 59 (1966), 133–51

——, *The Learned Doctor William Ames* (Urbana: University of Illinois Press, 1972)

——, *Dutch Puritanism: A History of English and Scottish Churches of the Netherlands in the Sixteenth and Seventeenth Centuries*, Studies in the History of Christian Thought 31 (Leiden: E.J. Brill, 1982)

van Stam, F.P., *The Controversy Over the Theology of Saumur, 1635–1650* (Amsterdam and Maarssen: APA-Holland University Press, 1988)

Staufenegger, Roger, *Église et société Genève au XVIIe siècle* (Geneva: Droz, 1983)

Steenblok, C., *Gisbertus Voetius: Zijn leven en werken* (Gouda: Gereformeerde, 1976²)

Stegmuller, F., *Reportorium Commentatorum in Sententias Petri Lombardi* (Wurzburg, 1947)

Steinmetz, David C., 'Luther and the Late Medieval Augustinians: Another Look', *Concordia Theological Monthly* 44 (1973), 245–60

—, *Luther and Staupitz: An Essay in the Intellectual Origins of the Protestant Reformation* (Durham: Duke University Press, 1980)

—, 'Calvin and the Absolute Power of God', *Journal of Medieval and Renaissance Studies* 18.1 (Spring, 1988), 65–79

—, *Calvin in Context* (New York and Oxford: Oxford University Press, 1995)

—, *Luther in Context* (Grand Rapids: Baker, 1995)

—, 'Divided by a Common Past: The Reshaping of the Christian Exegetical Tradition in the Sixteenth Century', *Journal of Medieval and Early Modern Studies* (forthcoming)

—, 'Luther and Formation in Faith' in the Acta of the Lilly Foundation Conference on the Formation of Peoples in Faith held at the University of Notre Dame in 1995 (forthcoming)

Stelling-Michaud, S. (ed.), *Le Livre Du Recteur de L'Académie de Genève (1559–1878)*, 2 vols. (Geneva: Droz, 1959)

Stoeffler, F. Ernest, *The Rise of Evangelical Pietism* (Leiden: E.J. Brill, 1965, 1971)

Strauss, Gerald, *Luther's House of Learning* (Baltimore: Johns Hopkins University Press, 1978)

Strehle, Stephen, *Calvinism, Federalism, and Scholasticism: A Study of the Reformed Doctrine of Covenant* (Berne: Peter Lang, 1988)

Sturm, Erdmann, *Der junge Zacharias Ursinus: Sein Weg vom Philippismus zum Calvinismus* (Neukirchen-Vluyn: Neukirchener, 1972)

Sturm, Klaus, *Die Theologie Peter Martyr Vermiglis während seines ersten Aufenthalts in Strassburg 1542–1547* (Neukirchen: Neukirchener, 1971)

Sudhoff, Karl, *C. Olevianus und Z. Ursinus: Leben und ausgewählte Schriften* (Elberfeld: Friderichs, 1857)

Thompson, John L., 'The Survival of Allegorical Argumentation in Peter Martyr Vermigli's Old Testament Exegesis' in Richard A. Muller and John L. Thompson (eds.), *Biblical Interpretation in the Era of the Reformation* (Grand Rapids: Eerdmans, 1996), 255–8

Todd, Margo, *Christian Humanism and the Puritan Social Order* (Cambridge: Cambridge University Press, 1987)

Torrance, James B., 'Strengths and Weaknesses of the Westminster Theology' in Alasdair Heron (ed.), *The Westminster Confession* (Edinburgh: St Andrews, 1982), 40–53

Toulouse, Teresa, *The Art of Prophesying: New England Sermons and the Shaping of Belief* (Athens, Ga.: University of Georgia Press, 1987)

Trapp, Damasus, 'Augustinian Theology of the Fourteenth Century: Notes on Editions, Marginalia, Opinions and Book-Lore', *Augustiniana* 6 (1956)

Trueman, Carl R., *The Claims of Truth: John Owen's Trinitarian Theology* (Carlisle: Paternoster, 1997)

—, 'John Owen's *Dissertation on Divine Justice*: An Exercise in Christocentric Scholasticism', *Calvin Theological Journal* (forthcoming)

Trusen, Winfried, 'Johannes Reuchlin und die Fakultäten', in G. Keil et al. (eds.), *Der Humanismus und die oberen Fakultäten* (Weinheim: Acta Humaniora, VCH, 1987)

Urban, W., 'Die "via moderna" an der Universität Erfurt am Vorabend der Reformation' in H.A. Oberman (ed.), *Gregor von Rimini: Werk und Wirkung bis zur Reformation* (Berlin and New York: De Gruyter, 1981), 311–30

Venema, Cornelis P., 'Heinrich Bullinger's Correspondence on Calvin's Doctrine of Predestination, 1551–1553', *Sixteenth Century Journal* 17/4 (1986), 435–50

Verbeek, Theo, *Descartes and the Dutch: Early Reactions to Cartesian Philosophy 1637–1650* (Carbondale and Edwardsville: Southern Illinois University Press, 1992)

—, 'From "Learned Ignorance" to Scepticism: Descartes and Calvinist Orthodoxy' in Popkin and Vanderjagt (eds.), *Scepticism and Irreligion* (1993)

Vignaux, Paul, *Luther, commentateur des Sentences (livre I, distinction XVII)* (Paris: J. Vrin, 1935)

Vind, Anna, ' "Men de har intet forstaaet om Kristus . . .": om Luthers opr med den skolastiske teologi', *Dansk Teologisk Tidsskrift* 59 (1996), 27–49

Visser, Derk, *Zacharias Ursinus, the Reluctant Reformer: His Life and Times* (New York: United Church, 1983)

—, 'Zacharias Ursinus and the Palatinate Reformation' in idem, *Controversy and Conciliation* (1986)

—, *Controversy and Conciliation: The Palatinate Reformation, 1559–1618*, (ed.), (Pittsburgh: Pickwick, 1986)

—, 'The Covenant in Zacharias Ursinus', *Sixteenth Century Journal* 18 (1987)

Visser, H.B., *De Geschiedenis van den Sabbatstrijd onder de Gereformeerden in de Zeventiende Eeuw* (Utrecht: Kemink, 1939)

Vos, Arvin, *Aquinas, Calvin and Contemporary Protestant Thought: A Critique of the Views of Thomas Aquinas* (Grand Rapids: Eerdmans, 1982)

Walker, Williston, *John Calvin: the Organizer of Reformed Protestantism (1509–1564)* (1906; New York: Schocken, 1969)

van der Wall, Ernestine, 'Orthodoxy and Scepticism in the Early Dutch Enlightenment' in Popkin & Vanderjagt (eds.), *Scepticism and Irreligion* (1993), 121–41

Wallace, Dewey, *Puritans and Predestination* (Chapel Hill, N.C.: University of North Carolina Press, 1982)

Walzer, Michael, *The Revolution of the Saints* (Cambridge, Mass.: Harvard University Press, 1965)

Weber, Hans Emil, *Reformation, Orthodoxie und Rationalismus*, 3 parts (Gütersloh: Bertelsmann, 1937–1951 / Darmstadt: Wissenschaftliche Buchgesellschaft, 1966)

Weir, David A., *Origins of the Federal Theology in Sixteenth Century Reformation Thought* (Oxford: Clarendon, 1990)

Weisheipl, J.A., 'Scholastic Method' in *The New Catholic Encyclopedia* 12 (New York: Catholic University of America Press, 1967), 1145–6

Wendel, F., *Calvin: the Origins and Development of his Religious Thought* (London: Fontana, 1963)

Wilbur, E.M., *A History of Unitarianism and its Antecedents* (Cambridge, Mass.: Harvard University Press, 1946)

Witt, R., *Hercules at the Crossroads: The Life, Works, and Thought of Coluccio Salutati* (Durham: Duke University Press, 1983)

Wolf, E., 'Zur wissenschaftsgeschichtlichen Bedeutung der Disputationen an der Wittenberger Universität im 16. Jahrhundert' in idem (ed.), *Peregrinatio II: Studien zur reformatorischen Theologie, zum Kirchenrecht und Sozialethik* (München: Kaiser, 1965), 38–51

Woolsey, Andrew, 'Unity and Continuity in Covenantal Thought: A Study in the Reformed Tradition to the Westminster Assembly', (PhD diss., Glasgow University, 1988)

Wundt, M., *Die Deutsche Schulmetaphysik des 17 Jahrhunderts* (Tübingen: Mohr, 1939)

Yardeni, Myriam, 'French Calvinist Political Thought, 1534–1715' in Menna Prestwich (ed.), *International Calvinism 1541–1715* (Oxford: Oxford University Press, 1985), 315–37

Zumkeller, Adolar, 'Die Augustinertheologien Simon Fidati von Cascia und Hugolin von Orvieto und Martin Luthers Kritik an Aristoteles', *Archiv für Reformationsgeschichte* 54 (1963), 13–37

Zur Mühlen, Karl-Heinz, 'Luther und Aristoteles', *Luther-Jahrbuch* 52 (1985), 263–6

Subject Index

Name Index